Natural
PROPOSITIONS

The Actuality of Peirce's
Doctrine of Dicisigns

FREDERIK STJERNFELT

Docent
Press

Docent Press
Boston, Massachusetts, USA
www.docentpress.com

Docent Press publishes books in the history of mathematics and computing about interesting people and intriguing ideas. The histories are told at many levels of detail and depth that can be explored at leisure by the general reader.

Cover design by Brenda Riddell, Graphic Details.

Produced with TEX. Textbody set in Garamond with titles and captions in Bernhard Modern.

ISBN-10: 0988744961
ISBN-13: 978-0-9887449-6-7

Contents

List of Figures

Preface

This volume integrates the work on Peircean logic, semiotics, and epistemology which has emerged as a continuation of my book *Diagrammatology* (2007) in which Peirce's notion of "diagrammatical reasoning" played a center role. It was never my intention to specialize as a Peirce scholar; the reason why I now publish this volume focused upon Peircean semiotics is simply because I kept finding important issues in the vast quarry which is Peirce's work, issues which I believe have a bearing on present and pressing issues in actual semiotics, linguistics, cognitive science, and philosophy. If reasoning with diagrams is the centerpiece of a Peircean epistemology, the simpler signs stating claims by means of diagrams will form the steps in such reasoning—they express propositions without being exclusively linguistic. This forms the basis of this book, arguing that Peirce's overlooked Dicisign doctrine forms a central node of an alternative panorama of the whole field of logic, language, knowledge, reasoning, perception, cutting it at other joints and along other dimensions than many received conceptions.

Important for the writing of this book have been good working conditions at the Center for Semiotics, Aarhus University, at the *Kolleg Bildakt und Verkörperung* at the Humboldt University, Berlin, and most recently the Epicenter, University of Copenhagen—aided also by the Danish Research Council grant "Joint Diagrammatical Reasoning in Language" and the Velux Foundation grant of "Humanomics".

Many colleagues and friends have supported and contradicted me in different ways in the process whom I would like to thank: Francesco Bellucci, Horst Bredekamp, James Robert Brown, David Budtz Pedersen, Peer Bundgaard, Andy Clark, Marcel Danesi, Terrence Deacon, Charbel El-Hani, Claus Emmeche, Franz Engel, Hans Fink, Tina Friis, Gary Fuhrman, Riccardo Fusaroli, Peter Harder, Vincent Hendricks, Jaakko Hintikka, Michael Hoffmann, Jesper Hoffmeyer, the Houghton Library staff at Harvard University, Jonathan Israel, Hans Siggaard Jensen, Cathrine Kietz, John Michael Krois, Kalevi Kull,

Jean Lassègue, Manfred Laubichler, Christina Ljungberg, Benjamin Meyer-Krahmer, Matthew Moore, Svend Østergaard, Helmut Pape, H.H. Pattee, Ahti-Veikko Pietarinen, Joao Queiroz, Moritz Queisner, Joanna Raczaszek-Leonardi, Thomas Riese, Andreas Roepstorff, Lucia Santaella, Theresa Schilhab, Karl Erik Schøllhammer, Sun-Joo Shin, Barry Smith, Jesper Sørensen, John Sowa, André de Tienne, Claudine Tiercelin, Ole Togeby, Kristian Tylén, Tommi Vekhavaara, Tullio Viola, Nikolaj Zeuthen.

A special thanks to the core of dedicated students at my Peirce class 2012–2013 at the Center for Semiotics, Aarhus University—and most of all my wife and daughters Agnete, Agnes, and Karoline.

Copenhagen, March 2014

Chapter 1

Introduction

> New classifications must result from such studies, the new classes
> being defined by new concepts; and the student naturally wishes to
> express his thoughts more precisely as he thinks them, and without
> the trammels of circumlocution.

("Rationale of Reasoning", 1910, Ms. 664, 1)

The title of this book—*Natural Propositions*—has been chosen in order to underline a desirable consequence of Charles Peirce's conception of propositions, that they are no strangers to a naturalist world-view and thus form natural inhabitants of reality. This is because propositions—in Peirce's generalization: *Dicisigns*—do not depend upon human language nor upon human consciousness or intentionality, contrary to most standard assumptions. Signs being able to carry a truth value are taken to encompass a much more wider array of phenomena than is indicated by normal philosophical examples—such as "The cat is on the mat" articulated in human language, everyday or formalized. Thus, propositions are taken to be expressible by means of a wide variety of semiotic tools—language, pictures, diagrams, gesture—involving a broad array of sensory modalities and conceptual models. The crucial approach in this expansion of the notion of proposition is Peirce's purely functional definition: it is a sign which makes a truth claim due to its double involvement—denotative and descriptive—with the same object. Much more about this definition follows below—here it suffices to call attention to the fact that this functional characterization crucially deflates the notion of proposition. When no longer presupposing human language, be it ordinary or formalized, nor human consciousness or intention, a purely functional conception of propositions allows us to grasp the unity of biosemiotic and semiotic phenomena much too often separated by hypostasized distinctions like language/picture, human/animal, conscious/preconscious. This more plastic conception of Dicisigns allows us to trace propositions deeply into biology on the one hand and widely into human forms of expression on the other. In biosemiotics, it ought not come as a big surprise that signs able to carry truths should be of greater survival value than signs without such abilities. In human semiotics, the recognition of the broadness of propositions gives a key to the understanding of a variegated range of "mixed media" phenomena drawing upon and connecting very different means of expression under the central aim of truth claiming.

Peirce's redefinition of propositions under the generalized notion of "Dicisign", however, forms but one central node in a vast redefinition of the whole field of cognition-perception-signs-language-thought-logic, so beset with received notions, misleading dualisms, spontaneous ontology, conflicting definitions, disciplinary wars and terminological and conceptual chaos as it is. Working in the early phase of modern logic, semiotics, and cognition, Peirce offers an alternative model of the overall intellectual topography of this whole domain—the "cognitive field" as we might call it—which may offer keys to evade many conceptual cul-de-sacs. Actually, such a reorientation is, to this author, among the most important lessons to be learned from Peirce's vast amount of published and unpublished material. It is less easy, however, to present such an alternative parsing of a vast area than to argue for a Peircean contribution to some specific detail in our conception of, say, iconic signs or logic representations.

This became clear to me after the publication of *Diagrammatology* (2007) in which I tried to give an account of the central role of diagrams in logic and reasoning as developed by the semiotics of the mature Peirce in the years after the turn of the century. Many readers found the presentation of Peirce's diagrammatology both challenging and compelling and I have no reason not to be satisfied with the overall reception of that book, yet, many failed to grasp the central point which is the *range* of Peirce's notion of diagram—more or less spontaneously preferring to restrict his claims as pertaining to the received, everyday notion of diagrams as stylized figures on paper. Such figures are indeed prototypical diagrams on Peirce's account—the important thing, however, is that he undertakes a vast generalization of the findings he makes in e.g. simple geometrical theorem proving with the use of diagrams. This allows Peirce to conceptualize phenomena normally taken to be worlds apart (algebras, images, maps, graphs, aspects of linguistic grammar, logic representations, etc.) as so many different subtypes of diagrams— the important distinguishing mark being that they are simplified spatial structures which may be used as general representations and, for that reason, furnish possibilities of reasoning by means of diagram experiment.

Thus, e.g., a topographical map of an area is a diagram, possessing an iconic relation to the landscape depicted—like in all icons, of course, iconic in some respects and not in others. But this diagram, at the very same time, functions as the predicative part of a proposition, a Dicisign. Map shapes serve to describe landscape shapes predicatively but the task of indicating which geographical area is referred to is undertaken by indices on the map—place names, scale indications, longitudes/latitudes, etc. In that sense, the topographical map is as good a representative of a Dicisign as any linguistically expressed proposition—it has a Predicate part (map shapes) and a Subject part (index indications) making it possible for the map to make true (or false) claims as to the properties of the landscape portrayed. Being a continuous predicate, of course, the diagram part of the map Dicisign may represent the landscape truthfully in some respects, falsely in others.

At the core of Peirce's rearticulation of the cognitive field, then, is a daring generalization. First, he proposed that all of mathematics is developed by diagrammatical reasoning. This proposal comes from the idea that mathematics concerns idealized, hypothetical forms of relations—and that it proceeds by experimenting with diagrams representing such idealized hypotheses.[1] This epistemology of mathematics makes of it a science of observation: mathematical ideality is grasped by the observation of diagram tokens which instantiate the selected properties of those ideal types which are investigated—such diagrams involving not only figures but all varieties of special notation. The possibility for mathematical to reach apodictic truth is thus bought at the price that such truths are possible only for idealized worlds with few, well-controlled properties (unlike the empirical world of which knowledge remains always more or less approximate). Such idealized objects have a hypothetical existence only—all of mathematics has an if-then structure of tracing the consequences of hypothetical assumptions given in initial diagrams subject to scrutiny. Second, he proposed that all deductive reasoning is undertaken by such diagrammatical reasoning. This implies, in turn, that also pieces of deductive reasoning where no explicit diagram is present involves an underlying diagrammatical structure. This also implies that ordinary deductive reasoning, in introspection, language, images, special sciences, etc. is diagrammatical. And, taken together with the first generalization, it implies that both everyday reasoning and empirical sci-

---

[1] The central papers of Peirce's scattered efforts within the philosophy of mathematics have recently been collected by Matthew Moore (Peirce (2010)) who has also edited an important volume addressing the characterization of Peirce's doctrine of philosophy of mathematics (Moore (2010)).

entific reasoning involve mathematical structure, even when not at all apparent for a first glance. This core of mathematical-diagrammatical deduction, however, is continuously connected, in the ongoing investigation process, to empirical findings by means of abductive guesses and inductive tests.

Such investigation process, however, is not restricted to its obvious and explicit versions in the sciences. In this introduction, I shall try to present a sketchlike overview of the broader implications of this overall reorganization of the cognitive field—of which further details will be found in the chapters of this book. Both Dicisigns and diagrams are signs—their definitions come out of Peirce's semiotics. Here, we find one, central if often overlooked, property of Peirce's overview—continuism. It should not be expected that conceptual distinctions— e.g. the famous trichotomy of icons, indices, and symbols—correspond to separate and autonomous species of signs out there, as if it were lions, tigers, and leopards. Rather, Peirce's distinctions are nested so that the more complicated signs contain, embed or involve specimens of the simpler signs. Thus symbols typically involve indices which, in turn, involve icons—conversely, icons are incomplete indices which are, again, incomplete symbols. The whole of Peirce's semiotics with all its distinctions thus serves to describe the functioning of the most complicated type of sign: the Argument. Arguments involve Dicisigns which involve terms—conversely, terms are incomplete Dicisigns which are incomplete Arguments. Dicisigns and the way Arguments lead from one Dicisign to the next are thus the connecting links between semiotics and logic. This link constitutes the Peircean doctrine that logic and thinking in general are instantiated in signs the structure of which forms the royal road to the understanding of cognition.

Dicisigns, like other signs, are conceived of as independent of the particular mental, psychological or other apparatus supporting them. Thus, Peirce's position shares a fundamental anti-psychologism with Frege and Husserl. But unlike them, his is an anti-psychologism without the linguistic turn. It is not (only) to language that we should turn in order to find logic and cognitive structure not psychologistically defined—it is to signs as vehicles for thoughts in general. Thus, signs are not analyzed as derivatives of more primary perceptions, like the narrow, phenomenological notion of signs found e.g. in Husserl and much philosophy of mind. Rather, many signs are indeed *simpler* than perceptions, as evidenced particularly by the biosemiotic sign use in simple animals without full perceptual field, sensory integration, central nervous systems, etc. Perception and consciousness are rather to be seen as evolutionarily later, more complicated phenomena, probably evolved so as to scaffold and enhance simpler cognitive semiotic processes already functioning.

The doctrine of logic as semiotics also has an important bearing upon what is taken to be central in cognition. Again, Peirce makes a daring generalization: *all* steps in cognition are taken to have the character of inference. This idea is constant in him from his earliest papers already in the 1860s:

> "Such being the nature of reality in general, in what does the reality of the mind consist? We have seen that the content of consciousness, the entire phenomenal manifestation of mind, is a sign resulting from inference. Upon our principle, therefore, that the absolutely incognizable does not exist, so that the phenomenal manifestation of a substance is the substance, we must conclude that the mind is a sign developing according to the laws of inference."
> ("Some Consequences of Four Incapacities", 1868, EP I 53, 5.313)

Again, the basic idea is functional—cognition has the purpose of leading from one Dicisign to another, drawing inferences with the horizon of stably guiding possible action which forms the ultimate truth value test. So, like the Dicisign, inference is not immediately a complicated, formal, conscious, deliberate, linguistic, second-order act (even if the versions of inference possessing such properties may prove particularly efficient). Rather, inference is the bread and butter of cognition, and all other aspects of cognition, from attention direction, mental maps and signal codes to externalized diagrams, notation systems, writing, etc. form, in this perspective, scaffolding systems evolved to support inference processes.

This particularly goes for perception. Perception does not begin, *ex nihilo*, with sense data—rather, perception continues the chain of inferences already taking its beginnings long before our individual births and long before the appearance of our species. This implies that perception appears for us as "perceptual judgments"—already logically formed and already containing a "propositional stance", claiming some statement about environment aspects. That is no later work of a higher-level logic or language module or anything of the sort—the whole visual system, already in the retina (contours, surfaces, etc.), is geared to stably extracting general aspects from the visual field. True, retrospectively we may analytically isolate "percepts" as simpler aspects of the perceptual judgment contributed by sensations—but they never had separate existence outside perceptual judgments. Thus, the very perception-action cycle of organisms possesses a primitive inference structure—even down to simple reflexive arc versions of it:

> "The cognition of a rule is not necessarily conscious, but is of the nature of a habit, acquired or congenital. The cognition of a case

is of the general nature of a sensation; that is to say, it is something which comes up into present consciousness. The cognition of a result is of the nature of a decision to act in a particular way on a given occasion. In point of fact, a syllogism in *Barbara* virtually takes place when we irritate the foot of a decapitated frog. The connection between the afferent and efferent nerve, whatever it may be, constitutes a nervous habit, a rule of action, which is the physiological analogue of the major premiss. The disturbance of the ganglionic equilibrium, owing to the irritation, is the physiological form of that which, psychologically considered, is a sensation; and, logically considered, is the occurrence of a case. The explosion through the efferent nerve is the physiological form of that which psychologically is a volition, and logically the inference of a result. When we pass from the lowest to the highest forms of innervation, the physiological equivalents escape our observation; but, psychologically, we still have, first, habit–which in its highest form is understanding, and which corresponds to the major premiss of *Barbara;* we have, second, feeling, or present consciousness, corresponding to the minor premiss of *Barbara;* and we have, third, volition, corresponding to the conclusion of the same mode of syllogism. Although these analogies, like all very broad generalizations, may seem very fanciful at first sight, yet the more the reader reflects upon them the more profoundly true I am confident they will appear. They give a significance to the ancient system of formal logic which no other can at all share." ("A Theory of Probable Inference", 1883, 2.711)

Thus, in the very same year as Peirce invents the first version of the modern standard notation of first-order logic, he presents this crucial biosemiotic argument pertaining to the extension of logic in reality (we shall return to this in ch. 5 below).

So as to the "cognitive field" as a whole, Peirce articulates a broad conception of cognition, not defined in opposition to perception, not presupposing language nor consciousness, which has the character of generalized inferences between generalized propositions called Dicisigns. As endemic to pragmatism, this conception is inimical to hypostasized dualisms often pervading the cognitive field: subject/object, sign/perception, image/language, animal/human, proposition/non-conceptual content— many of which are even often coupled on top of one another to large lumps of presuppositions such as that of man and animal differing so that man only has the privileges of objects, signs, language, propositions... Not that Peirce's doctrine lack distinctions; anti-Cartesianist as he is, however, he avoids taking such distinctions to refer to nicely separated ontological realms which invariably lead to artificial conceptual problems of how to reconnect again what was once cut apart—rather reality is taken to display continuous transformation and intermediary forms between the phenomena distinguished.

This permits a wholly original conception of the whole field of sign use, language, pictures, perception, reasoning, now partitioned along very different joints and fault lines and connected through neglected continua—different from those which have evolved and sedimented themselves in the academic parsing of the field into logic, psychology, cognitive science, linguistics, metaphysics, image studies, etc. ... and the different folk psychologies and folk metaphysics which have deposited around received dualisms and discipline self-assertions.

We can sum up the ambition of rearticulating the cognitive field by this late quote from the introduction to a planned volume on the Meaning of Signs:

> "A great desideratum is a general theory of all possible kinds of signs, their modes of signification, of denotation, and of information; and their whole behaviour and properties, so far as these are not accidental. The task of supplying this need should be undertaken by some group of investigators; and since pretty much all that has hitherto been accomplished in this direction has been the work of logicians, among whom may be instanced indiscriminately George Boole, Mary Everest Boole, Victoria Welby, M. Couturat, Alfred Bray Kempe, Alfred Peano [sic], Bertrand Russell, and since a large division of this work ought to be regarded as constituting the bulk of the logician's business, it would seem proper that in the present state [of] our knowledge logic should be regarded as coëxtensive with General Semeiotic, the *a priori* theory of signs.
>
> All these essays, as the title-page says, relate to the Meaning of Signs, generally. For just as medical men in opening up the secrets of the zymotic, or yeastly, diseases, derived invaluable hints from the study of other kinds of yeast than those which make the substance of disease, so students of reasoning ought to widen their field of view so as to include anything that may come within their ken that bears any real analogy to reasoning, and must examine it in those of its features wherein it agrees with reasoning without by any means neglecting those wherein it contrasts with reasoning; (...) It considers Signs in general, a class which includes pictures, symptoms, words, sentences, books, libraries, signals, orders of command, microscopes, legislative representatives, musical concertos, performances of these, in short, whatever is adapted

to mentally transmitting to a person an impression that virtually emanates from something external to itself: the definition will be worked out more carefully when the method of doing so shall have been more carefully considered." (Ms. 634, 14-18, 1909)

In this book, we begin with a chapter (2) revisiting the importance of anti-psychologism to semiotics. Frege and Husserl are widely known as the two central anti-psychologists, unknowingly emerging as fountainheads of the analytical and continental traditions in 20 C philosophy, respectively. Less well known is Peirce's anti-psychologism which is earlier than either of the two—and in a certain respect even more ambitious. With the rearticulation of the cognitive field, not only logic in the narrow sense should be kept free of psychologism: also the details of semiotics prerequisite to logic as well as the structures of scientific research strategies are taken to be independent of the psychological specificities of beings who make use of them.

This takes us to the first centerpiece of the book: chapter 3's critical reconstruction of Peirce's theory of the Dicisign—the generalization of the notion of propositions. Here, the central and often-overlooked place of the Dicisign in Peirce's semiotics is analyzed, and the many aspects of the Dicisign doctrine and its connections to other aspects of Peirce's semiotics, logic and cognition theory are outlined. The pragmatical importance of the notion of signs able to express truths has not been realized by most Peirce scholars, strangely little interested in the logical function of signs (with notable exceptions such as Hilpinen, Short, Houser, Pietarinen, Bellucci) which is why it seems necessary to present a thorough account of the more convoluted corners of the Dicisign doctrine.

In chapter 4, some important corollaries to the Dicisign doctrine are elaborated. The characterization of Dicisigns as natural propositions is developed vis-à-vis current discussions of naturalization, and the basic idea of a pre-linguistic Dicisign syntax of co-localization is isolated and analyzed. The virtual Peircean contribution to the actual discussion of "non-conceptual content" is charted, and the implications of a generalized doctrine of "inference" covering also perception are investigated.

Chapter 5 confronts the Dicisign doctrine with a recent attempt at integrating basic notions of logic with (animal) cognition—the linguist James Hurford's bold hypothesis that the split between ventral-dorsal visual streams found in primates has the function of performing a propositional analysis of visual material. Hurford's original proposal is critically investigated and it is argued that Peircean logic fits better the integration task than Hurford's psychologically grounded interpretation of Frege. Chapter 6 continues the biosemiotic investigation initiated by chapter 5—broadening the scope to biosemiotics as such.

The old semiotic question of how to characterize sign use simpler than that of human beings has sometimes given rise to ideas that evolution should go through iconic, indexical and symbolic phases, in that order, so that evolutionary later signs are composed from earlier, simpler signs. This, at a first glance tempting, idea is counter-argued from the Peircean point of view, privileging Dicisigns and their chaining into Arguments. That gives rise to an opposite viewpoint: simple biological sign use is full pragmatic Arguments taking the shape of Perception-Action loops—but they have little internal differentiation nor are they subject to individual shaping, recoding and reinterpretation. Semiotic evolution is then taken to rest upon the ongoing differentiation, articulation and subdivision of simple Argument structure, facilitating the growth of semiotic freedom and cognitive capabilities over the course of evolution.

Chapter 6 having charted the generalization of Dicisigns over biology, chapter 7 continues with the parallel generalization of Dicisigns over human expressions. A first issue is the central role played by pictures and diagrams, both as predicates in truth claims and in reasoning directly in the diagrammatical structure. Another is that an important dimension of differences between Dicisigns comes from the variety of predicates—so that a new taxonomy of subtypes of predicates appear as a major semiotic task. A third is the wide variety of different combinations of perception modes, sign types and media satisfying the functional definition of Dicisigns. A fourth is that the Dicisign doctrine appears as an important, on some points radical, version of Andy Clark's actual "Extended Mind" hypothesis. Finally, the conception of language itself will also undergo transformation in the Dicisign perspective: it emerges as a special, multi-purpose diagrammatical tool, combining loosely coupled parts of highly differing universality to allow for the application to an indefinite range of tasks.

Chapter 8 focuses on the special issue of the iconicity of propositions using diagrams. The Peircean use of "iconic" is found to be double. One use of the term refers to operations, to what may be performed, experimentally, in order to extract further information from an iconically represented Dicisign. Another use of the same word, however, points to the fact that even signs with the same power as to operation may possess different degrees of iconicity in terms of their similarity with the objectivities they represent—hence "operational" vs. "optimal" iconicity.

Chapter 9 goes back into the roots of Peirce's Dicisign theory in the discussion of the extension and comprehension of propositions in his 1860s papers. In an unpublished rejoinder to those papers—Ms. 725, from around 1870—Peirce presents some hitherto unexplained diagram experiments with the aim of establishing a conception of natural kinds based on these structures of propositions.

The chapter claims that those diagrams experiments ultimately fail—but that they throw an important light upon the connection between Dicisigns and an ontology of kinds.

Chapter 10 goes into the central distinction which Peirce made within diagrammatical reasoning—that between "corollarial" and "theorematic" reasoning, a distinction which he himself hailed as his first "real discovery", recently celebrated by Jaakko Hintikka to actually constitute one of Peirce's most important results. In corollarial reasoning, the conclusion is more or less directly read off of the diagram, once it has been constructed, synthesizing the premises; in theorematic reasoning, some further addition to the diagram, often requiring ingenious experimentation, is required for assessing the theorem to be proved. This chapter presents and discusses Peirce's different examples and descriptions of what makes theorematic reasoning differ, and it concludes by proposing a further subdivision among theorematic reasonings.

Chapter 11 approaches the most general level of Peirce's logico-semiotic reorientation of the cognitive field—that of his strategic theory-of-science deliberations of the general structure of investigations—the "methodeutics" as he would have it. Maxims like the Pragmatic Maxim, "Symbols Grow" or "Do Not Block the Way of Inquiry" form heuristic, strategic additions to logic proper—much like Hintikka's distinction between chess rules and chess strategies. Simultaneously, they form Peirce's overlooked Enlightenment credentials, outlining the self-correcting behavior of the community of researchers against received doctrines in their institutional embeddings.

While in several senses a reconstruction of central parts of Peirce's philosophy of propositions, this volume is not intended as a Peirce introduction. Many such introductions, some of them very good, exist. My aim is to bring worthwhile Peircean ideas into play in contemporary contexts, of cognitive science, cognitive semiotics, biosemiotics, epistemology and philosophy of logic. For that reason this volume also takes the liberty of developing further the Peircean Dicisign doctrine in these directions, taking it sometimes far away from Peirce's original formulations—e.g. when discussing biological or mixed-media Dicisigns—as well as bringing Peircean conceptions in play in relation to present issues and discussions. Much to the annoyance of my friend Barry Smith, I have not been able to do this by translating Peircean terminology exhaustively into ordinary philosophical lingo. This has the reason that it is precisely the overall conceptual reorientation of a whole field which I find most pregnant with possibilities—I fear this may be occluded by attempting to present it in terms most readers will associate with received senses primarily.

I hope to convince the reader that Peirce's semiotics is important not only as a piece of intellectual history and an important anticipation of things to come, not only as a piecemeal contribution to details of actual semiotics, philosophy, and cognitive science—but that its most important offering is that of a renewed outlook of the whole of the "cognitive field", enabling us to envision the exploration of routes not taken, both in terms of further conceptual development and experimental investigations.

Chapter 2

The Generality of Signs

2.1 The Actual Relevance of Anti-Psychologism

Anti-psychologism is basic for semiotics as such. During the founding period
of modern semiotics in the decades around 1900, the refusal of taking signs
to be reducible to psychological phenomena was crucial for the establishing
of logical and semiotic phenomena and structures as autonomous objects of
research. Thus, it plays center stage in Peirce, Frege, and Husserl—the three
of them forming a virtual trinity of anti-psychologism. From the three of them,
anti-psychologism became central to logic, semiotics and phenomenology of the
20th century—importantly making the study of propositions in these traditions
independent from psychology. It is well-known how the anti-psychologism of
Frege fed into the nascent currents of formal logic and analytical philosophy
from late 19th century onwards to the extent that this virtually forms the birth
certificate of those disciplines[1]—it seems more exposed to oblivion, however,
how the very notion of signs and semiotics as domains of research crucially
depends on anti-psychologism.

But what is this "psychologism" which anti-psychologism takes as its critical
target? Narrowly taken, it is the idea that logic is the empirical study of how
minds and brains behave while thinking[2]—more generally, it is the idea that
the study of the content and structure of thought and signs forms part of the

---

[1] As charted, inter alia, in Coffa 1991 or Dummett 1993.

[2] "Psychologism" in English is the translation of German "Psychologismus" which was
invented in 1866 by Johann Erdmann to critically characterize the work of Eduard Beneke
(Kusch 1995, 101) who became later himself the target of similar attacks. Subsequently, the
term became commonplace in the "Psychologismusstreit", the struggle over psychologism, in
German academia around 1900.

domain of psychology—so that the empirical investigation of minds and brains forms the primary or even the only way of accessing these issues. A basic problem in psychologism is that it immediately allows for relativism. If one mind holds one thing to be true while another prefers another, both minds are equally entitled to be investigated by psychology—who are we to judge, if psychology is taken to be the deepest or even the only access to those claims? Psychology studies psychic processes in general—with no distinction as to whether particular claims made by those psyches are true or false, and the truth or falsity of a claim may not be decided from investigating the psychological process bringing forth that claim. To make a caricature: If mathematical entities were really of a purely psychological nature, then truths about them should be attained by means of psychological investigations. The upshot of psychologism might thus be that a proper way of deciding the truth of the claim that $2+2=4$ would be to make an empirical investigation of a large number of individual, psychological assessments of that claim. So, if we amass data of, say, 100.000 individual records of calculating $2+2$, we might find that a small but significant amount of persons take the result to be 3—which would give us an average measure of around 3.999 as the result. This might now be celebrated as the most exact and scientific investigation yet of the troubling issue of $2+2$— far more precise than the traditional, metaphysical claims of the result being 4, which must now be left behind as merely the coarse and approximate result of centuries of dogmatic mathematicians indulging in armchair philosophy and folk theories, not caring to investigate psychological reality empirically.

Another implication of psychologism may be that signs and their meaning are nothing more than the individual psychic or neuronal phenomena supporting them or associated with them. This makes it difficult to describe the majority of signs which are repeatable and thus assumed to be identical from one use to the next. For how could two different mental experiences be assumed to be identical? Thus, the meaning of a word in a language may be taken to be the sum or average of the set of individual mental representations of that word's meaning (something similar goes for the acoustic or graphic image of the word which is also identically repeatable or multiply realizable).[3] An immediate problem in such a conception is that an object to which we have fairly direct access—word meaning as accessed by linguistics, dictionaries, encyclopædias, public definitions, introspection, common action, intersubjective agreement in everyday speech—is replaced by an object to which we have no access (or very limited access), namely a sum of different bundles of associations in the minds of a vast array of individual persons. This problem is of

---

[3] The fact that word meanings may vary from one context of use to another forms another issue which must not be confused with psychologism.

immediate concern for the scientific study of meaning— how are we to establish the meaning of a lexeme if it consists in nothing but millions of vague, fleeting, instantaneous, mental events which we are only able to address via the insecure roundabout way of trusting people's own introspective reports about their mental experiences? And the same problem holds for the individual language learner's access to word meaning: the user has even less access to the myriad of mental events in other persons' heads assumed to constitute word meaning—how could we ever learn language if the prerequisite was the child's laborious summing up of the psychic imagery of many other persons? Anti-psychologism in semiotics has approached this conundrum by claiming that the expression, the content as well of the reference of semiotic structures cannot be thus reduced to individual mental representations—rather, the sign vehicle, its content and reference are seen as objective, general types which are instantiated in tokens in the concrete processes of cognition and communication. Of course, such tokens may, in turn, give rise to widely differing mental associations in the single sign user without those associations being central to the objectivity of the sign. Thus, the fact that yours truly is a synaesthete and imagines the equation $2 + 2 = 4$ as involving two light blue "2" digits and a claret red digit "4" has absolutely no bearing on the fact that the meaning, reference and truth of that equation is exactly the same in me as in another individual who may associate the very same general claim and state-of-affairs with other colors or with different imaginary means such as Roman numerals, two dots alongside two dots or any other mental way of adorning that basic claim.

Here, we shall make a concise presentation and comparison of classical anti-psychologism in the semiotics of Peirce and Husserl in order to actualize anti-psychologism. Focusing upon propositions and reasoning, it is vital to make clear that the fact that minds and brains may make statements and arguments is not the same thing as taking such statements and arguments, their meanings and references, to be products of mental activity. A reason why this seems again necessary to argue is the introduction of cognitive science and the neurosciences in semiotics, linguistics and philosophy. This is not to claim that this development with any necessity leads to psychologism. The important study of the relations between semiotics and cognition and the many investigations of how the brain and mind process many different aspects of sign use form central and important parts of actual cognitive semiotics— yet, the neglect of anti-psychologism may, in some cases, lead researchers to assume untenable dreams of the complete reduction of things semiotic to psychology, thereby unknowingly repeating late 19C cul-de-sacs of psychologism and leading to erroneous or exaggerated interpretations of experimental findings. Unlike the case in early psychologism, however, such claims only rarely appear as explicit programs of reducing logic and semiotics to psychology—much more often, such ideas appear implicitly, in constructivist folk ontologies, in the definition of experimental aims or in ambitious extensions of conclusions drawn from empirical investigations. The logical argument against psychologism makes evident the dangers in such hasty psychologizations.

2.2 Husserl's Anti-Psychologism

Let us begin with Husserl's anti-psychologism which gave birth to the whole movement of European phenomenology, taking the objective description of ideal structures[4]—whether intended by a mind or not—as its object.

A well-worn myth in the history of philosophy tells us that it was Frege's scathing review of Husserl's first book *Philosophie der Aritmetik* (1890) which prompted Husserl to a volte-face, repudiating his earlier psychologism in favor of the staunch anti-psychologism of *Logische Untersuchungen* (1900–1901) whose 300-pages Prolegomena counts as Husserl's major statement against psychologism.[5] A strong case can be made, however, that Husserl was never a psychologicist and that the parts of *Philosophie der Aritmetik* mistaken for psychologism rather aimed at establishing an epistemology of numbers, not the psychological reduction of them.[6] In any case, the attacks prompted Husserl to introduce *Logische Untersuchungen* by his most thorough statement against psychologism—a statement which proved central to the ensuing debate over psychologism in the first decades of the 20th century. Figures attacked for

---

[4]Many people immediately frown when faced with the notion of "ideal" and "ideality". The wording is not important, notions as "typical" or "general" may just as well be used; "ideal" in Husserl's sense of the word does not in any way imply subjectivism, quite on the contrary.

[5] Kusch 1995 provides a detailed account of the *Psychologismusstreit* in German philosophy and psychology up to 1930. A social constructivist, Kusch attempts to find the roots of the controversy in fights for university chairs between the two sciences—and he even sides with psychologism for the basic reason that it forms an ally to his own sociologism, both of them willing to reduce the issue of truth to the relativity of psyches and societies. His final argument—that the victory of anti-psychologism in the 1920s was due to the antiscientific welding of phenomenology with Lebensphilosophie in order to fit irrational "Weimar mentality"—completely overlooks Husserl's stance against the Lebensphilosophie, also in its phenomenological guise in Heidegger. Even worse, it overlooks that irrationalist vitalism more often sides with psychologism rather than with anti-psychologism. Still, Kusch's book is highly valuable, not only does it give a useful and detailed comparison of Frege's and Husserl's antipsychologisms, it also gives a detailed overview over the wide variety of positions on the psychologism issue among different contemporary schools of philosophy and psychology. Peirce, on the margins of these European struggles, is not mentioned.

[6]See Smith 1978.

psychologism in the Prolegomena include Eduard Beneke, Benno Erdmann, John Stuart Mill, Christoph Sigwart and other logicians, and the main line of arguments in his refusal of psychologism runs as follows.

The Prolegomena embeds the criticism of psychologism in the outline of an ambitious and important theory of science—the central argument of which is that any science forms a body of knowledge expressed in propositions which, in turn, are connected to form a theory by means of logical relations holding between them. Thus, logic constitutes a basic prerequisite to any science. This implies, on the other hand, that the theoretical doctrines of the single sciences are never, in themselves, complete (§5). They require completion through this doctrine of a theory of science ("Wissenschaftslehre") as well as a metaphysics (in the sense of a doctrine accounting for the basic concepts and entities of the science in question). The latter two require that a science must constitute a unity given by the system of propositions it embraces (§6). Only a few of these propositions, however, facilitate immediate evidence—and other propositions regarding other states-of-affairs more remote from experience must be logically founded on those evident propositions. Here, the close affinity of the early Husserl to early analytical philosophy is obvious. Thus, logic linking all the propositions of a discipline together forms a basic, normative tool of science—a tool which must be, in turn, based on logic as a descriptive doctrine. This meta-scientific prolegomena to the Prolegomena is important for its insistence on the role of logical normativity in any science whatsoever—and it forms the frame of the whole psychologism refutation as Husserl returns to this theory in his conclusion. Some combinations of propositions are logically valid, others not so—and this validity cannot be established psychologically, because psychology indiscriminately studies psychic processes without regard to the validity of their claims.

Husserl's argument, however, differs from ordinary arguments against psychologism, he claims. They include the distinction between normative logic and descriptive psychology as well as the circularity argument: psychology depends upon logic, hence it cannot found the study of logic (Hermann Lotze, Carl Stumpf). Husserl does not embrace these arguments (§19): he refuses to accept the characterization of logic as being normative only, and thus the former piece of anti-psychologism may be repudiated merely by taking logic to form a very special subset of psychology. The latter may be rejected by admitting that psychology does indeed use the rules of logic, but does not take logic as a premise (a scientist may proceed logically without explicitly relying upon logic, just like the painter does not need to be an expert on aesthetics). The latter part of this argument Peirce would also embrace with his distinction between use-embedded *logica utens* and the explicit study of logic in the *logica docens.* Husserl takes this to imply that only if the scientist argues *from* logic, not *with* logic, a *circulus vitiosus* will appear.[7] The validity of this argument seems doubtful, however; even if the artist does not explicitly know aesthetics, his practice tacitly presupposes it to the extent that he must conform to it; the degree of explicit, conscious knowledge in the subject cannot be decisive for the logical relations between the claims he makes or the phenomena they address. Degrees of consciousness form a psychological issue and cannot decide logical issues (cf. Husserl himself on this issue in §23, below). The vagueness of this argument is also evident from the fact that Husserl does not otherwise refrain from using the circularity argument.

Husserl's own argumentation takes another direction with a pre-Popperian argument attacking the empiricist implications of psychologism. Psychological regularities are empirical laws and thus necessarily inexact—which is why they fail to form a possible base of support for the exact laws of logic: Induction is never able to prove the validity of an empirical law, only its probability (§21).[8] Secondly, psychologism confuses logical laws in themselves with the psychological acts of judgment using those laws—a confusion between the ideal and the real, the distinction between which becomes crucial to Husserl's overall argument. Thus—a proto-Searlean argument—a computer does not understand its own calculations; their logical validity does not depend upon whether they are accompanied by conscious acts of judgment or not.[9] Thirdly, if logical regularities were, as claim the psychologicists, natural laws of the mind, they should have a psychological content and presuppose the existence of minds. But no logical law implies the existence of any matter of fact—we cannot pass from any truth of logic (or mathematics) to the existence of any empirical fact, be it in psychology or elsewhere. Unlike the ideal truths of logic and mathematics, the general laws of the empirical sciences are idealized fictions *cum fundamento in re* (§23).

---

[7]It may be argued, though, that the degree of explicitness to which logic is taken as a premise, should not play a role for the issue of a possible *circulus vitiosus*. Science presupposes that the arguments of a theory may be checked by any other well-informed scientist—the ideal, logical stability and repeatability of the theory is presupposed in such an assumption. If a scientific theory were merely a vague, approximate, subjective content, ever-shifting in its wandering from one mind to the next, one scientist would be unable to control the other's work.

[8] Kusch 1995 refers Moritz Schlick for the counterargument that if logic is indeed a part of psychology, then psychology eo ipso *does* contain exact laws, namely those of logic. This, of course, raises other issues—how could these then be the only empirical laws escaping inexactitude?

[9]Husserl's argument is that the logical validity is independent of the presence or absence of consciousness accompanying the process; Searle, of course, makes the same argument with another aim, that of arguing against the claim that ordinary computers may have conscious states.

A large argument bearing on the real-ideal distinction is devoted to the Law of Contradiction as it is explained in different psychologicists, Mill, Sigwart, F.A. Lange, Herbert Spencer, psychological renderings of Kant, etc. (§25ff). Contradiction cannot be explained by the (claimed) empirical impossibility of minds to have mutually exclusive experiences at the same time—for that description presupposes the idea of mutual exclusivity which is the same as contradiction. This issue leads Husserl to an important observation regarding empiricism (§26): the belief in nothing but singular empirical propositions bars it from even defending its own principles, because it rejects the important possibility of reaching mediate knowledge from immediate knowledge. It thus confuses the origin of knowledge with its legitimation (*Genesis* and *Geltung*, as it were)—as Reichenbach was later to distinguish in his famous contrasting context of discovery vs. context of justification.

The example of syllogisms is important (§30)—few psychologists venture into a psychological version of them, because any fallacy would immediately count as a counterexample: if logic was really a "physics of thought" (Th. Lipps) the validity of logic would be rejected by any person committing a fallacy.

Husserl's most crucial point against psychologism, however, is that it leads to relativism or skepticism—as argued in his conclusive return to his basic theory of science (§32). Theory-construction, according to him, has two basic, correlative sets of conditions of possibility: a) subjectively: the experience of evidence, the ideal presuppositions for the possibility of immediate and mediate knowledge and their legitimation in any possible knowing subject whatever; b) objectively: the set of propositions of the theory and the logical inference structure binding them together. If the possibility of either of these is denied, we are left with variants of skepticism. The refusal of the former leads to noetic skepticism, the refusal of the latter leads to logical skepticism (no knowledge is possible; no truth is possible, respectively)—both of which are inherently contradictory, because they form theoretical doctrines denying the possibility of true theories. Again, these skepticisms must be distinguished from so-called "metaphysical" skepticism which is not thus contradictory, but which denies the possibility of knowledge of certain realms of reality, an example being Kant's refusal of knowledge of things-in-themselves to be possible.

Relativist psychologism may take the shape of noetic or metaphysical skepticism—in both cases claiming that truth and knowledge are always relative to the judging subject. Such relativism comes in two variants, depending upon its notion of subject. An individual relativism may ensue, tied to the subjectivity of the single person and with solipsism as the result—or, on the other hand, a specific (species-related) relativism focusing on the idea that any species of judging beings possess their own unique set of thought-laws (§34), admitting "truth for this and that species" only. The former is quickly dealt with—by a variant of the classic argument against solipsism for being self-refuting. The latter is taken more seriously—more scientific-seeming as it is, referring to the knowledge structures of whole species, particularly human beings. This is characterized as "anthropologism", the anthropocentric claim that knowledge and truth are relative to the human species.[10] The basic argument against it is that the same content of thoughts cannot be true and false at the same time—no matter whether expressed in different thought-laws or languages or not. So there are only two possibilities—either other species use words corresponding to "true" and "false" in a way like us—or they use similar words differently, and then it is a strife about words. The problem in the "anthropologicist" argument is that the existence of the human species is a fact, and from facts come only facts—not logical truth. If truth had its origin in the specific constitution of human beings, no truth would exist without man, and the relativity of truth would entail the relativity of the existence of the world—that is, make science impossible.[11]

Psychologism, in all its forms, now constitutes such a type of relativism (§38). Sigwart, again, is taken as an example (§39): for him it is a fiction that a truth may be true without anyone thinking it. But then Newton's Second Law would not be true before Newton, Husserl argues: Truth is not a subjective phenomenon. Any truth is a unity of validity in the atemporal realm of ideas (parallel to Frege's argument for a "Third Realm" of ideal structures), and you cannot at the same time relativize truth and maintain the objectivity of being, because the two of them are correlative. Similarly Benno Erdmann: he imagines a superspecies of thinking beings might exist whose highly sophisticated concepts would be as alien to us as ours are to our children—and their logic would be both superior to ours and unintelligible to us. Husserl's counterargument: even such supermen would be bound by the law of contradiction—and by logic and mathematics in general.

Thus, the set of three basic prejudices of psychologism is listed (§41):

---

[10]This central argument was already in Peirce (below), and crops up again in cognitive science—Clark 2008 warns against "anthropocentrism" and "neurocentrism" (93) where accidental aspects of human neural cognition are taken to form basic properties of cognitive processes in general.

[11] Kusch (2007) claims that Husserl here and in the following confuses truth and reality. Husserl indeed seems to vacillate between taking truth to be the correspondence relation between a proposition expressed in a sentence and a state-of-affairs on the one hand, and to simply *be* that state-of-affairs on the other. If it is taken to be the former, then it is correct that truths did not exist before man or other species uttering sentences, even if the reality referred to did exist. This, however, seems to be a strife of words, and it seems evident Husserl's position may be consistently redescribed using either of the two truth definitions.

1) *The idea that prescriptions for the regulation of psychic processes are themselves psychologically grounded.* Against this, rules for norms must be distinguished from what is governed by those norms. Concepts like truths, sentences, subject/predicate, implication etc. are general norms prerequisite to any science—and must be distinguished from empirical norms inherent in instruments and tools related to human scientists.

2) Second prejudice (§44): *Logical concepts are psychic formations.* If that were true, the whole of mathematics would become a mere branch of psychology. But even if we cannot access numbers without counting, sums without addition, products without multiplication—nobody would say that mathematicians are psychologists. The act of counting is located in space-time, but the ideal form type of a number is nothing existing in time and space, and the former is a psychological tool for grasping the latter. An important observation here is that "Vorstellung" ('idea') is a misleading word since it tacitly presumes that all objects of the mind share an equally psychic character.[12] Here, specifically logical concepts are not psychic or mental—rather, they are the *objects* of mental acts, just like external objects are not parts of the mind. So this prejudice tends to make invisible an important tripartite distinction: that between 1) the psychic connections between mental experiences *vs.* 2) the real connections between theoretically known states-of-affairs *vs.* 3) logical connections between propositions—a distinction between connections in mind, reality, and logic, respectively.

3) A third prejudice (§49) is that *All truth lies in judgment.* But we only recognize a proposition as true due to its evidence. And evidence is not merely a psychological feeling. There are non-mental ideal conditions for evidence: "the experience in which a judging person realize the truth of his judgment, its suitability to truth"—while the task of psychology, by contrast, is to study the natural, empirical conditions for the experience of evidence: degrees of concentration, alertness, practice, etc.[13]

The decisive lesson is thus the distinction between real and ideal (§51). Any proposition involves claims of meaning and validity and it would be absurd to split up the concept into some extension of single cases. Truth is the idea of a fit between the meaning of a proposition and a state-of-affairs; and evidence

---

[12] John Deely (2001) argues that it is the appearance of the notion of "idea" in both empiricism and rationalism in early 17th century which leads to the strange fact that at the same time as modern realist science is expanding, modern anti-realist, nominalist epistemology sees the light. To Deely, "idea" unfortunately replaces "sign" with its ineradicable connection to referent objects.

[13] It is well-known that Husserl was himself attacked for psychologism in the LU—one reason was his doctrine of intentional acts in the 5th LU—another was his reference to evidence in his truth theory. He does not, however, identify evidence with a psychological feeling but with the experience of an ideal fit between a claim and a state of affairs.

is not a mere psychological feeling, but the experience of this very fit. The distinction between real and ideal gives two types of truths (§63): individual truths pertaining to real existence on the one hand—and general truths on the other.[14] The concrete sciences addressing empirical facts must attach to the lower principles of the nomological and abstract sciences.[15]

Science is, at one and the same time, an anthropological unity of thought acts and thought dispositions and external arrangements on the one hand, involving psychological states—and, on the other hand, an objective, ideal connection between truths. Truth is the ideal correlate of the fleeting subjective acts of knowledge in different individuals in time and space (§62)—we may say, using later terminology, that the former has a multiple realizability in different subjects and may thus be incarnated in many different particular versions of the latter. This is why the aprioric study of real possibilities—cut off from all connection to particular thinking subjects and the idea of subjectivity— may be accomplished. Such real possibilities may then, in turn, be applied on empirical single cases (§65).

A theory, ideally conceived of, just consists of logically connected propositions. This characterization finally opens the vista for an ambitious "Theory of theories": if all "givenness", all material/empirical content, is erased from a theory, its pure logical skeleton form will remain (this is taken to be the procedure by which notions like concept, truth, sentence, subject, predicate, etc. have been isolated in the first place). To these concepts of logic, concepts of formal ontology may be added, which pertain to any sort of object domain whatever: concepts like object, state-of-affairs, unity, plurality, number, connection... —formal categories of objects (§67). Thus, different possible theory structures can be investigated—and one may be transformed into the other by the controlled variation of certain factors—so that any particular theory ideally may be assigned to a form class among other form classes of theories (§69).

---

[14]It is important to add that general truths may have very different types of objects. The prototypical case, as it were, is logical and mathematical truths, referring to ideal objects with no amount of factual matter involved. Another set is general claims about matters of facts, e.g. laws, patterns, tendencies, universals, properties charted by science or everyday knowledge—these may even come in two types, material ontological concepts like matter, organism, society, language, etc., and empirical universals like bacteria, elephants, telephones, etc.. A third set is general claims about restricted universes of discourses, such as thought experiments or fictions, such as addressed by Husserl's important follower Ingarden; see Stjernfelt 2007, ch 17.

[15]A section critically addresses the then current idea that logic are techniques of thought economy only; we skip these arguments as they do not add much to the central issue of psychologism.

The object correlate of these pure theories is what Husserl calls "the theory of multiplicity" (the integration of recent results of general mathematics: general geometry, the topology of Grassmann and Hamilton, Lie group theory, Cantorian set theory etc.) on the object level. The important upshot of this idea is that all theories are taken to contain mathematical structure, simple or complex, implicit or explicit—so that all empirical theories form material specifications of selections of this "theory of multiplicity". Perceptual judgments—the bread and butter of empirical science—are thus taken to be integrated into theories governed by the ideal norm of the unity of science facilitated by logic (§72).

Thus, Husserl's overall argument is that psychologism in logic leads to relativism and consequently to the impossibility of science—while the theory of science proves the necessity of scientific theories to be carried by logically connected propositions. With the focus upon logic (and mathematics) in the Prolegomena, Husserl's antipsychologism may seem not to have a direct bearing on semiotic issues more broadly conceived. This is not so. We do not have the space here to run through its wide consequences in what follows in the *Logical Investigations*; suffice it to say that antipsychologism is a guiding light all through the work. In the first investigation, general expression signs ("Ausdrücke" as opposed to non-general, indicative "Anzeichen") are investigated; in the second, an anti-empiricist theory of abstractions (as due to a change in attitude distinct from the issue of induction) is outlined. In the important third investigation, a doctrine of parts and wholes is outlined, and the central distinction between formal ontology (holding for all objects) and different material ontologies (holding for the special sciences) is sketched—the upshot being that the foundation of any science is constituted by the set of dependencies holding between the specific parts and wholes studied. The fourth investigation applies this to language, giving the outline of an a priori grammar for any empirical language. The fifth investigation, famously introducing Husserl's concept of "intention", was already during the reception of the book mistaken for reintroducing psychologism because of its emphasis on subjective intentions; the resulting theory is, quite on the contrary, the outline of a material ontology of any possible subjectivity, expressed in the terminology of the dependence ontology of the third investigation. The long sixth investigation draws further consequences for science and the relation between the conceptual and perceptual aspects of it. The overall result, then, is that Husserl's antipsychologism forms the very basis of his early phenomenology and underlines the irreducibility to psychology not only of the central core of logical and mathematical propositions, but also of a whole array of general phenomena which may involve mental acts and be addressed by them, such as signs, abstractions, part-whole structures, grammar, intentionality, and science as such.

When Husserl returns to the issue of anti-psychologism many years later, in the *Formale und transzendentale Logik* (1929), the basic real-ideal argument of the *Prolegomena* is repeated, now phrased in the terminology of the possibility of objects of mental acts—like propositions—to be numerically identical. I may address exactly the same object in two different mental acts—such objects must be ideal, as all real objects are ever-changing and never numerically identical. This terminology may be confusing, because "ideal" nowadays is often associated with "subjective". As should be evident, Husserl's use of "ideal" is almost the opposite. As we shall see, Peirce would call such entities "generals" and "universals", but it is important to notice that the same issue keeps cropping up in different guises, also in current cognitive science. Here, concepts such as "schemata", "coarse-graining", "insensitivity", "multiple realizability", "abstraction", "types", etc. address the same issues: that it is possible for the mind to use signs to address entities which are not fully determinate without assuming such objects are mere figments of the mind. The notion of "ideal" may frighten scientists of our day, but the central idea that cognition relies upon schemata is exactly the same idea expressed in a different dialect. And that it is exactly because such entities are not fully determinate that they may be simpler than real objects, allowing for their identical repetition.

2.3 Peirce's Anti-Psychologism

It seems considerably less well-known that Peirce was no less an ardent anti-psychologist than were Frege and Husserl. Did he not refer to minds when pragmatically defining meaning as the conceived effects of an idea—and did he not make psychological experiments himself, counting among the first to investigate "subliminal perception" experimentally? Indeed he did—and this goes to show that antipsychologism is not in any way incompatible with deep interests in profound psychological issues such as the way empirical minds use and intend ideal entities. Peirce's anti-psychologism even predated not only Husserl's but also that of Frege—it simply formed a central concern already in his very first papers from the 1860s, and it remained with him over the years, even in an increasingly radical form, following the well-known growth in Peirce's realism as traced by Max Fisch in an influential paper (Fisch 1986).[16]

---

[16]Not much has been written about Peirce's anti-psychologism; Colapietro (2003) reconstructs his general stance on the issue and notices a possible tension with Peirce's polemical embracing of "anthropomorphism"; Kasser (1999) argues that Peirce's 1878 pragmatism

As early as 1865, in the first of his "Harvard Lectures", the young Peirce states that "Logic has nothing at all to do with the operations of the understanding, acts of the mind, or facts of the intellect. This has been repeatedly shown by the Kantians. But I will go a step further and say that we ought to adopt a thoroughly unpsychological view of logic ..." (W1 164). Peirce proceeded to write a syllogism on the blackboard and insisted on distiguishing between its meaning—its "logical character"—on the one hand, and the different thoughts accompanying individual graspings of it, on the other: "Now, this has a particular character to me as I write it; it has the same to all of you as you read it; it will have the same if you read it tomorrow (...) Now is this logical character a form of thought only? My thought when I wrote it was a different event from each one of your thoughts, and your thoughts will be each different if you read it again from what they were when you read it just now. The thoughts were many, but this form was one" (ibid. 164-65). This distinction between individual thoughts and logical form anticipates Peirce's later distinction between existing Secondness and real Thirdness, just as it anticipates Husserl's between real and ideal.[17] Peirce's wording directly points to the relation of multiple realizability between the two: one and the same general logical form may be realized in many different, individual psychological thought processes.

So, in the very papers where Peirce first set the course for his lifelong quest in logic and semiotics, well before his pragmatic maxim of 1878 and his formalizations of propositional and predicate logic in the early 1880s, well before Frege's *Begriffsschrift* of 1879 and his attack on psychological logic in the 1884 *Grundlagen*, and well before even the coinage of the term "psychologism" in Germany, Peirce emphatically rejected psychologism in logic.[18] It is not our aim here to chart all occurrences of antipscyhologism in the development of Peirce's thought; let us focus upon how antipsychologism becomes central in the mature Peirce, exactly in the period after the turn of the century when he

---

papers do not deviate from his overall anti-psychologism, Amini (2008) discusses Peirce's argument from logical machines against psychologism.

[17]The possibility of terminological confusion is vast, as it appears. Husserl uses "real" about empirical matter-of-fact being—where the later Peirce would use "existence". Husserl uses "ideal" about a subset of what the later Peirce would call "real"—general structures of thought and reality.

[18]As to Peirce, antipsychologism is even repeated in one of his very last papers, "An Essay toward Reasoning in Security and Uberty" (1913) and thus spans the whole of Peirce's career: "So, it in no degree conflicts with my admiration of modern psychology that I at once express the opinion that (at least, as far as I am acquainted with it) it can afford no aid whatever in laying the foundation of a sane psychology of reasoning, albeit it has been and can still be of the most precious service in planning and executing the observations on which the reasonings depend and from which they spring." (EPII, 471).

developed the detailed version of his phenomenology and semiotics, including the doctrine of propositions as Dicisigns. An important line of argument here is Peirce's extension of logic from the formal study of truth-preservation between propositions to a much broader field. This extension is based on the Kantian idea that the only metaphysics possible is that mirroring logic:

> "The first question, and it was a question of supreme importance requiring not only utter abandonment of all bias, but also a most cautious yet vigorously active research, was whether or not the fundamental categories of thought really have that sort of dependence upon formal logic that Kant asserted. I became thoroughly convinced that such a relation really did and must exist. After a series of inquiries, I came to see that Kant ought not to have confined himself to divisions of propositions, or "judgments," as the Germans confuse the subject by calling them, but ought to have taken account of all elementary and significant differences of form among signs of all sorts, and that, above all, he ought not to have left out of account fundamental forms of reasonings." ("Pragmatism", 1906 EP II 424, 1.561)[19]

Peirce thus extends the study of logic in two directions, as it were, "downwards" and "upwards"; the former leading him to include the host of different semiotic tools by means of which logical propositions are functioning—the latter leading him to include the scientific linking of propositions in the process of research, studied by "methodeutic"—we would rather nowadays call it heuristics or theory of science. This extension of logic downwards to semiotics and upwards to heuristics immediately extends antipsychologism to cover them as well: semiotic structures, logical structures, structures of scientific discovery—all of those are accessible independently of the psychology of the particular minds which happen to realize them. Semiotics, logic proper, and theory of science all are to be conceived of anti-psychologistically—an important parallel to Husserl, in whom we also saw basic semiotic issues and the structure of whole theories as being beyond psychology. Thus it comes as no surprise when we find him articulating the basic stance of psychologism in logic and a rejection of it along a similar line as when Husserl refuses that the exactitudes of logic could be based in the inexactitudes of psychology:

> "It is almost universally held that logic is a science of thought (so far as it is a science at all), that thought is a modification of con-

---

[19]In this section, I present fairly elaborate Peirce quotes to substantiate my claim that Peirce's psychologism is on the same level of thoroughness as Frege's or Husserl's more famous versions—and to give an idea of its original character.

sciousness, and that consciousness is the object of the science of psychology. The effect of this, were it perceived, is to make logic logically dependent upon the very one of all the special sciences which most stands in logical need of a science of logic." ("Carnegie Application", 1902, Ms. L75, 233)

In central papers of this period (such as "Minute Logic" from 1902, the pragmatism lectures and the *Syllabus* from 1903 the "Prolegomena for an Apology to Pragmaticism" of 1906), Peirce's antipsychologism is developed in detail. Many of his arguments echo Husserl's[20]—thus, in the *Syllabus*, we find Peirce arguing in parallel to Husserl when stating that intelligible logical structures are badly explained by referring to much more obscure mental phenomena:

"To explain the judgment in terms of the 'proposition' is to explain it by that which is essentially intelligible. To explain the proposition in terms of the 'judgment' is to explain the self-intelligible in terms of a psychical act, which is the most obscure of phenomena or facts." (*Syllabus* 1902 EPII, 275n, 2.309n1)

And just like Husserl, Peirce pinpoints Sigwart's psychological theory of contradiction as an especially fragile piece of psychologism. While Husserl argued that Sigwart presupposed the contradiction he was out to explain, Peirce takes another road—that of dissociating the everchanging tendencies of the human mind from logical validity. As a fallibilist, he picks the case of Euclidean geometry which was perceived as unshakably evident by innumerable scholars over many centuries until the appearance of doubts about the parallel postulate and the growth of non-Euclidean geometries during the 19 C. The psychological feeling of evidence perceived by generations of expert Euclid scholars thus formed no guarantee against logical fallacy:

"The appeal to direct consciousness consists in pronouncing certain reasoning to be good or bad because it is felt to be so. This is a very common method. Sigwart, for example, bases all logic upon our invincible mental repulsion against contradiction, or, as he calls it, "the immediate feeling of necessity" (*Logic,* §3, 2). Those who think it worth while to make any defence at all of this proceeding urge, in effect, that, however far the logician may push his criticisms of reasoning, still, in doing so, he must reason, and so must ultimately rely upon his instinctive recognition of good and bad reasoning.

---

[20] Peirce's scattered references to Husserl and LU in this period are mostly pejorative—but some inspiration can not be precluded. Mostly, it seems as if both of the two mistook the other for a psychologicist (see Stjernfelt 2007, ch. 6).

Whence it follows that, in Sigwart's words, "every system of logic must rest upon this principle." It is, however, to be noted that among the dicta of direct consciousness, many pronounce certain reasonings to be bad. If, therefore, such dicta are to be relied upon, man not only usually has a tendency to reason right, but also sometimes has a tendency to reason wrong; and if that be so, the validity of a reasoning cannot *consist* in a man's having a tendency to reason in that way. Some say that the validity of reasoning consists in the "definitive dictum" of consciousness; but it has been replied that certain propositions in Euclid were studied for two thousand years by countless keen minds, all of whom had an immediate feeling of evidence concerning their proofs, until at last flaws were detected in those proofs, and are now admitted by all competent persons; and it is claimed that this illustrates how far from possible it is to make direct appeal to a definitive pronouncement." ("Minute Logic", 1902, 2.209)

Thus "tendencies" of the human mind may prove wrong even after having persisted for millennia and hence cannot be taken as foundational definitions of logical validity—quite on the contrary, it is the latter which are necessary in order to investigate the former and which may, in the longer run, prove the former to be mistaken.

In shaping the final versions of his system after the turn of the century, Peirce famously looks back and admits that his original Pragmatic Maxim of 1878 was coined in too psychological terms which is why he now rephrases it as a logical principle:

"Thus, when you say that you have faith in reasoning, what you mean is that the belief-habit formed in the imagination will determine your actions in the real case. This is looking upon the matter from the psychological point of view. Under a logical aspect your opinion in question is that general cognitions of potentialities *in futuro*, if duly constructed, will under imaginary conditions determine *schemata* or imaginary skeleton diagrams with which percepts will accord when the real conditions accord with those imaginary conditions; or, stating the essence of the matter in a nutshell, you opine that percepts follow certain general laws. Exactly how far you hold that the percepts are determined by law is a matter of individual opinion. The mere fact that you hold reasoning to be useful only supposes that you think that *to some useful extent* percepts are under the governance of law." ("Minute Logic" 1902, 2.148)

The Maxim's emphasis on future conduct makes Peirce realize that as all conceptions of the future must be, to some extent, general, such conceptions must involve general, schematic, ideal signs whose multiple realizability makes them fit to refer, at once, to many related particular future developments. This is in accordance with his idea that symbols are signs with general meaning—and whose generality entails they have an *esse in futuro* because they pertain not only to the finite amount of past and present realizations but also to indefinite future realizations of that meaning. Peirce's anti-psychologism thus importantly insists that logic requires of semiotics the involvement of schematic, general or unsaturated signs[21] facilitating diagrammatic reasoning:

> "Diagrammatic reasoning is the only really fertile reasoning. If logicians would only embrace this method, we should no longer see attempts to base their science on the fragile foundations of metaphysics or a psychology not based on logical theory; and there would soon be such an advance in logic that every science would feel the benefit of it." ("Prolegomena for an Apology to Pragmaticism", 1906, 4.570)

Here, an important difference between Husserl's and Peirce's antipsychologisms becomes evident. Husserl, as a mathematician inspired by Weierstrass and Kronecker, was suspicious against diagrams and considered them to form a mere part of the mental imagery connected to the psychological instantiation of reasoning in particular minds—and thus inevitably forming part of a psychologistic account for logic. Peirce, quite on the contrary, saw diagrams as the crucial means giving access to pure logical form beyond individual (or species-bound) psychologies. And unlike Husserl who vacillated faced with the *circulus vitiosus* argument against psychologism, Peirce presents the psychologistic stance and argues that it invariably leads to such a circle:

> "Another mark of our philosophy is the disposition to make psychology the key to philosophy—categories, aesthetics, ethics, logic, and metaphysics. Something of this has existed since Descartes; but since about 1863[22] every student of philosophy, even though he be one of those who consider the present psychological tendency

---

[21] Peirce, as a chemist, took unsaturatedness of many signs—like Rhemes, his version of propositional functions—to be central. Here, he parallels Frege, although with some differences addressed in the next chapter.

[22] Peirce's pinpointing of the year 1863 as the victory of experimental psychology seems to point to Fechner's *Psychophysik* (1860) followed by Wundt's *Beiträge zur Theorie der Sinneswahrnehmung* (1862) and *Vorlesungen über die Menschen- und Thierseele* (1863); cf. Peirce's review of the English Wundt volume *Principles of Physiological Psychology* (1905, 8.196).

excessive, has placed a new and higher estimate than before upon the scientific value of psychology. Here was seen one science, than which no branch of philosophy, in the days when men disputed about the *primum cognitum,* was more enveloped in metaphysical fog, which yet almost suddenly, that mist lifting, had come out bright and clear as a June forenoon. How could it but happen, as it certainly did, that men should think that the best way to resolve any problem of philosophy would be to reduce it to a question of psychology? The future must determine precisely what the value of this method may be. It has its opponents. For some years after the movement once became general, no strong voice was raised against it; and ten or fifteen years ago psychologists of the first rank could dream of establishing the truths of their science without any metaphysical assumptions whatsoever. Some writers use such language even yet; but careful examination has convinced the better part that even physics has its metaphysical postulates, and that psychology is peculiarly dependent upon them. That being the case, some writers urge that if psychology needs to rest upon metaphysics, and metaphysics upon logic, especially if, as some contend, logic rests upon ethics, then to found ethics, logic, and metaphysics in their turn upon a basis of psychology, this self-supporting cycle would rest on nothing. The reply is that the philosophical sciences will support each other, like two drunken sailors. Suffice it to say that the mutual support theory and with it the theory that psychology is the proper foundation for philosophy are not now without vigorous opponents." (Draft of a review of Baldwin's Dictionary, 1901, 8.167)

Who is Peirce thinking of here when talking about present vigorous opponents to psychologism? It could not be himself who is "now" a vigorous opponent—for he has been an opponent for some 35 years at this point. It could not be Frege, whom he did not know about; it could not be Bolzano who was long since gone. Maybe after all Peirce did recognize the strong antipsychologism of Husserl's Prolegomena, recently published? In his mature period, Peirce argued—just like Husserl—in the crucial two steps that 1) logic is primary to psychology, while, in turn, 2) phenomenology is primary to logic (commenting upon a paper James has sent him):

"Perhaps the most important aspect of the series of papers of which the one you send me is the first, will prove to be that it shows so clearly that phenomenology is one science and psychology a very different one. I know that you are not inclined to see much value in distinguishing between one science and another. But my opinion is that it is absolutely necessary to any progress. The standards of certainty must be different in different sciences, the principles to which one science appeals altogether different from those of the other. From the point of view of logic and methodical development the distinctions are of the greatest concern. Phenomenology has no right to appeal to logic, except to deductive logic. On the contrary, logic must be founded on phenomenology. Psychology, you may say, observes the same facts as phenomenology does. No. It does not *observe* the same facts. It looks upon the same world;—the same world that the astronomer looks at. But what it *observes* in that world is different. Psychology of all sciences stands most in need of the discoveries of the logician, which he makes by the aid of the phenomenologist." (Letter to James, Oct 3 1904, 8.297)

While the anti-relativist argument and the threat from skepticism are central to Husserl's anti-psychologism, Peirce rarely explicitly addresses psychologism as a species of relativism, probably because relativism was less present as a danger in 1900 New England than it was in post-idealist Germany, ever ready to embrace reductive origin explanations. Yet, Peirce addresses two of the issues implied in relativism—the non-relative validity of logical truth as well as the non-anthropocentric view of logic. The former is addressed many times, for instance in this earlier quote:

"It was shown in the first of these papers that the validity of an inference does not depend on any tendency of the mind to accept it, however strong such tendency may be; but consists in the real fact that, when premises like those of the argument in question are true, conclusions related to them like that of this argument are also true." ("The Doctrine of Chances" 1878, 2.649)

The latter is addressed on many occasions when Peirce underlines that his concept of mind is not delimited to the human mind (or any other specific domain of minds, for that matter), thus arguing against what Husserl would call anthropologism:

"A subtle and almost ineradicable narrowness in the conception of Normative Science runs through almost all modern philosophy in making it relate exclusively to the human mind. The beautiful is conceived to be relative to human taste, right and wrong concern human conduct alone, logic deals with human reasoning. Now in the truest sense these sciences certainly are indeed sciences of mind. Only, modern philosophy has never been able quite to shake off the Cartesian idea of the mind, as something that "resides"—such is the term—in the pineal gland. Everybody laughs at this nowadays, and yet everybody continues to think of mind in this same general way, as something within this person or that, belonging to him and correlative to the real world." ("Lectures on Pragmatism", 1903, 5.128)

In one of his late masterworks, "Prolegomena for an Apology to Pragmaticism" (1906), Peirce broadens his notion of mind not only to encompass possible non-human occurrences of subjectivity (like Husserl), but to a generalized conception of mind being at work in a germ-like form already in inanimate nature, only to develop during the process of evolution. The mere functional connection of signs are thus taken to constitute "quasi-minds". We saw how Husserl, in his theory of science, was also preoccupied with the logical connection structure of propositions—but in his case, a more fixed notion of subjectivity was taken to form the prerequisite of the epistemological access to such sign connection structures. In Peirce, the related idea is turned the other way around, as it were: the very logical connection between instantiated signs constitutes, in itself, a quasi-mind:

> "Thought is not necessarily connected with a brain. It appears in the work of bees, of crystals, and throughout the purely physical world; and one can no more deny that it is really there, than that the colors, the shapes, etc., of objects are really there. Consistently adhere to that unwarrantable denial, and you will be driven to some form of idealistic nominalism akin to Fichte's. Not only is thought in the organic world, but it develops there. But as there cannot be a General without Instances embodying it, so there cannot be thought without Signs. We must here give "Sign" a very wide sense, no doubt, but not too wide a sense to come within our definition. Admitting that connected Signs must have a Quasi-mind, it may further be declared that there can be no isolated sign. Moreover, signs require at least two Quasi-minds; a *Quasi-utterer* and a *Quasi-interpreter*; and although these two are at one (*i.e.*, are one mind) in the sign itself, they must nevertheless be distinct. In the Sign they are, so to say, *welded*. Accordingly, it is not merely a fact of human Psychology, but a necessity of Logic, that every logical evolution of thought should be dialogic." ("Prolegomena for an Apology to Pragmaticism" 1906, 4.551)

As it appears, Peirce took the elaboration of such functional sign connections to require at least two minds (maybe only in the shape of two phases of one and the same mind)—and saw this as a truth of logic in his broad sense, presumably as part of the logic of discovery; Husserl only later addressed related issues in his notion of intersubjectivity.

Thus, many themes overlap in the antipsychologism of the two, including the *Genesis-Geltung* argument that validity of logic cannot be derived from empirical facts, and the anti-anthropologism argument that psychology only studies the human mind, while logic and semiotics are valid for minds as such (no matter which empirical array of beings may prove to be subsumed under this concept). The *circulus vitiosus* argument is refused in its simple form by Husserl, but restated in a more sophisticated form and also marshaled by Peirce. The normative-descriptive argument is refused by Husserl, but supported by Peirce; yet, the latter's distinction between *logica utens* (normative, implicit) and *logica docens* (descriptive, explicit) serves, to some extent, the same purpose as Husserl's distinction between logic as normative art of reasoning ("Kunstlehre") and logic as a descriptive discipline. Important differences between the two include their opposite stances to diagrams, taken by Peirce to form the royal road to mathematics, to logical form, and to general regularities overall, taken by Husserl to form part of untenable psychologistic accounts of reasoning. Another important difference regards the relation between signs and conscious subjectivity, the former depending upon the latter in Husserl, the latter on the former in Peirce.

Taken together, the two of them strongly argue for a conception of logic, semiotics, and mathematics which is independent of the individual mind able to intend those entities as well as independent of particular kinds of mind with this ability. But how much more comes along with it? In Husserl, all ideality, that is, all issues of generality—comprising issues studied in the rest of the *Logische Untersuchungen*, indeed in the rest of his work—are taken to form objective structures not dependent upon empirical psychology. In Peirce, his logical idealism also covers much more than mathematics and logic narrowly conceived; thus semiotics as the study of the broad sign machinery necessary to construct propositions, on the one hand, and the whole logic of discovery and heuristics ("methodeutic"), on the other, are taken to form part of structures not dependent upon the particularities of human psychology.[23] Even if propositional logic, to both of them, forms the core of ideality which most

---

[23]In both of them, the issue of certain universals of the special sciences is also included in the array of general entities—in Husserl under the headline of "material" or "regional" ontologies; in Peirce under the headline of the special metaphysics of each of the single sciences.

evidently is irreducible to psychology, the zoo of general entities covered by such irreducibility proves much vaster. Semiotics, in particular, concerns signs which—as identically repeatable—possess the same ideality—or generality—as the logical propositions constructible from signs.

An important agreement between the two sets them against Frege's anti-psychologism as it came to be interpreted by nascent analytical philosophy. Dummett (1993), in his comparison of Frege and Husserl, is interested in locating which small but seminal difference between the parallel doctrines of the two made it possible, over time, that they became grandfathers of the very different traditions of analytical philosophy and phenomenology, respectively. His observation is that "Husserl *generalized* the notion of sense or meaning. Something like sense, but more general, must inform every mental act; not merely those invoking linguistic expression or capable of linguistic expression but acts of sensory perception for example" (1993, 26–27). This "vague analogy", to Dummett, is a generalization which "precludes the linguistic turn" (1993, 27) and which would, over the years, lead Husserl into a relapse of psychologism. Dummett celebrates the linguistic turn as the founding axiom of analytical philosophy—even if his embrace of it takes the somewhat weakened shape of the claim that "The two notions, of the structure of the sentence and of the structure of the thought, must be developed together" (7).[24] There is much to be said for this basic difference between Frege and Husserl. But where does Peirce fit into the picture? He too rejects the focus on linguistic sentence structure as the royal road to logic which facilitated the linguistic turn—he rather claims that the structure of thought and that of *signs in general* should be developed together, taking language to be a particular sign system only. In this, he parallels Husserl. But as against him, we already noticed his emphasis on *external* sign vehicles like diagrams, etc. Husserl's rejection of these as being part and parcel of psychologism made him favour the Brentanist emphasis on (conscious) intentionality, over the years leading him to locate all relevant structures in the depths of "transcendental subjectivity". Peirce's emphasis on spatial intuition in logic[25] and in the manipulation with diagrams in reasoning,

---

[24]The language-centered Frege interpretation in analytical philosophy smoothed over what was less unanimous in Frege himself. After all, the *Begriffsschrift* was a graphical logic notation rather than a linguistic formalism (for a comparison to Peirce's graphical notations, Shin 2013), and in his later years, Frege increasingly focused upon the analysis of thought itself rather than language, cf. his 1906 comment to Husserl: "The main task of the logician consists in liberation from language" (cit. from Dummett 1993, 6).

[25]Here, Peirce differed from both Frege and Husserl in developing further Kant's emphasis on schematism as uniting understanding and intuition. He attacked Kant for separating too drastically the two domains which Peirce saw as continuous, and on top of this Kant interpretation, he added, as Bellucci (2013) emphasizes, F.A.Lange's extension of spatial intuition from mathematics to cover logic as well (Lange 1877).

on the other hand, was modeled upon the laboratory experiments of empirical scientists, as a trial-and-error logical inference structure. This made his view of logic as semiotics closely connected to *action* and its effects, in turn leading to pragmatism. Dummett's comparison of Frege and Husserl with the Danube and the Rhine, springing close to each other in the depths of the Schwarzwald but following diverging directions, should add Peirce as a distinctive third river. The first thorough anti-psychologist of the three, he emerges in the very same area, diverging to form the current of pragmatism and semiotics with the intertwined emphasis on action and signs.

2.4 Barsalou's "Perceptual Symbol" Theory—An Example of Contemporary Psychologism

Many examples of psychologism may be found in contemporary studies of cognition—here I pick as a case Lawrence Barsalou's much-discussed theory of "perceptual symbols" and his ensuing theory of abstraction. Barsalou's basic idea is that word meaning appears due to "perceptual symbols" based in perception and memory. Perception is taken to leave traces, called simulators, in long-term memory, and the reactivation of those simulators gives rise to a renewed appearance of some of the traces of an object. The object has left a perceptual multi-modality of traces, and which of them are later simulated depends on the actual task, which is why there is no general conception of, say, dogs, but only different profiles, sounds, smells, etc. which may be simulated for different purposes. This idea of the multi-modality of (some empirical) universals is a good idea (not unlike Umberto Eco's proposal of basic "cognitive types" in *Kant and the Platypus*), just like the idea of selective realization of aspects of the concept in concrete cases. Another related good idea is to go against the linguistic turn tendency to claim that general concepts have nothing to do with images—here, they are taken to involve schematic representations as part of the simulators. Abstraction, now, is taken to form "summary representations" (2003, 1178ff) described as follows: "...behavioural abstractions reflect underlying summary representations of category members in long-term memory. According to these views, when people generalize behaviourally, they describe an underlying summary representation, such as a declarative rule, a statistical prototype or a connectionist attractor" (2003, 1177). "Summary representations" thus have three characteristics: they 1) facilitate "type-token interpretation" (the ability to categorize a particular object as belonging to a species, e.g. a lamp), they 2) give rise to "structured representations" (propositions like "this computer is on top of this table"), and they 3) enable "dynamic realizations" changing from one use of an abstract category to the next. This latter property is taken to explain what is seen as a major deficit in abstract empirical concepts—that no exhaustive definition of them may be given.[26] Now, such summary representations of empirical universals are taken to be sufficient, in turn, to explain all other types or aspects of abstraction, such as categorical knowledge, behavioral abilities to generalize across category members, schematic representations, flexible representation, and abstract concepts. Such "summary representations" are taken to arise out of the modality-specific "simulators" of Perceptual Symbol theory described as follows: "A simulator is *not* a static representation of a category. Instead, it is a generator of representations. Specifically, a simulator re-enacts small subsets of its content as specific *simulations* on particular occasions to represent the respective category. The simulator's entire content is never activated all at once—only a small subset becomes active that is tailored to the constraints of the current situation (cf. Barsalou 1987, 1989, 1993)" (2003, 1180). The first sentence cannot but remind one of Kant's famous notion of Schema, which is also not a picture of the concept, but rather that which makes the production of pictures possible. Adding to that, the simulator is claimed to form a sort of ungraspable depth of possibility of which only parts may be activated in any single use.[27]

In many ways, this theory adds interesting ideas to the discussion of concepts of empirical universals (which form a subset only of the issue of abstract concepts, to be sure): the insistence that such concepts involve schematic representations of features of the object, and that such representations also contain aspects specific to various perception modalities. The problem, however, is the focus upon perception as detached from action, from language, from reasoning—as well as the consequent understatement of the delicate relation between the particular and the general aspects of cognition. The most remarkable thing is that the simulator concept completely glosses over how the selection of abstract multimodal "traces" in the simulator is processed from the allegedly non-abstract perception preceding it—the crucial process of generalization. The only explanation offered is a sort of rehash of the traditional empiricist account for abstraction by induction: "If attention focuses repeatedly on a particular component of experience across occasions, a simulator

---

[26]In some sense, this complaint is strange. Why should we expect exhaustive definitions or descriptions of abstract empirical concepts? The fact we do not find such descriptions might rather be taken as a token of their reality—particulars famously do not admit exhaustive descriptions either.

[27]It seems strange how such a fuzzy notion escaping exhaustive description should be able to serve as a response to Barsalou's complaint that abstract concepts have no exhaustive definition.

comes to represent it. As a result, simulators develop for various types of object, location, event, action, mental state and so forth" (ibid.). In these two brief periods, the whole of the problem is contained, rather than resolved. Central ontological categories are presumed to come for free in this process: "In the theory developed here, *property* simulators and *relation* simulators are central to the abstraction process. Each is addressed in turn. A property simulator arises from repeatedly processing a property of a category's members" (ibid., italics added). Properties and relations, just like objects, locations, events, actions referred to above, are, of course, classical formal ontological categories—how could they, all of a sudden, "arise" from the simple photocopying device of trace-leaving particular perceptions in simulators? It is not evident how the mere copy-and-replay device of perception-close simulators in long-term memory is suddenly able to not only to generalize and categorize features and collect them into multimodal abstractions—but also to sort them into ontologically relevant categories such as properties and relations—before allegedly combining these into higher-order concepts.

Here, the distinction between the particular experience of a single dog and the general concept of dog—token and type—is glossed over by means of the "trace" and "simulator" notions. It is simply not made explicit whether the simulator left in memory constitutes a token or a type—seemingly, the type is taken to be made out of a sum of individual, remembered sense impression tokens. This seems insufficient—this does not account for the cohesion between those impressions in categories, granting they refer to one and the same type; it does not account for the plastic applicability of the type to future cases not identical to any single one of those impressions; it does not account for the mutual understanding of the same type between different persons, necessarily holding very different such sets of personal, perceptual impressions.

The fact that no simple criterion exists for what the exhaustive description of an abstract empirical concept amounts to is taken by Barsalou as the decisive argument that such concepts are problematic (as if such criteria existed for the exhaustive description of *anything* empirical, including particular objects), but the "simulator" concept is, as we saw, little more exhaustive. The fact that a dog may be abstractly referred to by different terms like "dog", "pet", "predator", "animal" and via different selections of its characteristic looks, sounds, and smells is taken to call for a "dynamic" theory of abstraction where the context is deemed responsible for such different reactivations of the same pool of traces. Instead of the comparatively "simple" theory that perception always already is attuned to general features of reality (an ability which may then be reused in intending abstract objects of logic and mathematics), a cumbersome theory—without empirical support—about neural clusters acting as simulators is constructed. The upshot of the theory is highly deflationist, tending to renounce the existence of anything corresponding to general concepts (even if depending itself upon a large array of such concepts, even including some additional home-made ones such as "perceptual symbol" or "simulator") in favor of the merely "summary representations". As so often in psychologism, ontological complexity is triumphantly renounced, only to be smuggled in again via the back door. How is it possible that different memory traces from different single experiences scattered across spacetime end up in the right ("dog") category—instead of being mixed with other contextual features from the same experience or from other among the bewildering array of fleeting perception experiences? How are "essential" features pertaining to the type sifted from ephemeral "accidental" features, to use the old Aristotelian terminology? This constitutes the very problem of categorization—but this theory presupposes without further notice that the "summary" representations automatically perform this "summing up" without any indication of how it takes place. It is as if the category (say "dog") is already there in the mind to take care of collecting its perceptual traces. A similar problem: where do the prominent terms "property", "relation", "object" etc. used for the further selection of traces for the elaboration of abstractions suddenly come from, if not from spontaneous ontology? Why should the brain be geared to isolate exactly these types of "simulators" especially if they did not enjoy ontological prominence? But most of all, its deficiency is apparent in the lack of any account of how the brain/mind is supposed to pass from allegedly completely particular perceptions of particular objects and to memory traces which seem to be already general. If perception is particular only, how come memory is already general? The whole problem of abstraction lies already here—long before the ensuing selection of traces for different purposes rendering the theory "dynamic". "Traces" seem to be particular and general at one and the same time, thus glossing over the whole of the issue of generalization, rather important for an abstraction theory. How is memory able to thus generalize traces from perceptions if they did not contain, in themselves, any such generality?

The idea seems to be that parts of the simulator are selected by means of an attention-like process (and attention is of course a standard part of many abstraction theories), but attention is not sufficient for an abstraction theory because all it can do is to select among perceptual material, not to generalize and abstract on the basis of those selections.

A recurrent and basic flaw in this brand of psychologism is the over-emphasis of the concreteness and particularity of perception—which gives the ensuing problems of ever ascending to abstractions, once you are caught into the quagmire of particularity.[28]   This is not the place to go deeply into alternative abstraction theories[29] but one basic idea could be that perception

---

[28]Alva Noë argues that the perceived "richness" of human visual perception is never actual—we do not in fact see all those details we imagine—but should rather be conceived of as a potential fact: we know we may always move closer in order to focus on selected details. Thus, even human vision is much more schematic and abstract than is often assumed.

[29]A referee of a paper version of this chapter argued that my criticism of psychologism obliges me to present an alternative abstraction theory. I happen to think this is no small feat which would require volumes rather than a paper, but I can give some hints to where I would look. One thing is that the "richness" of perception is a peculiarity of higher animals. In most of biology, sensing and perception are very sparse and abstract, typically selecting few general pieces of environmental information relevant for survival, cf. the simplicity of the *Umwelten* of lower animals. So perception has its biological origin in abstraction and still bears much more traces from it than the misleading idea of the full particularity of rich perception admits. Thus, there is generality already in perception, and, to take visual perception, edge detection and object construction take place already in the retina and early visual cortex long before conscious perception. So perception is already much more general than assumed in many empiricist theories and their metaphysical assumption of fully detailed "sense-data", and it is geared to detect gestalts, general patterns and similarities, already in the present now of perceptual experience and in working memory, long before any simulators in long-term memory. On top of that comes the innate character of some very basic aspects of categorization, like object constancy, cross-modal pattern perception, recognition of conspecifics, of faces, of biological movement vs. physical movement, subitizing the size of small sets, etc. Innate content of this sort, however, only provides some basic structures of abstraction. Equally important is the generality of action—as emphasized by the pragmatist tradition for connecting meaning closely to possible action. Basic biological actions have goals which are general (food, drink, sleep, sex, escape, fight, hunt, etc.)—general in the sense that very many different concrete perception-action chains and many different supporting objects of the environment may afford the realization of one identical action goal. So actions are already generalizing in their interface with the surroundings, governing the direction of perception in the quick action-perception cycles of higher animals, including humans. Perception-action cycles are a basic feature of animal life, phylogenetically as well as ontogenetically, and preclude the idea that we should somehow only begin abstraction "in the head" based on particular perceptions and some simulators only. Rather, perception and action are wired together in a way which makes the general purposes of action select in the general patterns constructed by perception. As to logic—so central to the strife over psychologism—it seems to be germ-like realized early in biology within the perception-action cyclus in the shape of inferences linking perception and action, governing what to do after a given partial perception—and where to direct you sensory organs after a given partial action (see ch. 6). So inference is just as basic as perception and action and is no late, higher-level result of abstraction processes (even if explicit, consciously controlled inference, to be sure, is a late growth). Perception typically detects general action affordances. There is no such thing (or, at least, only as a late and marginal spinoff) as a pure perception completely decoupled from action. So the problem is simply wrongly stated as the psychological issue of how to abstract from a pure perception. In such perception-action cycles, relevant aspects of world structure impose themselves on the organism—the *a priori* structures of simple logic and mathematics, the material ontologies of biology, communication, and sociology, and the enormous amount of empirical universals from mice to armchairs.

Regarding abstract concepts supported by language, they acquire stability from further sources— one is common action and the experience of successful communication and refer-is generally geared to extract general features of the environment and thus recognize colors, shapes, individuals (as James Hurford insists (see ch. 5), as simple objects as individuals are also generalizations from instantaneous impressions). This becomes even more evident if a comparison is made to simple animals without central nervous systems—their cognitive abilities are generally restricted to the detection of the presence of few, very general qualities of the environment, qualities closely connected to important kinds of nutrition and danger relevant for the survival. In that sense, feature abstraction is biologically much simpler and widespread than full, rich, detailed perception which should rather be seen as a highly developed ability in complex organisms with central nervous systems and moveable perception organs facilitating quick perception-action cycles, integration of modalities, and the construction of environmental maps. So the issue is not so much that of finding out how to come from perception to abstraction. It is, rather, how to come, during evolution, from abstraction to perception.

A related issue is that perceptual symbols are conceived of in isolation from their appearances in propositions—their natural habitat, so to speak. Used in connection with action, it is biologically crucial that perceptual symbols may be used to assess *correct* states-of-affairs upon which to act. Perceptual symbols with linguistic representation thus have their normal function appearing

---

ence, forcing language users to distinguish between sharable concepts in themselves on the one hand and the individual psychological imagery each user and his simulators may adorn concepts with, on the other. The "numerical identity" of concepts across language users is achieved, moreover, by the normative character of linguistic concepts indicated by the common agreed-upon labeling by means of the word expression, forcing every language user to distinguish between ideal, common meaning and his own particular imagery, the reality of the ideal meaning being granted by the fact that other language users address the same type of objects, forming a collective knowledge transgressing the individual sum of experiences (and forming forerunners of scientific concepts). Every language user knows this distinction, knows other language users know it, knows other language users know other language users ...forming an obligation of each user to attune himself to the common general concept. This makes possible the explicitation of the connection between meaning and the truth value of a proposition expressed by a sentence using it. If language users may agree not only approximately but completely that "Kennedy was shot dead in 1963", it is because they agree upon the general, and in the Husserlian sense ideal semantics of "shooting", despite the fact that each user may have highly different psychological imagery, memories and simulators of their own experiences with shooting, not to talk about that particular day in 1963. Thus, language forms a collective, objectifying and stabilizing support of general concepts already existing in pre-linguistic biology. A specifically important part of this is the ability of language to support "hypostatic abstractions", a special class of abstractions creating higher-level objects of thought (such as "redness", "gravity", "trajectory", "oxygen", "phlogiston", etc.) some of which may refer to general regularities of reality. I cover some of these ideas in Stjernfelt 2007, ch. 8-9, 11, and later in this volume.

in sentences expressing propositions—Peircean Dicisigns[30] This is also where children normally encounter words for empirical universals during language learning. Thus, the identity of concepts across language users—difficult to understand for a Barsalovian approach where each language user has his own idiosyncratic concept closely tied to his own sensory experiences with, say, dogs—is tied to the fact that language users are able to agree upon the truth value of propositions, say "That dog is gray". The reason why language users may agree not only approximately but completely upon such a sentence is the *schematic* character of the involved perceptual symbols of "dog" and "gray".[31] It is precisely because such concepts are underdetermined, schematic, unsaturated, general, multiply realizable,—or involve "ideal objects" to use Husserl's terminology—that they may appear identically in the minds of different language users—notwithstanding their very different experiences with particular dogs etc. and their different mental imagery when using the concepts.

A further problem—also noted by many of the commentaries to Barsalou's original 1999 target paper—is that if perceptual symbol theory does in fact explain anything at all, it would only be abstractions directly from perceptions, forming a rather small subset of abstractions. Murat Aydede thus asks whether all concepts are really perceptual symbols: "Without an independent and noncircular account of what this sense is, of what it is that makes symbols exclusively perceptual, I am not sure how to understand this claim, let alone evaluate its truth" (611). Barsalou's account thus leaves most ordinary concepts outside of the reach of explanation, as William F. Brewer remarks: "Barsalou argues that all cognitive representation is carried out with perceptual symbols. A list of things the theory has no convincing way to represent: (1) abstract constructs such as entropy, democracy, and abstract; (2) (non model) scientific theories such as evolution and quantum mechanics; (3) gist recall in abstract sentences (Brewer 1975); (4) logical words such as "but," "therefore," and "because"; (5) language form; (6) the underlying argument structure of

---

[30]They may also occur in propositions outside of language, of course, in perceptual judgments as when some object is judged to be of a specific type without expressing it in language. In pre-human higher animals, such quasi-propositions occur in cognition (as argued by Hurford 2007, cf. ch. 6) and will also be the natural locus of occurrence of perceptual symbols.

[31]The referee of this paper thus claims that word meanings must be individual in each language user, although often rather similar to one another. Against this, the ability of language users to agree completely upon propositions involving general concepts must be argued. The semantics of words can be measured on their contribution to the truth-value of propositions in which they appear; this truth-value being independent of the individual imagery of language users. Thus, successful co-reference, agreement upon states-of-affairs and common action across language users is the relevant criteria for concept identity, not individual associations.

his own article" (612).[32] To such a list, mathematics and logic, the classical strongholds of anti-psychologism, may easily be added.[33] Barsalou's type of psychologism is one of simply not mentioning many of the important problems left unadressed—claiming that the assumed psychological act type of "summary representations" solve them all. One is the identity of concepts across persons—how is that possible when each of us has an indefinite amount (as Barsalou claims) of simulators in our brain, individually built from finite experience? Thomas K. Landauer in his comment addresses this issue: "A critical aspect of human concepts is their mutual comprehensibility; the sharable properties are what we want to understand first and foremost" (624–25). Similarly, the conspicuous absence of inference and reasoning from Barsalou's account also seems to indicate he assumes they may be explained away by perceptual symbols along with all other issues of abstraction, as Landauer continues: "The most primitive sensitivity to touch is useless without inference. There is nothing more physiologically or logically real about perception than about abstract cognition. Both are neural processes designed to promote adaptive function, only some of which needs to depend on perceptual input or feedback. It makes as much sense to speak of perception as grounded in inference as the other way around" (ibid.).

Thus, in Barsalou's theory, generalization, abstraction, the numerical identity of concepts across subjects, concepts not directly related to perception, inference, logic, mathematics—all of these central issues are more or less explicitly taken to be eliminated to the simple perception-and-memory processes of simulators. It is not necessary to be as harsh as Stellan Ohlsson to judge this piece of psychologism unsatisfactory: "There is not now, and there never was, any positive reason to be interested in empiricist theories of cognition.

---

[32]Barbara Landau, in her comment, accuses Barsalou of "Reinventing the Broken Wheel" (624) and just renaming traditional accounts: "Simulation is essentially equivalent to the notion of a concept, frame, or theory. As such, it has all of the same virtues (being able to explain the dynamic, structured, and interpretive nature of concepts), and inherits all of the same flaws. Consider Barsalou's claim to have made progress in understanding how we represent Truth (sect. 3.4.3): a simulated event sequence frames the concept. But what is the concept? Simulations devoid of content do no better at characterizing our knowledge than concepts devoid of content. Without understanding the underlying notions of even such modest concepts as Bird, Hat, or Above, we are in no better position to understand how it is that we manage to gain, generalize, or ground our knowledge." (the first word of the quote is rendered as "Stimulation" in the text; the context seems to indicate it should be "Simulation")

[33]To this list, James Hurford (621) adds an example which is important in this context: Even stable individuals are, in themselves, abstractions from fleeting experience– so they cannot be taken as unproblematical point of departure for a symbol or abstraction theory. This example would have amused Peirce who also insisted on absolute individuals as being an abstract idea.

Empiricists are forever arguing, as does Barsalou, to survive the obvious objections. Better be done with such theories once and for all and focus on the fundamental and remarkable fact that humans are capable of forming abstractions. The most natural explanation for this fact is that abstract concepts are exactly what they appear to be: internally generated patterns that are applied to perceptual experience to interpret the latter" (631).

In the final conclusion of the abstraction paper, Barsalou writes: "By applying loose collections of property and relation simulators to perceived and simulated category members, interpretation, structure and flexibility arise naturally in the abstraction process" (1185). Flexibility indeed sounds much more appealing than rigidity—but the theory's emphasis on dynamicity and different instantiations of simulators seemingly has no answer to the basic problem of every abstraction theory—namely how subjects may agree upon discussing the very same concepts and propositions (and not only concepts which just flexibly seem similar), how "property" and "relation" and other ontological categories emerge as organizing concepts out of perception, how general categories are established out of category members, how perception is related to reasoning and action—not, again, to speak about the vast issues of logic, semiotics, and mathematics. So, flexibility is bought at an enormous price. Even if adding some good ideas to the structure of one particular kind of abstract concepts—those referring to empirical universals—the theory's psychologism makes it assume this same process accounts for all other abstract contents of the mind, if not the world.

It is remarkable how this allegedly empiricist theory of symbols is no less theoretical than the anti-psychologism theories it seeks to explain away. Without explicitly stating it, like many psychologism-influenced theories, it seems to be founded on a metaphysical theory claiming that the world consists of particulars, and the grouping together of them into generals is something exclusively created by the mind.[34] On the basis of this more or less implicit

---

[34]This immediately hands over the issue of explaining the ubiquity of general concepts in everyday thought and language as well as in science to psychology itself—which is thus forced to come up with some theory of abstraction, now taken to be a purely psychological process, creating abstractions rather than grasping them. This consequence is apparent, of course, in the British empiricists, and reappears in a latter-day version in Barsalou's abstraction account. It should be noted that this psychologism leads nominalists to a strange composite (even if rarely admitted) ontology. On the one hand, nature is taken to consist of particulars only. General concepts are taken to be the results of general labels generated by the mind. But as the mind must also—cf. naturalism—form part of nature, generality, absent from material nature, is taken to appear only there, in the mind. So nominalist ontology ends with no less than three different regions of being: 1) matter, consisting of particulars; 2) mind, naturalistically consisting of particulars but with the peculiar ability of being able to give rise to 3) the third constituent of the world: general labels. As compared with this

nominalist metaphysics—common to many psychologisms—are built the hypotheses of the particularity of perception and its primacy as compared to abstraction and inference structures. A metaphysics according to which general structures are just as ordinary inhabitants of the furniture of the world as are individual objects seems much more able to understand not only empirical abstractions but also the mind's grasp of non-empirical abstractions in semiotics, logic, and mathematics. Such a metaphysics, it is true, may seem less parsimonious. But, with Einstein's famous quip, we should make our theory as simple as possible—but no simpler.

2.5 The Indispensability of the Generality of Signs

Both Peirce's and Husserl's antipsychologicist semiotics are based on the observation that even if simple, singular signs exist, most interesting signs, beyond a certain degree of complexity, are tokens of types, and many of these, in turn, refer to general objects (Peirce) or ideal objects (Husserl).

A very important rule here is the Frege-Peircean idea that the semiotic access to generality is made possible by general signs being unsaturated and schematic: the predicate function "___ *is blue*", for instance, is general 1) because referring possibly to all things blue, 2) because of the generality of the predicate blue, having a schematic granularity allowing for a continuum of different particular blue shades.[35]

This generality is what makes it possible for the sign to be used with identical—general—meaning, at the same time as the individual users are free to adorn their use with a richness of individual mental imagery and associations (like Ingardenian filling-in during literary reading) without this imagery in any way *constituting* meaning—sameness of meaning in language being granted by successful intersubjective communication, reference, and action.

The identical repetition of signs and their meanings is possible only in virtue of their being general (or Husserl: ideal) objects. Individual, particular

---

ontology, an ontology like Peirce's or Husserl's finding aspects of generality in the world as well as the mind, may seem not only more parsimonious, but also considerably less strange, cf. ch. 4. Moreover, the ubiquity of general concepts in the sciences ("gravity", "electron", "metabolism", "inflation", etc.) receive a more natural interpretation when taken to refer to ideal objects—general features—of the world, than when taken to refer to psychological labeling only.

[35]The culturalist argument that "blue" and similar words covers different parts of the color spectrum in different languages and thus precludes mutual understanding, does not hold. Exactly the fact that it can be proven that different color name systems exist, shows that there is a common underlying structure the color terms of all languages refer to—and any one of the different cultural "blue"s may be taken as reference term, defining the limits of the category in terms of spectrum wavelenghts.

objects or events may, of course, never be repeated completely identically, any particular object necessarily differing from any other in space and time and its indefinite amount of properties. But schematic representations employed by signs importantly differ by highlighting only a restricted and controllable domain of properties. As to the sign vehicles, this explains why different tokens may incarnate exactly the same type—that the spoken "A" in English may come in an indefinite amount of different acoustic pronunciations, pitches and volumes and still remain the same A, or that the word "the" is exactly the same no matter the typography—accessible for speakers by means of "categorical perception". And as to sign meaning and reference, it is the sparseness of this generality/ideality which makes it is possible for people to agree fully (and not approximately only) on the meaning of propositions like "$2 + 2 = 4$" or "Kennedy was shot in Texas in 1963" or "A man took his red hat and walked along the street" or "A soldier came marching along the high road: "Left, right—left, right"" (to take a fictional example) or "A UFO landed at Roswell in 1953" (to take a fallacious example)—even if the different users of those sentences may add extremely varying mental imagery of those propositions in their individual psychological acts of intending them. In most cases, the individual sign users without further ado realize that other sign users may have their very own imagery—without getting the idea of confusing meaning with different uses and images associated with it.

This is also why any attempt to *define* the sign in terms of sets of mental representations or averages over mental representations is doomed to fail. Not only are the mental imagery of other persons (or organisms in general) notoriously inaccessible, and not only do they come in an indefinite number making the ensuing description of sign meaning fluctuating and impossible—but even if they were, in fact, accessible and we were able, in some way, to collect them all, such sums or averages would include misunderstandings and idiosyncratic mental imagery irrelevant or even foreign to the general meaning of propositions.

As to the important current experimental research of semiotics, by means of questionnaires, tests, eye-tracking, brain-imaging, behavior experiments, and so on, all such procedures importantly add to our general understanding of how signs, meanings, and references are processed by human beings and their brains and minds—in some cases by different groups of human beings. But such results can never hope to reduce the generality of signs to any mere sum of such individual processings. This lies already in the fact that the setup of the very experiments themselves and their interpretation crucially rely upon preceding semiotic idealizations. This lies in the very logic of experimenting. Experiments as such address general relations expressed in hypotheses.

As to psychological experiments specifically, the instructions given to a range of different subjects in the scanner, for instance, is presumed to remain the same, ideal instruction, understood as pertaining to the same, ideal task by all participating subjects. Such instructions are expressed in everyday language, but rely upon pre-experimental general hypotheses about, e.g. the linguistic behaviour of the subjects. The investigation of the specific uses of adverbs and which parts of the brain participate in such use presuppose, of course, the notion of "adverb" and its general meaning and applicability. Subsequent statistical averaging across participants is supposed to weed out individual deviations—but this takes place on the basic assumption that such deviations are still atypical and irrelevant and that the general pattern of the task remains behind them, granted by the statistical significance of the data. In the scanner example, e.g., the results obtained are processed by means of sophisticated mathematical statistics—the ideal regularities of which are applied indiscriminately across different uses, and in this case, over different subjects. We expect these mathematical signs, their meaning and reference, to stay identical and valid over time, over large amount of data, and over different scientists using them—so the very idea and procedure of statistical data processing *presupposes* the ideality/generality of mathematical signs and structures. Ideality does not stop here, however. The crucial comparison of brain activity signals across subjects is calibrated using an idealized representation of the human brain. One such representation is the so-called Talairach Atlas of the human brain, warping individual brain shapes and sizes to fit the Talairach coordinates in order to make them comparable. The Talairach Atlas, thus, forms an idealization of the human brain (constructed from postmortem sections of a 60-year-old French woman whose brain size was smaller than average—which means that most individual brains must be considerably transformed to fit the rather small size of the ideal atlas). Other competing such atlases have been developed, such as the MNI (Montreal Neurological Institute) brain—but the ideality of the general brain structure it represents of course remains the same. The generality, ideality, and stability of this scientific sign system are indispensable for the very comparison of single brain scannings—and, moreover, it presupposes that there exists, in reality, an isomorphism mapping between the functional parts and connections from one human brain to another—a hypothesis about the empirical reality of universal human brain structure.[36] Lastly,

---

[36]Such idealizations, of course, may fail or prove to be incorrect in details but the important issue is that they can not be assumed to be conventional through and through—they must correspond to existing general neural structures *in re*. If fallacies in such scientific idealizations should prove sufficiently strong, they will have to be given up completely, which would, in this case, prove fatal for cognitive neuroscience; in the more ordinary case, fallacies remain in the details, and the erroneous idealizations will give way to better idealizations

the findings—typically plotted as colored spots indicating activity sites in the idealized brain—are given a universal interpretation as to which brain functions generally participate in the task investigated, summed up in the general conclusion to the experiment. The generality of the result, the significance of the result for human beings in general, apart from the particular sample of test persons, is granted by mathematical statistics. So the ideality, generality, and identity of signs are presupposed in every single phase of empirical brain scanning experiments—which is why such experiments could never hope to disprove the existence of such general signs. Brain imaging, of course, is only picked here as a conspicuous example; the whole idea of (not only psychological) experimenting presupposes both the repeatable generality of the setup and the hypothesis of a general finding expressed in general terms. [37]

Semiotics is impossible without anti-psychologism. If signs were only particular, fleeting and ever-shifting epiphenomena of brains and minds, this would not only give up signs as such as stable objects of scientific study—but it would, in turn, destroy even psychology itself along with all other sciences, because sciences, as already Aristotle realized, always intend general structures, even when they describe particular objects.

The central structure taken by modern logicians to realize such generality is that of the proposition. Taking propositions as ideal entities, or types, go back to Bolzano, but forms, since late 19 C, the backbone of modern formal logic and philosophy of logic. Peirce, in his mature doctrine, developed a doctrine of propositions and their expressions not confined to human languages which, at the same time, forms a good candidate for a naturalization of logic. In this theory, he referred to propositions as "Dicisigns".

(such as the recent tendency to prefer the MNI to the Talairach map). Bottom line is that the project of neuroscience as such is impossible without reference to such ideal diagrams as the Talairach and MNI map—which is why cognitive neuroscience fits badly with a psychologistic metaphysics claiming all generality to be a mere product of the mind (see Roepstorff 2007).

[37] A strong defense for the commitment of scientific theories as such to general terms and their reference to (empirical) universals can be found in Smith and Ceusters 2010.

Chapter 3

Dicisigns

3.1 Peirce's Semiotic Doctrine of Propositions

> I do not, for my part, regard the usages of language as forming a satisfactory basis for logical doctrine. Logic, for me, is the study of the essential conditions to which signs must conform in order to function as such.

Kaina Stoicheia, 1904[1]

Peirce's doctrine of propositions—"Dicisigns"—has been strangely neglected. To take an example: no single paper title in the 50-odd years of publication history of *Transactions of the Charles S. Peirce Society* involves the notion of Dicisign, and only a small handful of papers address the doctrine under the headline of "propositions".[2] Compared to the voluminous literature on Peircean sign types such as the icon-index-symbol trichotomy, the type-token distinction, or the types of inferences, Dicisigns are close to being neglected. In the development of 20 C logic, Peirce's philosophy of propositions—unlike his logic formalizations and other results in Peircean logic—has had little influence, if any.

---

[1] This important concise presentation of Peirce's semiotics as of 1904 has the Greek title of Καινα στοιχεια, meaning "New Elements"—here we refer to the title in Latin letters.

[2] Major contributions include Tom Short's 1984 paper "Some Problems Concerning Peirce's Conceptions of Concepts and Propositions" (*Transactions* XX, No. 1 Winter 1984) which leads up to his treatment of the issue in his *Peirce's Theory of Signs* (2008), as well as and the two related 1992 papers by Risto Hilpinen, "On Peirce's Philosophical Logic: Propositions and Their Objects" (*Transactions* XXVIII, no. 3, Summer 1992, 467-488) and Nathan Houser, "On Peirce's Theory of Propositions: A Response to Hilpinen" (ibid. 489-504).

Yet, Dicisigns not only form an early and fairly elaborated doctrine of propositions—independent of that of Bolzano, contemporaneous with those of Brentano and Frege, and earlier than those of Russell, Wittgenstein, the Vienna positivists, etc. Dicisigns also take a very central place in the mature Peirce's semiotics and epistemology, closely related to his doctrine of diagrammatical reasoning. Peircean Dicisigns differ, in important respects, from received doctrines of propositions, and it is our contention that Peirce's semiotic doctrine of Dicisigns, while maintaining antipsychologism and the independence of logic, forms a unique, functionalist, and in a certain sense naturalist theory of propositions.

Already in the period from 1880–85, Peirce constructed his linear formalizations of propositional logic and first order predicate logic— following immediately, but unknowingly, in Frege's 1879 footsteps.[3] These few years apart, Frege and Peirce independently discovered predicate logic with polyvalent predicates and quantification. As has gradually become known, it was Peirce's rather than Frege's much more cumbersome formalization of the *Begriffsschrift* which came, via Schröder, Peano, and Russell, to be taken as the basis for modern formal logic.[4] So Peirce's elaborated doctrine of the Dicisign, primarily developed only in the years around 1900, takes these formal logical breakthroughs of the years around 1880 as their background: the distinction between a quantification part and a Boolean part of propositions (today: the prefix and matrix parts, respectively) became central to Peirce's later analysis of the two functions of Dicisigns in general. But why did Peirce actually care to develop, on top of his early achievements in formal logic, a doctrine of Dicisigns? Two reasons may be inferred. One is that, during the same period, he developed the competing set of logical formalizations known as Existential Graphs, giving, on several points, a new perspective on propositions. The other is that, in this period, he developed his general semiotics, highlighting an interest in which sign vehicles are capable of performing which logical functions, leading him to reformulate and generalize basic sets of distinctions to cover all signs, thus his old icon-index-symbol trichotomy and the classical logical term-proposition-argument triad.[5]

---

[3]It can not be excluded that Peirce knew about the *Begriffsschrift* but did not care to read it due to the many unfavorable reviews of it at the time; his student Christine Ladd mentions it in the 1883 *Studies in Logic* by Peirce and his students (cf. Anellis 2012). Frege probably learned Peirce's name from Schröder's (disparaging) 1880 review, but neither of the two explicitly faced the other's ideas nor referred to them.

[4]Cf. Putnam's "Peirce the Logician", in Putnam (1982), 252–260; Anelllis (2012).

[5]A third, more hypothetical, reason might be the appearance of Russell's *Principles of Mathematics* (1903) presenting his early doctrine of propositions. The annotations in Peirce's copy, now at the Houghton Library at Harvard, shows he took some interest in it, although his, mostly disdainful, margin notes primarily are to be found in the beginning of the book

In this chapter I shall reconstruct and discuss, to some degree of detail, Peirce's theory of Dicisigns with a special emphasis on the extension of empirical sign vehicles capable of instantiating propositions or quasi-propositions—as Peirce's interest in this issue forms the most important difference between his doctrine and mainstream ideas of propositions. So let me begin by outlining the extension of Peirce's Dicisign concept.

3.2 The Extension of the Dicisign Concept

Dicisigns are signs, to put it bluntly, which say something about something. This is, for a pragmatist, absolutely central—which is why Dicisigns are taken to be central among "genuine signs" while simpler signs like icons and indices are taken by Peirce to be "degenerate" signs, and unsaturated propositional functions—so-called Rhemes—are characterized as "fragmentary" signs (in the "Kaina Stoicheia", 1904, EP II, NEM IV).[6] The fine-grained varieties of degenerate signs regularly appear as parts or aspects of propositions, but they do not, in themselves, satisfy the basic semiotic task of Dicisigns, namely, to convey information: "...no sign of a thing or kind of thing—the ideas of signs to which concepts belong—can arise except in a proposition; and no logical operation upon a proposition can result in anything but a proposition; so that non-propositional signs can only exist as constituents of propositions" ("An Improvement on the Gamma graphs" 1906, 4.583).

Thus, Peirce's doctrine of Dicisigns constitutes an original and far-reaching account for the semiotics of propositions—also when compared to the doctrines of Frege, Russell, Wittgenstein and the tradition to which they gave rise. Most importantly, Peirce's semiotic theory of Dicisigns does not tie propositions to

---

(in pp. 12–24 of the ch. "Symbolic Logic") and so do not cover ch. 4-5 where Russell's theory of propositions is outlined.

[6]Peirce's initial argument here is that symbols are genuine signs in contradistinction to the degenerate sign types of icons and indices. The notion of "degeneracy" comes from the geometry of conic sections where certain sections (the point, two crossing lines, the circle, the parabola) only obtain with particular, non-generic values of the variables, simplifying the equations, as opposed to the generic sections giving ellipses and hyperbolas. Degenerate cases are thus limit phenomena only. Peirce develops the notions of generic and degenerate in relation to his categories in "A Guess at the Riddle" (1888), generalizing the terms from their use in geometry and the study of conic sections. In the "Minute Logic" (1902) and "Kaina Stoicheia" (1904), he applies them to signs. From symbols, Peirce moves to the central type of genuine signs which is propositions—the main issue of "Kaina Stoicheia"—able to express facts: "What we call a 'fact' is something having the structure of a proposition, but supposed to be an element of the very universe itself. The purpose of every sign is to express 'fact,' and by being joined with other signs, to approach as nearly as possible to determining an interpretant which would be the *perfect Truth* (...)" (p. 304). Not all Dicisigns, however, are symbols, cf. below.

human language exclusively, neither in the shape of ordinary language nor of special, formalized languages. This more general doctrine of Dicisigns has several important merits. First, it allows for the consideration of the role played by Dicisigns in pre-human cognition and communication in biology—and thus to envisage an evolutionary account for the development of propositions from very simple biological versions of quasi-propositions and to the much more explicit, articulated, nested, and varied propositions in human cognition and communication.[7] Second, it allows for the investigation of a broad range of human Dicisigns which do not involve language—or which only partially involve language. This makes possible the study of how pictures, diagrams, gestures, movies, etc. may constitute propositions or participate in propositions—highlighting how non-linguistic signs may facilitate reasoning and appear in speech acts taken in a wider sense, including what could be called picture acts. Third, it connects propositions closely to perception, cf. Peirce's doctrine of "perceptual judgments" realized in the act of perception. Fourth, Peirce's functional definition of Dicisigns liberates them from the idea that conscious intentions, "propositional stances", and the like form an indispensable presupposition for propositions to appear. And fifth, it embeds Dicisigns and their development in a social setting, Peirce taking the step from proposition to proposition in thought to be dialogical and to presuppose the knowledge of a Universe of Discourse shared among dialogue participants. This further allows for a plasticity of interpretation of Dicisigns, relative to the Universe of Discourse in which they partake. This radical extension of Dicisigns, embracing animal sign use on the one hand and non-linguistic human semiotics, perception and dialogical reasoning on the other, does not come without problems, though. The Dicisigns at stake here may appear more implicit, indirect, and vague as compared to the explicitness of declarative sentences in the indicative, expressed in human language, ordinary or formalized, and thus form a notion of propositions which is, in important respects, deflated.

Peirce's doctrine of Dicisigns comprehends propositions proper, linguistically represented and objects of fully conscious propositional attitudes on the one hand—as well as what he himself calls "quasi-propositions", Dicisigns which are not necessarily Symbols, on the other. This is why I generally stick to the term "Dicisign" addressing Peirce's broad notion of propositions—while using "proposition" about the received notion as well as "proposition" as opposed to "quasi-proposition" when these more specific subtypes come up.[8] In this

---

[7]Thus, most if not all animal sign use displays the characteristic double function of Dicisigns, cf. below.

[8]It should be added that Peirce's terminology referring to Dicisigns varies, to say the least. Taking his departure in the classic logical trichotomy of Terms, Propositions, Arguments, he invents new terminology in order to indicate his own generalization of that trichotomy

chapter, my aim is threefold. First, to give an account of Peirce's notion of propositions as it appears in the mature version of his semiotics in the years after 1900, peaking in his Dicisign doctrine of 1903 presented in the Pragmatism and Lowell lectures and the *Syllabus*, further elaborated in the 1904 "Kaina Stoicheia", the 1905–6 Monist papers and the letters to Lady Welby 1904–08. Second, to indicate its relation to other central tenets of his theory, particularly that of diagrams and diagrammatical reasoning. Third, to trace the possible contributions of Peirce's doctrine to actual issues of structured propositions, their meaning, objects, type of existence, etc.

3.3   Dicisigns: Signs Separately Indicating their Object

A striking peculiarity of Peirce's logic is its emphasis on logic *as semiotics*— and, correspondingly, the status of all logic entities and figures as signs—as he expresses it by a recurring onion metaphor: "A pure idea without metaphor or other significant clothing is an onion without a peel" ("The Basis of Pragmatism", ca. 1906, EPII, 392). At the same time, Peirce holds a Bolzanian idea of propositions in themselves as ideal entities—as types—facilitating the appearance of tokens of one and the same proposition in very different semiotic acts. The existence mode of propositions is not that of numerical, hic et nunc individual existence, but that of sign types, of mere possibilities—which is why they need semiotic machinery to be able to appear in sign tokens and play a role in actual discourse. For that same reason, the character of that machinery comes to center stage in Peirce's Dicisign doctrine.

True to Peirce's general way of investigating sign types, he describes Dicisigns compositionally, functionally, and systematically. As Hilpinen (1992) says, Peirce's recurrent and "standard" definition of Dicisigns is given in the following italicized passage from "Kaina stoicheia":

> "It is remarkable that while neither a pure icon or a pure index can assert anything, an index which forces something to be an icon, as a weathercock does, or which forces us to regard it as an icon, as the legend under the portrait does, does make an assertion, and forms a proposition. This suggests a true definition of a proposition, which is a question in much dispute at the moment. *A proposition is a*

to cover all signs. That gives terminological results like "Rhemes, Dicisigns, Arguments", "Semes, Phemes, Delomes", or "Sumisigns, Dicisigns, Suadisigns", just like the parallel version of "Dicent Signs" to "Dicisigns". Here, we shall generally stick to the "Rhemes, Dicisigns, Arguments" version. Peircean concepts explicitly being the focus of discussion—like Rhemes, Dicisign, Arguments—shall be capitalized.

sign which separately, or independently, indicates its object." (EP
II, 307, emphasis Hilpinen's)[9]

This definition implicitly posits propositions against predicates without any
reference indicated, "Rhemes" (cf. the Dicisign "The sky is blue" vs the unsaturated Rheme or propositional function "_ is blue"). And it sets Dicisigns
apart from simple indices which do nothing but exactly indicate their object
(the pointing gesture, the proper name, the pronoun, etc.), thus not performing their indicating *separately* from other aspects of their functioning. Moreover, it is this definition which implies that Dicisigns comprehend more than
full-blown general, symbolic propositions and also involve quasi-propositions
like Dicent Sinsigns and Dicent Legisigns[10]—they qualify for the basic reason
that they, too, separately indicate their object. Photographs, for instance,
may function as Dicent Sinsigns, just like statements of identity, location or
naming may function as Dicent Legisigns. Such quasi-propositions, like the
pointing of a weathercock, even give the core of the definition: "It is, thus,
clear that the vital spark of every proposition, the peculiar propositional element of the proposition, is an indexical proposition, *an index involving an
icon*" ("Kaina Stoicheia", 1904, EPII, 310, italics added). The weathercock is a
quasi-proposition because of its indexical connection with the wind, involving
the icon of turning in the wind's direction. Full-fledged linguistic propositions
realize this same structure by grammatical means—but this is no special capacity of language as such. Rather, language is adapted to fit Dicisign structure.
Thus, this basic definition makes clear the large extension of Peirce's Dicisign
category. This maybe surprising definition of the Dicisign is closely connected,
however, to the basic function of the Dicisign, namely to convey information—
to relay claims, assert statements, true or false. Only by separately indicating
an object does it become possible for a sign to convey information about that
object, correctly or not:

> "...the essential nature of the *Dicisign*, in general, that is, the kind
> of sign that *conveys* information, in contradistinction to a sign from
> which information may be derived. The readiest characteristic test
> showing whether a sign is a Dicisign or not, is that a Dicisign is
> either true or false, but does not directly furnish reasons for its
> being so." (*Syllabus*, 1903, EPII, 276)

---

[9]This idea is present already in "On a New List of Categories" (1868) where Peirce out-
lines the classic distinction term-proposition-argument and defines propositions as follows:
"Symbols which also [in addition to determining imputed qualities, FS] independently determine their *objects* by means of other term or terms, and thus, expressing their own objective
validity, become capable of truth and falsehood, that is, are *propositions*." (EP I, 8)

[10]In the ten-sign taxonomy of the *Syllabus*.

Dicisigns are thus signs which may be assigned a truth value—without providing, themselves, reasons for that value. The implicit countercategory here is the Argument, involving more than one Dicisign and explictly giving reasons for its being true. The distinction between signs conveying information and signs from which information may be derived points to the possibility of deriving information from icons—crucial to diagrammatical reasoning. When such information is actually derived, however, it will be structured as a Dicisign. The most simple example of this is perceptual judgment (see next chapter). I see a certain configuration of crafted wood and derive the information "This is a chair", linguistically expressed or not. Even if I do not convey this information to anybody else but myself in an act of communication, Peirce insists that individual reasoning also takes the shape of dialogic communication. When concluding "This is a chair", I communicate this to myself, that is, to a version of myself existing a moment later, thus conveying information to myself in the shape of a Dicisign.

3.4   The Double Function of the Dicisign

The function of expressing truth or falsity is possible only by means of the Dicisign having a particular double structure which Peirce describes in various ways, already in the early nineties:

> "Every assertion is an assertion that two different signs have the same object." ("Short Logic", 1893, 2.437)

An assertion is the speech act of claiming that a proposition is true.[11] As a sign, the proposition must involve those two different signs: it must, at the same time, fulfill two functions connecting it in two different ways to the same object, the index and the icon mentioned above. This is the reason why many propositions possess an internal structure composed from two separate parts, each fulfilling its specific function. Oftentimes, Peirce generalizes the classical notions of subject and predicate to account for these two aspects of Dicisigns:

> "It must, in order to be understood, be considered as containing two parts. Of these, the one, *which may be called the Subject,* is or represents an Index of a Second existing independently of its being represented, while the other, *which may be called the Predicate,* is or represents an Icon of a Firstness." (*Syllabus,* 1903, EPII, 277; 2.312)

---

[11] Despite Austin's famous claim to the contrary, Peirce does in fact distinguish between a proposition, the tokens representing it (sentences), the belief of a proposition (the assent to it), and the public claim of a proposition (the assertion of it), cf. below.

A Dicisign thus may perform its double function by means of having two parts, a subject part referring by means of some version of an index (maybe indirectly by an indexical symbol like a pronoun or a quantifier or an indexical legisign like a proper noun) to the object of the Dicisign, and a predicate part, describing that object by means of an icon of some quality (maybe indirectly by an iconical symbol like a linguistic predicate). As Hilpinen remarks, this is an Ockhamist idea, William of Ockham defining the possible truth of a proposition by the possibility that the subject and the predicate "supposit for the same thing" (Hilpinen 1992, 475), that is, refer to the same object. So the doubleness of the Dicisign is what enables it to express truth: it is true in case the predicate actually does apply to the subject—which is the claim made by the Dicisign.

> "That is to say, in order to understand the Dicisign, it must be regarded as composed of two such parts whether it be in itself so composed or not. It is difficult to see how this can be, unless it really have two such parts; but perhaps this may be possible."
> (*Syllabus* 1903, EPII, 276; 2.311)

Central examples—for instance, that of a photograph—do indeed indicate that the Dicisign may play those two independent roles without explicitly being articulated in two separately identifiable parts of the sign, as Peirce realizes a bit later in the *Syllabus*. The photograph's indexical connection to its object via focused light rays stemming from that object, influencing a photographic plate, whether chemically or electronically, plays the subject role of the Dicisign, granting the connection of reference between sign and object; while the shapes, colours and other qualities formed on that plate play the predicate role—even if those two roles are not explicitly separated as distinct parts of the photographic sign itself. Still, the two are clearly functionally separate, constituting two aspects of the sign rather than two distinct physical parts of the sign vehicle.

Peirce's analysis of the predicate part or aspect of the Dicisign is closely connected to the Russian-doll structure of the Rheme-Dicisign-Argument triad, where Dicisigns in a certain sense contain Rhemes and Arguments similarly contain Dicisigns. Rhemes are what is left if one or several Subjects of a Dicisign are erased:

> 'If parts of a proposition be erased so as to leave blanks in their places, and if these blanks are of such a nature that if each of them be filled by a proper name the result will be a proposition, then the blank form of proposition which was first produced by the erasures is termed a *rheme*. According as the number of blanks in a rheme is 0, 1, 2, 3, etc., it may be termed a *medad* (from μηδαν,

nothing), *monad, dyad, triad,* etc., rheme." (*Syllabus,* 1903, EPII, 299; 2.272)

Thus, Rhemes correspond to what is now often called propositional functions with the caveat that they comprehend also a vast range of non-linguistic predicates.[12] Peirce, originally a chemist, made this analysis of polyadic predicates modeled upon the notion of chemical valency. For the same reason he saw predicates as unsaturated, calling for saturation by indices in one or more of their blanks. For instance, in the proposition "Peer gives an answer to Svend", one or several of the subjects "Peer", "answer", and "Svend" may be erased to give Rhemes like " ___ gives an answer to Svend", "Peer gives a ___ to ___ ", " ___ gives a ___ to ___ ", etc. To Peirce, unlike Frege or Russell, the predicate includes the copula—in "The sky is blue", the predicate Rheme will be " _ is blue".[13] This allows for him to include a wide variety of expression types under the Rheme predicate category—linguistically, verbs as well as adjectives and common nouns, with the copula added, constitute Rhemes. Outside of linguistics, pictures, images, diagrams, gestures, etc. may form Rhemes and thus appear as the predicative, propositional-function part of Dicisigns. Common to all predicate Rhemes is that they involve an iconic, descriptive sign. So, the important basis of this double aspect theory of the proposition is that one and the same complex sign—the Dicisign—in some way indicates an object by a direct index or by some more indirect identification procedure for

---

[12]Later in the *Syllabus,* Peirce realizes that the Subject terms of propositions must *also* be classified as Rhemes (in the ten-sign combinatory, e.g., proper names are classified as Rhematic Indexical Legisigns). This seems to imply that they, too, must be considered as unsaturated. That all constituents of propositions must be Rhemes follows immediately from the idea that Rheme-Dicisign-Argument is Term-Proposition-Argument generalized so as to be a tripartition of all signs—as Peirce later says "A rheme is any sign that is not true nor false," (Letter to Lady Welby 12 Oct 1904, 8.337). A corollary of this, as Bellucci argues (2013a), is that Peirce's analysis of propositions differs from Frege's in an important respect: while Frege saw predicates (Fregean functions) as unsaturated, he did not see subjects (Fregean arguments) as unsaturated. In Peirce's doctrine, *both* must be unsaturated and, in some sense, in need of completion by means of each other. He even compares them to the groups of halogens and alkali metals in the periodic table of elements, with the chemical valencies of -1 and 1, respectively, known to form stable compounds (Na^+ and Cl^-, eg., forming $NaCl$, salt).To Peirce the chemist, it seemed obvious that both atoms of a molecule must possess matching valencies, plus and minus, respectively. A corollary of this idea is that proper names do not, as little as predicates, form autonomous signs outside of their saturation in Dicisigns, and thus also qualify as Rhemes. Despite this generalized notion of Rheme, however, it may be a source of confusion that Peirce continues to use "Rheme" simultaneously in the more restricted sense referring to predicates or propositional functions specifically.

[13]The traditional role of the copula of asserting the proposition is, in Peirce's account, analyzed as external to the structure of the proposition itself; assertion is performed by a speech act affirming the proposition in a social setting.

retrieving the object or set of objects referred to (maybe involving a proper name or other symbolic index, a common noun, quantification, etc.) and, at the same time, furnishes a description of that object given in the predicative, Rheme aspect of the Dicisign. These two aspects form the basis of the purely *functional* definition of propositions:

> "Thus, every proposition is a compound of two signs, of which one functions significantly, the other denotatively. The former is intended to create something like a picture in the mind of the interpreter, the latter to point to what he is to think of that picture as being a picture of." ("Basis of Pragmatism" 1905, Ms. 284, 43)

So, the basic function of the predicative aspect of the Dicisign is to yield an iconic description of the sign's object. This, however, is not all. By including the copula and the number of blanks involved in the predicate given, the predicative side of the Dicisign includes all that is not immediately indexical:

> "The most perfectly thorough analysis throws the whole substance of the Dicisign into the Predicate." (*Syllabus* 1903, EPII, 281; 2.318)

This implies that the predicate also includes the *syntax* of the Dicisign making of the predicate-subject composite a claim, cf. the idea that the predicate is "...representing (or being) an Icon of the Dicisign in some respect" (*Syllabus*, EPII 279, 2.316), cf. below. The predicate not only depicts certain characters of the object, it also depicts the Dicisign claiming those characters to pertain to the object. The predicate iconically describes that very aspect of the Dicisign— its syntax. So, the predicate operates on two levels simultaneously, on the object and metalanguage level, as it were. We shall return to this syntax below.

The fact that Peirce chose the age-old terminology of subject-predicate from Aristotelian logic in his structured proposition doctrine of Dicisigns hid, to some degree, the radicality of it and did not help the spread of it. Jean van Heijenoort's influential history of logic (1967) constructed the "Fregean revolution" as leading almost directly from the *Begriffsschrift* to Russell and modern formal logic, thereby sidelining the strong role played, also in Peano and Russell, by the tradition of algebraical logic: Boole, de Morgan, Jevons, Peirce, Schröder etc. (cf. Anellis 1995; 2012).[14] Among Heijenoort's major claims was that the latter aimed at a mere calculus for logical computing, not a representational language for inferencing; that the algebraists did not grasp quantification (even if Peirce and his student O.H. Mitchell were, in 1883, the

---

[14]Cf. also Shin 2013.

first to introduce a version of the modern notation of it), and, decisively, that the algebraists stuck to Aristotelian subject-predicate logic and failed to follow Frege's ground-breaking function-argument distinction instead. Peirce's idea of "throwing all" of the analysis of the Dicisign into the predicate, however, parallels Frege's function-argument strategy for carving up propositions—but sticking to the old surface terminology, Peirce did not immediately signal this radicality of his doctrine. As is already evident, Peirce's logic did not address calculation only and functions as a representative language just as much as the Frege tradition—albeit in a broader sense of "language". To him, calculation is the root of the understanding of inference as diagram experimentation:

> "But to say of the one notation or the other that it is of *no use* except for the working of the machinery of a calculus is to betray complete ignorance of the method of mathematical research. This is performed by experimentation upon diagrams; and the utility of the notations for this purpose consists in their enabling us to supply the bricks for building diagrams." ("The Basis of Pragmaticism," 1905, Ms. 283, 117 of one variant)

It is true Peirce did distinguish logic as practical calculation from logic as a science—but that is different from any distinction between calculus and representative language. It is rather the distinction between *logica utens*, logic for practical purposes, and *logica docens*, logic as the study of the steps of reasoning where Peirce saw the motive of his Existential Graphs as the latter rather than the former.

The algebraic tradition, moreover, was what allowed Peirce's doctrine to be even more radical than Frege regarding the extension of predicates far beyond language. Despite his graphical notation, Frege was interpreted as staying close to the idea of logic as a language—while Peirce's adherence to the algebraic tradition was what permitted him to transcend human language as basis for logic and, in fact, more so than Frege, to integrate both computational and inferential aspects of logic.

3.5   The Indexical Side of Dicisigns

As already noted, Peirce's first formalization of logic—in (1883) and the two "Algebra of Logic" papers in the 1880s—formed the first version of standard modern formal logic which later adopted Peirce's ideas via the intermediaries of Schröder and Peano. Thus, the central idea is to separate completely the two aspects of the proposition, quantification of variables on the one hand, predicates and their interrelations on the other—the indexical and iconical parts, as it were. In our day's terminology, the prenex normal form of the proposition, distinguishing the quantifier prefix part of it from its quantifier-free matrix part. Thus the isolation of the indexical part in the shape of a pointing gesture, a proper name, a constant or a quantified variable makes possible the corresponding isolation of the predicate and syntax—the idea of throwing all of the substance of the Dicisign into the predicate.

In the simplest cases, the index is simply the drawing of attention to the objet of the Dicisign—by a pointing gesture, an adverb, pronoun or a proper name identifying the object, or any other way of indicating the object of the proposition:

> "Thus the subject of a proposition if not an index is a precept prescribing the conditions under which an index is to be had."
> ("Lectures on Pragmatism", III, 1903, EPII, 168)

An index putting the receiver in a direct, immediate, causal contact with the object referred to thus forms the prototypical version of the subject part of a proposition (cf. the simple examples of a weathercock causally connected to the wind)—and all more complicated propositions in principle furnish information about how to retrieve such an index; that is the task, e.g., of proper names and quantifiers. Proper names are connected to the objects by means of an early version of rigid designation:

> "A proper name, when one meets with it for the first time, is existentially connected with some percept or other equivalent individual knowledge of the individual it names. It is *then*, and then only, a genuine Index. The next time one meets with it, one regards it as an Icon of that Index. The habitual acquaintance with it having been acquired, it becomes a Symbol whose Interpretant represents it as an Icon of an Index of the Individual named." (*Syllabus*, 1903, EPII, 286)

Quantification is now analyzed in dialogic terms. Existential quantification reserves the right to select an appropriate object to the speaker of the Dicisign, while universal quantification hands over the right to the selection of appropriate objects to the receiver of the Dicisign—forming the kernel of Peirce's early version of game–theoretical semantics (cf. Hilpinen, Pietarinen, etc.).[15]

An important, pragmatic difference to the standard theories, however, is that the indexical part of the proposition is subject to interpretation given the context of the utterance. In many cases, there is a tacit understanding

---

[15]See ch. 6.

(cf. below on "collateral information") which objects are indicated so that the explicit reference to them in the shape of indices may be underdetermined:

> "When we express a proposition in words we leave most of its singular subjects unexpressed; for the circumstances of the enunciation sufficiently show what subject is intended and words, owing to their usual generality, are not well-adapted to designating singulars. The pronoun, which may be defined as a part of speech intended to fulfil the function of an index, is never intelligible taken by itself apart from the circumstances of its utterance; and the noun, which may be defined as a part of speech put in place of a pronoun, is always liable to be equivocal." ("Lectures on Pragmatism", VI, 1903, EPII, 209; 5.153)

Thus, Peirce's insistence that Dicisigns are indeed signs gives his theory an important flexibility where implicit information agreed upon by the interlocutors and the specific Universe of Discourse they address may form part of the interpretation of Dicisigns. We shall return to this in more detail below.

3.6   The Iconical Side of Dicisigns

As to the predicate side of the Dicisign, it "... only conveys its signification by exciting in the mind some image or, as it were, a composite photograph of images, like the Firstness meant" (*Syllabus* 1903, EPII, 281; 2.317). This idea is that a central function of the predicate is to invoke a *general* image of the property signified. This should not, of course, be mistaken for psychological imagery subject to the fancy of the individual.[16] Rather, the important and controversial idea here is that *general,* schematic images play a central role in logic and cognition. This comes to the fore in Peirce's theory of diagrams and diagrammatical reasoning— diagrams being relational icon *types* capable of instantiation in different tokens, just like linguistic entities may be so instantiated. In the quote given, Peirce uses the metaphor of the photographic technique of the time known as "composite photograph" (cf. Hookway (2002)), the practice of subjecting the same photographic plate to subsequent exposures of related objects giving rise to a generalized picture subsuming the individual contributions as instances and blurring individual detail. Sometimes such procedures are still used, e.g. to give an idea of the "woman of the year", superposing images of a series of celebrity fashion models to give a general image

---

[16]Peirce was just as much opposed to psychologism as was Frege, and even antedated him on this issue in his 1860s papers (cf. ch. 2).

of the ideal woman of the moment. Composite photographs here function as an example of schematic images with general content as such.

This idea lies behind the enormous variety of predicate signs admitted in Peirce's Dicisign doctrine, one of the most important differences to the standard logical tradition. Photographs, paintings, moving pictures, diagrams, graphs, algebras, gestures, object samples—in short, all possible description devices may enter into Dicisigns to perform the functional task of predicative iconicity in the Dicisign: "All icons, from mirror-images to algebraic formulae, are much alike, committing themselves to nothing at all, yet the source of all our information. They play in knowledge a part iconized by that played in evolution according to the Darwinian theory, by fortuitous variations in reproduction" ("Reason's Rules," 1902, Ms. 599, 42). Indices, by contrast, would then play the role of connecting certain selected icons to reality, granting them existence and thus ensuring their survival over others.

Very often, Peirce takes as the immediate example of a proposition the painting with a legend[17]—such as in the short version of his 1903 list of ten signs given in a letter to Lady Welby (12 Oct 1904) where it forms the example of the seventh category of "Dicent Sinsigns"—one-shot quasi-propositions, as it were:

"7. Dicent Sinsigns (as a portrait with a legend)" (8.341)

In the *Syllabus*, this idea is elaborated:

"A proposition is, in short, a Dicisign that is a Symbol. But an Index, likewise, may be a Dicisign. A man's portrait with a man's name written under it is strictly a proposition, although its syntax is not that of speech, and although the portrait itself not only represents, but is a Hypoicon. But the proper name so nearly approximates to the nature of an Index, that this might suffice to give an idea of an informational Index. A better example is a photograph. The mere print does not, in itself, convey any information. But the fact that it is virtually a section of rays projected from an object *otherwise known*, renders it a *Dicisign*. Every Dicisign, as the system of Existential Graphs fully recognizes, is a further determination of an already known sign of the same object. (...) It will be remarked that this connection of the print, which is the quasi-predicate of the photograph, with the section of the rays, which is the quasi-subject, is the Syntax of the Dicisign; and like

---

[17]This has rarely been elaborated in Peirce scholarship. Jappy's introduction to Peircean visual semiotics (2013), however, includes cross-modal Dicisigns under the headline "Pictura Loquens" (150-51).

the Syntax of the proposition, it is a *fact* concerning the Dicisign considered as a First, that is, in itself, irrespective of its being a sign. Every informational sign thus involves a fact, which is its Syntax." (*Syllabus*, EPII 282, 2.320)

The idea, of course, is that the portrait painting forms the predicate part of the Dicisign, while the title of the painting provides the subject part, informing about which person it is who is claimed to possess (some of) the visual properties showed by the canvas. The very physical painting is, of course, a sinsign,[18] but it should be mentioned that—especially in an era of easy picture reproduction—similar replicas of the painting may exist in abundance so that the portrait, taken in a generic sense, may be used not only as a sinsign but also as a Dicent Symbol. Without a title or legend, the isolated painting is but an unsaturated predicate—a rheme:

"But a pure picture without a legend only says 'something is like this: '" (Review of Lady Welby, 1903, 8.183)

This requires, of course, that we add to the pure unsaturated predicate the vague index "something"; the erasure of the indexical part is taken to be equivalent to the positing of the vaguest index possible, existential quantification. In general, the large variety of possible predicate types is argued by the following argument:

"A proposition never prescribes any particular mode of iconization, although the form of expression may suggest some mode. [...] ...it is true (and a significant truth) that every proposition is capable of expression either by means of a photograph, or composite photograph, with or without stereoscopic or cinetoscopic elaborations, together with some *sign* which shall show the connection of these images with the object of some index or sign or experience forcing the attention, or bringing some information, or indicating some possible source of information; or else by means of some analogous icon appealing to other senses than that of sight, together with analogous forceful indications, and a sign connecting the *icons* with those *indices*." ("Reason's Rules", 1902, Ms 599 5-7)

It is unclear, however, in what sense the Dicisign expressed by means of a photographic predicate could be said to be the *same* as a Dicisign about the same object using, e.g., linguistic or algebraic predicates. It is easy to see that

---

[18] Referring to his first trichotomy (pertaining to the quality, the existence and the type of the sign itself), Peirce uses tone/token/type and qualisign/sinsign/legisign interchangeably.

there may be considerable overlap between such predicates and that collateral information may add to the identification of the relevant aspects of the predicates to be picked out, but still the painting of Louis XIV with a legend conveys much more information of his looks than does, e.g., the linguistically expressed Dicisign saying "That day, Louis XIV wore a grey wig" which may communicate only a minor subset of the information rendered by the painting.[19] Here, Peirce's theory of pictorial predicates certainly is in need of further development; we shall return to that below. A vast field of predicates is furnished by diagrams. In Peirce's philosophy of mathematics, the access to mathematical objectivities is granted by diagrams in general—but also in everyday reasoning diagrams, in the shape of maps, tables, matrices, graphs, schemas, scenarios, etc. form a wide variety of simple and complex predicates for use in propositions, sometimes, as in maps, furnishing continuous, complex Dicisigns which may give rise, in turn, to the inference of an indefinite number of linguistic propositions.

A very important corollary of the breadth of predicate possibilities for Dicisigns is the much more widespread appearance of propositions and quasi-propositions in human semiotic life than is apparent from the classic linguistics-centered view of propositions. Newspaper articles with photographs, TV news items with film clips and voice-over speak, cartoon frames with images and dialogue, algebraic equations, maps with locations and events indicated, artworks with titles, internet combinations of pictures and text of many sorts may, on this view, constitute Dicisigns conveying information, true or false; cf. ch. 7.

3.7 The Syntax of the Dicisign

A classic query pertaining to structured propositions, given the analysis of them into characteristic parts, is what keeps these parts together. The mere sum of the two elements, of course, does not constitute a proposition. To Frege, it seems to have been a composition of senses, resulting in the overall sense of the proposition, in turn picking out its reference (to Frege, a truth value). Propositional functions require saturation, which they receive by arguments—corresponding to Peirce's subjects. Russell's solution (1903; before he abandoned propositions and reinterpreted them as multiple relations kept together by judgments (1910)) dispenses with sense or meaning altogether, taking parts of the sentence expressing a proposition to be directly connected to reality counterparts: the proposition consists of objects and relations, so-

---

[19]A recent version of this argument: Kitcher and Varzi (2000).

called Russellian propositions.[20] The sentence expressing it is composed from "terms" of which there are essentially proper names and verbs. Verbs are, by nature, unsaturated and thus the composition of the proposition sentence is prompted by their saturation. But verbs and terms directly correspond to real relations and objects making up the proposition. Verbs, simultaneously, are taken to be responsible for the assertion of the proposition. Russell's account, of course, is restricted to languages, and he does not solve the deeper and more general issue of the unity of the proposition by relying upon the linguistic example of word class categories. Wittgenstein famously took the logical form of the proposition to be ineffable. Peirce addresses this issue in

---

[20] Peirce increasingly turned against the purely extensional definition of sets in early set theory, giving rise to the idea of extensional semantics that a term may be defined by the set of individuals falling under it. Instead, Peirce restricted the notion of sets (here: "class") to collections of elements defined by some intension: "Whatever ~~collection gath~~ sam there may be to whose members, and to them alone, any sign applies, to is called the *breadth* of the sign. [...] Now the *breadth* of a descriptive appellation has an *essence*, or Imputed Firstness; which is the signification, or *Depth*, of the appellation. Take the word *phenix*. No such thing exists. One naturally says that the name has no *breadth*. That, however, is not strictly correct. We should say *its breadth is nothing*. That breadth is precisely what I mean by a *sam*. Therefore I define a *sam* as an *ens rationis* having two grades of being, its essence, which is the being of a definite quality imputed to the sam, and its existence which is the existence of whatever subject may exist that possesses that quality. A *gath*, on the other hand is a subject having only one mode of being which is the *compound of* the existence of subjects called the *members* of the *gath*.
You may remark that a sam is thus defined with[out] any reference at all to a gath. I repeat the definition, so that you may observe this:
A *sam* is an *ens rationis* whose essence is the being of a definite quality (imputed to the *sam*) and whose existence is the existence of whatever subject there may be possessing that quality.
On the other hand, it is impossible to define a gath without reference to a sam. For when I say that a gath is a subject whose only mode of being is the compounded existence of definite individuals called its members, what is the meaning of this *compounded* existence? It is plain that the idea of a compound is a triadic idea. It implies that there is some sign, or something like a sign, which picks out and unites these members. Now the fact that they are all united in that compound is a quality belonging to them all and to nothing else. There is thus here a reference to a possible *sam* which does this. Thus, we might as well at once define a *gath* as a subject which has but one mode of being which is the existence of a *sam*. From this fact, that a gath cannot be defined except in terms of a sam, it follows that if by a collection be meant, as ordinarily is meant, a gath; while a gath is not distinguished from a sam, it becomes utterly impossible to define what is meant by a collection." (Ms. 469. Lowell Lectures. 1903. Lecture 5. Vol. 1, 16)
Gaths are extensionally defined sets which may only artificially be loosened from their foundation in Sams, in intensionally defined sets. Even the classical way of defining a set— by means of a list—is taken to be intensional which sounds strange indeed for finite sets. Of course, as soon as you reach infinite sets, no definitive list may be given, so some algorithm or other intensional description must be given in order to indicate the extension. This, of course, effectively excludes any purely extensionalist semantics for non-finite sets.

some of his most convoluted developments of the Dicisign doctrine, especially in the *Syllabus* and "Kaina Stoicheia". As is already evident, Peirce does not—against tradition—accord any special place to the copula as a third constituent of the proposition. The assertion sometimes attributed to the copula or the predicate is relegated to the speech act use of propositions, external to their inner structure. The verbal aspect of the proposition is taken to be part of the predicate, and so the syntax of the proposition is inherent in the structure of the predicate. Not any old combination of an index and an icon necessarily constitutes a Dicisign—the two should be represented as involving the same object by means of some syntactic connection between the two aspects of the Dicisign:

> "Finally, our conclusions require that the proposition should have an actual *Syntax*, which is represented to be the Index of those elements of the fact represented that corresponds to the Subject and Predicate." (*Syllabus*, 1903, EPII, 282)

Thus, the syntax claims that the Dicisign is *really* indexically connected to the real fact to which subject and predicate correspond. How could the syntax be said to make such a claim? What is often taken to be the function of the copula, Peirce instead analyzes as an index connecting the tokens of the subject and the predicate, respectively, in the sign:

> "It may be asked what is the nature of the sign which joins 'Socrates' to '_ is wise,' so as to make the proposition 'Socrates is wise.' I reply that it is an index. But, it may be objected, an index has for its object a thing hic et nunc, while a sign is not such a thing. This is true, if under 'thing' we include singular events, which are the only things that are strictly hic et nunc. But it is not the two signs 'Socrates' and 'wise' that are connected, but the replicas of them used in the sentence. [...] No other kind of sign would answer this purpose; no general verb 'is' can express it." ("Kaina Stoicheia", EPII, 310)

So the very combination, in the actual, expressed proposition token, joining the token of the predicate icon and the token of the subject index is taken to be, in itself, indexical. This index—as always in a proposition—involves an icon which is, in turn, the very spatial *juxtaposition* of the two sign tokens: "... it is the juxtaposition which connects words. Otherwise they might be left in their places in the dictionary" (ibid.). The very filling-in of the predicate token blanks by means of token subjects is, in itself, the iconical device showing their indexical connection claimed by the Dicisign. This, of course, places a special emphasis on the notion of "juxtaposition" of which grammatical connection is only one possibility.

Other examples include an object used as a sample, endowed with a label naming it (like a stuffed animal with a caption indicating the species):

> "It is sometimes written upon the object to show the nature of that object; but in such case, the appearance of that object is an index of that object; and the two taken together from a proposition." ("Kaina Stoicheia", EPII 310)

So, in general, co-localization seems to form a primitive, pre-linguistic syntax sufficient to connecting the subject and predicate tokens as a sign of the combination of the subject and predicates themselves in a proposition.[21] In human languages, such co-localization has further developed into the detailed conventions of grammar, word order, case, inflections and other grammatical devices to govern the composition of linguistic propositions. Already in pre-linguistic or mixed-media Dicisigns, however, simple co-localization may give rise to conventionalizations, such as the two different types of co-localizations using proper names in much Western painting (here, "symbol" is referring to propositions):

> "So, if a symbol is to signify anything, and not be mere verbiage, or an empty logical form, it must ultimately appeal to *icons* to *monstrate* the elementary characters, both of sense and of conception. One of the simplest examples of a symbol that can readily be found is, say, the portrait of a man having printed under it AN-DREAS ACHENBACH. This form of conjunction of an icon and an index is a symbol telling me that the celebrated artist looked like that. It has that signification, because of the rule that names so prominently printed under portraits are those of the subjects of the portraits. Were the same name to be found written small upon the portrait in one of the lower corners, something altogether different, and not so simple, would be conveyed." (Ms. 1147, the largest of several drafts of the article "Exact Logic" for the Baldwin dictionary, 12)

---

[21] Interestingly, the analysis in King's recent (2007) book-length defense of structured propositions ends with assuming the "syntactic concetanation" (34) as a primitive, resulting in this description of the proposition: "...we can think of this bit of syntax as giving the instruction to map an object o (the semantic value of the expression at its left terminal node) and a property P (the semantic value of an expression at its right terminal node) to true (at a world) iff o instantiates P (at that world)." (ibid.)—close to the Peircean assumption of co-localization syntax as primitive (without referring to Peirce's arguments).

Two different locations relative to the painting predicate indicate different grammatical roles of the proper names given there: that of the subject of the proposition, on the frame, and that of the maker or utterer of the picture sign, in the corner (sometimes elsewhere on the painting surface or on its back side).

The syntax of the proposition is also the starting-point of the investigation of its interpretant in *Syllabus*. The object of the Dicisign, of course, is the entity referred to by the subject. The interpretant is not merely the predicate, but the claim, made possible by the syntax, that the predicate actually holds about an existing object:

> "...the Interpretant represents a real existential relation, or genuine Secondness, as subsisting between the Dicisign and the Dicisign's real object." (*Syllabus*, 1903, EPII, 276; 2.310)

This leads Peirce to the surprising conclusion that—since the object of the interpretant is the same as that of the sign itself—this existential relation between Dicisign and object forms, *in itself*, part of the object of the Dicisign. Consequently, the Dicisign has *two* objects; one, primary, is the object referred to—another, secondary, is the very reference relation claimed to exist between the Dicisign and that object:

> "Hence this same existential relation [between Sign and Object] must be an Object of the Dicisign, if the latter have any real Object. This represented existential relation, in being an Object of the Dicisign, makes that real Object, which is correlate of this relation, also an Object of the Dicisign. This latter Object may be distinguished as the *Primary Object,* the other being termed the *Secondary Object.*" (*Syllabus*, 1903, EPII 276; 2.310)

What is here called Primary/Secondary object is what is later developed into the doctrine of Dynamic/Immediate Object, cf. below. Correspondingly, the predicative part describes some character of the Primary Object—at the same time as it depicts the indexical relation which the Dicisign claims to hold between itself and its object. This is, in short, the truth claim of the proposition—which can be analyzed as the Dicisign saying there exists indeed an indexical relation between itself and its object. This is why the Dicisign, in its interpretant, is represented as having two parts, one referring to the object, and the other—the predicate—referring to the relation between the sign itself and the object. And, in turn, this is why

> "...in order to understand the Dicisign, it must be regarded as composed of two such parts whether it be in itself so composed or not." (ibid.)

Hence, the Dicisign must, at the same time, present, iconically, the connection between those two parts:

> "...the Dicisign must exhibit a connection between these parts of itself, and must represent this connection to correspond to a connection in the Object between the Secundal Primary Object and Firstness indicated by the part corresponding to the Dicisign." (ibid., 277)

This implies Peirce's second conclusion. The co-localization of predicate and subject tokens in the expression of a proposition not only functions as a picture of their co-presence in the object—it also functions as a representation of the indexical relation between the sign itself and the object:

> "Second: These two parts must be represented as connected; and that in such a way that if the Dicisign has any Object, it [the Dicisign] must be an Index of a Secondness subsisting between the Real Object represented in one represented part of the Dicisign to be indicated and a Firstness represented in the other represented part of the Dicisign to be Iconized." (*Syllabus* 1903, EPII 277; 2.312)

So, the syntax of the Dicisign connecting its two parts mirrors 1) that of the combination of its real object and its alleged property into a fact, as well as 2) the indexical relation which the Dicisign claims to exist between itself and the object. This also explains what lay in Peirce's idea of "throwing all" of the analysis of the Dicisign into the predicate. It is not only an unsaturated predicate icon describing some relational property in the object—it also involves the truth claim part of the proposition, picturing the claimed connections between this property and some object(s) to be specified by subject(s) in its blanks.

We may sum up this complicated analysis as follows:

Dicisign:		
Index Tokens (of the Subject Indices)	—*co-localized in the sign with an*—	Icon Token (of the Predicate Icon)
referring to:		describing:
1) Primary Objects	—*co-localized in reality with the*—	Depicted Character
2) Secondary Object: The Indexical Connection Dicisign-Objects	—*claimed by the*—	Depiction of The Connection Dicisign-Objects (by co-localization of index tokens within the icon token)

In the simplest Dicisigns—Peirce's recurring examples being Dicent Sinsigns like the weathercock and the painting with a legend—these syntactic relations appear in a causal and purposive variant, respectively. The weathercock causally forces an icon of the direction of the wind to appear—so here the primary object is the wind, and the depicted character its direction. The secondary object is the causal relation between the two, granted by the mechanical structure of the weathercock, giving the iconical co-appearance of the wind and its represented direction. In the painting, the connection between the icon and index is purposive: the primary object is Louis XIV and the depicted characters the shapes and colors which the painting represents him to possess. The addition of a subject index on a blank part of the predicate (the frame) provides the iconic co-localization which is taken as a sign of the secondary object: the alleged real, indexical relation between the legend and the picture.[22]

---

[22] As mentioned, one can compare Peirce's account with recent investigations of structured propositions like King (2007). King proposes that propositions *are* a certain sort of facts, so that the proposition expressed in English as "Rebecca swims" *is* the fact that "there is a context c and there are lexical items a and b of some language L such that a has as its semantic value in c Rebecca and occurs at the left terminal node of the sentential relation R that in L encodes the instantiation function and b occurs at R's right terminal node and has as its semantic value in c the property of swimming" (39). This fact is thus different from the fact—Rebecca swims—which is the truth-maker of the proposition (King himself realizes the strange corollary that the fact which the proposition claims is the case is not immediately given by his redescription of the proposition; the same may be said about Peirce's redescription). King's definition involves the whole linguistic machinery in the virtual expression and reference of the proposition: the possibility of expressing a sinsign

As Bellucci (in prep.) argues, Peirce's presentation in the *Syllabus* intends to "...deduce the proposition's structure from its basic conception as 'bearer of truth-values'." (16). A long, complicated argument spanning several pages—a maze of abstractions, Peirce himself admits—is taken to undertake this deduction (*Syllabus*, 1903, EPII 275–77). The double structure of the Dicisign—as well as its double object and the co-localization of its parts as an iconic sign of the Dicisign's claim to be an index—all this is taken to follow with necessity from the basic capability of the Dicisign to take a truth value. As Bellucci rightly remarks, "...nothing substantially new is achieved by the deduction which was not already part of the picture presented (...)" (ibid.)—the interest of the deduction is to develop all of its aspects from its truth value capability solely. The deduction takes three steps: 1) an initial definition of Dicisigns with the emphasis on truth; 2) the argument that this definition requires Dicisigns to possess a specific double structure; 3) the detailed description of those two parts. The first step is Peirce's analysis of the truth claim of the Dicisign to be equivalent to the fact that the interpretant of the proposition "...represents the proposition to be a genuine Index of a Real Object, independent of the representation" (*Syllabus*, 1903, EPII, 278; 2.315). Thus, the Dicisign's claim to truth is equivalent to it claiming to be a real index of what it represents. The second and most labyrinthine step is that for this reason, the Dicisign must have two parts. The first step established that the interpretant of the Dicisign claims it to be an index—but, as that interpretant must have the same object as the sign it is an interpretant of, this connection between Dicisign and

---

in a certain language with a certain syntax and with a certain interpretations of its noun and verb phrases. Peirce's taking propositions to be Dicisigns immediately requires they are types which it should be possible to express in sinsigns with a certain double structure. Peirce, of course, differs in allowing for a far wider array of semiotic expression types than King's binding propositions to some language. Remarkable, however, is that King independently reaches certain results paralleled in Peirce's doctrine. Thus, King unknowingly reinvents Peircean "lines of identity" to represent the identification between different occurrences of the same variable in predicate logic expressions (42); even more interesting is King's insistence that at the deepest level, the syntactic combination relation R remains as yet undefined—as the very basis of all more specific syntactic relations. He vacillates between the possibilities of taking it as a primitive relation or taking it to be explained in terms of other, nonsyntactical concepts (presumably mental or neurological). Peirce's notion of "continuous predicates" (below) aims at essentially the same issue, the explanation of the fundamental syntax of co-localization—preferring instead the ontological explanation in terms of the continuity of real relations. King's relation R is equally fundamental as his hypothesis rests on the idea that the proposition "inherits" the relation R and its "instantiation function" (its ability to be saturated by suitably semantic entities) from the sentence embedded in the proposition. In Peircean lingo, this would mean that the colocalization syntax of the sinsign expressing the proposition is inherited by the structure of the proposition itself; again Peirce would prefer an ontological motivation (in the structure of facts) of the primitive syntax rather than a linguistic (or neuro-mental) one.

object must *also* be an object of the Dicisign. Bellucci: "Therefore, that which the interpretant represents—the secondness between the proposition and its object—is also represented by the proposition." (19). In order to achieve this, the Dicisign must have two parts—one representing the Object, and the other, more surprisingly, representing a part of the Dicisign itself (namely its claim that it is connected to its object). The third step, then, analyzes these two parts. The first part is easy: it is the normal purported object reference of the Dicisign, called its Subject—now doubled to include also the object relation of the sign itself (cf. below on objects and meanings of Dicisigns). The other is the more complicated part: it will now have to "represent how the proposition itself represents the object" (Bellucci, 22). In a certain sense, it is the Dicisign's self-description relating in which way the Dicisign describes its object. For a first glance, the Dicisign says: 'Here is an object O, and it has the property P'; the *Syllabus* deduction now claims that this is only a shorthand, made possible by an underlying, more complicated structure which may be given the following colloquial paraphrase: 'Here is an object O, really connected to this sign, and this connection grants the truth of this sign's further claim that this predicate holds of that object: P'. So the surface predicate of the Dicisign is embedded in an implied, more complicated predicate describing the Dicisign itself.

As Bellucci remarks, Peirce's earlier description of the Dicisign—also in discarded sketches of the *Syllabus*—directly derives the double structure of the Dicisign from the double structure (object/property) of the facts depicted. Peirce then seems to prefer the more complicated argument because it presupposes less—the truth claim of the Dicisign only. You could add that the simpler argument does not address the syntactic and claim aspects of the Dicisign and thus also achieves less than the complicated deduction aims for.

This is how we should understand the difficult doctrine of the double object of Peircean Dicisigns—which paves the way for the relation between Dicisigns and facts.

3.8   Facts as Truth-makers of Dicisigns

"What we call a 'fact' is something having the structure of a proposition, but supposed to be an element of the very universe itself" ("Kaina Stoicheia", 1904, EPII 304), Peirce claims, and this fact theory is what explains the ability of propositions to depict facts. Facts are the truth-makers of Dicisigns—if a Dicisign is true, the corresponding fact is the case.

Thus, the fact depicted by the Dicisign is different from the object reference of the Dicisign.[23] This distinction allows for an obvious way of explaining the existence of false Dicisigns—something which may sometimes be a challenge for picture-oriented theories of the expression of propositions (cf. G.E. Moore; the early Russell). The syntax keeping together the Dicisign in itself functions as an index of the two aspects of the fact corresponding to the two aspects of the Dicisign: "Every informational sign thus involves a Fact, which is its Syntax" (*Syllabus*, 1903, EP II 282; 2.321). Peirce thus maintains a theory of facts or state-of-things to account for what was later called the truth-makers of propositions. Thus, he distinguishes the object or referent of the Dicisign—given by its indexical subject part, on the one hand—and the truth-maker making true the Dicisign as a truth-bearer—given by the fact structured in the same way as the syntax of the proposition. This plastic theory permits Peirce's account to escape problems encountered by proposition theories taking states-of-affairs or facts to be not only the truth-makers of propositions but also their referents. Such simpler doctrines immediately, of course, run into trouble because of their difficulty in accounting for false propositions.

But even theories admitting false propositions may encounter problems. False propositions refer to non-existing facts, but the same thing is achieved by meaningless propositions. The difference between propositions such as "Barack Obama is the president of China" and "The present king of France is bald" tend to evaporate in such a theory. Russell, as is well known, concluded that the latter—just like the former—must be counted as false. In Peirce's account, we should rather take the former proposition as a false claim about an existing person and the latter as a meaningless claim about a non-existing person because it fails to make an object reference for the proposition in the Universe of Discourse—even if both have non-existing truth-makers. (In the framework of bivalent logic, Peirce tended to count meaningless propositions as true, reserving "false" to refer to ascriptions of erroneous predicates to potentially existing entities only.)

Facts, in Peirce's doctrine, are certain simple states of things:

> "A *state of things* is an abstract constituent part of reality, of such a nature that a proposition is needed to represent it. There is but one *individual,* or completely determinate, state of things, namely, the all of reality. A *fact* is so highly a prescissively abstract state of things, that it can be wholly represented in a simple proposition, and the term "simple," here, has no absolute meaning, but is merely a comparative expression." ("The Basis of Pragmaticism in the Normative Sciences", EPII, 378, 5.549–50)

---

[23] As already remarked by Hilpinen (1992).

Thus, simplicity here pertains to the relevant level of observation—not to any supposedly basic level of reality, such as was the case in Wittgenstein's in some respects similar picture theory of language in the *Tractatus* which famously led him to found his whole theory upon logical atoms without being able to point out a single example of one. Even if Peirce's theory of Dicisigns may, even in a very strong sense, be called a picture theory of propositions, it does not follow that the objects and properties singled out by a proposition be simple in any absolute sense. This is because states-of-things or facts in Peirce's account are *structures* of reality, distinct from simple subsets of reality:

> "... I must first point out the distinction between a Fact and what in other connexions, is often called an *Event** [Foot note* Or at least the temporal element of it is not the whole of it since [the] thing to which the event happens [is] an element of the event.], but which, owing to that word being used in the Doctrine of Chances in its stricter sense of the way in which a doubt about what *will* happen is ultimately resolved, must be here called an *Occurrence*. If from the Universe of the Actual we cut out in thought all that, between two instances of time, influences or involves in any considerable degree certain Existent Persons and Things, this Actual fragment of what exists and actually happens, so cut out, I call an Actual Occurrence which Thought analizes into Things and Happenings. It is necessarily Real; but it can never be known or even imagined in all its infinite detail. A *Fact*, on the other hand is so much of the Real Universe as can be represented in a Proposition, and instead of being, like an Occurrence, a *slice* of the Universe, it is rather to be compared to a chemical principle *extracted* therefrom by the power of Thought; and though it is, or may be, Real, yet, in its Real Existence, it is inseparably combined with an infinite swarm of circumstances, which make no part of the Fact itself." (Ms. 647 "Definition", 5th draught 16–18 Feb. 1910, p. 8–11, discussing Laplace)

Thus, facts or states-of-things are "principles", structures extracted from reality—explaining their Janus-headed doubleness, consisting at the same time of particular objects (secondnesses, referred to by the indices of the proposition) and general properties (firstnesses, described by the icons of the proposition). Scientifically traceable causal relations hold between facts, *not* between occurrences.[24] Thus, Peirce's version of scientific realism (and scholastic realism, assuming the reality of some predicates) is dependent upon this ability of

---

[24]Peirce continues: "It is impossible to thread our way through the Logical intricacies of Being unless we keep these two things, the *Occurrence*, and the *Real Fact*, separate in our

Dicisigns to depict extracted, structured aspects of reality. Here, the ability of Dicisigns to involve the large array of iconic predicate possibilities of maps, diagrams, graphs, etc., becomes central to his notion of diagrammatical reasoning in the sciences. The important claim above, that the simplicity of facts is relative only, gives an easy way of understanding why simple Dicisigns may express facts stemming from very different levels of ontology (from "$2 + 2 = 4$" to "There are two classes of elementary particles", "This chair is white" to "The Movement of Enlightenment took place in the 17th and 18th centuries") where the objects involved have highly different ontology and complexity, cf. on diagrams and language in ch. 7. This simplicity pertains to fact structure only, not to the objects and events co-constituting those facts.

3.9   The Relation of Dicisigns to Rhemes and Arguments

The systematic characterization of the Dicisign as compared to Rhemes and Arguments is a task to which Peirce returns over and over, with changing (but not necessarily contradictory) results in his deliberations concerning sign taxonomies in the decade after the turn of the century. One takes the idea of the Dicisign as the sign separately indicating its object as paradigm. Measured on this property, Rhemes are signs which lack such separate parts, while Arguments, on the other hand, are signs which add a further separate function, namely that of separately expressing its interpretant—the conclusion of the Argument, of course, fulfilling that function:

> "A representamen is either a *rhema*, a *proposition*, or an *argument*.
> An *argument* is a representamen which separately shows what interpretant it is intended to determine. A *proposition* is a represen-

Thoughts. John Stuart Mill did not do so; since he argues as if an *Occurrence* could have a *Cause*. In truth, both the *Cause* and its *Effect* are Facts, and no man will ever understand the subject of causation rightly until he sees that they are so. It is not, for example, the Motion of the Earth, as an Occurrence, that is caused by its momentum and by the gravitational attractions of the Sun and of the other bodies of the Solar System considered as Occurrences; for none of these things *are* Occurrences. It is the Fact of the motion of the Earth's centre of gravity of which one component is due to the Fact that it has not ceased to move with a certain velocity in a certain direction, while other components are due to the Facts that the various other bodies, by virtue of their several masses and the gravitating power that resides in every unit of mass, continually communicating, at the distances which they severally are from the Earth's center of gravity, several component accelerations, to its motion. Mill's not making the needful distinction between Facts and Occurrences drives him to the declaration that the complete cause of any happening is the aggregate of all its antecedents, a principle which, though it is a necessary result of his views, he utterly ignores from the moment of enunciating it; for the excellent reason that its recognition would eviscerate the conception of Cause of all utility." (ibid.)

tamen which is not an argument, but which separately indicates what object it is intended to represent. A *rhema* is a simple representation without such separate parts." ("The three normative sciences", "Lectures on Pragmatism", IV, 1903, EPII 204)

This idea may be expressed more simply in the beautiful (but maybe, for a first glance, more bewildering) definition:

"The second trichotomy of representamens is [divided] into: first, simple signs, substitutive signs, or *Sumisigns*; second, double signs, informational signs, quasi-propositions, or *Dicisigns*; third, triple signs, rationally persuasive signs, *arguments*, or *Suadisigns*." (*Syllabus* 1903, EPII, 275; 2.309)

Thus Rhemes-Dicisigns-Arguments are simple-double-triple signs, respectively. Peirce here introduces a different terminology, that of Sumisigns-Dicisigns-Suadisigns (on other occasions, he experiments with Seme-Pheme-Delome). These terminological neologisms are all intended to indicate the generalization of the concepts involved from the standard, linguistic-logic acceptance to the broader, semiotic interpretation indicating the intended exhaustive tripartition of *all* signs, following the generalization strategy for all basic trichotomies of Peirce's semiotics. The triple structure of the Argument refers to the idea that it not only is a sign for its object by means of the Rheme and the Dicisign presented in the premise, but also involves the same object a third time, now appearing as that to which the conclusion pertains.[25] This is obvious from yet another description of the same triad:

"Or we may say that a Rheme is a sign which is understood to represent its Object in its characters merely; that a Dicisign is a sign which is understood to represent its Object in respect to actual existence; and that an Argument is a sign which is understood to represent its Object in its character as sign." (*Syllabus* 1903, EPII, 292; 2.252)

Rhemes potentially refer to any object (or *n*-tuple of objects in case of polyadic Rhemes) displaying the character iconically presented in the rheme; in addition to that, Dicisigns indexically point out their object, and, again in addition to that, Arguments represent their object as signifying the conclusion.[26] This

---

[25]Correlatively, Arguments add to the syntax of Dicisigns the higher-level syntax of deriving one Dicisign from the other in a way so that deriving is represented as lawful and general.

[26]Peirce sometimes speaks as if all Dicisigns refer to actual existence: "Thus every kind of proposition is either meaningless or has a real Secondness as its object. This is a fact

may easily give the idea close to the received one, that the relation between the three is compositional, so that Dicisigns are constructed from Rhemes, while Arguments are constructed from Dicisigns. Peirce's redefinition, however, goes against such simple compositionality:

"It is only the terminology, and the extension of the division to *all* signs, (with the consequent necessary modifications,) that is not to be found in every treatise on Logic. Every such book tells about the triplet, *Term, Proposition, Argument*; but not every book makes it quite clear what it is that there is a division of. If we are to say that it is a division of all signs, we shall have to change the definitions of the three classes, not to their very bottom, but superficially, and so much that precision demands that new terms should be substituted for 'term', 'proposition', and 'argument'. (...) Now until I constructed the System of Existential Graphs, and for longer after than it would be agreeable to me to confess, I never so much as dreamed of there being any fault to be found with the doctrine of the books which goes back to the time of *Abelard*, and without doubt much earlier, that a Syllogism is composed of three Propositions, and a Proposition of two Terms. But after this system had been constructed, and after I had found by experience that its teachings are trustworthy, it one day attracted my notice that this system represents the relations of Terms, Propositions, and Arguments quite differently. The exposition of this can wait until the Reader is in possession of the system. I will now only say that, while this system does present Semes, yet it would not be incorrect to say that everything scribed according to this system, down to its smallest parts, is a Pheme, and is not only a Pheme, but is a Proposition. Delomes (dee'loamz) also are brought to view. Yet no Delome (dee'loam) is ever on the diagram, A Graph in this system is a type which expresses a single proposition. Without just now troubling you with an adequate description of the Delome (dee'loam), I may point out that it represents no statical determi-

that every reader of philosophy should constantly bear in mind, translating every abstractly expressed proposition into its precise meaning in reference to an individual experience." (*Syllabus* 1903, EPII, 276, 2.315)

Such simple Dicisigns form the core of his doctrine, and from this center, Dicisigns more remote from actual existence may be defined, such as ordinary universal propositions not involving existence ("All Englishmen are gentlemen"), propositions referring to fictional universes ("Donald Duck wears a sailor's sweater"), modal propositions, imperatives, interrogatives, requiring each their set of logical rules.

nation of thought but a process of change from one state of belief to another." ("πλ", 1906, Ms. 295, alternate version 26ff)

Peirce here uses Seme-Pheme-Delome for Rheme-Dicisign-Argument. His argument is built on how Existential Graphs represent propositions (see ch. 8), but it has a broader scope. The upshot is that every part of the formalism, from the smallest to the largest graph, is a Dicisign, simple or complex, and in a certain sense any part of a Dicisign is already a Dicisign. Such a claim may appear strange, as linguistically expressed Dicisigns may not have parts in the sense mentioned; it is easier to apply to Dicisigns with continuously articulated predicates such as pictures or diagrams—any part of such a predicate is still a predicate (up to coarse-graining), and a Dicisign using such a predicate consequently allows for Dicisign parts: a part of a map is also a map, albeit of a smaller domain. Arguments, by contrast, are movements from one Dicisign to another, cf. the central idea of reasoning as experimenting and manipulating with diagrams. Such experimenting, of course, may be charted in a higher-level diagram along another dimension, but not on the same level of Dicisign representation. Thus, Dicisigns are not built from Rhemes, and Arguments not from Dicisigns—even if they do contain them. Their relation should rather be described by continuity, cf. the metaphor from kinematics:

> "But in the last sense, which alone is the essential one, an Argument is no more built up of Propositions than a motion is built up of positions. So to regard it is to neglect the very essence of it. (...) ...Positions are either vaguely described states of motion of small range, or else (what is the better view,) are *entia rationis* (i.e. fictions recognized to be fictions, and thus no longer fictions) invented for the purposes of clear descriptions of states of motion; so likewise, Thought (I am not talking Psychology, but Logic, or the essence of Semiotics) cannot, from the nature of it, be at rest, or be anything but inferential process; and propositions are either roughly described states of thought-motion, or are artificial creations intended to render the description of thought-motion possible; and Names are creations of a second order in service to render the representation of propositions possible. An Argument may be defined as a Sign which intends itself to be understood as fulfilling its function." ("πλ", 1906, Ms. 295, 102)

Thus, the reasoning process as such is taken as primitive in the sense that arguments form the basis and frame for the description of the machinery that makes it possible. Dicisigns, then, are tools for the description of phases of reasoning—we may add: tools for making explicit propositions with the aim of conducting arguments.[27] Thus both Rhemes and Dicisigns may be seen as potential or truncated Arguments rather than autonomous figures:

> "I have maintained since 1867 that there is but one primary and fundamental logical relation, that of illation, expressed by *ergo*. A proposition, for me, is but an argumentation divested of the assertoriness of its premiss and conclusion. This makes every proposition a conditional proposition at bottom. In like manner a "term," or class-name, is for me nothing but a proposition with its indices or subjects left blank, or indefinite." ("The Regenerated Logic", 1896, 3.440)

This has the important corollary that all propositions are equivalent to conditionals. All universally quantified propositions are equivalent to conditionals (All humans are mortal $\Rightarrow$ If x is a human, then x is mortal)—existentially quantified propositions are similarly instantiated conditionals: (Socrates is mortal $\Rightarrow$ If there is an x such that the x is Socrates, then x is mortal).[28] All such a conditional lacks in order to be an argument is the assertion of the premise and the assertion that the conclusion follows. Thus Peirce can say that a proposition is an argument deprived of its assertiveness (*Syllabus*, 1903, 2.344), just like a Rheme is a proposition deprived of its subject (or its predicate). So, all three parts of the Rheme-Dicisign-Argument distinction are conceived of functionally, in their relation to the ongoing chain of inference.

This has the corollary that the Rheme-Dicisign-Argument relation is not that of compositionality. Even if Rhemes can be derived from Dicisigns and Dicisigns from Arguments, and even if the Dicisign requires the involvement of (at least) two Rhemes and the Argument that of (at least) two Dicisigns, it would be erroneous to say the Dicisign is composed from two Rhemes and the Argument from two Dicisigns. This is because the syntaxes of Dicisigns and Arguments, again, are taken to be *continuous* so that both Dicisign and Argument may be parsed in different ways and with different reinterpretations of their constituents. This continuity, granting the unities of the functions of Dicisigns and Arguments, respectively, is the basic level of which the functional parts form but aspects—cf. the idea that any genuine part of a Dicisign must be, in itself, a Dicisign.

---

[27]Taking the chain of reasoning as primitive may give a new idea of biological sign evolution. Instead of assuming simple organisms use very simple signs which then compose to more complex sign during evoution, we can assume that simple organisms use unarticulated, implicit arguments so that semiotic sophistication during evoution rather has the character of the ongoing articulating and making explicit the semiotic machinery, such as the two functions of Dicisigns, cf. ch. 6.

[28]Cf. Goudge 1950, 249.

3.10 "Collateral Information" and the Interpretability of the S-P Distinction

Sometimes, Peirce takes the reference frame of propositions to be simply all of reality—not unlike the Frege-Russell tradition—but at other times he takes care to underline that propositions may refer to selected subsets of that reality only, agreed upon by the communication partners—or even to fictitious universes (which could be said also to exist, in another sense, as peculiar subsets of reality). This relation of propositions to a selected Universe of Discourse is important for several reasons. One is the relativity of indexical reference to such universes, making much sign use dependent upon the implicit knowledge about the objects indicated by the proposition—the issue of what Peirce calls "collateral information". Another is that the exact borderline between reference and description in a proposition is also open to interpretation and may, with the same proposition, vary from one use to the next. Finally, a consequence underlined by Jaakko Hintikka is that the truth of the proposition becomes relative to the Universe of Discourse discussed—which makes possible a plurality of representations of the same objects and, consequently, avoids the ineffability of truth which is often the implication of accepting a one-to-one reference of logic to one universe only.

We already touched upon the role of collateral knowledge discussing the indexical half of the proposition. The issue is not, however, marginal in Peirce's doctrine. Quite on the contrary, no subject of a Dicisign is identifiable at all without some collateral information about the relevant object referred to:

> "I think by this time you must understand what I mean when I say that no sign can be understood—or at least that no *proposition* can be understood—unless the interpreter has 'collateral acquaintance' with every Object of it." (Draft of a Letter to William James, February 26th 1909, EPII 496, 8.183)

The idea is that propositions never occur as isolated entities but form part of ongoing processes of inference, and in order to assume their place in such processes, they must refer to objects already introduced earlier in the reasoning process:

> "At this point it must be noticed that the simplest assertion uses two signs. This is true even of so simple a proposition as 'pluit', where one of the signs is the totality of the circumstances of the interview between the interlocutors, which makes the auditor think that what is happening out of doors is referred to. This is evident,

since if he simply heard the word 'pluit' pronounced, though he might be ever so determined to believe what was meant, yet if he knew not at all whence the sound came, whether from somebody recounting a dream or telling a story or from a planet of a distant star, and did not know at what time the word was uttered, he could not in the least guess what he was expected to believe. Nor could any mere *words* tell him, unless they referred to something in his immediate experience, as a sign (and if he were, for example, told that the rain was 'fifty miles north of *where you are standing.*') It must be something common to the experience of both interlocutors." ("Basis of Pragmatism", 1905, Ms. 284, 42-3)

The very role of the index part of the proposition is not only to point out an object—this involves also connecting it to existent objects and reference frames. This does not mean, of course, that no new objects may ever appear—only that their appearance is possible only with reference to the framework of already known objects. This comes from Peirce's unvarying, Kantian insistence that existence is no predicate; that is, no amount of descriptive machinery will ever be sufficient uniquely to indicate an existing object or event:

"...every correlate of an existential relation is a single object which may be indefinite, or may be distributed; (...) that is, may be chosen from a class by the interpreter of the assertion of which the relation or relationship is the predicate, or may be designated by a proper name, but in itself, though in some guise or under some mask, it can always be perceived, yet never can it be unmistakably identified by any sign whatever, without collateral observation. Far less can it be defined. It is *existent,* in that its being does not consist in any *qualities,* but in its effects—in its actually acting and being acted on, so long as this action and suffering endures. Those who experience its effects perceive and know it in that action; and just that constitutes its very being. It is not in perceiving its qualities that they know it, but in hefting its insistency then and there, which Duns called its *haecceitas*—or, if he didn't, it was this that he was groping after." ("Some Amazing Mazes, Fourth Curiosity", c. 1909, 6.318)

A recurrent example taken by Peirce is the assertion of the proposition that a house is burning. If a person hears this claim, he will not scrutinize world history and the geography of the globe in order to sum up all examples of burning houses to find the right one; he will, as the first thing, look around in order to discover the burning house in the immediate vicinity of the here-and-now of the communication partners. Acting thus is, of course, following elementary communication maxims later charted by Grice recommending information given to be relevant. But Peirce's idea is even more basic: if no possibility of locating the reference of the index part of the Dicisign is at hand, it simply does not convey any information as such:

> "All that part of the understanding of the Sign which the Interpreting Mind has needed collateral observation for is outside the Interpretant. I do not mean by 'collateral observation' acquaintance with the system of signs. What is so gathered is *not* COLLATERAL. It is on the contrary the prerequisite for getting any idea signified by the sign. But by collateral observation, I mean previous acquaintance with what the sign denotes." (Review of Lady Welby, 1903 8.179)

On the other hand, given the presence of collateral information, even subtle aspects of the predicative part of the proposition may perform the indexical function to a sufficient degree for information to be conveyed. This is why a simple photograph may function as a full-fledged proposition, given the right amount of collateral information. If I see a photo of President Obama as a young man, easily recognizable by the features of his face, smoking a cigarette, I am in a position to retrieve the propositional information that Obama has been smoking. I might not be able to see what he smoked (or whether he inhaled)— if I do not possess the collateral information making me able to identify the brand of cigarettes. Thus, much visual communication is able—as against often-heard claims that pictures are not able to make statements—to state propositions, provided the relevant collateral information is accessible to the receiver. And to Peirce's Dicisign doctrine, this is no special feature for images or anything of the kind, because even the most formalized, scientific proposition is only understandable given a relevant amount of collateral information— which is part of the reason why proofs using mathematical formulae need accompanying information in ordinary language. This aspect of the Dicisign doctrine is connected, of course, to Peirce's ontology of epistemology: his view of the reasoning process as a continuous whole, having begun long before man and continuing into an indefinite future: the single proposition is only really understandable in its context of this ongoing process (see below). Thus, it is possible to communicate surprising Dicisigns by means of pictures alone. Take a constructed example: you find in your mailbox an envelope containing nothing but a photograph of yourself, easily recognizable, in an embarrassing, sexual situation. This is sufficient to convey the propositional information that somebody has caught you in that situation, is able to prove it, and intends you to share that knowledge—most probably wishing to blackmail you and pressure you to subject to some demands not expressed in the sign (like all Dicisigns, of course, such a sign may be false and rely upon photo manipulation). So the proposition "X took part in such-and-such erotic scenes" forms the core of the speech act of a threat (or should we call it a picture act, no language being involved at all as yet). Maybe you even faintly suspect who the sender may be and what the intended *quid pro quo* might amount to. An empirical example of such a sign has recently appeared in the context of the so-called Ergenekon scandal where the Turkish islamist government allegedly tried to compromise some of its secularist opponents by the use of such videotaped pictures:[29]

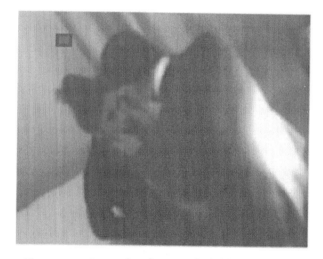

Figure 3.1: Screenshot from Turkish blackmail video

You may say such collateral information belongs to the pragmatics of proposition utterances rather than to the study of propositions themselves. In Peirce's Dicisign doctrine, however, no such distinction prevails because of the close connection between the index part of any proposition and the relevant collateral knowledge. The index part is simply there in order to activate that knowledge—if it does not succeed, the sign will not be able to function as a Dicisign at all.

The possibility of Dicisigns with no explicit articulation of the parts responsible for each of its two basic semiotic functions—as in the photograph

---

[29]Here reproduced from a screenshot of "The Daily Beast"—www.thedailybeast.com, 27 May 2011.

case—has the corollary that the distinction between these two functions may vary with context, even pertaining to exactly the same Dicisign. If the same photograph as just discussed were sent to another identifiable participant in the orgy depicted, it would function, in the same way, as a threat—but now based on the singling out the depiction of this other person as the relevant index in the photography instead of yourself. And, again, if the very same photograph was sent to a third party, e.g., an expert on pornography, he might take as the relevant object the present ocurrence of rare erotic practices there displayed while the individual identity of the participants may lose relevance. But reinterpretability not only pertains to the primary object of the sign—also to the secondary or immediate object of the sign. Take again the Louis XIV painting—to some observers, the special smile may be that piece of collateral knowledge enabling to abductively identify the subject as that French king; to other observers it may be the special wig playing the role of immediate object identifying the subject; both of them features which may, in other cases be taken as part of the predicative, descriptive side of the Dicisign. This relativity or indeterminacy in the precise delimitation of the subject/predicate aspects of the Dicisign is remarked upon by Hilpinen (476), observing the crucial fact that this idea takes Peirce's analysis far away from the logical atomism of Russell or Wittgenstein,[30] claiming that only one correct parsing of a proposition exists. Even if the distinction between subject and predicate remains indispensable for the Dicisign and thus *must* be drawn somewhere in each single usage, the context may decide where the exact dividing line goes in each single case:

> "The interpretant of a proposition is its predicate; its object is the things denoted by its subject or subjects (including its grammatical objects, direct and indirect, etc.). Take the proposition "Burnt child shuns fire." Its predicate might be regarded as all that is expressed, or as 'has either not been burned or shuns fire', or 'has not been burned', or 'shuns fire', or 'shuns', or 'is true'; nor is this enumeration exhaustive. But where shall the line be most truly drawn? I reply that the purpose of this sentence being understood to be to communicate information, anything belongs to the interpretant that describes the quality or character of the fact, anything to the object that, without doing that, distinguishes this fact from others like it; ..." ("Pragmatism", 1907 5.473)

This implies that the reinterpretability of the S-P distinction may go as far as inverting completely the two functions in the same sign. The painting (P)

---

[30] Russell (1903) mentions that a sentence may be analyzed in subject/assertion in as many was as it has subjects (44), but this is a far cry from the plasticity of Peirce's conception.

with a legend (S) was Peirce's staple example of a proposition—but given the relevant collateral knowledge, the two functions may be inverted. Take the improbable situation of a person which is well acquainted with the visual appearance of Louis XIV but never learned about his name or position. To such a person, the painted canvas may function as a subject—distinguisting its object from others like it—while the name tag "Louis XIV" would be the new, predicative information, describing his name and royal status (the painting-with-legend thus functioning, as a whole, as a Dicent Indexical Legisign, cf. our discussion below).[31]

Both of these issues—the need for collateral information and the reinterpretability of the S-P distinction—are connected to the central issue in Peircean logic that the reference of a Dicisign is taken to be relative to a selected universe of discourse—a model—consisting of a delimited set of objects and a delimited set of predicates, agreed upon by the reasoners or communicating parties, often only implicitly so.[32]

The radicality of the plasticity inherent in the reinterpretability of Dicisigns becomes obvious when Peirce attempts the opposite move of his standard anal-

---

[31] Of course, this invertibility comes from the fact that the character of the name, apart from its indication function, also belongs to the predicate: "There is an x with the name $N(x)$ and the visual appearance $P(x)$", cf. the idea of throwing everything into the predicate. The indexical relation between x and the name N is then presupposed in Peirce's early version of rigid designation, cf. above. The Immediate Object granting the indexical subject-object connection always also has iconical qualities.

[32] Reinterpretability and plasticity of the Universe of Discourse is taken to be central in Hintikka's generalization of the distinction between the algebraists' logic as a reinterpretable calculus and the Fregeans' logic as a universal language. This distinction, Hintikka sees as constitutitve to 20 C philosophy as such. In logic, he finds it in the algebraic tradition from Boole through Peirce to Schröder to Löwenheim, to Carnap and model theory (and to himself) versus the more well-known Frege-Peano-Russell-Wittgenstein tradition. More generally, in philosophy, the calculus tradition will be found in figures like Husserl or Cassirer focusing upon the plurality of phenomenological and semiotic means to express the same propositions—while the universal medium tradition will unite Russell, early Wittgenstein and Quine with continental philosophers like Heidegger and Derrida, all agreeing upon the ineffability of truth and impossibility of translation. In Peirce's doctrine of Dicisigns, the plurality of representations is evident in the fact that the same objects may be addressed using different semiotic tools, highlighting different aspects of them. To Hintikka, these virtues of the calculus tradition also imply that the ineffability of truth of the universal-medium tradition evaporates. If you accept only one language, the question of the relation of this language to its object cannot be posed outside of this language—and truth becomes ineffable. If several different, parallel approaches to the same object are possible, you can discuss the properties of one language in another, and you may use the results of one semiotic tool to criticize or complement those of another. Even taking logic itself as the object, Peirce famously did this, developing several different logic formalisms (most notably the Algebra of Logic and the Existential Graphs), unproblematically discussing the pro and cons of these different representation systems.

ysis: throwing as much of it as possible into the subjects instead of the predicate. In the fall of 1908 he develops this idea, developing a concept of as stripped-off a predicate as possible, the so-called "continuous predicate":

> "1908 Oct 18
>
> The second remark about the subject of an assertion is that more or fewer objects may be regarded as subjects while the remainder of the assertion is the predicate. Moreover instead of regarding the subjects are plural one may regard the whole set as forming the *Collective Dynamical Subject*. The *Complete* Collective Dynamical subject includes *all* that is necessary to be acquainted with in order to understand the assertion, excepting the forms of connection between the different Single Subjects. Thus in the assertion "Every catholic adores some woman," the complete subject embraces 1. the character of being catholic, 2. the character of the relation of adoring, 3. the character of being a woman; and the proposition is that, the character of being catholic determines anything to be in the relation of adoring to something having the character of a woman." (Ms. 339, "Logic Notebook")

Speaking about collateral knowledge, Peirce observed that it is not only the referent objects which the Dicisign reader needs preliminary knowledge about—that also goes for the characters and types of relations involved in the predicate. Now, Peirce constructs the structure of all subjects of a proposition, calling it the "Complete Collective Dynamical Subject" or "Subject-System"—involving all aspects of the predicate which requires collateral knowledge beforehand. Already Murphey pointed to the following quotation, but since then only few scholars have investigated this idea (see Pietarinen 2006a; Bellucci 2013a):

> "... I mean by the Subject (capitalized) of an assertion or question not the name or description so called by the grammarians, but that which is named, described, or referred to, to which the predicate relates. In the second place, the grammarians usually limit the term to the subject nominative, while I term anything named in the assertion a Subject, and although I do not always express myself so accurately, I regard everything to which the assertion relates and to which reference can be removed from the predicate, although what is referred to be a quality, relation, state of things, etc., as a Subject. Thus one assertion may have any number of Subjects. Thus, in the assertion 'Some roses are red,' i.e. possess the color redness, the

color redness is one of the Subjects; but I do not make 'possession' a Subject, as if the assertion were 'Some roses are in the relation of possession to redness,' because this would not remove relation from the predicate, since the words 'are in' are here equivalent to 'are subjects of,' that is, are related to the relation of possession of redness. For to be in a relation to X, and to be in a relation to a relation to X, mean the same thing. If therefore I were to put 'relation' into the subject at all, I ought in consistency to put it infinitely many times, and indeed, this would not be sufficient. It is like a continuous line: no matter what one cuts off from it a line remains. So I do not attempt to regard 'A is B' as meaning 'A is identical with something that is B.' I call 'is in the relation to' and 'is identical with' Continuous Relations, and I leave such in the Predicate. The Predicate is that part of the assertion which is signified as the logical connexion between the Subjects. But I sometimes term the whole set of Subjects the Subject-System." ("Common Ground", Ms. 611, 1908; Murphey (1961), 317-318)

Translating characters of the predicate to second-order objects by means of hypostatic abstraction ("is red $\Rightarrow$ possesses redness"), the total number of subjects in the proposition (and the valency of the predicate) increases correspondingly. In a letter to Lady Welby, a dyadic example is picked to illustrate what is left of the predicate when such an abstraction process is completed:

"When we have analyzed a proposition so as to throw into the subject everything that can be removed from the predicate, all that it remains for the predicate to represent is the form of connection between the different subjects as expressed in the propositional *form*. What I mean by 'everything that can be removed from the predicate' is best explained by giving an example of something not so removable. But first take something removable. 'Cain kills Abel.' Here the predicate appears as '___kills ___.' But we can remove killing from the predicate and make the latter '— stands in the relation ___to ___.' Suppose we attempt to remove more from the predicate and put the last into the form '___exercises the function of relate of the relation ___to ___' and then putting 'the function of relate to the relation' into another subject [to] leave as predicate '___exercises ___in respect to ___to ___.' But this 'exercises' expresses 'exercises the function'. Nay more, it expresses 'exercises the function of relate', so that we find that though we may put this into a separate subject, it continues in the predicate just the same. Stating this in another form, to say that 'A is in the relation R to B' is to say that A is in a certain relation to R. Let us separate this out thus: 'A is in the relation R^1(where R^1 is the relation of a relate to the relation of which it is the relate) to R to B'. But A is here said to be in a certain relation to the relation R^1. So that we can express the same fact by saying, 'A is in the relation R^1 to the relation R^1 to the relation R to B', and so on *ad infinitum*. A predicate which can thus be analyzed into parts all homogeneous with the whole I call a *continuous predicate*. It is very important in logical analysis, because a continuous predicate obviously cannot be a *compound* except of continuous predicates, and thus when we have carried analysis so far as to leave only a continuous predicate, we have carried it to its ultimate elements." ("Letters to Lady Welby" (14 December 1908), Peirce (1966) 396–397; the 'to' in brackets seems to be missing in the text)

What is left is the pure, relational structure of the predicate. Why does Peirce pick the term "continuous predicate" for this relational structure? His idea is connected to the often-quoted quip "Nota notae est nota rei ipsius"—the predicate of a predicate is a predicate of the thing itself. In the article "Nota Notae" in *Baldwin's Dictionary*, Peirce traces the wording to Kant and Wolff; the idea itself to Aristotle's Categories. In the context of polyadic predicates— relations—the *Nota Notae* of course implies that the relation of a relation to a thing is a relation to the thing itself. Just like the original idea, this may be repeated so that a connection of any number of relational steps from an object is, in itself, a relation to the object, cf. the quote above. So the *Nota Notae* grants there is an end to this cleansing process of all relational predicates. When reached, all the extra-relational semantics of the predicate is thrown into an enlarged Subject category, now comprising not only objects, but also reified aspects of relations, more or less general. Why is this purely relational predicate, left after the process, called "continuous"? This is because the *Nota Notae* identifies a multitude of connected relations with one relation—just like a multiplum of connected continuous line segments constitutes another continuous line segment. Thus, Peirce conceives of relatedness as such as essentially continuous. What remains of the predicate, then, is merely the structure of relations (which, cf. the reduction theorem, may again be analyzed as a composition of relations with valencies no higher than three). Bellucci (2013a) argues that the continuous predicate is, in the final analysis, what keeps the proposition together and grants its unity. In that sense, throwing all having to do with collateral knowledge into the subject system reveals that the structure left in the predicate is really what keeps the proposition together: the relational structure is what connects the subjects and the nonlogical parts of the predicate. Already Murphey, in his comments, saw the deep connection between this result and Peirce's metaphysical continuism—the idea that identity, co-existence, and relation are "continuous predicates" provides the deepest key to logical form. In Peirce's Existential Graphs, this continuity appears in both the blank Sheet of Assertion representing the relevant Universe of Discourse and in the notation known as the Line of Identity. This, then, is why co-localization comes naturally as the EG notation for conjunction: belonging to the same continuum is an obvious icon for logical conjunction.[33] This throws a light on Pietarinen's important observation that the Line of Identity notation reunites, in fact, the four functions of the copula triumphantly distinguished in the Fregean tradition: identity, predication, existence, and class inclusion: the convention of Lines of Identity fulfills all of these functions in the formalism; the outer end of the Line representing Existential Quantification, the continuity of the Line representing identity between differently named objects; the labeled Line of Identity represents the structure of the predicate, the hooks at its end points the unsaturated slots facilitating saturation by subject indices or class names. Thus, Peirce's argument—not knowing about Frege's and Russell's dissociation of them—goes to show the deep interrelation of the four. As Bellucci (2013a) remarks, this forms an important solution as to the "glue" of structured propositions, different from (but close to) Frege's complete arguments/incomplete functions solution, different from Russell's various solutions with judgment or logical form as unifying functions, different from Wittgenstein's ineffable logical form solution.

In the context of the reinterpretability of Dicisigns, the cleansing of predicates for all collateral knowledge shows the extreme plasticity of that notion. In certain contexts, all except for one subject variable may be thrown into the predicate (x as the subject saturating the predicate "___killed Abel", as when asking the Biblical question of "Who killed Abel?"); at the other extreme, the subject-system of Cain, Killing and Abel saturates the predicate of "___stand in the relation of ___ to ___", effectively throwing as much as possible into the Subject-System.

We said above that Peirce did not offer an analysis of predicates. As is evident from the doctrine of "continuous predicates" this is not completely true—

---

[33]Before constructing the Existential Graphs, Peirce toyed with a dual variant called Entitative Graphs, in which co-localization represented disjunction, while the outer end of the Identity Line represented Universal Quantification. He gave up that notation and switched to its dual exactly for iconicity reasons: it seemed more natural that the single end point of a line represented Existential than Universal Quantification, just like the continuous connection more naturally represented conjunction.

the idea of "continuous predicates" is an attempt at distinguishing in predicates that which is analyzable (their relational structure), and that which is not (the closer semantical character of the relation). In the PAP (Ms. 293, 1906), Peirce also took "killing" as an example of a predicate which does not permit a thoroughly rational analysis. What is diagrammatizable—translatable into spatial structure—of the predicate is, also in Peirce's own EG's, the relational structure with specified subject slots. The semantic, nonlogical surplus of the predicate may then—if needed—be thrown into the "Subject-System". This plasticity of reinterpretation becomes important in order to understand the function of non-linguistic predicates like diagrams, pictures, and gestures, in Dicisigns, cf. ch. 7 below.

3.11 Two Arguments for the Unity of Propositions

Peirce thus seems to present two different accounts for the logical form granting the unity of propositions. One is the deduction of the double structure from the proposition's truth claim in the 1903 *Syllabus*; the other is the 1908 argument from continuous predicates for the unity of the relational predicate. The first one centers upon the proposition as truth claim lending itself to assertion; the second centers upon the unity of what is claimed in the predicate. How, if at all, do these two arguments relate? Bellucci, in his two detailed papers (2013a; in prep.) address each of the two separately, but seems to assume, without further notice, that they go together.

They certainly differ. The first argument is centered upon the predicate part being primarily an icon of the Dicisign itself—only secondarily containing a traditional predicate characterizing the object(s) referred to. This argument takes as its starting point the capacity of Dicisigns to have truth values and presupposes the principle of throwing the whole analysis of the Dicisign, including its claim aspect, into the predicate. The second is centered upon the predicate part as depicting possible object relations outside of the sign—not at all addressing the Dicisign's icon of itself which played center stage in the first argument. The second argument takes as its starting point the predicate as interrelating different semantic contents along with objects—hardly mentioning its truth claim—and presupposes the abstraction of all non-logical content *away* from the predicate, throwing it into the subject.

In a nutshell, the first argument focuses upon the predicate as an icon of the Dicisign itself, the second upon the predicate as an icon of object characteristics. These two unities are thus not the same. The first pertains to the semiotics of signs capable of truth claims; the second of the ontology of relations. This may give us a key to the relationship between the two: the latter pertains to relations as such - whether they are depicted in the Dicisign or not. In this sense, the unity of "Cain killed Abel" lies in the continuous predicate of "X stands in the relation of Y to Z"—the fact it is possible at all for entities to entertain triadic relationships. It is, so to speak, the *fundamentum in re* of relational logic. It would hold even if there were nobody around to assert Dicisigns. It is what grants the possibility of there being references for polyadic predicates. The first argument addresses the conditions of possibility of there being truth-claiming signs. Unlike the second argument, then, it presupposes the existence of such signs. Through the intricate *Syllabus* argument, the double structure of the Dicisign was developed, seeing the predicate as primarily a claim about the referring and depicting abilities of the sign itself. Here, the predicate as depicting the object is merely a corollary of Dicisign structure. But the Dicisign could not be true if it was not somehow the case that the relational structure of its predicate really was able to depict existing relations represented. So, the existence of the Dicisign presupposes relational realism, to put it shortly. The converse does not seem to hold. So, the two arguments actually seem to be independent—but both of them are necessary for Peirce's account for the unity of propositions. The realism of continuous predicates is necessary for the possibility of there being real relations, and so for polyadic predicates to apply; the double structure, syntax and truth claim are necessary for there being Dicisigns. One establishes the unity of polyadic predicates; the other the saturated, claim-making use of them in Dicisigns.

3.12 Types of Dicisigns

Not only is the span of predicate types extremely wide in Peircean Dicisigns, they also come in widely differing degrees of generality. In Peirce's 1903 ten-sign classification (resulting from the combination of his three basic trichotomies), no less than three types are Dicisigns.[34] Let us quote his three

---

[34]A basic idea in Peirce's mature semiotics is that each basic trichotomy is exhaustive, so that any sign is either a qualisign/sinsign/legisign, just like it is an icon/index/symbol and a rheme/dicisign/argument. From this principle follows that the three combine. Of the 27 resulting possible combinations, only 10 are deemed realizable because a higher sign from a higher trichotomy does not combine with a lower sign from a lower trichotomy. Peirce gave two different versions of this list. The standard list occurs in the *Syllabus* 1903 (EPII, 294-5):

1. Qualisign
2. Iconic Sinsign
3. Rhematic Indexical Sinsign
4. Dicent Sinsign
5. Iconic Legisign
6. Rhematic Indexical Legisign

descriptions of those signs (the square brackets are insertions by the CP editors citing Peirce's own examples).

> "Fourth: A Dicent Sinsign [*e.g.,* a weathercock] is any object of direct experience, in so far as it is a sign, and, as such, affords information concerning its Object. This it can only do by being really affected by its Object; so that it is necessarily an Index. The only information it can afford is of actual fact. Such a Sign must involve an Iconic Sinsign to embody the information and a Rhematic Indexical Sinsign to indicate the Object to which the information refers. But the mode of combination, or *Syntax,* of these two must also be significant." (*Syllabus* 1903, EP II, 294; 2.257)

> "Seventh: A Dicent Indexical Legisign [*e.g.,* a street cry] is any general type or law, however established, which requires each instance of it to be really affected by its Object in such a manner as

---

7. Dicent Indexical Legisign
8. Rhematic Symbol— Symbolic Rheme
9. Dicent Symbol—Proposition
10. Argument

Another version appears in the letter to Lady Welby Oct 12 1904 (8.341):

1. Qualisigns
2. Iconic Sinsigns
3. Iconic Legisigns
4. *Vestiges,* or Rhematic Indexical Sinsigns
5. *Proper Names,* or Rhematic Indexical Legisigns
6. Rhematic Symbols
7. Dicent Sinsigns (as a portrait with a legend)–
8. Dicent Indexical Legisigns
9. *Propositions,* or Dicent Symbols
10. Arguments.

Here, the sequence 3 to 8 has been changed. In 1903, the list takes the quali-sin-legisign sequence as fundamental, so that the priority of the three trichotomies is 1-2-3; in 1904 the overall structure follows the Rheme-Dicisign-Argument sequence, so the priority is rather 3-2-1. No argument is given for the change, but the implicit reason must be taken to be that the function of signs in reasoning (given by Rheme-Dicisign-argument) is decisive. This naturally groups Dicisigns together (7-10) while the no less than six Rhemes—fragmentary, unsaturated signs—make up the first six types of the list. The 1904 list also has the merit that legisigns are preceded by their sinsign replicas pairwise (2-3, 4-5, 7-8). It is remarkable that none of the two lists chooses the most well-known, second trichotomy of icon-index-symbol as its organizing principle. The 1908 version of the triangle depicting the ten combined signs (from the Dec 24 letter to Lady Welby, EPII, 491) is a mirror version of that of the *Syllabus,* now with Arguments in the upper left corner, maybe indicating that the corresponding list should now begin with the *most* complicated (or complete) sign type, that of the Argument, effectively inverting one of the lists given.

to furnish definite information concerning that Object. It must involve an Iconic Legisign to signify the information and a Rhematic Indexical Legisign to denote the subject of that information. Each Replica of it will be a Dicent Sinsign of a peculiar kind." (*Syllabus,* 1903, EP II 294, 2.260)

"Ninth: A Dicent Symbol, or ordinary Proposition, is a sign connected with its object by an association of general ideas, and acting like a Rhematic Symbol, except that its intended interpretant represents the Dicent Symbol as being, in respect to what it signifies, really affected by its Object, so that the existence or law which it calls to mind must be actually connected with the indicated Object. Thus, the intended Interpretant looks upon the Dicent Symbol as a Dicent Indexical Legisign; and if it be true, it does partake of this nature, although this does not represent its whole nature. Like the Rhematic Symbol, it is necessarily a Legisign. Like the Dicent Sinsign it is composite inasmuch as it necessarily involves a Rhematic Symbol (and thus is for its Interpretant an Iconic Legisign) to express its information and a Rhematic Indexical Legisign to indicate the subject of that information. But its Syntax of these is significant. The Replica of the Dicent Symbol is a Dicent Sinsign of a peculiar kind. This is easily seen to be true when the information the Dicent Symbol conveys is of actual fact. When that information is of a real law, it is not true in the same fullness. For a Dicent Sinsign cannot convey information of law. It is, therefore, true of the Replica of such a Dicent Symbol only in so far as the law has its being in instances." (*Syllabus* 1903, EP II 295, 2.262)

The Dicent symbol, of course, is Peirce's version of ordinary propositions involving predicates expressing general ideas, such as linguistic adjectives, verbs, common nouns, etc. But language is not the only source of such predicates. A wider array of icons may have general qualities, most conspicuously in their function as diagrams. Thus, a diagram with a label— say, a geometrical figure with a legend—may express a Dicent symbol, a full-fledged proposition, and the manipulation of that diagram, in turn, may express an Argument. The same goes for many types of maps, scientific diagrams and illustrations, tables, graphs. The obvious contrast category here, of course, is that of Dicent Sinsigns, not involving any general idea but rather actual fact only. It is interesting here to compare Peirce's examples of such signs. It involves the recurring weathercock, the painting with a legend, but also perfectly naturally occurring shapes such as footprints.[35] So the simplest Dicent Sinsign is a natural process functioning as a sign for some interpreter by indexically producing an icon of the object. The object must be a singular, individual object. That does not imply the sign immediately facilitates the recognition of that object. Peirce's own example is Robinson seeing for the first time Friday's footprint. He realizes this track stems from an existing person—but he has as yet no idea which person. So this sign is indefinite, implicitly having an existential quantifier 'Some person made this footprint'. The weathercock is a simple example of a measurement device, constructed so as to select, isolate, magnify, render clear some iconic information through an indexical process. Individual measurements made with such tools then qualify as Dicent Sinsigns.[36] The

---

[35]"Dicisigns are either symbols, when they become genuine *propositions*, or they are *informational indices*. Almost all indices are either informational or are elements of informational indices. Thus, when Robinson Crusoe found the footprint generally spoken of as Friday's, we may suppose that his attention was first attracted to an indentation of the sand. So far it was a mere *substitutive index*, a mere something apparently a sign of something else. But on examination he found that 'there was the print of toes, heel, and every part of a foot', in short, an icon converted into an index; and the connection of this with its presence on the shore, could only be interpreted as an index of a corresponding presence of a man. We thus see clearly that a dicisign, or information-bearing sign, is a sign that indicates a Secondness in its object by a corresponding secondness in its own composition." (Ms. 478, 46–47, alternative version of *Syllabus*, 1903)

[36]The most thorough analysis of the weathercock is found in Ms. 7 ("On the Foundations of Mathematics", around 1903): "The reference of a sign to its object is brought into special prominence in a kind of sign whose fitness to be a sign is due to its being in a real reactive relation,—generally, a physical and dynamical relation,—with the object. Such a sign I term an *index*. As an example, take a weather-cock. This is a sign of the wind because the wind actively moves it. It faces in the very direction from which the wind blows. In so far as it does that, it involves an icon. The wind forces it to be an icon. A photograph which is compelled by optical laws to be an *icon* of its object which is before the camera is another example. It is in this way that these indices convey information. They are *propositions*. That is they separately indicate their objects; the weather-cock because it turns with the wind and is known by its interpretant to do so; the photograph for a like reason. If the weathercock sticks and fails to turn, or if the camera lens is bad, the one or the other will be *false*. But if this is known to be the case, they sink at once to mere icons, at best. It is not essential to an index that it should thus involve an icon. Only, if it does not, it will convey no information." The fact that the weathercock is constructed for its purpose is not central, however. It adds to the clarity, precision and usefulness of the tool, but the crucial issue—an icon produced by an index—is shared with objects not so constructed such as grass or trees bending in the wind and thus indicating its direction. Thus, a fossil contains in itself the possible propositions which science may once be able to construct from the investigation of it: "...if, for example, there be a certain fossil fish, certain observations upon which, made by a skilled paleontologist, and taken in connection with chemical analyses of the bones and of the rock in which they were embedded, will one day furnish that paleontologist with the keystone of an argumentative arch upon which he will securely erect a solid proof of a conclusion of great importance, then, in my view, in the true logical sense, that thought has already all the reality it ever will have, although as yet the quarries have not been opened

painting with a legend, however, is more complicated. Not only does it have an explicit syntax which we discussed above—it is also not as evident that the predicate is without general qualities. Very often, painters idealize the person portrayed, not only in the sense that they beautify him but also in the sense that they seek to capture typical expressions, looks, postures, etc. so that the painting not only communicates actual fact, but also more general information about its object. In that sense, paintings may contain different degrees of generalities, on a continuous gradient scale from pure images to diagrams. Photographs may also display such generality, not by means of the photographic process alone and not only by means of techniques like the "composite photographs" discussed, but also aided by the very selection process of the "best" photo among many available. This may be seen, e.g., in more or less scientific illustrations, such as those in an atlas of mushrooms. The watercolor painting of a mushroom in such a book should depict all of the *typical* visual properties of the species in order to aid identification—resulting in a painting which may be *more* typical than any particular, existing specimen of the species in reality. Also photographs used in such books must be selected so as to display all typical features of the appearances of the mushroom species in question, thus embodying general qualities, even if actually depicting individual organisms. Retouching, 'photoshopping' and related processing of photographs, of course, may aid in the production of photographs serving as more general predicates describing types. Thus, there seems to be a continuous gradient from completely singular Dicent Sinsigns on the one end to fully Dicent Symbols with general predicates, be they linguistic or diagrammatic or otherwise, on the other end.

This analysis leaves us with the seemingly intermediary category of Dicent Indexical Legisigns. At a first glance, it may appear as an artifice of Peirce's system of combining the three trichotomies. His examples of this category, in any case, seem strangely wanting and peripheral. One is the type of a "street cry", supposedly a ritualized shout, as that of a street vendor, facilitating the recognition of the individual uttering it; the other is the answer to the question "Whose statue is this?"—*"It is Farragut"*. The reason it is not, like the full proposition, a symbol is that it has, like the sinsign, no general predicate while, on the other side, the sign *itself, qua* legisign, is general. The predicate should

that will enable human minds to perform that reasoning. For the fish is there, and the actual composition of the stone already in fact determines what the chemist and the paleontologists will one day read in them (...) It is, therefore, true, in the logicians sense of the words, although not in that of the psychologists, that the thought is already expressed there" ("A Sketch of Logical Critics", 1911, EP II, 455). Peirce's picture theory of Dicisigns implies that facts in reality already have the structure of the Dicisign that may represent them.

be typical as a sign, but not general as to its contents—this is why individuals, proper names (or, supposedly, pronouns) are involved in the examples given.

There are some strange discrepancies here, though. "It must involve an Iconic Legisign to signify the information and a Rhematic Indexical Legisign to denote the subject of that information", Peirce said in the definition of this category of Dicisigns above, and the latter category is identified simply with proper nouns while the former can be examplified in diagram types, apart form their individual appearance in diagram tokens (sinsigns). But in the examples given, the proper name does not appear as the subject but as the *predicate* slot of the proposition. What would a sign look like actually fitting the description quoted? It would have a proper noun (or pronoun) as a subject, and a diagram type as the predicate. It might be a map with a legend—such as a map of Rome (the diagram predicate part) with the name "Rome" and other geographical names indicated in the map (the proper name subject part). But why would such a sign not simply be a Dicent Symbol?— every map is, to some degree, general and provides information not only about the geographical layout of an area at a particular point of time like a photo snapshot would do.

The examples which Peirce himself gives are thus quite different from this analysis. They pertain to information about object names—identification statements (the street cry identifying the person yelling it; "It is Farragut", identifying the individual depicted). These examples give the idea that the category of Dicent Indexical Legisigns should rather be categorized as Dicisigns in which names or indices occupy the predicate slot, supposedly including also naming speech acts ("This is known as a Z" "I refer to this as an X", "I baptize thou Y", "Let me present you to Mr. W", "This is called a 'tree'"). If we take that to be the case, the otherwise hazy category of Dicent indexical legisigns would occupy an important role. On a gradient between this category and full-fledged propositions would then appear signs which not only name or identify individual objects, but classes or continua of such objects ("I define a line as that which has length and no breadth", "Element nr. 92 is Uranium"), that is definitions, claims about class-names, etc.

3.13   Meanings and Objects of Dicisigns

Dicisigns being the central type of *efficient* signs, the establishing of their meaning is naturally important to a pragmatist semiotics like Peirce's. The relation between sign and meaning in Peirce generally being one of inference, the meaning of a Dicisign is described in terms of which inferences it is possible to draw from it. Thus, in the Lectures on Pragmatism, Peirce simply says:

"...what we call the *meaning* of a proposition embraces every obvious necessary deduction from it." ("The nature of meaning", Lectures on Pragmatism 1903, EPII 214, 5.165)

So, assessing the meaning of a sign is effectively conducting an Argument. The important constraint here is to *obvious* deductions from the Dicisign only, ruling out less obvious, maybe yet never performed deductions, e.g. theorematic deductions from it (cf. ch. 10). In the same lecture, we find a bit different definition of Dicisign meaning:

"On the whole, then, if by the *meaning* of a term, proposition, or argument, we understand the entire general intended interpretant, then the meaning of an argument is explicit. It is its conclusion, while the meaning of a proposition is all that that proposition or term could contribute to the conclusion of a demonstrative argument." ("The nature of meaning", 1903, EPII, 220)

Here, the "obvious" criterion has vanished, and the meaning instead is defined as the sum of possible contributions of that Dicisign to the conclusion of an Argument—not ruling out, e.g. non-obvious, theorematic deductions from it, requiring construction, experiment, and proof. This vacillation or ambiguity probably lies behind the development, in the mature Peirce, of the doctrine of *two* objects and *three* meanings (or interpretants) of signs. We already saw how an early version (primary/secondary object) was prompted by the analysis of the syntax of Dicisigns in the *Syllabus* deduction. It evolves into Peirce's general distinction between Immediate and Dynamical Objects of a sign:

"As to the Object, that may mean the Object as cognized in the Sign and therefore an Idea, or it may be the Object as it is regardless of any particular aspect of it, the Object in such relations as unlimited and final study would show it to be. The former I call the *Immediate* Object, the latter the *Dynamical* Object. For the latter is the Object that Dynamical Science (or what at this day would be called 'Objective' science,) can investigate." (Review of Lady Welby, 1903, 8.183)

The Dynamical Object, hence, is the object including all of its aspects, such as potentially laid bare by scientific investigation in the limit. This, of course, cf. Peirce's realism, is, at the same time, the object in itself, as it exists independently of perception or participation in any semiotic investigation processes. The Immediate Object has posed more problems to many interpreters. In what follows after the quote, Peirce explains that the Immediate Object is the object "as cognized in the Sign" in terms of "the occasion of sundry sensations". At other occasions, Peirce has described the Immediate Object as "...the object as the sign itself represents it".[37] This has taken some interpreters to surmise the Immediate Object should be the object as it is depicted, described, imagined, or signified in the sign. But in that case, it would no longer be an object category, but a meaning category. And as there are already three interpretant categories, cf. below, it would seem to overpopulate the field of interpretants if the Immediate Object should also count as part of the sign's meaning.

But the fact that the Dicisign's subject is claimed to be indexically connected to its referent object provides the relevant interpretation of what is the Immediate Object. Thus, the Immediate Object has nothing to do with describing the characters of the object, rather, the Immediate Object *is* the claimed indexical connection of the sign with its object, that which in the *Syllabus* deduction was taken to be the secondary object of the Dicisign, the object category corresponding to the meaning category of the icon of the sign itself in the predicate. This becomes obvious from the following reflection where Peirce imagines his wife asking him, one morning, about the weather: "I reply, let us suppose: "It is a stormy day." Here is another sign. Its *Immediate Object* is the notion of the present weather so far as this is common to her mind and mine—not the *character* of it, but the *identity* of it. *The Dynamical Object* is the *identity* of the actual or Real meteorological conditions at the moment" (Letter to James, March 14, 1909, 8.314). Neither the Immediate Object nor the Dynamic Object is concerned with descriptive characters—this is left to the meaning categories. Both deal with the *identity* of the reference.

---

[37]The full quote is interesting in itself: "But it remains to point out that there are usually two Objects, and more than two Interpretants. Namely, we have to distinguish the Immediate Object, which is the Object as the Sign itself represents it, and whose Being is thus dependent upon the Representation of it in the Sign, from the Dynamical Object, which is the Reality which by some means contrives to determine the Sign to its Representation. In regard to the Interpretant we have equally to distinguish, in the first place, the Immediate Interpretant, which is the interpretant as it is revealed in the right understanding of the Sign itself, and is ordinarily called the *meaning of the sign;* while in the second place, we have to take note of the Dynamical Interpretant which is the actual effect which the Sign, as a Sign, really determines. Finally there is what I provisionally term the Final Interpretant, which refers to the manner in which the Sign tends to represent itself to be related to its Object. I confess that my own conception of this third interpretant is not yet quite free from mist." ("Prolegomena to an Apology for Pragmaticism", 1906, 4.533)

Here, the Immediate Object is not only defined in terms of "Representation" but also as something whose being is dependent upon the sign. These ways of arguing may easily be mistaken for saying the sign creates a description of the object which is the IO. But "representation" in Peirce generally means denotation rather than signification, and the dependence of the IO on the sign does not exclude the dependence of both upon the DO—but must be taken to mean that the cutting out or selection of IO from the DO is due to the interaction with the sign—rather than taking the IO as being a meaning created by the sign.

So the Immediate Object is rather those parts or aspects of the Dynamical Object with which the sign claims to stand in indexical connection—including that very connection itself. Thus, the complex of light rays informing the eye about the visual structure of an object is the Immediate Object of that visual sign—or, to be more precise, the aspects of those light rays which are indexically influenced by the object and so informing about its appearance. In our interaction with objects, we rarely if ever interact distinctively with the whole of an object, with all of its parts and aspects, simultaneously. Rather, we stand in different, specific causal relations with aspects of the object, and it is the specific selection of those aspects and parts which forms the Immediate Object of the Dicisign. In that sense, the Immediate Object includes a part of the Dynamical Object—the part standing in indexical relation to the sign. And for both of them it holds that "...acquaintance cannot be given by a Picture or a Description ..." (ibid.), but only by indexical connection to the object.[38] Unlike Russell's distinction between knowledge by Acquaintance and by Description, Peirce's version claims that *both* must be present in any true Dicisign, because indexical Acquaintance, taken by itself, is stripped of all descriptive capacity which is reserved for the predicate aspect of the Dicisign:

> "It is usual and proper to distinguish two Objects of a Sign, the Mediate without, and the Immediate within the Sign. Its Interpretant is all that the Sign conveys: acquaintance with its Object must be gained by collateral experience. The Mediate Object is the Object outside of the Sign; I call it the *Dynamoid* Object. The Sign must indicate it by a hint; and this hint, or its substance, is the *Immediate* Object. Each of these two Objects may be said to be capable of either of the three Modalities, though in the case of the Immediate Object, this is not quite literally true." (Letter to Lady Welby, SS 83, 1908)

This implies, of course, that the Immediate Object must leave certain aspects of the Dynamical Object unspecified. In an outline of a trichotomy of signs according to their Immediate Object, Peirce distinguishes between indefinite, singular, and distributive (elsewhere, vague, singular, and general) signs; the former and the latter both being characterized by leaving parts of the Dynamic Object not directly referred to. In indefinite signs, "...the immediate object is only a possible presentment of a dynamic object, a fragment of it, the rest

---

[38] But do we need another index in order to connect to this index-object complex? Peirce does not address this, but we may assume this worry is ruled out for continuity reasons: an index of an index of an index ...of an object will still be an index of the object for continuity reasons similar to the *Nota Notae*.

being held in reserve, so that there is nothing in the immediate object to prevent contradictory attributes being separately possible of it. Thus 'A certain man' may turn out to be rich. He may turn out to be poor" (Ms. 339, "Logic Notebook", 256r 1905 Oct 10). Conversely, in distributive or general signs, the Immediate Object may be substituted for any Dynamic Object fitting the Immediate Object—as in "Any man". The Immediate Object, in both cases, involves a fragment of the Dynamical Object only and is hence necessarily incomplete and contains some degree of vagueness or generality, respectively. Even in the case of singular signs, where the sign precisely denotes its object (a limit case only, according to Peirce), the Immediate Object is but the end of a singular indexical connection terminating in the Dynamic Object. For this reason, Hilpinen has rightly compared the Immediate Object to Meinong's notion of "incomplete objects" whose function is as auxiliary objects (*Hilfsobjekte*) in connecting to the full, complex objects which it is impossible to intend every aspect of (Hilpinen, in press).

The Immediate Object may vary, of course, in degrees of elaboration. The same entity may be the object of several Dicisigns forming "collateral observations" relative to each other. The Dynamic Object always exceeds the sum of moments of causal interaction connecting it to Dicisigns—which is seen from the fact that a visual object has an infinity of profile shapes in between any two perceived such shapes. For that reason, it is "... plainly impractible, therefore, to restrict the meaning of the term 'object of a sign' to the Object strictly so called. For, after all, collateral observation, aided by imagination and thought, will usually result in some idea, though this need not be particularly determinate; but may be indefinite in some regards and general in others. Such an apprehension, approaching, however distantly, that of the Object strictly so called, ought to be, and usually is, termed the "immediate object" of the sign in the intention of its utterer. It may be that there is no such thing or fact in existence, or in any other mode of reality; but one surely shall not deny to the common picture of a Phoenix or to a figure of naked truth in their well the name of a "sign", simply because the bird is a fiction and Truth an *ens rationis*" ("Pragmatism", 1907, Ms. 318, one of several parallel drafts, 40-41, EP II 409).

In such cases, however, no real index connects the alleged Immediate Object to any existing Dynamic Object. Here, the doctrine must assume an as-if index to make believe it so refers (to reality in a lie, to an agreed-upon imaginary world in the case of fiction), or the index points to a general object of thought.

This division of the Dicisign's object throws light upon the triadic differentiation of its meanings. The above-mentioned "obvious" deductions from a Dicisign constituting the Immediate Interpretant now correspond to the Immediate Object in the sense that they also remain a meaning incomplete, as a subset of all possible deductions from the Dicisign. That ideal set of all such deductions rather corresponds to what Peirce calls the "Final" Interpretant—the sum total meaning of the Dicisign which investigation would reveal in the limit only. The "Dynamic" Interpretant, then, is the meaning such as it is actualized in any particular, concrete use of the Dicisign, always only another subset of the Final Interpretant (plus erroneous, actual inferences as well). So the Dynamic Object and the Dynamic Interpretant do not correspond to each other, confusingly, and the puzzle stemming from their terminological similarity has the reason that "dynamic" used about objects is taken to mean "at the end of dynamic scientific investigation" while "dynamic" used about interpretants is rather taken to mean "in actual existent dynamic sign exchange".

In the continuation of the quote where Peirce informs his wife about stormy weather, the three interpretants of that Dicisign are presented as follows: "The *Immediate Interpretant* is the *schema* in her imagination, i.e. the vague Image of what there is in common to the different Images of a stormy day. The *Dynamical Interpretant* is the disappointment or whatever actual effect it at once has upon her. The *Final Interpretant* is the sum of the *Lessons* of the reply, Moral, Scientific, etc." (8.314)[39] The three meaning categories are taken to be 1) the immediate schema presenting the general picture of a stormy day,—adding, in the blank of that predicate, the reference to the particular occasion of utterance, it should be noted (the meaning of a Dicisign is not only its iconic-predicative part but what can be inferred from the application of that part to a given subject)—the 'obvious' inferences from it; 2) the actual interpretation made by a sign interpreter in the situation of communication— in this case, the wife's change in emotion and action upon learning the fact reported by the Dicisign, deciding to stay inside and light the fireplaces etc.; 3) the Final—in other cases, the 'Normal'—Interpretant of the Dicisign is all which may be inferred from it, by all means of investigation in the limit. The three meaning categories thus may be compared as follows: 1) lies close to dictionary meaning in a broad sense (but comprising also other signs, of course, than linguistic signs), close to the normal use of the word 'meaning'; 2) equals pragmatic meaning relative to a situation of communication, determined by the dialogic string preceding it and the collateral knowledge involved in the situation; 3) corresponds to the ideal limit of all possible knowledge to which the Dicisign in question may, in the future, contribute.

---

[39] The CP erroneously has '...the vague Image *or* what there is in common to the different Images of a stormy day.'

3.14   Conclusion

Peirce's doctrine of Dicisigns, when pieced together from his different writings around 1900, constitutes an early and fairly elaborated doctrine of propositions. My claim, however, is that it is not only of historical interest. Recent philosophical discussion has focused upon issues such as: are propositions structured—or are they some sort of primitives (like mappings from sentences to sets of possible worlds)? Do they exist in any sense at all—already Russell famously ended up finding it burdensome to accept the commitment to any kind of existence of all false propositions, this prompting him to give up the idea of propositions. Does their existence depend upon the existence of human language and its syntactical and semantic devices?

Peirce's doctrine articulates a strong claim for what are nowadays called "structured propositions". His analysis of what keeps propositional structure together forms a sophisticated doctrine not far from some present positions (such as King 2007): the syntactical connection between predicate and subjects in a proposition functions as an icon of the actual, indexical connection between their correlates in terms of objects and relations. It is a picture theory of Dicisigns—but it lacks the insistence of Wittgensteinian picture theories on a foundational level of logical atomism, taking instead the facts referred to by true propositions to be structural aspects of reality on any given level of description. The functional definition of Dicisigns— signs performing two simultaneous, different functions relating to the same objects, those of reference and description, transgresses the idea that propositions should depend upon the syntax of human language exclusively, opening the investigation of other syntactical combination strategies fulfilling the function to be charted in non-linguistic signs in human and non-human semiotics. As to the mode of existence of propositions, Peirce's doctrine is not completely clear—I think, however, its lack of clarity may be easily sanitized. As Short (2007; 231ff, 242ff) points out, two different ideas seem to compete in Peirce's doctrine. One claims propositions are signs—which may enter into more compound signs when those signs are asserted, assented to or subjected to other speech acts.[40]

---

[40]Space does not allow us to discuss here Peirce's embryonic speech act theory according to which propositions are signs fit to be asserted—or to be the objects of other propositional attitudes like utterances, judgments, assents, interrogatives, imperatives, etc.: "One and the same proposition may be affirmed, denied, judged, doubted, inwardly inquired into, put as a question, wished, asked for, effectively commanded, taught, or merely expressed, and does not thereby become a different proposition", "Kaina Stoicheia", 1904, EP II 312; cf. Brock 1981. The important thing in our context is that propositions are ideal signs types which, in order to have actual effects, must be expressed in sign tokens in one of many possible ways. As to the central act type of assertion, Peirce identifies it with the willingness publicly to accept responsibility for the truth of the proposition involved and thus expose oneself to

Another claims propositions are ideal entities existing outside of space-time as mere possibilities. How could these two doctrines be reconciled? Short thinks the problem is "easily rectified" by preferring the ideal interpretation so that propositions are what may be abstracted from various types of Dicent Symbols—but not themselves being signs (245).[41] But do we have to make this choice? The idea of Dicisigns as signs is the source of much of the strength of Peirce's doctrine, so we would hesitate to give up that idea. In the ten-sign typology of the *Syllabus* combining the three basic trichotomies, the six most complicated signs are all legisigns, types, that is, none of them are actually existing signs but general sign types which appear in actuality only as instantiated in tokens, of which only three types of sinsigns exist. The four sign types involving Dicisigns—Arguments, Dicent Symbols, Dicent Indexical Legisigns, and Dicent Sinsigns—thus only have certain subtypes of Dicent sinsigns as their instantiating "outlet" to actual discourse, so to speak. Any actual use—such as an assertion—of a Dicisign requires its tokening in a sinsign. But that implies that Dicisigns, apart from the special case of Dicent Sinsigns, do possess the ideality of types, of legisigns. So the idea that Dicisigns are indeed signs need not be as remote from their ideality as Short presupposes. Short seems here to identify signs with tokens, sinsigns, only. Here Peirce's argument for their ideality: "A sentence, in the sense here used, is a single object. Every time it is copied or pronounced, a new sentence is made. But a proposition is not a single thing and cannot properly be said to have any *existence*. Its mode of being consists in its possibility. A proposition which might be expressed has all the being that belongs to propositions although nobody ever expresses it or thinks it. It is the same proposition every time it is thought, spoken or written, whether in English, German, Spanish, Tagálog, or how. A proposition consists in a meaning, whether adopted or not, and however expressed. That meaning is the meaning of any sign which should signify that a certain iconic representation, or image (or any equivalent of it) is a sign of something indicated by a certain indexical sign, or any equivalent thereof" ("RR" 1902, Ms. 599, 5–7).

The token sinsigns—sentences or other instantiations by means of gesture, picture, diagram tokens—are actual, existent entities, but the Dicisigns they

---

the punishments and other social effects normally enacted upon liars. The act of assertion, thereby, differs not only from the proposition asserted as well as from the expression of it, but also from the act of assent whereby an individual personally accepts the truth of it. Thus, as Short also points out, Austin's famous quip that "With all his 66 division of signs, Peirce does not, I believe, distinguish between a sentence and a statement" (Austin 1961, p. 87n1, quoted by Short 2007, 242) is simply besides the point.

[41] It even leads Short into attempting a distinction between the Rheme/Dicisign/Argument trichotomy and the Seme/Pheme/Delome trichotomy (which are synonymous in Peirce).

instantiate are not. They are mere possibilities. But still they are structured possibilities—possessing the structured syntax of Peirce's doctrine: the syntactical coupling of the two functional constituent signs. That propositions, in that sense, are ideal signs, is expressed by the Legisign-Sinsign (Type-Token) distinction. Should this confuse us and give us Ockhamist headaches that this commits us to accept an infinity of possible propositions, combining merely possible subjects with merely possible predicates, including lots of meaningless and false combinations? Not more, I think, than we should take it as a heavy ontological burden to accept the infinitely recursive composition possibilities of human language or the indefinite range of yet unrealized compound possibilities of organic chemistry.

All in all, much can be learnt from Peirce's Dicisign doctrine, not only pertaining to the history of logic. The liberation of propositions from the iron cages of human language in the Frege-Russell tradition allows us to begin to grasp the logic and cognitive abilities of other animals as well as those of human beings freely mixing language with images, pictures, diagrams, gesture in order to understand and express Dicisigns. In the next chapters we shall attempt to distill such actual implications of Peirce's doctrine of propositions.

Chapter 4

Some Consequences of the Dicisign Doctrine

4.1 Naturalization of Propositions

A most remarkable implication of a Peircean notion of Dicisigns is the possible naturalization of propositions. Propositions are taken to function without the intermediary of language or consciousness, and propositions are taken to exist before the existence of human beings—in short, the expression of propositions seem to be natural inhabitants of any system or process of signs imaginable. This, of course, immediately raises the issue of *which* naturalization. If naturalization means the reduction to an ontology admitting no other existence than that of physical individuals, or if naturalization means the reduction of all content of thought to psychic processes—then a Peircean doctrine of propositions could not be amenable to naturalization. Peircean scholastic realism prevents the former step; anti-psychologism precludes the latter. But if naturalization means the reformulation of knowledge so it fits into a naturalist evolutionist world-view based on the reality of laws of nature, then the Dicisign doctrine offers a double advantage over existing doctrines of propositions. One advantage is that the purely functional definition of propositions liberates Dicisigns from the confinement to human language, intention, and consciousness, that is, beyond linguistic-turn philosophy as well as philosophy of mind. This implies propositions are no artifice of special structures of the human mind and brain but that they are rather naturally occurring as part and parcel of any possible cognitive process, human or not:

"Granting that there may be some general concepts which are not perceptual, that is, not elements of perceptual judgments, these may make a kind of music in the soul, or they may in some mysterious way subserve some end; but in order to be of any *cognitive* service, it is plain that they must enter into propositions. For cognition proper is true, or at any rate is either true or false, and it is propositions alone that are either true or false." ("Lectures on Pragmatism", VI, 1903, Ms. 316, 56–57)

This leads to the second advantage. Given the purely functional, deflated notion of propositions, it becomes possible to envision a biological evolution of signs so that the structure of Dicisigns has been realized in evolution, allowing for the gradually more sophisticated mastery of Dicisigns in higher species, culminating so far in certain avians and mammals.

It is well known that Peirce was trained as a chemist, worked professionally as a practising scientist for a 30-year period—and at the same time was a strong realist, in a double sense of the word. He was a realist in the simple sense that he took reality to be what is unaffected by what anybody thinks about it. He was also a realist in the medieval "Scotist" sense of taking certain universals to be real, certain predicates to correspond to patterns in the world—the sense of realism opposed to nominalism. As a working scientist, Peirce witnessed with surprise the dominant philosophy of science of his day to side with nominalism, often connected with psychologism, and from early on, he analyzed and attacked nominalism.[1] To Peirce, all results of science, experimental or rational, had to be general, as no knowledge of isolated particulars can amount to the synthesis characteristic of scientific knowledge. Natural laws, tendencies, patterns, regularities form the backbone of all science which is why he was immediately realist as to such structures. Taking the Millian refuge and restricting oneself to speak about "uniformity" or "regularity" of nature was, to him, begging the question. Again, logic was his tutor. Kant's idea that the only metaphysics allowed should be that which is built upon logic was developed and extended by Peirce. The fact that a proposition like "Socrates is a man" is true prompts us to accept not only the existence of Socrates but also the reality of being a man. Already in "Some Consequences of Four Incapacities" (1868) Peirce based himself on the Kantian principle that any assumptions of metaphysical existence must be based upon logic: "...a realist is simply one who knows no more recondite reality than that which is represented in a true representation. Since, therefore, the word 'man' is true of something, that which "man" means is real. The nominalist must admit that

---

[1]See Forster 2011.

man is truly applicable to something; but he believes that there is beneath this a thing in itself, an incognizable reality. His is the metaphysical figment" (EP I, 53; 5.312). This is truth-maker realism: what makes a true proposition true is what must be taken to exist. To Peirce, no scientist in his heart doubts the reality of the general results of his research. We shall not, at this place, go deeply into Peirce's "scholastic realism" (see Stjernfelt 2007, ch. 2–3); suffice it to say that taking both possibilities, particular here-now existence and lawlike structures to form part of the natural universe gives us a naturalism which avoids many of the problems of would-be parsimonious nominalism. It must be added that such nominalisms invariably end up with an ontology failing to reach the austerity they aim for, partly because of the metaphysical figment of an incognizable reality which Peirce referred to, and partly because everything which is driven out of ontology invariably is resurrected in the human mind. If no universals refer to real structures, then all universals are but labels invented by the human mind. If propositions do not exist in reality they, as well, must be creations of the human mind. If causes are not real, etc. The implication is that one the one hand, we get an emaciated natural world consisting of isolated particulars only, bereft of any generality. On the other hand, in the very same universe, one particular, strange kind of object is supposed to stand out—the mind—which alone has the ability to create general objects and syntheses, namely those labels assumed identical from one use to the next, the *names* of the nominalists. So ontological stinginess as to the natural world automatically seems to imply the abnormal and extreme ontological overpopulation of the human psyche—otherwise assumed to form part of the very same natural world. Philosophers may be satisfied with bracketing that psyche, leaving the problem to psychologists—but that only leaves the road open for exactly psychologism, the tendency to locate ontological and logical structure in the mind of the beholder and take psychology to be the science studying them. So nominalism and psychologism often, if not always, go together. Peirce refused both—with the upshot that his naturalism automatically includes thought, logic, semiotics, and mind as intrinsic aspects. Nowhere is this more apparent than in his idea that propositions may be defined purely functionally. The deflation inherent in taking function to be the core of propositions implies at least four things: 1) propositions do not require an explicit linguistic system in order to function; 2) propositions are no human privilege; 3) propositions need no conscious intention in order to function; 4) propositions are relevant for cognitive as well as communicative processes in general. This deflation goes hand in hand with the fact that the functional definition of propositions is *semiotic*: propositions are signs and find expression in sign tokens. This implies that it is the investigation of the structure of semiotic processes which may establish which Dicisigns—if any—partake in that process. In this chapter, we shall chart a bundle of possible, immediate developments of the Peircean Dicisign doctrine.

4.2 Co-localization as the Basis of Syntax

We saw how Peirce analyzed the Dicisign with an emphasis on its syntax, partially given by the "continuous predicate" of relation connecting the subjects involved, partially by the Dicisign's self-reference inherent in its truth-claim. The Dicisign, involving two signs relating each in their way to the same object, has a syntax in order to assess that these two signs do, in fact, involve the same object, the Dicisign claiming, about itself, that its iconic representation holds for a specified object. The indication of the sign object is realized by the subject index part of the Dicisign while the description of the same object is realized by part of the predicate icon part of it. They analyze the fact depicted into two parts, existence and relational properties, respectively. The claim that these two are, in fact, related in a real fact is expressed by the syntax of the Dicisign which, deceptively simply, represents this relation by *co-localizing* the Subject Index and the Predicate Icon: "It has to contain two parts both representing the same object, exhibited in a secondness to one another so that this Secondness shall be interpretable as an index of a corresponding secondness in the object" (*Syllabus* draft pages on Dicisigns, 1903, Ms. 478, 43). The real connection making up a fact in reality is mirrored in a real connection on the level of the expression of the Dicisign itself, and, what is more, the very connection claimed by the Dicisign to hold between itself and this object, is depicted in the unsaturated predicate structure. This co-localization is the foundation for signs to be able to claim anything at all—and so it is in some sense the mother of all syntax and may be developed in many different directions and subtypes of co-localization. Because of the far more elaborate and conventionalized syntax of human language it may be difficult to appreciate the extreme simplicity and basic status of co-localization in primitive Dicisigns. We find it, however, to be fundamental in the processing of simple, non-linguistic Dicisigns—just like traces of it may be found in parts and aspects of human language and thought with little or absent explicit grammatical structure.

Co-localization as a primitive semiotic phenomenon may be viewed as part of Peirce's overall spatialization-of-logic hypothesis. In a certain sense, it is connected to the so-called localism hypothesis in linguistics—that basic semantic and grammatical relations are fundamentally motivated in spatial relations. Peirce never makes it explicit as a hypothesis, but as Bellucci (2013) has recently argued, it comes out of his interpretation of F.A. Lange's 1877 *Logische*

Studien, in which Lange argues for the principle that "...die Anschauung der Begriffsverhältnisse in Raumbildern die eigentliche Grundlage aller logischen Technik bildet ..." (74)[2]. Lange thus generalizes Kant's idea that mathematics is constructive and presupposes the pure intuition of space to embrace also logic. Here, Lange celebrates Kant's famous schematism, uniting intuition and understanding, with the only proviso that it is not a product of understanding, but of imagination, producing series of images incarnating conceptual rules (134). This synthesis, to Lange, is what already involves intuition and understanding (which should never have been separated in the first place), and the "Raumvorstellung", the presentation of space, is the origin of all syntheses (137). Spatial syntheses, then, are the root of all understanding, including subjective self-understanding and temporal imagination, Kantian "inner sense" which is possible only by this objectifying detour. To Lange, spatiality makes the apriori synthesis *objective* rather than subjective—which is why we may be in error about apriori relations (cf. Smith's much later notion of "fallibilistic apriorism")—we possess the same distance to them as to empirical objectivities. Peirce obviously was deeply influenced by Lange's insistence on "überall Raumbilder" (spatial imagery everywhere, 139) in his logic and epistemology. Lange's syllogistic notion of logic, however, remains much narrower than Peirce's who took Lange's important principle and let it accompany his own vast generalization of logic to cover semiotics and theory of science.[3] This forms the basis for Peirce's doctrine of diagrams (see ch. 7ff), generalizing it to a general epistemology of ideal objects and deductive inferences—so that spatial imagination is what makes possible a priori and necessary reasoning. This makes logical deduction mathematical ("Validity", in Baldwin's Dictionary 1901, 2.782)—cf. Peirce's adherence to the tradition seeing logic formalizations as algebraic. Later, in the Existential Graphs, Peirce develops a topological formalization of logic; both of these, however, rely upon different spatial diagrams, algebraic and topological, respectively. It is important to note that

---

[2]"...the depiction of conceptual relations in spatial imagery forms the proper basis of all logical technique..."

[3]"The chief source of logical truth, though never recognized by logicians, always has been and always must be the same as the source of mathematical truth. This was well shown in a little book entitled *Logische Studien* by the historian of materialism, Friedrich Albert Lange, published in 1877, having been unfortunately left unfinished at the author's death in 1875. I have found few books on logic so instructive. I do not mean that the reader will find Lange's views exactly reproduced in this work, by any means, upon a single topic. But it has influenced me considerably, and I can recommend it as one of the very few works on logic that I have found too short. (...) I will merely state here that my conclusion agrees substantially with Lange's, that mathematical truth is derived from observation of creations of our own visual imagination, which we may set down on paper in form of diagrams" ("Minute Logic", 1902, 2.77).

Peirce's embrace of the Kant-Lange hypothesis does not commit him to any particular conceptualization of space (as did Kant's idea of the apriori status of Euclidean geometry). Rather, Peirce assumes a generalized, fundamental notion of space which may receive very different formal interpretations—non-Euclidean geometries, topologies, algebras.[4] In his fertile period after 1900, Peirce returns to this Langean inspiration over and over again.

Peirce's most thorough analysis of the Dicisign in the *Syllabus*, as we saw, took co-localization as the fundamental aspect of its syntax—even intended, self-represented co-localization. In a certain sense, this forms the diagram of Dicisign syntax itself, thus providing the spatial starting point of logic (while much of the diagrammatical reasoning doctrine deals with the many different modes of diagrammaticity of predicates).

As an example of co-localization in Dicisigns, Peirce's painting-with-a-legend is basic. The legend must be in some sense phenomenologically *close* to the picture in order to function as the subject index saturating the picture predicate. Very often, the legend or title is physically attached to the picture object, to the frame, or is inscribed on its flip side. In art exhibitions, the legend is often printed on a separate table displayed immediately besides the painting. Sometimes it may, for different reasons, have some distance to the painting; in those cases additional indices typically will be necessary to insure the unanimous connection between the two (as in cases where, e.g., the titles of three paintings are given in the same table, in that case the order of the paintings in the wall may be mirrored iconically by the order of the titles in the table, numbers on the frames may correspond to numbers in the table, or positions on the wall may be indicated by a small drawing or by arrows or direction instructions ("to the left", "in the middle", "to the right")). As soon as predicate and subject are not immediately co-localized, some additional indexical-iconical machinery must emerge in order to ensure their syntatical continuity.

A classic example of semiotics is road signs. How do we know *where* a given sign makes its signification present and exerts its force? Road signs, as is well known, realize different speech acts: some are declarative, some imperative prohibitions, some imperative instructions, some suggestive, etc. Let us take the standard road sign meaning "Parking Prohibited". The very *position* of the sign is what indicates where the sign is valid. The conventional symbolic-iconic sign on the metal post, obviously, is in need of saturation by

---

[4]As Shin (1997) says, Peirce's appropriation of Kant's view on the syntheticity of mathematics leaves behind Kant's idea that this syntheticity resides *in specific domains*—it rather resides in the *necessity of construction* in certain problems, cf Peirce's distinction between corollarial and theorematic reasoning (see ch. 10) which Shin takes as a candidate for a Peircean distinction between analyticity and syntheticity (see also Stjernfelt 2007, ch. 8).

a subject index in order actually to function as a Dicisign. If the sign were placed on a living room wall as a decoration, it would sink to an iconic rheme, an isolated, unsaturated propositional function, and no longer indicate that parking is prohibited. It takes a certain environment, namely one in which cars have regular access, for it to function. In that case, the very location of the sign vehicle functions as the subject index which saturates the sign and realizes the imperative Dicisign. It is here, in the immediate environment of the sign, that the validity of the Dicisign is claimed - it is the surroundings and the car drivers potentially going about there which form the subject of the imperative Dicisign "Parking prohibited": YOU who read this should not park your CAR, HERE. If the surroundings of the sign are vague as to delimitation, e.g. along a road, additional information may be necessary in the sign, making explicit the topographical range of the surroundings where it is valid (often using arrows, distance indications, etc.). But these are supplementary signs adding detail precision to the more fundamental Dicisign subject given by the sign's own placement: "*Referring to cars in the area around this sign*, Parking is Prohibited". It is important that the sign's claim is *conspicuous*— otherwise the guy parking his car may rightfully claim he was not informed about the prohibition. This is why road signs are 1) composed from flashy colors standing out on the background, 2) use a particular road sign code making them easily recognizable *as* road signs. These two properties make up the second requirement of the Dicisign syntax which Peirce developed in his *Syllabus* deduction: the road sign is conspicuous *as a sign*. This is what gives it the required self-reference: "This is a sign, and it states that the parking of cars is prohibited in this sign's surroundings". Peirce, in a small text, analyzes a parallel example: "Every proposition has three elements. 1st an indication of the universe to which it relates, 2nd its general terms, 3rd connection of the terms [...] Every proposition relates to something which can only be pointed out or designated but cannot be specified in general terms. "No admittance, except on business." over a door is a general proposition, but it relates to that door which may have no qualities different from these of some other door in some other planet or in some other tri-dimensional space of which there may be any number scattered through a quinqui-dimensional continuum without anywhere touching one another. But the hanging of the sign over this door indicates that this is the one referred to. The indescribable but designatable object to which a proposition refers always has connected with it a variety of possibilities, often an endless variety. In the example we have taken, these possibilities are all the actions that can have a relation to that door. The proposition declares that among all these actions there is not to be found any permitted passage through the door except on business" (Ms. 789, no date).

Such elementary syntax, the combination of the sign with its environment localization, is so fundamental and easily processed as often to escape notice. It forms the basis for a vast amount of sign use—if a shop sports a sign saying "Alimentation", it is a Dicisign referring to the food present in the room under the sign (and, per convention, the fact that this food is not only present, but also for sale from this shop). The party responsible for uttering the sign, of course, is the shopkeeper who is also juridically responsible to the extent that a customer can claim his liability if something sold under the pretext of food turns out to be inedible. In the road sign: the authority granting the traffic imperative's validity as law (and the connected conditions of prosecution and fines in case the imperative is not obeyed) depends, of course, upon the jurisdiction and, behind that, the political power exercised in the area where the sign is posted, ultimately local sovereignty based on Weberian monopoly of violence —but that is the further pragmatic environment to the basic syntax of co-localization. Linguists might find this is an issue of pragmatic sign interpretation having nothing to do with real syntax. Quite on the contrary, the Peircean viewpoint would take this prelinguistic syntax to be so basic as to precede Morris' syntax-semantics-pragmatics distinction,[5] and to form the basis for the more sophisticated grammars built on top of it in human and other languages.

Simple co-localization also is apparent in language, e.g., in the transphrastic composition of periods. Typically, this is seen as the locus where syntax and semantics yield and pragmatics take over. The composition of periods is not subject to grammar of the same strictness as NP-VP sentence syntax, word order, inflection of lexemes, etc. The very co-localization of sentences on the page or in the current of speech is enough to grant they address the same issue, and the sequence of periods very often forms an icon of the temporal, logical, psychological or other sequence of the contents related. But also within sentence grammar, remnants of simple co-localization may be found when explicit semantic and syntactic regularity becomes sparse. Such an issue is formed by compound nouns in many languages—like "gold ring", "house boat", "boat house" etc. in English (cf. Bundgaard, Østergaard, Stjernfelt 2006, 2007). It is a well-known linguistic fact that the semantic relation between the two parts of a compound noun is grammatically underdetermined. A gold ring is a ring consisting of gold, but a house boat is not a boat consisting of house, it is a boat usable as a house. A boat house, however, is not a house usable as a boat, it is a house to protect a boat. The semantic relations between the two terms comprehend a wide variety of matter, shape,

---

[5]Which was, of course, Morris' rearticulation of Peirce's Grammatica Speculativa, Critical Logic, Methodeutic trichotomy.

surface, function, purpose,—classical ontological categories, not indicated by grammatical or morphological devices (even if they may, of course, in case of doubt, be made explicit, e.g. by prepositions and verbal nominalizations: "ring of gold", "boat for housing", "house for boat keeping", etc.). In the absence of such determinations, however, the only syntax in compound nouns seems to be that (in English, Danish and other Germanic languages) the second noun takes the functional role as subject while the first noun takes that of the predicate (in Romance and other languages it may be vice-versa) modifying the subject. A gold ring is a gold-like ring in some sense, a house boat is a house-like boat, the boat house a boat-like house, etc. The semantics of the relation between the two nouns is not made explicit—the relation here is a pure Peircean "continuous predicate"—but is left to the receiver's pragmatic sense, and in some cases several different interpretations of the connection may be possible. There are trains in a train station, but (hopefully) there's no fire in a fire station. Here, the semantic relation is not explicitly indicated but must just be learned or guessed. This may pose problems in cases of neologisms: "Dolphin safe" might immediately be thought of as something being safe against attacks from dolphins, but it is actually used about tuna fish meat caught in a way (allegedly) posing no danger for simultaneous catch of dolphins. This semantic underdetermination is due to the fact that the syntax of compound nouns approaches simple co-localization. It is the very fact that two nouns are placed besides each other which gives the information that they should be read as a predicate-subject structure, the only grammatical conventionalization being word order to tell which is which.

This extreme simplicity of the syntax of co-localization, of course, has its basis in the very parsing of perceptions—cf. Hurford's idea that already animal perception parses its contents in subjects and predicates (next chapter). In that sense, there is a basic continuum from simple perception—the fact that you have an indexical relation to what you perceive and you adorn that relation with an iconic predicate *at the same location* in the field of perception which your indexical relation connects you to. It is the structure of existent entities entertaining relations—or, to speak in terms of more classic ontology objects entertaining properties—which forms the ultimate basis of co-localization syntax. Pietarinen's observation that co-localization as operationalized in Peirce's EG notation breaks with the Frege-Russell ambiguity analysis of the copula[6] gives us a key to the fertility and reinterpretability of co-localization. Co-localization may, in fact, iconically be taken to represent all of the continuous predicates, identity, co-existence, predication, relation, existence, class subsumption, implication . . . and it may do so without explicit convention,

---

[6] Pietarinen (2011) 276–77; (in prep.), 5

dependent upon the local function of the sign. Examples: A sign on a building *identifies* this building as the "House of Commons" at the same time as claiming the existence of this institution. Two co-localized signs on a building may indicate the *co-existence* of two functions in that building "Ministry of Education. Ministry of Science". A plate on a building may make a *predication* "Goethe Haus"—the house where Goethe once lived. Two co-localized signs may—using a slight convention of order—indicate *subsumtion*: "Ministry of Education. Department of Primary Schools". A sign showing two faces, one sad and shabby, one happy and well-shaven, may indicate, again with the slight convention of order, *implication*: if you go to this barber, you get a good shave. One sign may *identify*—or *subsume*—several buildings: "University of Oxford", cf. Ryle's old puzzle. Of course, as Kierkegaard once observed, even such simple signs may lie: in a Copenhagen shop window he observed a sign saying (in Danish): "Her rulles" ('Mangling here'). The shop displaying the sign, however, was a junk dealer, the sign was for sale and no mangling took place there—Kierkegaard used it as a parable of the explanations of philosophy not really offering any explanations after all. As the examples will show, there are no sharp distinctions, at this elementary level, between the meanings distinguished in the Frege-Russell ambiguity hypothesis. The Peircean conclusion, then, will be that the ambiguity does exist, but it has a very good reason: the metaphysical fact that continuous predicates emerge from one and the same spatially conceived local continuum.

4.3 Nonconceptual Content

An important implication of Dicisigns is that because not confined to linguistics they cut across the much-discussed distinction between conceptual and non-conceptual representative content. In a largely Fregean framework, much discussion has taken place during the last thirty years pertaining to which kind of content may be ascribed to human intentions such as perceptions which are not explicitly or only partially conceptual. The distinction originated with Gareth Evans (1982) addressing particularly the distinction between perception and judgments (in turn, based upon conception): "The informational states which a subject acquires through perception are non-conceptual, or non-conceptualized. Judgments based upon such states necessarily involve conceptualization: in moving from a perceptual experience to a judgement about the world (usually expressible in some verbal form), one will be exercising basic conceptual skills." (227). Thus, the notion generally pertains to the idea that while the "reasoning and concept-applying system" of human beings can be described by means of conceptual content, perceptual states, by contrast, cannot be so described because perception represents the environment independently of the perceiver's conceptual repertoire, has richness, a finer granularity, etc.: "Nonconceptualists argue that, while propositional attitudes represent the world in digital form, perceptual states represent the world in analog form" (Bermúdez and Cahen (2012)). Conceptualists, on the other hand, claim that even perceptual representational content must be conceptual in order to be able to function as warrant for beliefs. Obviously, any solution to this issue will depend on how narrow or wide your concept of "concept" and "conceptual content" is, as the opposed concept of "non-conceptual content" is defined purely by negative contrast. We shall not here go deeply into the wide debate in the wake of Evans' book[7]—apart from observing that much of the discussion seems to rest upon a notion of perception not only cleansed of concepts but also alien to propositions. Immediately, nonconceptualists are right when claiming that the contents of perception (and of signs rich with iconicity like pictures, diagrams, etc.) cannot be reduced or translated to compositions of concepts unless you embrace an extremely wide redefinition of concepts.[8] Such claims, however, are important to keep distinct from other basic notions such as reasoning, belief, generality, and propositions.

Nonconceptualism much too often argues by adding further dichotomies to that of conceptual/nonconceptual, like that between reasoning, generality and propositions on the one hand and perception on the other, so that non-conceptual content should, simultaneously, be taken to be reasoning- and proposition-free, and very often "propositional" and "conceptual" immediately seem to be taken as synonyms so that only conceptual content should be able to contain articulated propositions.[9] Such claims seem to rest upon a theory of perception where perceptual content is immediately not only non-linguistic

---

[7]Positions like McDowell for conceptualism, Byrne for conceptualism but against experience justifying beliefs, Tye for non-conceptualism, Crane for non-conceptualism in the sense perceptions are not propositional attitudes—and many more.

[8]Bermúdez and Cahen (2012) point to this dependence of "non-conceptual" on your definition of conceptuality: "As we saw earlier, on the most minimal view of concepts, a thinker can be credited with a concept of Fs provided that he can discriminate things that are F from things that are not F. A richer view of concepts might demand that the thinker have a full appreciation of the grounds on which one might judge something to be an F. The most demanding view of concepts might require the thinker to be able to justify and defend the judgment that something is an F. Clearly, different locations on this broad spectrum will generate different ways of thinking about what is to count as nonconceptual content—as well as different assessments of the overall significance of the notion."

[9] Raftopoulos and Müller claim that "the existence of cognitively impenetrable mechanisms is a necessary and sufficient condition for nonconceptual content" (2006, p. 190). Bermúdez and Cahen (2012) interpret this as the "...insulation from the propositional attitudes of the person ..." but this does not follow, unless you presuppose a very close connection between conceptual content, propositions and conscious attitudes.

but non-conceptual in the sense of non-general, and non-propositional—and that language, concepts and propositions are connected, later elaborations of sense-data-like perceptions. The Dicisign doctrine, of course, basically refuses to accept such an opposition, claiming instead there are quasi-propositions already in perception and that perception, consequently, involves "propositional stances". The same goes for externalized Dicisigns in books, pictures, computers and elsewhere which may display parts which are not exhaustible by concepts—such as gestures, images, diagrams, etc. Thus, it is a source of error to assume propositions are conceptual through and through—they may involve both conceptual and non-conceptual representational contents.

Peircean continuism, however, would hesitate to accept any sharp distinction between conceptual and non-conceptual content, also because of the often not very explicit doctrine of what counts as "conceptual". Rather, Peircean continuism would assume a continuum from very diagrammatic, schematic and "thin" content to very image-like, perceptual, "thick" content, *both* of those with the capacity to participate in quasi-propositions, and with general aspects structuring and participating in even the most "thick" perceptual content.

Some of this discussion seems to rely upon a preconception of "concepts" as necessarily linguistically expressed concepts. Here, the whole cognitive semantics and cognitive linguistic current (Talmy, Lakoff, Langacker, etc.) would assume the existence of pre-linguistic conceptual content to be further shaped by language. Similarly, the Peircean conception, obviously, would not tie conceptual ability to language, especially not human language, exclusively. Rather, the Peircean approach would separate the ability to shape propositions, with its characteristic double function giving rise to truth conditions, from the ability to form different degrees of conceptual content, the latter depending upon which types of predicates are admitted in the functional role of description of the Dicisign ... posing a continuum between very rich contents and very poor contents already in perception (based on the fact that perceptions always-already contain general aspects). Bermúdez and Cahen write (2012): "The information loss in the transition from perception to perceptual belief is not a sign that there are two different types of content in play, but should rather be understood as a transition from a more determinate type of conceptual content (e.g., *that is colored thus*) to a less determinate type of conceptual content (e.g., *that is red*)." From our viewpoint, the very distinction between non-conceptual and conceptual content *is* such a matter of degree of determination, not a distinction between two completely different kinds of content. But, as indirectly indicated in the quote by the fact that the paraphrases of contents in parentheses *both* take propositional shape, it could not possibly be an issue of something pre-propositional versus something propositional. There are Dicisigns on many levels, differing in degrees of determination of content, ("that is colored thus"/"that is red") just like the passing from the portrait painting claiming "Louis XIV looked like this" to, e.g., the linguistically expressed claim that "Louis XIV wore a gray wig".

In the discussions of nonconceptual content, it is referred to as nonconceptual *mental* content and nonconceptual *representational* content, interchangeably. From our position, however, these terms are not synonymous. The Dicisign doctrine makes it evident that nonconceptual representational content is ubiquitous also beyond perception—in pictures, images, diagrams, movies, photographs, paintings, gesture, iconic aspects of language, etc.—and that such external representations are not inherently mental even if their use may involve mental processing. Mental nonconceptual content, rather, is but a subset of representational nonconceptual content, and there is no reason to delimit the investigation of nonconceptual content to mental representations only. Dicisigns may take external nonconceptual content as their predicates (pictures) just as well as mental nonconceptual content (perceptions)—cf. the discussion of Clark's "extended mind" doctrine in ch. 7 below. So, the spontaneous dichotomies involved in much discussion of nonconceptual content are part of the problematic setup: the assumption that perception is non-propositional, non-inferential, and non-conceptual; the idea that language only is conceptual and distinguished by a clear borderline from non-conceptual content. Rather, conceptual and non-conceptual content are related across a continuum, and both of them may form part of propositions and quasi-propositions.

4.4   Inference as the Fundamental Concept of Cognition

An important advantage in Peirce's deflated notion of proposition is its dispensing with consciousness as a defining feature in bringing about propositions. The whole of Peirce's semiotics emphatically brackets the issue of consciousness as any precondition for signs to be produced and interpreted:

> "In fact, in the present condition of philosophy, consciousness seems to be a mere quality of feeling which a formal science will do best to leave out of account. But a sign only functions as a sign when it is interpreted. It is therefore essential that it should be capable of determining an interpretant sign." (Ms. 7 "On the Foundations of Mathematics", around 1903)

The production of interpretants unites, in Peirce's semiotics, meaning (cf. our discussion of types of interpretants above) and inference. Peirce's theory of meaning is basically inferential, cf. his insistence on symbolic propositions to be "genuine" signs. Already in a very early paper (1868), Peirce takes inference to be *the* basic cognitive procedure:

> "... we must, as far as we can do so without additional hypotheses, reduce all kinds of mental action to one general type. (...) We must begin, then, with a *process of cognition, and with that* process whose laws are best understood and most closely follow external facts. This is no other than the process of valid inference, which proceeds from its premiss, A, to its conclusion, B, only if, as a matter of fact, such a proposition as B is always or usually true when such a proposition as A is true." ("Some Consequences of Four Incapacities", 1868, 5.266-267)

Premises and conclusions both, of course, are propositional—so the idea of taking the chain of inferences to form the backbone of cognition makes of Dicisigns its joints. Thirty years later, the doctrine is explained as follows:

> "... the purpose of signs—which is the purpose of thought—is to bring truth to expression. The law under which a sign must be true is the law of inference; and the signs of a scientific intelligence must, above all other conditions, be such as to lend themselves to inference. Hence, the illative relation is the primary and paramount semiotic relation. It might be objected that to say that the purpose of thought is to bring the truth to expression is to say that the production of propositions, rather than that of inferences, is the primary object. But the production of propositions is of the general nature of inference, so that inference is the essential function of the cognitive mind." ("On Signs", c. 1897, 2.444n)

What would this radical claim entail? For two reasons, it implies a vast generalization—and deflation—of the concept of inference, related to that of propositions in the Dicisign doctrine. One is that many different aspects of cognitive acts—in the arc from perception to action, involving the contributions to it of will, emotion, memory, etc.—will have to be reconceptualized under the inference notion, thereby broadening it considerably. Every aspect of cognition—however remote its contribution may seem—is taken to serve, in the last account, the inference chain from perception to action. Another is that inference is seen under the headline of *action* habits rather than the specific habit subtype which is mental representation. Central to the pragmatist doctrine, namely, is that the conclusions of inferences are primarily *action habits* rather than psychic or mental representations only—such representations, when occurring, probably serve to support the more primary purpose of giving rise to reasoned behaviour. Thus, some of those habits, of course, will be mental, or some of their parts or phases may be mental, but this is not their essentially defining property.

As to the chain of reasoning, Peirce early made an important pragmatic proposal for its status in the sciences: ".. reasoning should not form a chain which is no stronger than its weakest link, but a cable whose fibers may be ever so slender, provided they are sufficiently numerous and intimately connected" ("Some Consequences of Four Incapacities", 1868, 5.265)—as against Cartesian beliefs in single inference chains, Peirce takes sound reasoning to consist of many connected inferences pointing in the same direction.

As to inferences being basically action habits rather than (only) mental representations, this leads Peirce to the important step of conceptually separating inference from consciousness. After having discussed the four-colour map problem in topology, Peirce concludes as to the general character of the future solution:

> "It is evident that when the problem is solved, the researcher will have acquired a new habit to which the various concepts, or general mental signs, that have arisen and been found valuable, are merely adjuvant. Meantime, the psychological assumption originally made is in great measure eliminated by the consideration that habit [is] by no means exclusively mental. Some plants take habits; and so do some things purely inorganic. The observed laws of habit follow necessarily from a definition of habit which takes no notice of consciousness. Thus the facts that great numbers of individuals which die and are replaced by reproduction is favourable to a marked prominence of habit, and that highly complex organisms of which multitudes of parts exercise interchangeable functions are so, follow from such a definition. Nevertheless, I am far from holding consciousness to be an "epiphenomenon", though the doctrine that it is so has aided the development of science. To my apprehension, the function of consciousness is to render self-control possible and efficient. For according to such analysis as I can make the true definition of consciousness is connection with an internal world; and the first impressions of sense are not conscious, but only their modified reproductions in the internal world.
>
> I do not deny that a concept, or general mental sign, may be a logical interpretant; only, it cannot be the ultimate logical interpretant, precisely because, being a sign, it has itself a logical interpretant. It partakes somewhat of the nature of a verbal definition, and is very inferior to the living definition that grows up

in the habit. Consequently, the most perfect account we can give of a concept will consist in a description of the habit that it will produce; and how otherwise can a habit be described than by a general statement of the kind of action it will give rise to under described circumstances?" ("Pragmatism" 1907, Ms. 318, NEM III/I, 493-494)

This conceptual separation of consciousness from the inference chain pits Peirce against standard assumptions in much cognitive science and philosophy that the expression of propositions should depend on mental acts involving consciousness. The ubiquity of propositions, on the other hand, implies that consciousness, when present, is basically oriented towards propositions and their implications. This most forcefully regards perceptual consciousness. This is not the place for a full-range discussion of Peirce's theory of perception; suffice it to say that perception always involves a perceptual judgment, that is, a proposition framed in perceptual matter which has truth conditions (and which, most of the time, we automatically assume to be true). Such perception depends, of course, on perceptual matter which is not, in itself, propositional. Such matter is only secondarily accessible by abstraction from perceptual judgments (focusing upon aspects of perception apart from their being the case)—so-called "percepts". These, however, should not be mistaken for particular, fully determinate sense-data. Rather, "Generality, Thirdness, pours in upon us in our very perceptual judgments, and all reasoning, so far as it depends on necessary reasoning, that is to say, mathematical reasoning, turns upon the perception of generality and continuity at every step" (*Lectures on Pragmatism*, 1903, EPII 207, 5.150). Perception is geared, from the outset, to extracting general features of the environment. This, then, is not a higher-level secondary-process cognitive achievement; rather reality has, in itself, general structures which perception is able to grasp. Higher-level abstractions and generalizations, it is true, will subsequently add to the contents of perceptual judgments. But that should not fool us into assuming a completely non-general starting point. Rather, we should imagine the chain of inference as constantly drawing perceptual material into it. Perceptual judgments are thus due to the immediate propositional stance assumed in perception, and Peirce characterizes the inference leading to them as an extreme case of abduction from which it only differs in not immediately being open to doubt (but of course mediately, if something calls for it).

How does this central role of inference in cognition square with the phenomenological tradition? In *Erfahrung und Urteil*, Husserl famously sought a phenomenological basis for logic. Also Peirce saw phenomenology— his doctrine of categories—as a prerequisite to logic in the system of sciences, but the centrality of inference in the cognitive process might seem to conflict with the Husserlian idea of the derived character of propositions in relation to "antepredicative" experience. Actually, Husserl finds the very same propositional structure from the higher levels of explicit scientific expressions and down to the "unterste Stufe" (59)—the deepest level—and in order to understand this "broadest concept of proposition" and its object correlate, it must be connected to life experience in its most concrete sense, as he says: "Alle Erfahrung in diesem konkreten Sinne ruht zuunterst auf der schlichten, letzten, schlicht erfaßbare Substrate vorgegebenen Urdoxa. Die in ihr vorgegebenen naturalen Körper sind letzte Substrate für alle weiteren Bestimmungen, sowohl die kognitiven wie auch die Wertbestimmungen und die praktischen Bestimmungen"[10] (60).

You should not naively assume perception and action to correspond to passivity/activity, for they are both active; rather a more radical concept of passivity (61) will focus upon the concept of the "... *rein affektiven Vorgegebenheit, der passiven Seinglaubens*, in dem noch nichts von Erkenntnisleistung ist: der bloße 'Reiz', der von einem umweltlich Seiendem ausgeht, wie z.B. das Hundegebell, 'das eben an unser Ohr dringt', ohne daß wir ihm bereits Aufmerksamkeit geschenkt und uns ihm als thematischen Gegenstand zugewendet haben"[11] (61). The sense impression impossible to reject—here the dog barking—strikingly corresponds to Peirce's definition of the percept as that which irresistibly enters perception. Husserl's description of the immediately following proposition goes as follows: "Jede erfassende Zuwendung, die das im Fluß der sinnlichen Erfahrung Gegebene festhält, sich ihm aufmerksam zuwendet, betrachtend in seine Eigenheiten eindringt, ist schon eine Leistung, eine Erkenntnisaktivität unterster Stufe, für die wir auch bereits von einen *Urteilen* sprechen können"[12] (62). Thus, Husserl concludes, there will be a proposition in the broadest sense already in any antepredicative objectifying act directed towards a being in the broadest sense—such as, in perceptual consciousness, when an object stands before us in its being. He even freely

---

[10]"All experience in this concrete sense rests deepest down on the simple, final, simply conceivable substrate of pre-given ur-doxa. The pre-given natural bodies within it are the final substrate for all further determinations, cognitive as well as value determinations and practical determinations." These and further translations by the author.

[11]"... *purely affective pre-givenness, the passive assumptions of being* in which there is no knowledge effort yet: the mere 'excitation' which originates from some being in the environment, such as e.g. the barking of a dog which 'just makes its way to our ear', without that we already directed attention to it and turned ourselves toward it as a thematic object."

[12]"Every grasping direction of attention which, in the current of sensory experience, retains something given, turns itself attentively towards it, enters observingly into its details, is already an effort, an activity of knowledge on the deepest level, about which we could also already speak of a *judgment*."

broadens such objectifying acts to include not only perceptions, but also practical actions.The decisive difference between Peirce's and Husserl's accounts for the relation between perception and proposition then rather lies in their respective conceptions of the *source and conditions* of perceptual judgments, Husserl taking them to presuppose antepredicative *consciousness* and forming part of the totality of *Ichakte*—ego acts—in the deepest levels of the ego (63). With his functional definition of Dicisigns, Peirce needs not presuppose such acts to be granted by any ego nor consciousness. Peirce preserves, it is true, a generalized notion of directedness in his interpretation of the Aristotelian notion of "final causation"—but takes care, again, to distinguish that from the attending of consciousness: "I hold that purpose, or rather, final causation, of which purpose is the conscious modification, is the essential subject of psychologists' own studies; and that consciousness is a special, and not a universal, accompaniment of mind" ("Minute Logic", 1902, 7.366).

With this proviso, the road is clear for considering Dicisigns in cases where consciousness can not necessarily be presumed, such as animal cognition.

Chapter 5

Dicisigns and Cognition

5.1 The Logical Interpretation of the Ventral-Dorsal Split in Perception

The sciences of logic, psychology, and linguistics have developed, to a large degree, independently during the 20th Century despite occasional more or less thorough attempts at interdisciplinarity between them. As discussed in ch. 2, modern logic only came into being in the decades around 1900 based on a stance against psychologism, that is, against the interpretation of logic as a sub-branch of psychology. Bolzano, Frege, Peirce, Husserl, Russell all, in different ways, insisted that logic could not be a part of psychology as that would undermine its claim to validity. Conversely, psychology has tended to take a disparaging view of logic, seeing it as "logicism", remote normative philosophical reifications of things better studied empirically (e.g. Elqayam & Evans 2011).

Thus, it is not without sense when the linguist James Hurford claims, in a BBS target article (2003), to be the first to drill a "... 'wormhole' between the hitherto mutually isolated universes of formal logic and empirical neuroscience" (Hurford 2003, 261)—continuing this initiative in his major two-volume work *The Origins of Meaning/ The Origins of Grammar* (2007; 2012) integrating logic, cognition, linguistics, neuroscience, ethology, and evolutionary biology in a grand synthesis. Here, let us focus upon his proposal as to the role of logic in prehuman cognition. Logic, of course, is chosen as the better candidate to chart prehuman thought because linguistic categories may be, to a large extent, human-specific and thus not immediately applicable to animal cognition, while logic has the broader scope of covering valid thought processes as such. Hurford's main idea is that prehuman cognition, particularly primate cognition, may be described in terms of a simplified version of first-order predicate logic. So, his argument is not that logical structure is needed for animal *communication* purposes—it is at stake already in the structure of animal *perception*. In Hurford (2007), he summarizes the idea there are two logico-neural links, as follows: "...(1) the link between dorsal stream, pre-attentional processes, which assign mental indices to a small number of tracked objects, and the individual variables of logic, w, x, y, z which I assume here to be in very limited supply—only up to four available at any one time; and (2) the link between ventral stream recognition areas, where categorization of tracked objects take place, and logical one-place predicates" (Hurford 2007, 103).

So the overall argument takes its basis in the neuropsychological finding that visual information, after its intial processing in the V1 area in the occipital lobe, is projected forward in the brain in two different streams.[1]

One, the ventral stream, projects to the temporal lobe, addressing categorization of visual features of the object seen—while the other, the dorsal stream, goes up to the posterior parietal lobe and concerns spatial localization of the object, connected to movement and grasping possibilities in egocen-

---

[1] Schneider (1969) proposed two visual systems for localization and identification, respectively. The classic paper establishing the ventral-dorsal split is Ungerleider and Mishkin (1982), which proposed the *What/Where* description of the two streams, taken to process object qualities and spatial location respectively. Goodale and Milner (1992) and Milner and Goodale (1995) proposed the alternative *What/How* distinction and claimed the streams to be functionally different rather than addressing different contents; thus both streams seem to process shape and spatial information but with different functional aims (functionality naturally fitting better Peircean Dicisigns). Norman (2002, 73) attempted to reconciliate approaches: "A dual-process approach to visual perception emerges from this analysis, with the ecological-dorsal process transpiring mainly without conscious awareness, while the constructivist-ventral process is normally conscious" and summed up the characteristics of the two streams in the following diagram:

FACTOR	VENTRAL SYSTEM	DORSAL SYSTEM
Function	Recognition/identification	Visually guided behaviour
Sensitivity	High spatial frequencies—details	High temporal frequencies—motion
Memory	Long term stored representations	Only very short-term storage
Speed	Relatively slow	Relatively fast
Consciousness	Typically high	Typically low
Frame of reference	Allocentric or object-centered	Egocentric or viewer-centered
Visual input	Mainly foveal or parafoveal	Across retina
Monocular vision	Generally reasonably small effects	Often large effects e.g. motion parallax

tric space. In the literature, the two streams are often called the WHAT and WHERE streams, respectively (sometimes WHAT/HOW), other description attempts include sensorimotor vs. cognitive processing or the "looking" vs. "seeing" stream. While the dorsal stream is fast, and to a large degree preconscious, the ventral stream is slower, seemingly prompted by and hence temporally sequential to the dorsal stream, and closer to consciousness. The overall picture is that the dorsal stream directs attention to locations and subsequently action affordances and objects in the visual field which are, in turn, analyzed and categorized by the ventral stream. The dorsal stream seems to provide a precise online analysis of egocentric visual action space, less subject to visual illusions than the more semantically heavy ventral stream, using general categories not tied to egocentric space.

Hurford's basic and ingenious observation is that these two streams seem to correspond approximately to standard basic notions in classical modern logic—Frege's distinction between function and argument in his analysis of propositions (analogous to Peirce's rearticulation of the predicate/subject distinction). Hurford terminologically selects a compromise vocabulary between the two—predicate/argument—mentioning Frege only intermittently and Peirce never. Hurford's argument builds on the summation of a comprehensive amount of neurocognitive findings and hypotheses. Important is Pylyshyn's idea (1989, 2000) that the posterior parietal cortex operates with a small amount of placeholders called FINSTs (for "FINgers of INSTantiation"), not more than 5 simultaneous foci of attention which may, all of the time, be updated and invested by new perceptual material. Thus, in processing a visual scene, the selected few important objects in it are highlighted for further investigation and analysis in terms of predicates by the ventral stream. Thus, visual cognition, in humans and higher animals alike, shapes its result in the logical form of $PREDICATE(x)$. Despite certain issues to which we shall turn below, Hurford's daring hypothesis seems convincing as a first, basic connection between logic and cognition.

This hypothesis fits surprisingly with the Peircean Dicisign doctrine, according to which all cognition able to express truth must functionally make use of the generalized predicate/subject structure. There are, however, a number of problems in Hurford's hypothesis (many of them, of course, brought out by the commentators in BBS's open review tradition). Our contention is that some of these issues may be better addressed in the Peircean framework which may considerably add to the synthesis which Hurford constructs from different scientific sources. Hurford, a linguist by profession, spends considerable energy in collecting and discussing recent neuropsychological findings to establish a knowledge base of current understanding of the ventral-dorsal split. Strangely, he does not offer the same attention to the other source of his construction—logic; Frege is mentioned cursorily but it is as if Hurford's edifice is primarily one of psycholinguistics where logic is called in only as a handmaiden to avoid linguistic anthropomorphic imperialism into the nonhuman realm. This implies that the very status of Hurford's wormhole never becomes entirely clear.

In the beginning of his BBS paper, Hurford attempts to make clear the role of logic in his synthesis: "... it is to be expected that the basic $PREDICATE(x)$ formalism is to some extent an idealization of what actually happens in the brain" (Hurford 2003, 261). This was certainly neither Frege's nor Peirce's idea, both of them taking logic in a strongly anti-psychologistic sense. They did not see logic as a simplistic representation of complex brain processes; rather they saw logic as normative and as a measure-stick which the thought processes of empirical brains would be expected very often *not* to live up to. Hurford's conception of logic is thus as a particular special science whose results do not impinge on other sciences: "Neuroscientists don't need logical formulae to represent the structures and processes that they find" (On "the bridge from logic to language", ibid. 262). The results of logic are rather conceived of as a sort of primitive brain science in a period before the investigation techniques developed by cognitive psychology: "Logical notations, on the other hand, were developed by scholars theorizing in the neurological dark about the structure of language and thought" (ibid. 262). Thus, Hurford misunderstands Tarski's famous truth definition as a fallacious piece of psychology: "But to say that 'Snow is white' describes the thought expressed by 'Snow is white' is either simply wrong (because description of a thought process and expression of a thought are not equivalent) or at best uninformative" (ibid.). What Tarski meant, of course, was that to understand the proposition 'Snow is white' is to know the conditions in which that proposition is true. Hurford, in general, is little preoccupied with what motivated both Frege and Peirce, namely logic as a means to investigate the structures involved in articulating truth claims, both in everyday and scientific propositions and inferences. Instead, maybe because of his linguistic background, Hurford thinks that "But, up to the present, the only route that one could trace from the logical notations to any empirically given facts was **back through** the ordinary language expressions which motivated them in the first place" (ibid. 262)—he takes logic as a sort of attempt to describe the mind based on ordinary language expressions. But modern logic was not motivated by ordinary linguistic expressions—quite on the contrary, it was motivated by structures of scientific thought and the need to find an unambiguous formalization for science, getting rid of the unclarities of ordinary language. Thus, Hurford misconstrues Frege when he says that

"Frege's new notation (but not its strictly graphological form which was awfully cumbersome) allowed one to explain thoughts and inferences involving a far greater range of natural sentences" (ibid. 262). This was not his aim—Hurford tends to see logic as a primitive sort of psycholinguistics, not realizing that all sciences depend on logic, be it implicitly or explicitly. In his (2007), Hurford seems even more insistent on full-blown psychologism, now as a basic assumption he contends that the "...logico-linguistic enterprise is essentially psychological" (124), implying that logic and language simply form objects of psychology. Which was precisely what the founding fathers of modern logic—Frege, Peirce, Husserl, Russell—denied.

So, initially, our articulation of Hurford's hypothesis would rather turn the other way, so to speak. The reason that basic structures of First Order Predicate Logic can be mapped onto certain brain processes is not that those results were a first approximation to neuroscience nor that logic is a sort of outcome of the brain's evolution and function. Rather, following the Peircean idea of adaptation to rationality,[2] we would say that it is no wonder that the brain functionally displays the logical doubleness of predicate and subject, as this double structure forms the prerequisite for the articulation and expression of truth (and that biological organisms have a basic survival interest in having a true grasp of aspects of their surroundings rather than none). So, the fact is rather that the brain has had to adapt, evolutionarily, to first order predicate logic in order to express truths. Hurford vacillates as to the precise status of his hypothesis; at the end of his BBS article, he articulates it in a different way, rather in the direction of the Adaption-to-Rationality hypothesis: "The

---

[2]Livingstone and Hubel (1987) take the division of processing back to early visual processing in the Thalamus where magnocellular and parvocellular areas seem to process location/movement and color/shape, respectively, informations ultimately deriving from rods and cones in the retina, respectively. This speaks for the claim that the split already can be found as a functional division of labor in the retina.

The Adaption to Rationality hypothesis finds a clear expression here: "But the views of all the leading schools of Logic of the present day, of which there are three or four, are all decidedly opposed to those of the present writer. That common tendency of them which he most of all opposes is that toward regarding human consciousness as the author of rationality, instead of as more or less conforming to rationality. Even if we can find no better definition of rationality than that it is that character of arguments to which experience and reflexion would tend indefinitely to make human approval conform, there still remains a world-wide difference between that idea and the opinion just mentioned. But the thinkers of our day seem to regard the distinction between being the product of the human mind and being that to which the human mind *would* approximate to thinking if sufficiently influenced by experience and reflection, as a distinction of altogether secondary importance, and hardly worth notice; while to the writer, no distinction appears more momentous than that between 'is' and 'would be'." ("Essays on Meaning. Preface (Meaning Preface)" 23 Oct 1909, Ms. 640.)

dorsal/ventral separation in higher mammals is, I argue, an evolved hardware implementation of predicate-argument structure" (Hurford 2003, 281).

An important observation supporting the idea of general structure informing the Ventral-Dorsal split is the fact, addressed by Hurford, that an analogous split is also found in the brain's processing of sound signals in the auditory system (e.g. Buchsbaum et al. 2005). Recently, it has been documented also in the domain of haptic perception, touch (Gardner 2008), as well as in olfactory perception, smell (Frasnelli et al. 2012), presumably the evolutionary oldest of the senses. Thus, the split seems to be no artifice of visual perception particularly, but rather a mode of cognitive organization across the sense modalities, probably relevant for the so-called "binding" problem addressing how the different modalities are connected, in cognition, to represent the same objects from which the relevant perceptions stem.

Among non-human animals, Hurford focuses particularly on primates. It is interesting, however, to consider recent findings that the dorsal-ventral split is found not only in "lower" mammals such as mice (Wang et al. 2012); a related split with a double visual pathway seems to be functioning also in the (otherwise rather differently constructed) avian brain (Nguyen et al. 2004) with a caudal stream for motion vision and a rostral stream for color and form.

This generality of the ventral-dorsal split across sensory modalities as well as across species wide apart in the ancestral tree points to two possibilities: either this split is evolutionarily very basic in a large range of higher animals, covering all sensory modalities and thus result of en early adaptation at the level of a common ancestor (as argued by Nguyen et al. 2004)—or, such a split is a fundamental propositional precondition in order for *any* sensory apparatus to be able to represent true facts in perception. The two possibilities obviously do not exclude each other: if the latter is the case, higher animal brains will simply have had to adapt to basic structures of First Order Predicate Logic. In the next chapter, we shall survey some cases across the animal kingdom to argue the spread of Dicisign structure in biology.[3]

For all its indubitable merits, Hurford's connection between logic and pre-human cognition comes with certain problems some of which might be eased in the light of the Dicisign doctrine. These issues include the treatment of log-

---

[3]Hurford is not the only scholar interpreting the Ventral-Dorsal split logically. Hintikka and Symons (2007) interpret the split as realizing two different modi of identification of objects earlier analyzed by Hintikka:perspectival, or subject-centered identification vs. public, or object-centered identification—exemplified in "Jane sees b" vs. "Jane sees who b is". To Hintikka and Symons, this analysis calls for two different types of quantifiers referring to the types of identification. The two do not, unlike Hurford, attempt to eliminate constants (b); the cross-identification of b across the two modes may make possible propositions of the shape *Predicate (b)* describing who it is Jane sees b as, simultaneously explaining the unity of the proposition across the two modes.

ical constants and proper names, the object character of the argument/subject reference, the analysis of polyadic predicates, the selection of quantifier types, and the failure to address kind universals, all of these leading Hurford to embrace a dubious feature-bundle ontology of prehuman logic. Let us investigate these problems.

5.2 The Logical Constant Problem

The first issue is that of logical constants where the variable of the propositional functions $PREDICATE(x)$ is saturated by a constant, say $PREDICATE(a)$— in the biological *Umwelt* interpretation typically an individual animal or other particular object of interest for the organism. Hurford sacrifices not a little effort to rule out the possibility of such a filling-in— which is strange as the cognition of individual entities and their properties in the animal Umwelt ought to be one of the primary purposes of animal cognition (is this particular object edible or not? is this organism predator or prey? is this conspecific in-group or out-group, dominant or subdominant, male or female, young or adult, etc.). Despite this, Hurford claims there can be no equivalent to constants or proper names in the protothoughts of animals: "In a formula such as *CAME(john)*, the individual constant argument term is interpreted as denoting a particular individual, the very same person on all occasions of use of the formula. FOPL [First Order Predicate Logic, fs] stipulates by fiat this absolutely fixed relationship between an individual constant and a particular individual entity. Note that the denotation of the term is a thing in the world, outside the mind of any user of the logical language. It is argued at length by Hurford (2001) that the mental representations of protohumans could not have included terms with this property. Protothought had no equivalent of proper names" (Hurford 2003, 265). Hurford's reason for thus excluding individual constants from animal cognition, surprisingly, is logical: "Control of a proper name in the logical sense requires Godlike omniscience. Creatures only have their sense organs to rely on when attempting to identify, and to re-identify, particular objects in the world. Where several distinct objects, identical to the senses, exist, a creature cannot reliably tell which is which, and therefore cannot guarantee control of the fixed relation between an object and its proper name that FOPL stipulates" (ibid.). In Hurford's 2007 paper, this claim is baptized and elevated into "The Principled Unknowability of Uniqueness" (128), and the thought experiment marshaled to support it is that of the possibility of identical twins. Here, the argument is psychological: "So, psychologically, individual constants, as logicians use them, that is as terms uniquely identifying individuals, are impossible because there is no guaranteed reliable procedure for getting to the 'right' referent" (ibid. 129). So, his overall argument is logical as well as psychological. He also relates ethological evidence. First, in the BBS paper, he discusses an observation of the presentation to a young tern of a loudspeaker sounding with the voice of its parents—the young approached the sound of the source and cheeped a response greeting. Hurford claims this shows the young tern is mistaking the loudspeaker for a parent, thus not able to identify uniquely even its own parent: "Obviously, the tern chicks in the experiment were *not* recognizing their individual parents—they were being fooled into treating a loudspeaker as a parent tern" (2003, 266). But the fact that animals (or people) can be fooled obviously is not an argument that they cannot, in other circumstances, be right. Actually, the tern chick *was* able to identify its parent, even by only a single one of its qualities of appearance, namely the individual voice; this would rather be an argument *for* its actual ability to recognize parent individuality. And approaching the loudspeaker is not equivalent to taking it to be a bird: maybe the chick just moved in the direction of the sound so as to approach the supposed parent, maybe hiding behind the loudspeaker. An additional argument in Hurford (2007) also involves birds: "The victims of parasitic birds such as the cuckoo cannot tell that the egg in the nest is not one that they laid." (131). But here, the deception is due to the spatiotemporal location of the egg, in the nest, along with the other eggs—not to any of its qualities. Famously, cuckoo eggs typically differ in size and color from the eggs of their hosts. So in this case, it is rather the spatial identification-by-location which is at work, in mammals relative to the dorsal identification of subjects by means of the variables of posterior parietal cortex. Hurford indiscriminately seems to imply his anti-uniqueness principle to cover both particular scenarios of perception—and several such temporally distinct scenarios. But within the frame of a single perception scene, the animal must be able to keep track of the object which is invested with (maybe changing) predicates supposedly, inter alia, by means of the independent spatial localization ability. The second issue is whether the animal is able to stably recognize individuals *across* independent local scenes—but in both of the bird cases, there is really nothing disproving that. So the ethological examples prove little. The reason why Hurford gives these examples, however, is that he finds that deception as such is irreconcilable with individual constants: ". . . a (hypothetical) organism with the equivalent of an individual constant in its mental repertoire **would never be deceived**—that is what is meant by 'individual constant'" (ibid. 135). Now, human beings *do* have access to individual constants in the shape of proper names, but surely are not for that reason immune to deception and mistaken identifications. So don't human beings have proper names? Indeed, Hurford's principled problem with constants and proper nouns seems to be of a logical nature, rather than psychological or ethological: "The logical notion of an individual constant permits no degree of tolerance over the assignment of these logical constants to individuals; this is why they are called "constants." It is an *a priori* fiat of the design of the logical language that individual constants pick out particular individuals with absolute consistency. In this sense, the logical language is practically unrealistic, requiring, as previously mentioned, Godlike omniscience on the part of its users, the kind of omniscience reflected in the biblical line "But even the very hairs of your head are all numbered" (Matthew, Ch.10)" (Hurford 2003, 266). The problem here is that Hurford inherits a conception of logical reference from Russell and Wittgenstein who thought, indeed, that the reference space for logical propositions was the whole of reality. And of course, an animal proto-thinking the equivalent to "There is a tiger" surely does not address the existence of tigers as a species of the world as such, but the fact that it perceives, now and here, a tiger in its perceptual field, in its *Umwelt*. This is what makes Hurford insist on taking a universe of discourse restricted to one (visual) scene (Hurford 2007, 125-26). This is obviously too narrow, because that would not allow animals to remember and compare individuals across such local scenes, as if they were not, actually, able to recognize close conspecifics, particular locations, etc., a problem Hurford later recognizes and attempts to solve with a feature-bundle theory (below). Here, however, Hurford's immediate obedience to the Frege-Russell tradition is the root of his conceptual problems: constants are taken to refer to fixed individuals in the unbounded space-time of all of reality. As observed by Hintikka, the alternative tradition which he calls logic-as-a-calculus (as opposed to the Frege-Russell tradition of logic-as-a-universal-language), actually permits the selection of Universes of Discourse of highly varied extensions. The very notion of Universe of Discourse goes back to the fountainheads of the algebraic tradition of logic, Augustus de Morgan (1846) and George Boole (1854).[4] Continuing on Boolean ground, of course, Peirce's Dicisign doctrine claims that propositions refer to a selected Universe of Discourse: "In every proposition the circumstances of its enunciation show that it refers to some collection of individuals or of possibilities, which cannot be adequately described, but can only be indicated as something familiar to

---

[4]"In every discourse, whether of the mind conversing with its own thoughts, or of the individual in his intercourse with others, there is an assumed or expressed limit within which the subjects of its operation are confined. The most unfettered discourse is that in which the words we use are understood in the widest possible application, and for them the limits of discourse are co-extensive with those of the universe itself. But more usually we confine ourselves to a less spacious field. (...) Now, whatever may be the extent of the field within which all objects of our discourse are found, that field may properly be termed the universe of discourse" (Boole (1854) 42).

both speaker and auditor. At one time it may be the physical universe, at another it may be the imaginary 'world' of some play or novel, at another a range of possibilities" (Peirce and Christine Ladd-Franklin, 1903, 2.536).[5]

Thus, constant reference in prehuman cognition needs not refer to the whole of the universe, requiring omniscience on the part of the animal (or the human being, for that matter). On the other hand, the relevant Universe of Discourse could hardly be only the particular visual scene of a single group of perceptions only; in that case the animal would not be able to recognize objects from one visual scene to the next. The relevant maximum Universe of Discourse probably varies considerably from species to species—depending upon and in any case never larger than what Uexküll addressed as the *Umwelt* of that species. Within that *Umwelt*, pragmatic situations may single out smaller Universes of Discourse; when the vervet monkey cries his alarm signal of "Leopard!" to the group of conspecifics nearby, the relevant Universe of Discourse will be the present situation for as long as that predator remains around. Parents will belong as constants to the Universe of Discourse of an animal for as long as he is able to recognize them as such, that is, for many higher animals a considerably longer period than a single visual scene. In short, given the more plastic logical notion of Universe of Discourse of the algebraic tradition, the very basis for Hurford's protracted problems with constants and proper nouns diminishes if not vanishes completely.

This is connected to related issues pertaining to what is the object of propositions. Hurford emphatically takes it to be physical objects as opposed to locations. This comes from his discussion of Pylyshyn variables in the dorsal stream. Initially, attention is drawn, in the pre-attention process, towards localizations in visual space, but as soon as an object is identified at a location, it is that object which occupies the variable slot for as long as it lasts. Here, Hurford seems hardhandedly to identify "objects" with closed physical entities bounded by a surface or something similar, able to bear properties. Most often, of course, logic examples use such mesoscopic physical objects or persons—but as the Dicisign doctrine makes clear, "object" should be taken broadly as an entity which something can be predicated about, psychologically speaking: all that which attention can be directed towards, shapes, locales, events, objects, figure/ground appearances ... Here, the Peircean distinction between Immediate and Dynamic Objects might clear up some of the confusion. When the tern chick reacts to the parental voice over the loudspeaker, it is, of course a replica of one of the Immediate Objects by means of which it usually identifies the Dynamic Object of one of his parents. Consequently, it approaches and answers this seeming Immediate Object when appearing, even if the Dynamic Object

---

[5]From Peirce and C. Ladd-Franklin "Universe" in Baldwin (1902), vol. 2, 742.

is in fact absent. Unique, individual Dynamic Objects are never encountered in all their aspects at once, but rather through one of several Immediate Objects given by the indices connecting proposition and Object. Interestingly, recent research seem to identify naturally occurring proper names in certain social species in the wild, such as the individual "whistling signature" used by bottle-nosed dolphins and recognized by conspecifics even over very long timescales.[6]

As mentioned, Hurford's attempt to eliminate constants and proper names from proto-thought leads him to embrace an Armstrongian feature-bundle theory of animal recognition (cf. Smith 2007). Hurford's strategy in (2007) is to make everything but the variable x itself into one-place predicates, including proper names which are taken to be just one further predicate among many changing predicates. Thus, in an imaginary social species, the dominant male may be "effectively distinguished by the following set of predicates: {SLANTY-EYED, SCAR-ON-LEFT-CHEEK, TORN-RIGHT-EAR, SWEATY-SMELLING, MALE, BIG, STRUTS}" (Hurford 2007, 132).[7] Hurford assumes this will solve the issue: "Presumably, a social animal will have such effectively distinctive bundles of features for all the members of its troop" (ibid.). Against this counts already the fact that in many species, individuals seem to be recognizable not only by a general reek of sweat, but by their own individual chemical transpiration profile. Yet on a more principled level, this theory runs into the same problems as feature-bundle theories in ontology in general: what is "distinctive"? What is it that keeps these predicate heaps together? If no stable object/individual/constant grants that these predicates hold for one and the same entity, it is difficult to see why intermittent properties would not make the alpha male mentioned change into a completely different individual. Not even the most dominant alpha male is capable of "strutting" all of the time—as soon as he relaxes on strutting, however, he will become, following Hurford's theory, a completely different individual, and the perceiver will be unable to recognize him. Maybe he only has a *disposition* for strutting, so that it is known that he *might* strut, just like it is know that he might attack you if you approach his harem or what he is eating—but in that case dispositions should be part of the feature-bundle as well. And this raises the issue how such dispositions should be distinguished from dispositions for other intermittent behaviours (EATING, SCRATCHING HIS BALLS, HAVING A FIT OF RAGE, SLEEPING, etc.) which are not parts of the relevant

---

[6]Cf. King and Janik (2013); Bruck (2013).

[7]Such a feature bundle would not even be able to grant individual reference in the whole world of possibilities. Hurford's own speculative "identical twin" thought experiment proves this. So the important thing is to establish a restricted Universe of Discourse where such a bundle could, in fact, be unique.

feature bundle because several or many or all of the troop may resort to these behaviours once in a while (this of course, corresponds to Aristotelian essences vs. accidents). They are not "distinctive", Hurford might say, but how do you notice they are distinctive for an individual if you cannot keep him constant while he incarnates changing predicates? Hurford quotes Steven Pinker for the wise observation that male animals "may not care what kind of female they mate with, but they are hypersensitive to which female they mate with" (ibid. 133)—in any case it would be unwise for any primate to attempt to mate with the alpha male's preferred female partner in his presence. Still, Hurford refuses to accept that any animals are able to make Pinker's distinction between individuals and categories, unless new evidence should indicate this ability. We have already indicated such empirical evidence, but the problem again seems logical rather than empirical. Hurford claims the problem is "uniqueness" and rightly says uniqueness can never be established from perception alone (his version of Kant's claim that existence is not a predicate). But Peirce's Dicisign doctrine takes another lesson from Kant's famous observation. What characterizes existence is not uniqueness in qualities, but its imperative insistence here-and-now. It is this insistence, appearing for the animals in the shape of indices in its perceptual field, which forms the basis of attention (psychologically speaking) and subject status in a quasi-proposition (logically speaking). So what connects the relevant feature bundles is the basic fact that they are insistently realized simultaneously in the here and now. It is the spatio-temporal coincidence of properties. After extensive discussion of his feature-bundle theory, Hurford seems, finally, also vaguely to realize the irreducibility of indexicality: "All that is left, after perceiving an object and taking in some of its properties, is the content of the information taken in, namely the properties, *plus the information that they all come from the same object.*" (ibid. 155, italics added). But the sameness of that object was what was supposed to be *established* by the bundle of properties in the first place! Now, the sameness of the object is taken as that which bundles the properties in the first place. This is circular.

Here, the Peircean stance would, just like Derek Bickerton (Hurford 2003, 286) against whom Hurford argues, admit both common noun predicates, and constants in the proto-language. Proper nouns in human language function as a device for keeping constants constant across situations. Which animal species may have developed equivalent devices seems to be an empirical issue—but the more basic issue of having constants in certain Universes of Discourse is probably that without constants there is no bundle to connect the features. Hurford, instead, proposes that proper nouns form a special subset of predicates. Of course, proper nouns, once they are established, may be used predicatively like everything else (cf. the discussion of Dicent Indexical Legisigns). Proper names depend on the basic level of "thisness". Hurford also seems to realize this much when discussing his own proto-logic formalizations with hiearchies of predicates bundled in boxes: "A box, remember, corresponds to a logical individual variable, such as x or y. These variables have no predicative content. Pure reference, as in deictic pointing, is descriptively uninformative. The predicates inside a box can then be said to make truth claims about the object referred to" (Hurford 2007, 156-7). This formalism necessitates the representation of more than an aggregate of predicates. Something must do the bundling—a box, in turn representing pure reference. But deictic pointing is exactly a here-and-now sign indicating the self-identical object *apart* from any of the predicates ascribed to it by the ventral stream (and assumed to be constant at least during the process of perceiving it, indicating it and having the addressee of the pointing perceive it as well). It is such pointing events (among indivduals understanding the pointing gesture, cf. the discussion of Tomasellian joint attention, next ch.) or indexical experiences of predicate coincidence which grants an animal access to constants in its restricted Universe of Discourse.

5.3 The Adicity of Predicates

Next problem on the list is that of polyadic predicates. The introduction of logical relations counts as one of the major progresses of modern logic, undertaken by Frege and Peirce independently. Both of them held that predicates were not only, as in the Aristotelian tradition, one-place, but could have any number of subject places. In human language, of course, most predicates have 3 or 4 places as their maximum, but there is no upper limit in principle to the possible valency of predicates in artificial languages. Hurford, of course, wants the simplest possible version of First Order Predicate Logic to account for animal behaviour, and we saw how he tried to reinterpret proper names to be just a further subset of 1-place predicates. The same thing goes for polyadic predicates which he takes to be, in animals, reducible to mere sums of 1-place predicates. This, of course, is a bold claim, as many 2-place predicates seem to characterize processes very central to animal life and survival: x mates with y; x eats y; x is a mother to y; x dominates y; x and y fight; x and y groom each other; x chases y; x kills y, etc. The elimination of such predicates is especially precarious, for they not only refer to processes in the animal's perceptual field—they also refer to processes many of which the animal knows from its own experience (and, we have reason to believe many higher animals are able to identify the character of events including itself with the character of the same events including others, cf. mirror neuron research). Also predicates with valencies higher than two may seem biologically important, maybe especially in certain higher animals: x and y fight over z; x gives y to z; x uses y to shape z; x uses y to retrieve z from w, etc.

This issue is also addressed by several of Hurford's BBS commentators. Peter F. Dominey rightly argues 1-place predicates are insufficient for event representation (Hurford 2003, 291f), while Shulan Lu and Donald R. Franceschetti (ibid. 295f) argue that 1-place predicates are incapable of representing Talmy configurations like figure, motion, path, ground, invariably requiring the integration of several entities in one proposition. Hurford's way of translating such predicates into 1-predicate bundles goes back to the attention-directing process of the dorsal stream. Pre-attention addresses and screens the whole scene, and only the ensuing attention makes explicit the single, located objects of the scene, facilitating, in turn, predications to be attached to each of them. But maybe, Hurford speculates, could scenes as such be the object of predicates? Such that a "grooming scene" (his example) is recognized before each of the participating groomers? This is obviously an empirical cognitive possibility in many, especially symmetric cases (there's a fight going on—how many and who are the participants?), but it seems difficult to imagine cognition should *always* characterize the scene before any of its constituents. This is not the major problem, however. The problem is rather that the animal is supposed to be able to recognize the character of the whole scene without *any* supposition about the valency of the action taking place in that scene. In some cases it might, of course, be cognitively plausible, as when seeing and hearing a remote grouplet jostling and uttering different screams and supposing this is a fighting scene. But it is really difficult to see how this could account for all cases. Seeing your nearest conspecific eating a carrot, the following first impression is strange: "There is some eating going on, this is an alimentation scenario, but there is *not* (yet) an eater and something eaten." Or "There is some fornicating going on, but there is *not* (yet) two partners mating." The cognitive implausibility in always being able to recognize the scene type without any of the participating objects and their relation, however, is not the only problem. There is also a logical problem. For how does the animal perceive actant roles: distinguishing the eater from the eaten, as it were? There must be no 2-place predicates with different subject slots, remember, so Hurford's analysis, again, is to devise two new one-place predicates: $AGENT(x)$ and $PATIENT(x)$. Hurford realizes the problem when he says that "...some predicates are more contextually relativized than others (...) AGENT, PATIENT, PART, and BIG, are mentally assigned to an object with much more consideration of the overall properties assigned to the scene in which they appear" (Hurford 2007, 149). But even if such consideration is taken, how do we know that the logic formalization saying "There's a BEATING event, John is AGENT, Mary is PATIENT" (Hurford's example) does not mean that John is beating into thin air while Mary is sitting passively watching? A visual scene may easily contain several objects unconnected— how do we know there is, in this case, a specific relation connecting John and Mary? Remember, we are not supposed to know that BEATING signifies a two-place relation, just that it characterizes an as yet undifferentiated scene. And remember, we are not supposed to know that AGENT and PATIENT are related in any closer way than, say, BLUE and BIG; they are taken to be isolated one-slot predicates. Coupling AGENT and PATIENT, of course, would smuggle in a two-place predicate through the back door. Classic logic, both in Frege's and Peirce's variants, of course, would claim that 2- and 3-place predicates are irreducible to combinations of predicates of lower valency (but, in Peirce, 4-place and higher predicates may be so reduced). Hurford's attempt to break down all predicates into conjunctions of 1-place predicates, in any case, is less than convincing. Rather, we would assume many higher animals have access to 2-place, maybe in some cases even 3-place predicates. It should immediately be added that Peirce's logic—and First Order Predicate Logic in general,—do not have any deeper analysis of predicates apart from their valency, including which types of relational predicates and relational roles there may be.

In Hurford's reduction, what more is left than one-place predicates? He explicitly admits he has not yet addressed the issues of negation, quantification, and inference (ibid. 164), issues of some importance for cognition, but that is not quite true. In the BBS paper, the elimination of constants left Hurford with variables only, and these must, of course, be quantified: "This leaves us with quantified formulae, as in $\exists x [MAN(x) \& TALL(x)]$. Surely we can discount the universal quantifier $\forall$ as a term in primitive mental representations. What remains is one quantifier, which we can take to be implicitly present and to bind the variable arguments of predicates" (Hurford 2003, 267).

This idea leaves us with some riddles. If a tiger or other dangerous predator appears in the perceptual field, it seems a bit odd to imagine the relevant representation in perceptual logic could be "Tigers exist " without any indication of the relevant Universe of Discourse—existential quantification saying nothing about the number or the spatiotemporal location of objects predicated, rather it claims the existence of at least one case of what is affirmed. Peirce—like others after him—referred to numbers as logically a sort of quantification. So a more plausible representation would be something like: "One tiger is in my vicinity"; subitizing research (which Hurford quotes extensively) establishes that most higher animals possess the ability to subitize (as opposed to count) numbers of objects up to around four. So another such scene might give rise to the even worse proposition that "Two tigers are in my vicinity". But they would not be distinct nor individually identifiable, given Hurford's reliance on existential quantification only—here simple numerical quantification would be needed as well. The same Hurford quote out of hand dismisses universal quantification. In the tiger example, however, the immediate action inference, in a monkey, from the perceptual judgments quoted would possibly be to flee up into a tree. But what is this inference by action based upon—probably a recognition, whether innate or acquired, that tigers are dangerous. Now, this is a universal statement: $\forall x[TIGER(x) \Rightarrow DANGEROUS(x)]$—or, at least, a weaker quantification like "$MOST\ x$". Again a conception of the universe of logical reference more modest than the Russell-Wittgensteinian reference to all of the world makes such an interpretation plausible. An innate, evolutionarily acquired fear of tigers has good reasons to be universal: if not, the danger of being eaten increases with the possibility of error (even if it might, in fact, be the case that some tigers are not dangerous). The relevant Universe of Discourse does not include zoo tigers, tame tigers, and other counterexamples which might falsify the universal. And even if the Universe of Discourse of the animal does in fact contain counterexamples, such as sick tigers, cubs or tigers not presently hungry, a strictly speaking false universal may serve the animal better than a scientifically more cautious expression with care for such exceptions. So from our point of view, we should strongly hesitate to eliminate the possibility of universal quantification from animal proto-thought. Rather, you could say its role becomes more important, the simpler the organism is: relying on instinct amounts to always reacting the same way to a given stimulus, that is quantifying universally.[8]

This is connected to the last of our logical problems with Hurford's reconstruction. The elimination of everything save 1-place predicates makes of everything an arbitrary and potentially ever-changing collection of such predicates. But would such an ontology, on the part of an animal, not prevent it from important actions related not to property predicates but to *kind* predicates—predicates like $TIGER(x)$? Hurford does not address the issue directly, and his unproblematic use of kind universals like MEAT or LIZARD or ROCK in his examples seems to indicate he takes them as predicates signifying simple properties not different from RED or BIG. But kind predicates, in human languages often expressed by common nouns, are cognitively much further from imme-

---

[8]Hurford's idea seems to rest upon the empiricist presupposition that animal minds are blank slates which build up all content from individual, particular perceptions. But evolutionarily, such perceptions seem to be a late and sophisticated capacity. Simpler animals seem to depend highly on quasi-automatic perception-action links—logically equivalent rather to instantiations of universally quantified propositions: For all x, if x is edible, eat x.

diate perception than (simple) property predicates. Lizards or Tigers may be encountered in a multitude of different ways in the visual field, in different profiles, from the front, side, or back, close or remote, with or without eye contact, night or day, and so on and so forth—not to mention their presence due to indices in other sensory modalities of the perceptual field, such as smell or hearing. Specific property bundles must be characterizing such concepts—the tiger concept (at least) consisting of STRIPED, ANIMAL, LARGE, SWIFT, DANGEROUS, CERTAIN SMELL, CERTAIN SOUNDS . . . But in such kind property bundles, universal quantification lies immediately: the bundle claims tigers in general have all of these properties, which is why DANGER can be deduced from the TIGER concept and abduced from some of its other components.

5.4 The Unity of the Proposition Revisited

A final issue of which Hurford is well aware is that it does not suffice to have two brain circuits responsible for the analyses of subject and predicate, respectively. The proposition as a whole unites the two in a characteristic way, the understanding of which has not yet been exhausted. In order to grasp this aspect of the proposition, it is necessary to look at 1) the interaction between the two streams, and 2) the ensuing action, either in terms of outward activity or in order of renewed proposition activity. Bruce Bridgeman says, in the BBS comments: "Anatomical connections between dorsal & ventral streams do not contradict the separability of their functions, any more than communication between two people contradicts their distinctness. Communication between the two streams is needed to initiate action (usually a cognitive-system function), to monitor progress in the execution of the action, and to modify goals of actions" (Hurford 2003, 287).

Here, Bruce Bridgeman points to another issue where the Peircean pragmatist conception of logic differs from Hurford's reliance upon Frege: the connection between logic and action which is also addressed by MacNeilage and Barbara Davis (ibid. 296f). To Peirce, the formation of habits is the general aim of reasoning, be it action habits or thought habits.[9] This is the same reason why Bridgeman addresses the important point of action taking place as a result of the proposition shaped by the ventral-dorsal pincer movement: "Plans for action exist separate from the sensory or motor worlds, and their steps must be executed in a particular order to be effective. Grammar may have appropriated an existing capability for planning of action sequences to

---

[9]Central to the pragmatist doctrine is that the conclusions of inferences in general are *action habits* rather than psychic representations. cf. ch. 4.

the planning of communicatory sequences (Bridgeman, 1992). Language, then, is a new capability built mostly of old parts, but the parts originate in motor planning, not in visual coding" (Hurford 2003, 287). Bridgeman's idea that action planning could be important for the linearization of grammar (there's no explicit order implied by the ventral-dorsal S-P processing) as well as for the reasoning sequence linking chains of propositions is promising. In simpler animals we may surmise much establishing of propositional *Umwelt* knowledge feeds directly into action, forming immediate feedback on the truth value of the proposition implied.

We have entered so deeply into the discussion of Hurford's application of logic in his theory of the proto-thought of animals because we recognize the bold, interdisciplinary character of his hypothesis and the wide-ranging importance it may hold. Logic is not an early piece of sketchy psychology only—rather, it addresses some of the prerequisites of how any cognitive system must be constructed in order to address *Umwelt* facts. And therefore, it becomes of seminal interest to chart how the possibilities for instantiating logic evolved biologically. Here, the virtues of Hurford's daring hypothesis emerge clearer when interpreted in the framework of Dicisigns, just as some of the logical shortcomings of the way he develops the hypothesis vanish or may be corrected, to some degree, in the Peircean picture of logic.

First of all, of course, this is evident from Peirce's non-linguistic take on logic which easily lends itself to exactly an attempt to chart the logic inherent in pre-human, pre-linguistic proto-thought. Furthermore, Peirce's logic, due to the functional definition of the Dicisign, does not need prerequisites like an explicit "propositional stance" taken by a conscious being. Signs satisfying the basic functional requirements will be categorized as propositions or quasi-propositions no matter whether accompanying phenomena of consciousness can be detected (which, of course, is difficult or impossible in most of non-human biology). This also opens the door to extending the Dicisign doctrine much further into biology than Hurford's primary focus on primates, an attempt we shall pursue in the next chapter.

Chapter 6

Natural Propositions—The Evolution of Semiotic Self-control

> Given the oxygen, hydrogen, carbon, nitrogen, sulphur, phosphorus, etc., in sufficient quantities and under proper radiations, and living protoplasm will be produced, will develop, will gain power of self-control, and the scientific passion is sure to be generated. Such is my guess.

("L", after 1902, Ms. 601, 7.50)

Many spontaneous ideas in biosemiotics and evolutionary epistemology presume that the earliest signs appearing in evolution must be simple in the sense that later, more complicated signs arise from the combinations of simpler signs. If biological cognition has evolved to fit parts of logical structure, however, the perspective should be turned 180 degrees. The "highest" Peircean sign types: propositions and their linking into arguments, are what represents aspects of reality (propositions) and give rise to inference to action (arguments)—they must be present from the very beginning of biosemiotics, albeit in a rudimentary indistinct proto-form, corresponding to Peirce's idea that propositions are genuine signs, and the whole periodic table of simpler signs are but degenerate signs which naturally occur *within* propositions. Selection forces the survival of truth-bearing signs—Dicisigns. Evolution then subdivides, sophisticates and articulates quasi-propositions, gradually achieving growing autonomy of its parts. So, instead of an ongoing construction from building-blocks, semiotic evolution is rather the ongoing subdivision, articulation and autonomization of a reasoning process having its very first proto-form in primitive metabolism.

Spontaneously, it might seem like a sound idea to presume primitive biological signs are simple signals, only later to combine into more complex signs. Such seems to be Terrence Deacon's idea that icons, indices, and symbols characterize large phases of biological evolution so that early biology was iconic, later to become indexical while only human beings process symbols. Hence, he reconstructs in his otherwise inspiring (1997) Peirce's notions compositionally, so that an index is taken to be a specific combination of icons while a symbol, in turn, is a specific combination of indices. I have discussed the problems in Deacon's reinterpretation of Peirce's icon-index-symbol triad elsewhere (Stjernfelt 2007, ch. 11) so I shall restrict myself to briefly summing up that discussion. Peircean symbols are not restricted to human sign use. Symbols are signs which are general as to their object; they possess an *esse in futuro*, referring to a potential continuity of future objects; they refer to their object by means of a habit, natural or cultural; they comprise icons for their understanding and indices for their object reference; and they have full propositions as an important subset. Thus, simple Pavlovian conditioning—dogs acquiring the habit of displaying eating behaviour by the ringing of a bell—will constitute a full-fledged Peircean symbol, not merely an indexical sign as Deacon would have it. It is not, like pure indices, a sign restricted to the here-and-now of actual connectedness between sign and object. The bell sound is a general type, referring, in turn, to another type, that of eating, a potential multitude of future eating situations. The here-and-now of the particular bell sound token in a particular instant functions as a Dicisign incarnating that general meaning in the actual moment of the ringing. Even a case as simple as coli bacteria (*Escherichia coli; E. coli*) swimming upstream in a sugar gradient as the result of its registration of molecules displaying a specific active site (cf. Berg 1988; Stjernfelt 2007) must be described as symbolic in Peirce's sense of the term: it is a habit (acquired phylogenetically, to be sure, in contrast to Pavlovian conditioning acquired ontogenetically), the habit connects a specific, typical aspect of molecular shape with a specific, typical action, that of oriented swimming and consumption. We shall argue this perception-action link is even the proto-form of an argument. The fact that the molecular configuration of the "active site" on the perimeter of the molecule is general may be seen from the fact that it is not unique to a specific carbohydrate but covers a wide range of different carbohydrates (cf. Adler et al. 1973). This generality is facilitated by the chemoreceptors of the cell being geared to detect sugars by means of weak interaction with the active site on the surface of the molecule.

And this generality, in turn, is what makes *E. coli* susceptible to being fooled by the same artificial sweeteners as may human beings. The ability to commit errors is, of course, what basically characterize Dicisigns. So, Peircean symbols are not a human prerequisite only, nor are Dicisigns.

Another related problem is that even if the icon-index-symbol triad is oriented from the simple towards the complex, it is not compositional. Deacon's reconstruction makes indices consist of a specific configuration of icons, and the symbol consist of a specific configuration of indices. But pure icons form a limit concept in Peirce—they will vaguely signify any possible object resembling them, because they are not connected to any actual object (that is the function of an index)—so an index could never result from any combination of such vague, dream-like signs only. The pure index is also a limit category—like a push in the back or a pointing gesture directing attention to an object. Such signs are indeed possible, but they remain limit cases, because neither the pure icon nor the pure index is able to communicate anything. In typical usage, as we have seen, indices are connected with icons in propositions, bearing information about the object which the index merely indicates without itself giving any information at all. Finally, a pure symbol bereft of any iconical or indexical qualities is equally marginal—something like the isolated x of algebra—in order to be understood, a symbol must bear information in the shape of an icon and relate that information to an object by means of an index.

Thus, the collaboration of icons and indices within symbols is a way of describing the triad much closer to the actual functioning of signs than the focusing upon rare, detached specimens of the three aspects of sign use. This forms the basic reason why the tempting idea of mapping the icon-index-symbol triad onto the process of evolution is doomed to fail: pure icons, indices, symbols are marginal phenomena. So, there could never have been an evolutionary period where purely iconic signs prevailed—they are much too vague to communicate any information of value for biological processes, because their content is merely possible and does not, in itself, relate to the actual world. And there could never have been a purely indexical period—indices being attention-directing and based on the here-and-now, they are unable to perform the central task of orienting and guiding biological activity into the future which requires the generality of the symbol. Rather, biological processes are characterized, from the very beginning, by the argumentative arc leading from one Dicisign to the next, typically, from primitive perception to primitive action—and the decisive criterion is that of being susceptible to deception.

6.1 Dicisigns in Biology

We have already seen how the deflated and naturalized notion of propositions in the Dicisign doctrine dispenses with any necessary connection between propositions on the one hand and human language as well as explicit, conscious intention on the other. The merely functional definition of the Dicisign as that sign which is able to convey truth by means of the double grasp of Subject indices and Predicate icons, makes it clear Dicisigns are indispensable for biological sign use. A very basic evolutionary argument may be invoked here: Signs which may not convey truth are hardly efficient in biology: isolated icons only indicating vague possibilities have little if any pragmatic efficiency in cognition and communication, just like isolated indices only able to indicate that something is happening at a location but not what it is, may be of restricted, local use but not much more than that. This is why Dicisigns are ubiquitous in biology.[1] This may seem hard for both biologists and biosemioticians to appreciate, probably because of the widespread idea that propositions require the judgment of a conscious "propositional stance" found only in human beings as well as the whole of the machinery of human language to express those propositions. Here, Peirce's purely semiotic definition of the proposition as a Dicisign combining two signs into one irreducible whole gives us a formal notion of Dicisign—neither presupposing consciousness nor explicit acts of judging.[2] We already saw in Hurford the argument for the existence of quasi-proposition in the cognition of higher animals. Given the functional definition of quasi-propositions, however, there is no need to restrict ourselves to higher animals. Pragmatically, the existence of Dicisigns will be displayed by

---

[1] Against this idea of truth in biology an argument may be made marshaling a deflated truth notion to be relevant for biology only. Thus, Cussins (1990), based on the investigation of categorization in connectionist networks, proposed that in biological organisms the notion of *success* may be substituted for that of truth. Such a conception gives a distinction between a success-governed level pertaining to proto-thoughts and the narrower, truth-governed level relevant only for full-fledged thoughts. The pragmatist conception of Dicisigns, however, already has deflated the notion of propositions so as to include quasi-propositions with action conclusions, just like pragmatism, in general, makes no sharp delimitation of truth from success. A problem in the distinction proposed would also be that many human phenomena would be difficult to categorize as there is no reason to believe that human beings do not, to a large extent, base their explicit truth claims upon proto-thoughts.

[2] Thus, our claim for the biological relevance of Dicisigns follows the naturalization of intentionality as argued in different ways by Millikan ("Aboutness is associated with a purpose only when the purpose is *explicitly represented*. On the other hand, for there to be an explicit representation of a purpose, *there must first be a purpose* to represent" (2000)—that purpose giving rise to signs whose meaning is not explicitly represented but may be induced from their having truth conditions) or Hoffmeyer (the notions of evolutionary and individual intentionality in organisms).

specific perception-action connections—in an organism's behavioral possibility of acting in a typical, categorized way prompted by the categorical perception of some biologically important, stable feature of its environment.

6.2 Dicisigns in Perception-Action Cycles

In the following, we shall run through a series of well-worn, classic examples of biosemiotics, establishing the role of quasi-propositions in each of them. Thus, when the *E. coli* reads the perimeter of the carbohydrate molecule, its subsequent oriented swimming counts as the behavioral proof that a Dicisign combining the abstract shape of the active site with a here-and-now presence of such a site has been processed by the bacterium. Of course, the molecular surface configuration of this "active site" exists in undetected sugar or other inert macromolecules without any Dicisign being realized—its "activity" is only granted by the bacterium's detecting activity. The decisive precondition is that the receptors of the *E. coli* make it possible for such detection to effect a change of behaviour in a characteristic and typical way, oriented towards the continuation of its metabolism (and hence its survival). This simple biological example gives us the important clue to what is semiotically basic in biology: the stable metabolism of an organism. The ingestion of basic nutrients enters the complicated structure of coupled cycles of the metabolism, one of the functions of which is the detection by the organism of further nutrient sources. The single phases of metabolism, may, of course, be described by purely biochemical means, but it is the functional fact that these phases form a circular, self-sustaining structure which provides the basic biological argument structure leading from perception to action. Metabolism is not only an internal process in the organism, it needs completion by the addition of external nourishment which evolution has taught the organism to detect and consume, completing the cyclical structure.[3] At the same time, this structure forms the prerequisite for adaptations towards sustaining this process better. This formed the basic insight in von Uexküll's early biosemiotic notion of the functional circle of animals, binding together perception signs with action signs to form the basic cyclic interweaving of perceptions with guided action. Thus, the perceptual Dicisign of reading the active site on a carbohydrate molecule—a proto-version of the proposition "This is sugar"—is followed by the action Dicisign of swimming in that direction—to form an argument: "If sugar, swim in its direction. This is sugar. So, swim in its direction". That this forms

---

[3]Metabolism as a process is thus intrinsically in need of completion. This forms the root of predicates, in themselves signs in need of completion; cf. Deacon's notion of "incomplete" nature (2012b).

a very primitive argument[4]—and not merely a cause-effect chain—can be induced from the fact that the *E. coli* may be fooled by artificial sweetener whose molecules possess the same molecular surface configuration as the active site in carbohydrates—but otherwise have a rather different chemistry without the easily releasable covalent binding energy of carbohydrates.

This is not to say, of course, that this process is not underpinned by causal relations. The semiotic aspect of the process lies in the fact that the weak, local interaction makes a whole class of surface stimuli from different sources give rise to the same, typical behaviour. Thus, it is the fact that the bacterium does *not* interact causally with the whole of the molecule (before consuming it, that is) but merely weakly interacts with a spot on its perimeter which is a precondition for its turning a semiotic and not merely causal process.[5] This argument structure binding together perception and action, of course, is close to being as simple as it may get—and the explicit analysis of it into two distinct Dicisign phases is possible for the observer equipped with the functional Dicisign definition, but surely not for the bacterium itself. It has no possibility to make any single aspect of the argument explicit nor autonomous—there are few chemical agents (besides carbohydrates, certain toxins) which the bacterium is able to categorize and react to. The automat-like character of the perception-action link testifies to its holist, not-yet-differentiated character. So the organism is not able to address the logical structure of its own perception-action chain as such nor to substitute other perceptions or conclusions for those of sugar and toxin, or eating and fleeing, respectively. Still this basic

---

[4]Calling it an argument is based on the fact that it displays the double structure of Dicisigns, triggering an action sign. Dealing with an idealized model in which the same active site regularly gives rise to the same action, it is a deductive argument. But it is important to add that it almost completely lacks the quality which Peirce requires for an inference structure to count as real, full-blown reasoning: namely that of self-control (see below). When I say "almost" it is because the argument may change, of course, over the long range of millions of generations due to the process of evolution. If the *Umwelt* of the bacterium were contaminated with a poisonous agent displaying the same "active site" as carbohydrates, this would be a grave challenge to *E. coli*. If a mutation occurs, however, making some bacteria able to distinguish sugar from this toxic substance by means of other active sites on the periphery of the relevant molecules, of course, a mutated group of *E. coli* might survive. Such adaptability could be interpreted as a sort of (very weak) self-control at the level of the lineage rather than on the organism level (organism and lineage levels, it could be added, are not distinct in bacteria to the same degree as in higher animals with sexual reproduction, due to bacterial genetic exchange and the absence of the condition of individual death).

[5]Thus, the difference between the weak interaction of "reading" the active site on the one hand and the binding and breaking covalent bonds in chemical reactions is semiotically important. The former allows for identifying the molecule without chemically interacting with it, due to the weak van der Waals bonds made possible by the variation of electric charge on the surface of the molecule.

argument structure is what makes it possible, during evolution, for higher animals to refine and spread perception-action cycles to much larger parts of
their surroundings, thereby enlarging their *Umwelt*, and, what is more, to isolate parts of the Argument as Dicisigns, and, in turn, parts of those Dicisigns
as Subject Indices and Predicate Icons. It is the fact that metabolism has
an active perception-action phase—marginal in plants and fungi, central in
animals—that introduces semiotics in the simple reasoning inherent in searching the environment for nutrients (and, in the *E. coli* case, escaping certain
toxins). The "reading" of carbohydrate and toxin gradients before a substantial
concentration of either is present is what allows the animal the conclusion of
going into the right direction for finding (or escaping) such concentrations.

That specific part of the object is Peirce's "Immediate Object" which stands
in direct contact with the organism. Thus, the split between Immediate and
Dynamic Object is the prerequisite for categorization by means of a predicate.
In human translation the *E. coli* predicate for carbohydrates would thus be
$SUGAR(x)$. Peirce's functional definition of the Dicisign here allows us to
acknowledge the quasi-proposition processed by the bacterium when it senses
the presense of carbohydrates due to its receptors weakly interacting with a
carbohydrate molecule. Temporal comparisons in the course of its movement
are what allows for the bacterium to compute the direction of the carbohydrate gradient and subsequently orient its swimming in that direction: $SUGAR$
$DIRECTION(y)$. Like most if not all primitive Dicisigns, this example thus
forms part of an argument from perception to action—from *Merkzeichen* to
Wirkzeichen, as von Uexküll would have it, from perception sign to action
sign. This allows us to grasp the role played by quasi-propositions in von
Uexküll's basic "functional circle", exactly taking the animal from a perception
Dicisign, involving the functional establishment that something is the case,
and to an imperative action Dicisign: swim in the sugar direction. Such simple arguments seem to involve imperative conclusions in the shape of action
which are, indeed, for a pragmatist viewpoint, the basic type of proposition.
Perception signs prompting action signs—belief as that which prepares for action. Simple animals do not, of course, have access to a range of different
propositional attitudes to the same propositional content; that is a privilege
for higher animals.

It is a very remarkable property in such primitive Dicisigns that they are
extremely general—they measure one property only. The semiotic interface
between the organism and its *Umwelt* is very restricted and covers only a few
predicates like $SUGAR\ DIRECTION(y)$ and $TOXIC\ DIRECTION(y)$. This
is why the perception part of such primitive *Umwelten* is aptly described in
sign terminology, rather than in full perception terminology. Unlike the case in

higher animals with high-resolution perceptual organs, fine-grained perceptual worlds, integration of sensory modalities, attention direction, etc., here is no detailed, phenomenal world at all. Rather, the *Umwelt* of the bacterium is confined to what can be caught in very few, general predicates. So the idea that biosemiotic signs in general are the result of abstraction processes and inductions from sets of individual, egocentric experiences is simply incorrect—it only holds for certain, ontogenetically acquired signs, possible for organisms with much more elaborated sense organs and corresponding *Umwelten*. The perceptions and predicates of *E. coli* are phylogenetically evolved and not subject to any modification or learning in the lifetime of a single organism (a concept, of course, which is relative due to reproduction by cell division). Only when ontogenetic learning becomes possible, the particular individual experiences of the organism can play any role. Such primitive signs are extremely stable and not subject to individual learning. The ability of higher animals, highly developed in humans, to make new signs by inductive learning from perception within individual lifetime should not, as it sometimes happens, be taken to characterize signs as such.

6.3   Firefly Signaling

Everything points to the fact that cognition—as in the *E. coli* example—is a much more simple process than communication, the former requiring only an organism and an environment, the latter requiring at least two organisms between which information is passed. Just like the true recognition of sugar in *E. coli* allows for the false recognition of sugar in artificial sweeteners, the communication of true quasi-propositions immediately allow for deception, the communication of false such Dicisigns with specific purposes. Firefly signaling, studied by James Lloyd and collaborators, gives an example of this much more complicated use of quasi-propositions.[6] Fireflies of the genus *Photinus* have species-specific signaling codes for mating. Typically, males fly in the evening, flashing the species-specific code in the dark, while females sit perched in the grass, to some extent responding to the male signaling. Given such responses, the males approach the females and mating may take place. Here, the quasi-proposition emitted by the courting male displays the two functional features of the Dicisign. The subject part of the Dicisign is played by the foreground-background structure of the flash itself, immediately drawing attention from the females (and from other observers, including other firefly species, human beings, etc.). The predicate function of the Dicisign is given by the species-

---

[6]Cf. El-Hani, Queiroz and Stjernfelt (2010).

specific flashing pattern allowing for the recognition of the flying flasher as a male of, e.g., the species *Photinus pyralis*. Translated into human language, then, the Dicisign in question will be equivalent to "Here is a male *Photinus* looking for girls". The female perched in the grass—if she answers—will, say, correspondingly "Here is a female *Photinus*, please come closer". Mating and ensuing reproduction and survival of the species, of course, function as the guarantee that these Dicisigns are, in fact, true in the functional sense of truth here discussed.

Not always, however, are such signs true. Another firefly genus, *Photuris*, has specialized in mimicking the love calls of other species. So if the female in the grass is not a *Photinus*, but a *Photuris*, the response signal claiming she is a female *Photinus*, will be false. This may be fatal for the male *Photinus* who reacts to the signal, approaches the female—and is immediately eaten by her. The development of the deception strategy of the species *Photuris* obviously presupposes the already established mating code of—among others— the species *Photinus*. When we speak of "false quasi-proposition", "deception" etc., of course, we are using these notions functionally, without any assumption of consciousness or explicit individual intention whatsoever. Our argument, however, is that such functional versions of true and false communication, deception etc. form the prerequisite for later evolution of consciousness in order to make more plastic and complex the processing and recognition of such quasi-propositions. Just like the cognitive case of the *E. coli*, the codes in use here are phylogenetically established and not subject to change by the individuals—but just as in their case, the actual use of the code in actual sign tokens takes place in the brief lives of individuals. Many scholars may hesitate to admit that cases such as those discussed here are examples of signs— because they prefer to reserve that notion to signals depending upon codes established by the individual in ontogenetic timescale. Such an argument, however, rests on a much too drastic distinction between phylogenesis and ontogenesis, also in the light of the emerging evo-devo synthesis with insights in the connections between the two in so-called Baldwinian evolution where already established behaviours in social species function as selection pressure on individuals. Thus, "teaching", "tradition", and "culture" are increasingly found in many species, not only in higher animals—provided, again that such notions are taken in a functional use rather than in a use presupposing explicit conscious intentions (cf. the classic paper by Caro and Hauser (1992) on the functional definition of biological teaching and the elaboration of that argument to biological tradition and culture in Whiten (2011)). There is no reason not to see habits established over the long run of phylogenetic evolution as semiotic codes, when the actual sign exchange takes place in ontogenetic time.

Moreover, already in the firefly case, that exchange requires a certain degree of interpretation in the situation requiring some degree of individual intelligence. The spatial negotiation making the two sexes meet, of course, requires the ability of navigating in the actual surroundings whose structure cannot be coded beforehand. And the possibility that the signaling female *Photinus* might, in reality, be a hungry *Photuris*, has given rise to a specific behaviour in the *Photinus* male. He does not land directly besides the female, but a certain distance away, and then slowly approaches the female, ready to break off his courtship if he senses anything is wrong. This behaviour, of course, is also inherited, but the very decision whether to break off his approach must involve a certain degree of acute perception and cognition of the female's properties on the part of the male.

6.4 Dicisigns in Aposematism

Already in the firefly case, Dicisign use is not restricted to intraspecies communication but spread in competitive use by other species. Such use of Dicisigns is widespread in aposematism—the use of conspicuous colors and patterns to warn predators. Darwin famously analyzed animal appearance under the headline of sexual selection but already Wallace pointed to the fact that this could not account for certain phenomena, such as coloring in larvae which are not sexually active. For such phenomena, he proposed the explanation that combined with bitter taste, noxious odour or poisonous chemicals, such appearances function as a warning signal, scaring away predators—what later, in 1890, was called *aposematism* by E. Poulton (from Greek *apo*, "away" and *sema*, "sign"). Such signaling is now known in a broad variety of invertebrate species, most conspicuously in insects. It is less widespread in vertebrates, but is found in certain fish, amphibia, reptiles, even a few mammals. The "scared" predator reaction, of course, may be an inherited code determining predator behaviour, in some cases; in other cases with predators capable of ontogenetic learning, especially among omnivorous predators, such coding may be due to individual experience in an organism. Preferred aposematic colors are black, yellow, and red, providing contrast vis-a-vis green foliage. Conspicuous color combinations and patterns have been proved to enhance the learning of avoidance behaviors in predators. A famous case communicating across many species and genera is the black-and-yellow striping known, for instance, in many wasps, *Vespidae,* e.g. *Vespula vulgaris.* By so-called Müllerian mimicry (after Fritz Müller, 1878), such sign use may spread among many species, such as honeybees—the common usage of the same sign enhancing the protection of both species. It is an interesting fact that not only immediate predators like birds may take notice of such sign use—also remote species such as human beings, never or rarely feeding upon wasps, know about the dangers from yellow-and-black striped insects. As in the firefly case, once a code is established, it may also be parasitically used, in this case by species which are not at all stinging, poisonous or ill-tasting, such as, e.g., many clearwing moths (*Sesiidae*). By using a similar sign, they enjoy some degree of protection from predators knowing the black-and-yellow stripe code—so-called Batesian mimicry (after Henry Walter Bates, 1861). Also in this case, then, the basic Dicisign character of the possibility of deception is apparent. Unlike species-specific firefly signaling, indicating the gender and species of the organism flashing, this predicate communicates a general, non-species-bound meaning approximating "Danger". The Dicisign, then is constituted by the localization and spectacular actualization of this general predicate on individual animal body appearances. Of course, standard biological description does not use anything resembling Dicisign terminology; here "warning signals", their degree of "conspicuousness", "distinctiveness" and "efficacy" form central parts of the standard terminology (Stevens and Ruxton 2012). Here the Dicisign speech act is referred to by the ordinary language notion of "warning" while the attention-drawing quality of the Dicisign subject is addressed as its "conspicuousness". Its predicative ability to give rise to typical behaviour in the receiver, of course, is addressed by "efficacy". More generally, "signals" are taken to be distinct from "cues" so that the former are evolved for their functional purpose, the latter not so, while "signals" comprise both constant appearances (like the wasp pattern) and on-and-off communicated signals (like the firefly signal) (Scott-Philips 2007). Some argue for a purely adaptational-behavioral definition of "signal", others invoke "information transfer" as alternative or supplementary definition (ibid.). This need not occupy us here, exactly because the Dicisign definition is indeed functional. The double character of the signal in attention-direction (subject) and behaviour-influence (predicate), the typicality of its predicate aspect, the behavioral reaction in terms of typical behaviour, suffice to establish it as a Dicisign in the Peircean sense. The fact that the signal satisfies these functional criteria for a Dicisign differentiates it from the mere physical-cause-like interpretation of signals. Communication as the co-evolved emitter-receiver connection between two adaptive systems, providing selective advantages for both of them (in some cases involving reciprocity, in other cases not so) is sufficient for Dicisign communicative structure, because primitive truth is at stake. Aposematism evolves only if the warning signals actually truthfully warn the receiver about some property worth avoiding in the emitter which is what, derivatively, permits the evolution of deceptive use of the same signal. This important distinction, crucial to the characterization of aposematisms as Dicisigns, is given in the biological literature with the distinction between Müllerian and Batesian mimicry.

6.5   Frischian Bee Signaling

A ground-breaking study in the sign use of invertebrates and an absolute classic in biosemiotics, of course, is the charting of the honeybee signaling system undertaken already in the 1920s by Karl von Frisch. Famously, von Frisch discovered that the European Honey Bee (*Apis mellifera carnica*) has an inherited code for communicating, in the hive, the location of nectar-rich flowers in the surroundings (1965, 1967). von Frisch found that, in the so-called "waggle dance" the direction and distance are communicated separately. The specific movement type of waggling shows that the bee in question is no longer moving around for transport, but for communication purposes, effectively saying: "This is a sign" and thus furnishing the syntax connecting predicate and subject. Now the length of the dance sequence proportionally indicates the distance from the cube, and the direction of the dance as related to vertical gives the angle of the direction as related to the sun's actual place in the sky. This is obviously a communicative quasi-proposition, expressing the bee equivalent to "there's nectar 200 meter from here, 13 degrees westerly to the direction towards the sun". The structure of this small semiotic system obviously is inherited, not ontogenetically acquired, but even more than in the firefly example, the actual use of it is dependent upon ontogenetically acquired and memorized information. The bee communicating inside the hive remembers the information it has computed during foraging, and translates relative distances in the environment to much smaller, relative distances in the map indicated by the waggle dance. There even seems to be "dialect" variations in the code between different subspecies. The use of these quasi-propositions is subject to surprising plasticity and variation. A location communicated may be used only later in the day, and in that case, the receiver is able to gauge her directions according to where the sun sat in the sky in the moment of communication, even if the sun has now moved considerably in its arc across the sky. If large obstructions are placed in the surrounding *Umwelt,* the bee searching the communicated flower location is able to negotiate its way around very large obstacles to find the right location. A communicating bee having found nectar behind such an obstacle gives information, when back in the hive, which is only partially correct. The direction is truthfully represented despite the obstacle, but the distance is given "too long" because of the prolonged route taken—but corresponds, of course, to the actual distance, which the next bee will have to travel around the obstacle. This implies that the two aspects of the waggle dance

Dicisign are computed independently by the bee. As always, the use of quasi-propositions gives the possibility of false 'belief'. If the nectar-holding flowers are removed, the bees will still go to the location they have learnt about and search there. An impressive experiment shows that the von Frisch direction communication depends on a whole mental map of the surroundings in which the bees navigate by landmarks like trees, bushes, buildings etc. (Gould 2002). In a flat area without conspicuous landmarks, a beehive was placed with four large alphabet letters indicating the general directions of the corners of the world. On an overcast day, the letters were turned ninety degrees around the compass—and subsequently, the flying pattern of the bees also turned ninety degrees. This showed, of course, that they were able to recognize the shapes of the four large, different letters, and use them as landmarks in their mental map of the surrounding; the same mental map to which the waggle dance implicitly refer. The recognition of those landmarks seems to have overruled the bees' normal estimation of the sun's position in cloudy weather. A cognitive map of the surroundings based on large landmarks constitutes, in itself, a complex Dicisign with a vast, topographical predicate showing the interrelation of those landmarks.

The honeybee example thus shows how both cognitive and communicated quasi-propositions may contain information gathered, kept and to some degree memorized by individual organisms in ontogenetic lifetime.

6.6 Vervet Monkey Alarm Calls

Much effort has been spent interpreting the findings of Seyfarth, Cheney et al. pertaining to the system of alarm calls in vervet monkeys (*Chlorocebus pygerythrus*)—a system variants of which have since then been found in many other primate species. Vervet monkeys typically face three natural predators: vultures; leopards and other large cats; python snakes and poisonous snakes. They have developed specific alarm calls referring to each of the three situations, and conspecifics nearby respond by different, specific flight behaviours. In addition to that, they have a fourth alarm call relating to what the first vervet call researcher Struhsaker called "minor mammalian predators", lions, hyenas, cheetahs and other mammals—minor in the sense that they only rarely hunt for vervets. Correspondingly, this call does not elicit flight, but merely vigilant behaviour (Seyfarth, Cheney, and Marler, 1980; Cheney and Seyfarth 1990, 102-103). These signals thus are quasi-proposititions saying "There's an eagle/leopard/snake. Beware!"—or, to be more precise: "There's one of those chasing from the sky/from the bushes/from the earth." As Cheney and Seyfarth add (1990, 170), such a characterization must be amended in the case of mammals where there is a further subdistinction among predators with the same strategy, depending upon whether the danger is major (leopards et al.) or minor (lions et al.). In this case, some degree of ontogenetic learning seems to take place, as pups do not master completely which calls to give on which occasions and only gradually acquire mastery of the code by imitating the adults (Seyfarth and Cheney 1986). The system of alarm calls seems to presuppose the ability to correctly categorize the three predator types, and to conclude the presence of predator individuals from perceptual cues involving sight, hearing, and smell. The wide variety of visual appearances of these species from different points of view, in different lightings and settings, seems to preclude any simple stimulus-response rote learning. Again, we do not need to assume the existence of individual, conscious, communicative intention, in order to recognize a case of functional quasi-propositions communicated.[7] Maybe, however, there is some reason to suspect a degree of metacognition at stake here. Cheney and Seyfarth report cases of "tactical deception"; at one occasion, when a vervet group was lunching in a fruit tree, one monkey gave an alarm call, causing the others to flee, after which the caller himself took over the fruit tree. Such cases, of course, depend on anecdotal evidence, because such behavior cannot easily be elicited, but it seems to rely on reports from experienced primate researchers. The degree of conscious intentionality in such behavior is contested and difficult to decide. Important, however, is that such deception is not a phylogenetically evolved habit as in the *Photuris*, but rather, to some degree, an individually learned strategy in ontogenetic lifetime. Whether it is learned by coincidence and just repeated because of earlier reinforcement or it is connected to some degree of intention, planning or even metacognition and a "theory of mind" of the mental state and ensuing reaction of conspecifics has not yet been settled. Given the functional definition of Dicisigns, however, this does not matter for the characterization of alarm calls, truthful or not, as Dicisigns.

6.7   Corvidae—'Feathered Apes'

The family of *Corvidae* has been the subject of much ethological and cognitive interest in recent decades. Corvids, involving ravens, crows, magpies, jackdaws, jays, etc. appear as the genera of birds which, along with *Psittaciformes* (e.g., parrots), have evolved the highest degree of intelligence. The brain/body weight ratio in ravens approaches that of chimpanzees, and some are now comparing corvids to primates, referring to corvids as "feathered apes"

---

[7]Cf. Queiroz (2012)

as to intelligent behaviours. Already Aesop has, in one of his fables, a crow filling a pitcher of water with small stones in order to make the water level rise so he could drink—a fable which now seems to have been experimentally confirmed (Bird and Emery 2009). In corvids, deception and counter-deception seems to have reached new heights. During food-saving in fall, some corvids cache thousands of kernels in individual hideouts, a large percentage of which they are able to retrieve from memory during winter due to landmark recognition. Some individuals are reliably reported to be aware whether conspecifics are watching them when they make their food storages, in which case they will later remove the food and find alternative storage for it when not observed. This seems to imply some version of functional quasi-propositional knowledge of the intentions of other minds. Individuals which are, themselves, experienced thieves foraging from the caches of other birds, are reported to be the most suspicious and most careful food cachers themselves—realizing *in actu* the old proverb "A thief believes everybody steals". Here, several quasi-propositions are at stake. The very memorizing of storage caches, often close to small landmarks, constitute so many Dicisigns: "This place contains food". The deception strategy must involve quasi-propositional knowledge that the observing conspecific is able to remember the cache location. Corvids are not able to communicate by means of voice, flashes or any specific sign-producing channel of communication, but the fake caching in the presence of peeping conspecifics is, in itself, a communicative act, a small piece of theatre play, falsely expressing, as it were, the quasi-proposition "I hide some food here"—knowing it will be hidden better elsewhere when the observer leaves. Some ethologists are careful with ascribing any mental states on the basis of behavioral observation and stick to descriptions in terms of adaptation: the corvids quickly adapt to the pressure of losing food by reshaping their behaviour. It is cautious thus to rephrase findings in the wording which presupposes the least degree of intelligence, but behavorist description is agnostic as to which processes lie behind a given behavioural adaptation so such cautiousness does not, itself, solve the issue of what takes place. At this level it is tempting to assume the contribution of some degree of conscious reasoning, but it is important that the Dicisign doctrine, again, does not require such a thing to be applicable.[8]

---

[8]In intelligent birds and apes trained by human researchers, the mastery of quasi-propositions may reach impressive levels and even give rise to the explicit expression of structured propositions. Sue Savage-Rumbaugh's bonobo Kanzi and Irene Pepperberg's now deceased grey parrot Alex are famous for their semiotic capabilities, mastering sign language, and some, truncated version of human language, respectively. Both of these individuals are able to express a long and seemingly indefinite amount of compositional quasi-propositions, not only in the imperative but also declarative (prompted, of course, by small snack rewards). Alex had a vocabulary of more than 100 words, and his ability to recognize properties in pre-

The recognition of the potential thief in the peeping conspecific may, again, be a purely functional Dicisign of the structure: "This conspecific may steal my cache."

6.8 Convergent Evolution

It is an important finding that the animals with highest intelligence have evolved in rather distant branches of the phylogenetic tree, not only in mammal genera like primates and cetaceans, but also different branches of avians like parrots and corvids. This phenomenon is investigated under the headline of "convergent evolution": it seems as if intelligence is not an ability closely connected to particular, species-specific brain or embodiment structures as has sometimes been assumed; rather, different neural structures seem able to support behaviours requiring comparable intelligence. In all cases, however, such intelligence seems to go along with a comparative growth in brain/body weight proportions. The relative independence of intelligence as to specific neural structures effectively seems to rule out, of course, that the evolution of such intelligence goes back to any common ancestor of the species involved. Rather, certain ethological similarities seem connected to high intelligence: all the species mentioned are social animals involved in power struggles and reciprocal manipulation games with conspecifics, many of them are omnivorous, requiring the ability of ontogenetical learning to distinguish a large array of edible and non-edible foods and deal with the different strategies for finding or catching it. Convergent evolution excludes assumptions that reasoning abilities should be specifically connected to very particular brain architectures and rather points to the fact that intelligence as such possesses structures which may be described, to some degree, independently of their neural instantiation. For us, of course, the Dicisign structure forms an obvious candidate to a basic structuring principle of intelligence, both in cognition and communication,

---

viously unseen objects was impressive. Shown such an object and asked, e.g. "What colour is it?", he would answer, truthfully: "It is blue", the same going for questions about other properties such as shape, size or number, with an 80% correctness rate of the answers. These results are contested, but it seems as if a simple interpretation in terms of stimulus-response is precluded, as the stimulus correctly categorized has not been encountered before and the answers would also be given in the absence of Pepperberg. Both Kanzi and Alex display considerable ability to express completely new quasi-propositions by composition from an acquired lexicon of proper names, common nouns and adjectives. Their communication results, of course, are possible only within the special symbioses they have developed as trainees of human scientists. Such communication capabilities, however, presuppose cognitive abilities to discern, structure, and recognize the quasi-propositional content communicated and so reveal a cognitive mastery of quasi-propositional perception and memory which may be more widespread in the species to which they belong.

and a central ingredient in reasoning, shaping one Dicisign out of another. The double function of Dicisigns seems to be what makes possible the articulation of truth, even in very simple organisms; the evolution of intelligence seems to be connected to an increase in the plasticity of quasi-propositions in ontogenetic learning. The growth of predicates more remote from immediate survival activity ("food", "sex", "predator" etc.) to more descriptive predicates only mediately connected to such activity is one dimension of growing intelligence, facilitating the construction of an *Umwelt* consisting of more neutral objects—worlds apart from simple *Umwelten* like that of *E.coli*, consisting of little more than nutrients and toxins. The ability to learn new predicates and associate them into kind universals during ontogenetic lifetime forms another dimension of intelligence growth. Probably deception may act as an important motor in such evolutions: the existence of the threat of deception from an ambiguous environment, from other species, or from conspecifics in social animals, acts as a strong selection pressure to evolve and develop abilities to see through the presentation of false Dicisigns. Conversely, collaboration as in honeybees, corvids, human beings, is a strong incentive to become able to communicate socially important knowledge reliably among conspecifics. Most animal Dicisigns seem to be simple, consisting of predicates taking rarely more than two variables and thus devoid of further syntactical variation. Dicisigns addressing episodic memory probably form a strong learning tool; rudimentary syntax seems to appear in some monkeys, even if not necessarily along with semantic relations governing syntactical combinations. Drawing inferences from Dicisigns is probably, in simple organisms, restricted to innate perception-action links; in animals with several different sensory modalities, this information must be synthesized as potentially adding predicates to one and the same object, and in animals with moveable sensory organs, quick perception-action cycles permit the swift zooming in of attention to Dicisign objects.

6.9   Sign Action—A Process Differentiated Through Evolution

This discussion of Dicisigns in selected examples of very different biological complexity, then, serves to state the basic argument that biologically simple signs could not be isolated icons or indices, only later to be composed into more complex signs—nor simple unstructured "signals", associations or stimulus-response mechanic reactions. Biologically simple signs, rather, are full-fledged perception-action arguments—only lacking explicit internal articulation—but bearing with them, due to their double function, the possibility of later segmentation, articulation, autonomization, adaptation to further purposes, making them flexible, potentially giving semiotic structure still more plasticity and eventually making the compositional combination of different Dicisigns, of predicates and subjects, possible. Parts of the metabolism may become relatively autonomous, forming organs—and parts of the perception part of metabolism may acquire their own parts, giving rise to cognitive plasticity, association learning, memory, recursivity and much more, just like the action part of metabolism may differentiate into motor limbs and tools able to support complicated action sequences, co-shaping the environment, depending in turn on this transformation. The basic argument for this ubiquity of simple propositions stretching into arguments in biology is thus based on the observation that phylogenetically acquired habits—like bacteria swimming in the direction of sugar—must be both simple, stable, and (most of the time) true in order to support survival. If not simple, it would be beyond simple organisms to process them. If not stable, they would not be able to address stable features of the environment (such as carbohydrate's combination of easily digestible binding energy and characteristic active sites). And if not more often true than false, they would lead to the perishing of the lineage rather than its survival. Dicisigns are signs able to express truths.

This points to a biosemiotic fact of potentially vast implication: that semiotic evolution should not be seen as going from the simple to the complex in terms of beginning with atomic signs which later serve as building blocks for more complex signs. The process from simple to complex should not be conceived of as a process of composition: the overall arc of the semiotic argument process structure is there from the metabolic beginning, only in a undifferentiated, general shape—and semiotic evolution rather takes the shape of the ongoing subdivision, articulation, and sophistication of primitive signs, an ongoing refinement of parts and aspects acquiring still more autonomy. Please permit an analogy here. To trace the origin of human architecture, you will have to turn to huts, to simple shelters and bivouacs and, before them, the nests of our biological cousins the great apes, and earlier, various biological hideouts and cavities, skins and shells as protection devices, phylogenetically and ontogenetically constructed, maybe all the way down to the cell membrane. Thus you begin with phenomena which perform the basic sheltering function of the whole edifice in a germlike form, rather than beginning with the development of bricks, planks and mortar which only much later would assemble into full buildings. The full building structure was there from the beginning, even if in a very primitive, unarticulated shape. Just like bricks, icons and indices primarily function within the wholes of Dicisigns linked up into action arguments—and they only acquire semi-autonomous status much later, during the ongoing sophistication of argument structure through evolution.

In biology, we would find a similar descent from simple, undifferentiated generality to articulated, explicit specificity in embroynic development. This was one of René Thom's core ideas, giving rise to Catastrophe Theory, and it originally formed the basis of Karl Ernst von Baer's revolutionary approach to epigenesis. The reason why early embryos are structurally much alike is not, as Haeckel later believed, that ontogenesis recapitulates phylogenesis, but rather that fertilized eggs are very simple and in a certain sense general while the ongoing development during embryogenesis forms the functional, specializing subdivision of an already functioning, metabolic whole into different cell-types and organs.[9] Hence, on this view, semiotic compositionality, as it appears in its highest degree of articulation in human language, forms an important *achievement* rather than a possible starting principle: the ongoing relative autonomization of parts and aspects of Dicisigns and their combinations may make them more and more compositional—resulting in a growth of combination possibilities, recursivity and hence increasing cognitive plasticity. Such segmentation of the argument process thus constitutes the overall shape of the increase in "semiotic freedom" during evolution, highlighted by Hoffmeyer (2010). The reason for taking, once again, the textbook example of *E. coli* to illustrate basic sign use, is thus to insist on the fact that the kernel of semiotic cognition is the extremely simple piece of reasoning which connects typified perception and typified action. The fundamental fact that this process may err is what displays its character of (simple) reasoning—and this formed the guideline for our quick reinterpretation of selected biosemiotic cases above. It also indicates that cognition begins long before organisms with central nervous systems evolve, and even longer before the appearance of organisms with attention-directing movable perception organs, binding of different sensory inputs into cross-modal perceptions and the construction of stable environment mappings apart from here-and-now perception. This should make us cautious with more or less automatic assumptions that nervous tissue such as found in the central nervous systems of higher animals should be the privileged or even only locus of cognitive processes. Such an idea is but a sort of magic, ascribing

---

[9] Thom (1978, 1988). In the tradition of semiotics, the linguist Viggo Brøndal had a similar intuition when he structurally composed all word classes from four basics (r,d,R,D), but maintaining that in the evolution of language, the four of them would have to have appeared together, entangled, yet undifferentiated, in the primitive word class of interjections which in some sense performs all of the functions of the specialized word classes at once, albeit indistinctively. Only the evolution of languages allowed, in his view, the emergence of the clear, distinct types of *r*, *d*, *R*, *D* and their ensuing compositional combination into specific word classes performing specialized functions (Brøndal 1948).

wonderfully special abilities to a specific type of cell tissue—overlooking the basic fact that cognition is a not merely a function of neural tissue but a process connecting the whole of an organism to aspects of its surroundings. Such an idea is what Clark (2008), pointing to the involvement of external elements of cognitive processes, calls "neurocentrism". Not only may "anthropocentrism" make us erroneously think that all accidental properties of human cognition are properties of cognition as such—but "neurocentrism" may repeat the error on a larger scale presuming that only properties found in nervous tissues are properties of cognition as such. Rather, cognition and inference are found in the shape of perception-action argument cycles long before the evolution of multicellular organisms and the ensuing evolution of central nervous systems. Such evolution processes should rather be conceived of as adaptations to make the interface between perception and action more plastic, more versatile by adding to the range and structure of Dicisigns which the organism is able to process before turning to action. So, the specialization of certain cells to become neurons, interlinked in the CNS in multicellular organisms, forms a way of both adapting the organism to its specific surroundings and keeping the surroundings temporarily at bay by achieving still more complicated logical structures and reasoning capabilities intervening between perception and action. Neurons and central nervous systems should thus be seen as special adaptations to the requirement of complicated cognitive and logic processes—which is why they have to adapt to necessary structures of such processes. As Peirce says—bearing in mind his objective notion of "mind":

> "For we must remember that the organism has not made the mind, but is only adapted to it. It has become adapted to it by an evolutionary process so that it is not far from correct to say that it is the mind that has made the organism." ("Abstract of 8 lectures", undated, NEM IV, 141)

The more varied the problems posed by the surroundings, including the social labyrinths of fellow conspecifics, become, the more complicated the intervening structure between perception and action must develop in order to adapt plastically—and the more that structure must conform to basic regularities of semiotics and logic: "Logic, for me, is the study of the essential conditions to which signs must conform in order to function as such" (Peirce, "Kaina Stoicheia", 1904). And, what is more, the more variation the environment presents within the small ontogenetic time-scale window of single organism life, the more of reasoning must be transported from the slow process of phylogenetic Darwinian adaption (teaching, e.g., bacteria, over millions of generations, the Argument habit of following sugar and avoiding certain toxins) to the comparatively extremely quick process of ontogenetic adaptive learning (teaching, e.g., apes, over a period of days, to acquire the habit of associating a specific location in the jungle with the presence of specific fruits). Here, biosemioticians must learn not to commit the time-scale error of automatically taking long-term habits for being non-semiotic while short-term habits are seen as having a semiotic nature.[10] The actual sign-exchange, both in the bacterium and the ape example, always takes place in the vanishing moments of individual ontogenetic lifetime—whether the underlying code habit is constituted in the vast timescale of phylogenetic adaptation or in the speedy timescale of ontogenetic learning or somewhere in between does not make any difference in principle (although it does make an enormous difference in behavioural plasticity).

Let us sum up then, the character of primitive, metabolic inference. It connects a perception Dicisign with an action Dicisign to an Argument which, again, forms a sub-section of the the overall metabolism of the cell. The reason for calling it an Argument is its ability to attain truth—and to err, respectively.[11] As an Argument, of course, it lacks a series of important aspects characterizing explicit Arguments made by human beings. The connection between its parts has been established over the phylogentic timescale of evolution and could only be changed in the same way. There is no ontogenetic freedom to exchange parts of it for other parts in an online trial-and-error process. No matter which consciousness definition you adhere to, there is no reason to assume any conscious access to the conclusion or to other parts or aspects of the Argument structure. The Argument appears as a behavioral gestalt, whose parts are only accessible as such to the external observer and analyst, not to the bacterium.

Finally, this overall argument implies that the distinction between man and animal must be sought elsewhere than in a distinction between icons/indices on the one hand and symbols on the other—namely in the growing degree of explicit control and metasemiotics, the ability for an organism to make explicit and control its own use of signs.

---

[10] Hoffmeyer (1996) makes a similar argument.

[11] The notion of truth implied here, of course, is weaker than your average truth definition in terms of correspondence between an explicit proposition and an aspect of reality. Primitive biological truth might be described as adequacy of perception and correlated action—measured on the perception-action link's support of metabolism. If that link does not support metabolism, of course, it will be weeded out in the long run of natural selection. The overall argument here claims that such primitive adequacy truth forms the root of more developed truth types in higher animals and human beings.

162

6.10 Hypostatic Abstraction

With the intensified research into human prehistory occupying many different disciplines, a Pandora's box of old questions has been reopened: the origin of language, the emergence of culture, the physical anthropology and evolution of human beings—and, conversely, the issue of communicative and cognitive abilities of other higher animals as compared to those of human beings. What is specific to human semiotic and cognitive abilities as compared to those of higher animals? A series of different answers to this issue of the semiotic or cognitive "missing link" between higher animals and human beings are already on the market: symbol use (Terrence Deacon), shared attention (Jerome Bruner, Michael Tomasello), language syntax (Chomsky), specific types of "blending" (Fauconnier and Turner), etc. The discussion is both electrified and muddled by the fact that these hypotheses range over different fields such as psychology, linguistics, semiotics, cognitive science, anthropology, etc. This implies that the proposals mentioned are not even directly comparable—in order to be compared, they should so to speak be translated into each others' terminology. What would, e.g., the psychological notion of "joint attention" amount to if translated into the terminology of linguistics, semiotics, or neuroscience? The possibility exists that it might turn out to mean approximately or even exactly the same as one or several of the other proposals—this could only be decided after such a reconstruction process which is, by no means, a simple translation issue but an interdisciplinary reorganization which will only be possible after a process of conceptual and empirical development and which will, in itself, constitute a main part of a solution.

I have aired the idea that a good candidate for this semiotic-cognitive "missing link" might be Peirce's notion of "hypostatic abstraction" (Stjernfelt 2007, ch. 11). Probably, no single semiotic feature may presumably be held responsible for all semiotic and cognitive differences between human beings and higher animals—still I find hypostatic abstraction to be one of the central candidate devices because it permits the making explicit and controling of various prehuman semiotic capacities and hence indispensable for the construction of human thought and language. Let us revisit Peirce's discussions of the term.[12] Peirce never wrote a comprehensive treatise on the issue but returns to it over and over again in his mature work around the turn of the century.

Here, it refers a process as well as a product, to be found in a bundle of related semio-cognitive events: *Linguistically*: the construction of an (ab-

---

[12] As with many of his interesting proposals, the discussions of "hypostatic abstraction" (or "hypostatis", "subjective abstraction", etc.) are scattered over his work, so a bit of reconstruction work is necessary.

stract) noun from more concrete expressions, such as adjectives ("hard" ⇒ "hardness"), a verb ("give" ⇒ "giver", "gift", "given"), or a (more concrete) noun ("object" ⇒ "objecthood"), etc. From the sentence "The sky is blue", the sentence "The sky possesses blueness" is constructed. *Logically*: the corresponding construction of a subject on the basis of a predicate, thus adding a new 2nd-order individual ("blueness") to the domain represented. *Mathematically*: the application of a meta-level operation or object regulating other, more basic operations or objects (e.g., passing from the existence of different types of connections between entities to forming the concept of "relation" as a new abstract object. The properties of this object now become open to investigation in higher-level hypostatic abstractions (the "symmetry", "transitivity", etc. of relations may now be investigated).[13] *Cognitively*: the process of taking a thought for a thing, so that a new cognitive object is constructed on the basis of a thought—alternatively described as the "stiffening" of transient, fleeting cognitive content into a stable shape facilitating further reasoning pertaining to this new, abstract object. *Perceptually*: the spatialization of a temporal perception process, such as forming the trajectory as an abstraction from the array of locations covered by the perceived movement of an object: going from "a point moves" to "the line traced by the moving point".[14]

---

[13] One of Peirce's own examples of hypostatic abstraction in mathematics concerns the successive abstractions of sets from elements, powers from sets, cardinal numbers from powers: "In order to get an inkling—though a very slight one—of the importance of this operation in mathematics, it will suffice to remember that a collection is an hypostatic abstraction, or ens rationis, that multitude is the hypostatic abstraction derived from a predicate of a collection, and that a cardinal number is an abstraction attached to a multitude. So an ordinal number is an abstraction attached to a place, which in its turn is a hypostatic abstraction from a relative character of a unit of a series, itself an abstraction again" ("Consequences of Critical Common-Sensism", 1905, 5.534; Peirce writes "collections" and "multitudes" for sets and powers).

[14] A Peirce quote giving many different examples of Hypostatic Abstraction is the following: "But hypostatic abstraction, the abstraction which transforms "it is light" into "there is light here," which is the sense which I shall commonly attach to the word abstraction (since prescission will do for precisive abstraction) is a very special mode of thought. It consists in taking a feature of a percept or percepts (after it has already been prescinded from the other elements of the percept), so as to take propositional form in a judgment (indeed, it may operate upon any judgment whatsoever), and in conceiving this fact to consist in the relation between the subject of that judgment and another subject, which has a mode of being that merely consists in the truth of propositions of which the corresponding concrete term is the predicate. Thus, we transform the proposition, "honey is sweet," into "honey possesses sweetness." "Sweetness" might be called a fictitious thing, in one sense. But since the mode of being attributed to it consists in no more than the fact that some things are sweet, and it is not pretended, or imagined, that it has any other mode of being, there is, after all, no fiction. The only profession made is that we consider the fact of honey being sweet under the form of a relation; and so we really can. I have selected sweetness as an instance of one of the least useful of abstractions. Yet even this is convenient. It facilitates

Peirce's ambitious idea is that these rather different examples constitute different occurrences of the same basic cognitive-logical structure and process characterized by their result: the emergence of a new, higher-level cognitive object. Most often, these aspects of hypostatic abstraction are merely mentioned as examples; they are not explicitly distinguished and interrelated as subtypes of the concept. The basic cognitive purposivity of hypostatic abstraction is this: it facilitates the explicit reasoning and investigation pertaining to general issues which would otherwise remain implicit, transient or lost in concrete particulars (of course, once the forming of hypostatic abstractions is possible it need not build on existing particulars and thus may refer to non-existing or fictive universals as well). The many different linguistic devices for hypostatic abstraction are tools which further develop, detail, and make explicit aspects of the ongoing cognitive process of reasoning. Thus, the adjective "red" basically refers to particular, concrete, here-and-now occurrences of that color and allows for their comparison, while the noun "redness" (or "the color red", "the red", etc.) constructs a new, stable, abstract object interconnecting these different occurrences and makes possible the further reasoning on this color as such, abstracted from its concrete occurrences, and on its relation to other colors, other properties etc.

Hypostatic abstraction may be described as a simple deduction from a premise "This object is red" to a conclusion "Redness exists (in this object)", so that it makes sense to say that the hypostatic abstraction is an entity whose being consists in the (purported) truth of a predicate expression:

---

such thoughts as that the sweetness of honey is particularly cloying; that the sweetness of honey is something like the sweetness of a honeymoon; etc. Abstractions are particularly congenial to mathematics. Everyday life first, for example, found the need of that class of abstractions which we call collections. Instead of saying that some human beings are males and all the rest females, it was found convenient to say that mankind consists of the male part and the female part. The same thought makes classes of collections, such as pairs, leashes, quatrains, hands, weeks, dozens, baker's dozens, sonnets, scores, quires, hundreds, long hundreds, gross, reams, thousands, myriads, lacs, millions, milliards, milliasses, etc. These have suggested a great branch of mathematics. Again, a point moves: it is by abstraction that the geometer says that it "describes a line." This line, though an abstraction, itself moves; and this is regarded as generating a surface; and so on. So likewise, when the analyst treats operations as themselves subjects of operations, a method whose utility will not be denied, this is another instance of abstraction. Maxwell's notion of a tension exercised upon lines of electrical force, transverse to them, is somewhat similar. These examples exhibit the great rolling billows of abstraction in the ocean of mathematical thought; but when we come to a minute examination of it, we shall find, in every department, incessant ripples of the same form of thought, of which the examples I have mentioned give no hint" ("Minute Logic", 1902, 4.235).

"For by means of abstraction the transitory elements of thought, the »επεα πτερ'οενα [epea pteroenta]",[15] are made substantive elements, as James terms them, "»επεα απτερ'οεντα [epea apteroenta]." It thus becomes possible to study their relations and to apply to these relations discoveries already made respecting analogous relations. In this way, for example, operations become themselves the subjects of operations.

To take a most elementary example—from the idea of a particle moving, we pass to the idea of a particle describing a line. This line is then thought as moving, and so as generating a surface; and so the relations of surfaces become the subject of thought. An abstraction is an ens rationis whose being consists in the truth of an ordinary predication." ("Relatives" in Baldwin's Dictionary, 1901, 3.642)

This should not be taken to imply that hypostatic abstraction expressions referring to non-existing objects may not exist. "Unicornicity" is a hypostatic abstraction from "unicorn" even if no unicorns exist—the implication of Peirce's definition is that, in this case, the hypostatic abstraction does not have any "being", that is, it does not refer to any real possibility like in the cases of "redness" or "hardness" or "trajectory". The deductive character of hypostatic abstraction is not changed by this observation—like any deduction, its validity dependes on the soundness of the premise invoked: "If and only if cases involving the predicate x exists, then x-ness has being".

Thus, if no x exists, x-ness has no being,—but in many cases the validity of this claim may be investigated both by investigating x's and investigating x-ness. Thus, the hypostatic abstractive deduction forms no guarantee that the resulting abstraction has a *fundamentum in re* and refers to really existing kinds—the wellknown examples of fallacious hypostatic abstractions in the history of science such as "phlogiston" or "caloric" testify to that. The fact that hypostatic abstraction is a deduction has often been confused with the possibly abductive character of the reasoning process in which a hypostatic abstraction may take part. Making a hypostatic abstraction may, in many cases, be part of a trial-and-error reasoning process where the abstraction made is subject to further investigation so as to determine its degree of reality. Thus, the deductive step of hypostatic abstraction forms, in this broader perspective, part of an abduction whose validity must be investigated by further de- or induction on the basis of the abstraction made. This is why hypostatic abstraction has

---

[15]"Epea pteroenta" is a Homeric metaphor meaning "winged words" (strong idioms);— James added the negative "Epea apteroenta", plucked words, to indicate nominalization.

sometimes been characterized as deduction, sometimes as abduction (cf. the papers of Pape and Short in Houser et al. 1997; cf. Stjernfelt 2007, 458).

It should immediately be added that Peirce takes great care to distinguish this process from what he calls "distinction", the attention ability which permits focusing on a particular part or aspect of an object at the expense of other parts or aspects of that object—and which is often confused with hypostatic abstraction (cf. Shin 2010). These focusing abilities come in three variants, nicknamed "dissociation", "prescission", and "discrimination", respectively. Dissociation is what permits the distinction between different independent qualities, such as "red" from "blue": prescission is what permits the distinction of a part which may be supposed to exist independently of another part, such as "space" from "color", while discrimination is what permits the distinction of a part which may be only imagined separately, such as "color" from "space". These two latter distinction types are important to the investigation of objects involving features dependent on each other in different patternings. The kind of attention they pertain to, however, involves imagining the object endowed with indeterminate parts:

> "In general, prescission is always accomplished by imagining ourselves in situations in which certain elements of fact cannot be ascertained. This is a different and more complicated operation than merely attending to one element and neglecting the rest." ("Terminology", 1893, 2.428)

According to Peirce, it is of paramount importance to keep the distinctions apart from hypostatic abstraction—while the former pertain to the degree of particularity and generality, the latter does not lead to higher generality but to the creation of new, abstract or ideal objects of thought or discourse.[16] The distinction between the two may be expressed as follows:

> "But even in the very first passage in which abstraction occurs as a term of logic, two distinct meanings of it are given, the one the contemplation of a form apart from matter, as when we think of whiteness, and the other the thinking of a nature indifferenter, or without regard to the differences of its individuals, as when we think of a white thing, generally. The latter process is called, also, precision (or better, prescission): and it would greatly contribute to perspicuity of thought and expression if we were to return to the usage of the best scholastic doctors and designate it by that

---

[16] As a realist, Peirce holds that some hypostatically abstract concepts refer to aspects of reality ("gravity") while others do not ("phlogiston").

name exclusively, restricting abstraction to the former process by which we obtain notions corresponding to the 'abstract nouns.'" ("Terminology" 1893, 2.428n)

In most concrete cases, of course, the two procedures work closely in tandem: before the hypostatic abstraction of "redness", a distinction is required to isolate the property of "red" in the object (more generally, hypostatic abstraction is impossible without a preceding distinction)—but still, the working of the two must be kept analytically distinct. In contrast to many empiricist theories of abstraction, moreover, it should be added that Peirce does not identify any of the two with induction as the statistical investigation of properties in a sample of objects. Abstraction does not presuppose induction and it is perfectly possible to perform a hypostatic abstraction on the basis of one observed object only (even if it may be wiser to perform it after an induction summing up knowledge of a wider sample of objects). An important aspect of hypostatic abstraction is that, in making a second-order object out of a thought, it gives it concrete form and thus facilitates cognitive and logic manipulation and investigation of it—as if it were a particular individual object:

"Intuition is the regarding of the abstract in a concrete form, by the realistic hypostatization of relations; that is the one sole method of valuable thought. Very shallow is the prevalent notion that this is something to be avoided. You might as well say at once that reasoning is to be avoided because it has led to so much error; quite in the same philistine line of thought would that be; and so well in accord with the spirit of nominalism that I wonder some one does not put it forward. The true precept is not to abstain from hypostatization, but to do it intelligently..." ("A Guess at the Riddle", c. 1890, EP II, 262; 1.383)

This implies that the hypostatically abstract object may be seen as if it shared some of the characteristics of particular individuals: it has properties, it stands in various relations to other such objects, it may be subsumed by still higher genera—in that sense hypostatic abstraction is a simplifying device involving cognitive economy because it permits to use some of the same means for their investigation which we use interacting with particulars. Peirce also ascribes abstractions a seminal role in his famous distinction between corollarial and theorematic deductions (see ch. 10); the former only relying upon definition of concepts appearing in the premises, the latter requiring the introduction of additional elements in the shape of postulates to conduct the proof. Theorematic reasoning, of course, requires creativity and guessing, even if being deductive—and the most challenging theorematic deductions are taken to involve the introduction of abstractions:

> "Deductions are of two kinds, which I call corollarial and theorematic. The corollarial are those reasonings by which all corollaries and the majority of what are called theorems are deduced; the theorematic are those by which the major theorems are deduced. If you take the thesis of a corollary,— i.e. the proposition to be proved, and carefully analyze its meaning, by substituting for each term its definition, you will find that its truth follows, in a straightforward manner, from previous propositions similarly analyzed. But when it comes to proving a major theorem, you will very often find you have need of a lemma, which is a demonstrable proposition about something outside the subject of inquiry; and even if a lemma does not have to be demonstrated, it is necessary to introduce the definition of something which the thesis of the theorem does not contemplate. In the most remarkable cases, this is some abstraction; that is to say, a subject whose existence consists in some fact about other things. Such, for example, are operations considered as in themselves subject to operation; lines, which are nothing but descriptions of the motion of a particle, considered as being themselves movable; collections; numbers; and the like. When the reform of mathematical reasoning now going on is complete, it will be seen that every such supposition ought to be supported by a proper postulate. At any rate Kant himself ought to admit, and would admit if he were alive today, that the conclusion of reasoning of this kind, although it is strictly deductive, does not flow from definitions alone, but that postulates are requisite for it." ("On the Logic of drawing History from Ancient Documents especially from Testimonies", 1901, 7.204)

As to the discussion of the semiotic "missing link" it should be mentioned that many higher animals are able to make prescissions—the ability to isolate features in an object is the precondition for associative learning, linking up co-occurrent such features—just as they are able to make deductions on the basis of phylogenetically inherited or ontogenetically acquired habits. Theorematic reasoning and Hypostatic abstractions, on the other hand, seem to be missing among animal proto-concepts.

6.11 Self-control by Abstraction in Human Semiotics

In a central argument, Peirce links the special semiotic and cognitive abilities in human beings to a higher degree of self-control which is, in turn, connected to the ability to make hypostatic abstractions. Let us first scrutinize this notion of "self-control". An important idea here is that self-control is crucial for inferences to count as real reasonings, as he may epigrammatically say: "...reasoning is thought subjected to self-control ..." ("Pragmaticism, Prag. [4]" c. 1905, 5.533). This is why computers ("logical machines") are not taken to be able to reason—even if their actions may formally realize inference structures and they are able to produce outputs which are interpretable as truths—they do not possess any self-control. The potentiality of performing a specific action is sufficient to count as a habit—but belief requires the self-control of habit: "[Readiness] to act in a certain way under given circumstances and when actuated by a given motive is a habit; and a deliberate, or self-controlled, habit is precisely a belief" ("A Survey of Pragmatism", 1907, 5.480). Fully realized self-control, on the other hand, may have as its result the formation of mechanical-like thought habits:

> "The power of self-control is certainly not a power over what one is doing at the very instant the operation of self-control is commenced. It consists (to mention only the leading constituents) first, in comparing one's past deeds with standards, second, in rational deliberation concerning how one will act in the future, in itself a highly complicated operation, third, in the formation of a resolve, fourth, in the creation, on the basis of the resolve, of a strong determination, or modification of habit. This operation of self-control is a process in which logical sequence is converted into mechanical sequence or something of the sort. How this happens, we are in my opinion as yet entirely ignorant. There is a class of signs in which the logical sequence is at the same time a mechanical sequence and very likely this fact enters into the explanation." (Letter to F.C.S. Schiller, undated, 8.320)

This, however, is only possible as the result of a complex process involving standards, future acts, and a decision to modify thought habits. Such self-control is required for full mastering of reasoning—but is, at the same time, the result of a long process with simpler biological antecedents. Thus, when speaking about simple perception-action loops as "inferences" with the structure of "arguments", we should not take this in the full value of self-controlled thought, the degree of control at stake primarily being performed by selection pressure. Importantly, Peirce sees a decisive aspect of self-control in the psychological ability to isolate a thought from other intrusions—a psychological equivalent to the logical notion of "distinction" discussed above:

> "Contemplation consists in using our self-control to remove us from the forcible intrusion of other thoughts, and in considering the interesting bearings of what may lie hidden in the icon, so as to cause the subjective intensity of it to increase." ("Short Logic", 1893, 7.555)

The isolation of the iconic sign—the predicate—may count as a first step in human self-control—to be followed by the hypostatic taking of that sign to be a thing in itself. Hypostatization, now, is crucially connected to the particularity of human reasoning. Peirce himself only rarely discusses hypostatic abstraction in connection to the man-animal issue. The most important locus is the following quote:

> "To return to self-control, which I can but slightly sketch, at this time, of course there are inhibitions and coördinations that entirely escape consciousness. There are, in the next place, modes of self-control which seem quite instinctive. Next, there is a kind of self-control which results from training. Next, a man can be his own training-master and thus control his self-control. When this point is reached much or all the training may be conducted in imagination. When a man trains himself, thus controlling control, he must have some moral rule in view, however special and irrational it may be. But next he may undertake to improve this rule; that is, to exercise a control over his control of control. To do this he must have in view something higher than an irrational rule. He must have some sort of moral principle. This, in turn, may be controlled by reference to an esthetic ideal of what is fine. There are certainly more grades than I have enumerated. Perhaps their number is indefinite. The brutes are certainly capable of more than one grade of control; but it seems to me that our superiority to them is more due to our greater number of grades of self-control than it is to our versatility.
>
> Doctor Y. Is it not due to our faculty of language?
>
> Pragmaticist. To my thinking that faculty is itself a phenomenon of self-control. For thinking is a kind of conduct, and is itself controllable, as everybody knows. Now the intellectual control of thinking takes place by thinking about thought. All thinking is by signs; and the brutes use signs. But they perhaps rarely think of them as

signs. To do so is manifestly a second step in the use of language. Brutes use language, and seem to exercise some little control over it. But they certainly do not carry this control to anything like the same grade that we do. They do not criticize their thought logically. One extremely important grade of thinking about thought, which my logical analyses have shown to be one of chief, if not the chief, explanation of the power of mathematical reasoning, is a stock topic of ridicule among the wits. This operation is performed when something, that one has thought about any subject, is itself made a subject of thought (. . .)"[17]("Pragmaticism, Prag. [4]" c. 1905, 5.533-34)

This long quote gives two important arguments. The first is that self-control comes in many grades which increase during evolution. Our hypothesis here will be that this increase corresponds to the increase of articulation and segmentation of the perception-action chain into detailed argument structures. Any relative autonomization of a part of that chain corresponds to an increase in self-control. On top of such grades of self-control which is already present in higher animals, Peirce presents an architecture of additional human self-control grades: 1) training; 2) self-training, controlling one's own self-control, involving imagination; 3) adoption of a rule guiding this meta-control; 4) improvement of that rule after some higher ethical standard, thus controlling the control over one's control; 5) controlling, in turn, that rule after some aesthetic standard (Peirce's notion of aesthetics pertaining to all goals which are worth pursuing).[18] Every such step, of course, takes the former step as its object,

---

[17]In the left-out part of the quote given, Peirce goes into his recurring example of hypostatic abstraction, Molière's joke from *Le malade imaginaire* about the idle inference from "opium puts people to sleep" and to "opium possesses a *virtus dormativa*" where Peirce argues that this ridiculed inference does in fact represent a step (albeit very small) forward in reasoning, because it opens the issue of what this dormitive power more exactly consists in, how strong it is as compared to that of other substances, etc., and thus facilitates further investigations. Without such further investigations, of course, the hypostatic abstraction remains idle.

[18]The special concept of aesthetics referred to here is discussed later in the quote: "And you, Doctor W., will see that since pragmaticism makes the purport to consist in a conditional proposition concerning conduct, a sufficiently deliberate consideration of that purport will reflect that the conditional conduct ought to be regulated by an ethical principle, which by further self-criticism may be made to accord with an esthetical ideal. For I cannot admit that any ideal can be too high for a duly transfigured esthetics. So, although I do not think that an esthetic valuation is essentially involved, actualiter (so to speak) in every intellectual purport, I do think that it is a virtual factor of a duly rationalized purport. That is to say, it really does belong to the purport, since conduct may depend upon its being appealed to. Yet in ordinary cases, it will not be needful that this should be done." (ibid., 5.535) That "duly transfigured" aesthetics is the generalized doctrine of all ideals possible to pursue; the idea is that such ideals may play a role in thought even if not explicitly addressed at all.

thus creating a new hypostatic abstraction subject to variation and evalua-
tion. Many higher animals, it is well-known, may be subject to training, but
the next, decisive step of self-training seems only rudimentarily accessible to
higher animals. The second crucial argument here is that such self-control is
seminal to human thought and language—and that this self-control is facilitated by thinking of our signs *as* signs, by thinking about thought and thereby
becoming able to criticize and control our own thought logically. Self-control
involves taking one's own thought as the object of a meta-level thought.[19] But
this is only possible by making the first thought an object—stiffening in the
shape of a hypostatic abstraction. Such self-control even makes possible language. How should this be interpreted?—it is well known that natural language
learning does not take place by the explicit memorizing of linguistic rules and
that practicing knowledge of grammar does not entail any explicit insight in
grammatical principles (much like Peirce's logical distinction between implicit
logica utens and explicit *logica docens* which differ in that the former is interested in the results of reasoning, not the process, the latter vice versa). The
work performed by self-control here is more basic—it is the ability to wonder
and check whether a particular sign is suitably used, focusing upon the relations between sign, object, and interpretant, upon its relation to other signs
and their objects and interpretants. Such ability is taken to be the prerequisite
to the establishment of grammar, fine-grained taxonomies, tuning of schematic
content, expression-content couplings, etc. in the development of languages.[20]

It is important to Peirce's notion of self-control, now, that such self-control
is a merely *restrictive* measure, selecting valuable inferences among less valuable inferences—thus, it presupposes the existence of inferences which it then,
subsequently, turns into reasoning by controlling them:

> "But self-control is the character which distinguishes reasonings
> from the processes by which perceptual judgments are formed, and
> self-control of any kind is purely inhibitory. It originates nothing.

---

[19] We remark in the passing that Peirce, in this nesting of control acts into higher-level
control acts, seems to subscribe to an Enlightenment ideal of the moral autonomy of human
reasoning, cf. ch. 11.

[20] Reasoning as opposed to mechanical computation is characterized by self-control. Given
the tower of control of control discussed here, however, self-control seems to appear as a
matter of degree. Even if perfect self-control may be achievable on one level, this hardly
involves all levels at the same time. Conversely, cases of intermediary control are possible,
Peirce muses in a psychological argument: "If, however, as the English suppose, the feeling of
rationality is the product of a sort of subconscious reasoning—by which I mean an operation
which would be a reasoning if it were fully conscious and deliberate—the accompanying feeling
of evidence may well be due to a dim recollection of the experimentation with diagrams"
("Minute Logic", 1902, 2.172). Subconscious diagram experiment—controlled only to some
degree—may lie behind non-substantiated evidence-feelings.

Therefore it cannot be in the act of adoption of an inference, in the pronouncing of it to be reasonable, that the formal conceptions in question can first emerge. It must be in the first perceiving that so one might conceivably reason. And what is the nature of that? I see that I have instinctively described the phenomenon as a 'perceiving.' I do not wish to argue from words; but a word may furnish a valuable suggestion. What can our first acquaintance with an inference, when it is not yet adopted, be but a perception of the world of ideas?" ("Lectures on Pragmatism" 1903, 5.194)

The question of the roots of inference is here answered phenomenologically—investigating the origin of inference structures as seen from the perspective of the human mind. Before subjecting an inference to control and evaluating it, we must first be able to perceive it in "the world of ideas". This idealist wording of course leaves out the fact that we access that world not by any direct, mystic, purely intuitive route, but only by the intermediary of diagrams, facilitated by imagination and experiment. The inhibitory work performed by the different levels of self-control, then, presupposes a wealth of possible inferences and abstract objects to chose between. The imaginative creation, variation and combination of such inferences and objects—at each of the control levels—is thus the prerequisite for inhibitory self-control to perform its function—Peirce's cognitive version of the Darwinian combination of variation with selection. And posed as an evolutionary question, the basic pool of such inference structure is found in the perception-action habits refined through the evolution of animals—habits which have been subjected to increasing degrees of control already over the course of evolution, before they are made, in turn, the object of the vastly increasing human processes of self-control by means of hypostatic abstraction and diagram experimentation.[21]

Thus, it is an important corollary of self-control, as described here, that it always involves (at least) two levels, that of imaginary creation, and that of inhibitory controlling. This implies that the focus of control must alternate between the levels, evolving inferences on the lower level and pruning them on the higher level. This makes self-control a special case of Peirce's important idea of the dialogicity of logic. This, I think, makes it possible to compare the Peircean notion of self-control by hypostatic abstraction with Tomasello's central ideas of joint attention.

---

[21] It goes without saying that this overall evolutionary increase in self-control recruits further capabilities to create higher level, more efficient cognition and action—such as consciousness, emotions, episodic memory, human language etc.

6.12   Hypostatic Abstraction and Joint Attention

How does Peirce's idea of hypostatic abstraction fit the Tomasellian idea of joint attention? For a first glance, the two ideas may seem wide apart, but for a closer glance important connections appear. Shared attention can not, of course, be reduced to two parties both of them intending the same object. It also involves the knowledge in each part of the other part's attention. But even that is not sufficient. As Frédéric Kaplan and Verena Hafner insist from the point of view of implementing joint attention in robot research, joint attention is not achieved even by robots tracking other robots' attention and coordinating that with their own attention (which is robotologically possible but does not entail shared attention):

> "To reach joint attention an agent must understand, monitor and direct the intentions underlying the attentional behaviour of the other agent. Attention can only be reached if both agents are aware of this coordination of 'perspectives' towards the world." (Kaplan and Hafner 2004, 68)

Joint attention thus requires for each agent to assume the famous "intentional stance" towards the other: the attention direction detected in the other agent is interpreted as a sign that an intention is directing that attention to some goal. But even that is not sufficient: each agent must be able to influence the other's attention, for instance by directing it by means of gesture, eye movements, linguistic cues, etc. And such influence is only possible based on a skill of social interaction: the agents must be able to master turn-taking, role-switching and ritualized games, as Kaplan underlines. If no turn-taking schema is active, the agents will not know who is directing whose attention at any given moment. Thus, the apparently simple phenomenon of "joint attention" entails a whole series of interrelated concepts—a molecule of social interaction. But something similar is the case with Peircean hypostatic abstraction. It forms, of course, one of the major techniques of letting "symbols grow", Peirce's brief version of the Enlightenment ideal of common, increasing knowledge construction (cf. ch. 11). It does so by means of its ability to take other signs as its object, thereby making their content and role explicit, and hence the possible object of scrutinizing, comparing and controlling them. And this whole process of thought, according to Peirce, has an irreducible dialogic structure: "Accordingly, it is not merely a fact of human Psychology, but a necessity of Logic, that every logical evolution of thought should be dialogic" ("Prolegomena", 1906, 4.551).

This necessity lies in the articulation of logic in signs fit to communicating them from a person in one moment to the same person (or other) in the next moment: "All thinking is dialogic in form. Your self of one instant appeals to your deeper self for his assent. Consequently, all thinking is conducted in signs..." ("Amazing Mazes" 4, 1909, 6.338). This gives rise to the possibility of performing logical arguments describable by a temporal sequence of propositions, the same person occupying alternately pro- and con-positions in an ongoing dialogic process. These important ideas have often been overlooked because Peirce's ideas on this are only scarcely represented in his published work and have not been much discussed in the Peirce literature, but it has been highlighted in the wake of the tradition of Hintikkan game-theoretical semantics (Hintikka, Hilpinen; most recently, Pietarinen 2006 has furthered the investigation of this issue). This idea occurs in the context of Peirce's logic representation systems known as Existential Graphs whose Alpha and Beta parts are isomorphic to propositional logic and first order predicate logic with identity, respectively. Peirce's idea is that these representations reveal a dialogic structure inherent in logical arguments. One agent, the so-called Grapheus, is responsible for the construction of the discursive world, while the other, the so-called Graphist, is responsible for counter-arguing the single steps of its construction. The two agents thus collaborate in critically investigating a logical issue and take it to conclusion, and they may, of course, often be instantiated in one and the same mind during soliloquious thought processes. In Pietarinen's Hintikkan interpretation, they may be seen as playing a semantic game against each other, and the existence of a winning strategy on the part of one of them is the game-theoretical equivalent to the truth of that part's argument. We shall not here go deeply into the specific means the two agents use when interacting in Peirce's elaboration of the existential graphs, but in our context, Peirce has some important general developments of what is involved:

> "Now nothing can be controlled that cannot be observed while it is in action. It is therefore requisite that both minds but especially the Graphist-mind should have a power of self-observation. Moreover, control supposes a capacity in that which is to be controlled of acting in accordance with definite general tendencies of a tolerable stable nature, which implies a reality in this governing principle. But these habits, so to call them, must be capable of being modified according to some ideal in the mind of the controlling agent; and this controlling agent is to be the very same as the agent controlled; the control extending even to the modes of control themselves, since we suppose that the interpreter-mind under the guidance of the Graphist-mind discusses the rationale of logic

itself." ("Basis of Pragmaticism," 1905, Ms. 280, 30–32, quoted from Pietarinen 2006)

The dialogic structure facilitates control of the thought process, because one part's utterance in the game takes the other part's utterance as its object in a hypostatic abstraction. What is visible, of course, is only the part's manifest utterance, but that utterance is the response to the whole preceding game and, in that respect, indirectly refers to it—much like a move in a chess game implicitly refers to the whole preceding game and one player's interpretation of the other's intention as perceived from his move sequence. Of course, hypostatic abstractions are not possible within the representation systems offered in the Alpha and Beta parts of the Existential Graphs (hypostatic abstractions quantify over other signs such as predicates and thus belong to second-order logic). Peirce envisaged this second order part in his Gamma graphs which were to comprise a part aimed at the explicit representation of hypostatic abstractions. But naturally, this representation of them takes place in a hypostatic abstraction of second order. If logical thinking necessarily possesses a dialogic structure, it forces the individual engaging in such thinking to divide so as to accommodate to it:

> "There is no reason why 'thought,' in what has just been said, should be taken in that narrow sense in which silence and darkness are favorable to thought. It should rather be understood as covering all rational life, so that an experiment shall be an operation of thought. Of course, that ultimate state of habit to which the action of self-control ultimately tends, where no room is left for further self-control, is, in the case of thought, the state of fixed belief, or perfect knowledge. Two things here are all-important to assure oneself of and to remember. The first is that a person is not absolutely an individual. His thoughts are what he is 'saying to himself,' that is, is saying to that other self that is just coming into life in the flow of time.
>
> When one reasons, it is that critical self that one is trying to persuade; and all thought whatsoever is a sign, and is mostly of the nature of language. The second thing to remember is that the man's circle of society (however widely or narrowly this phrase may be understood), is a sort of loosely compacted person, in some respects of higher rank than the person of an individual organism. It is these two things alone that render it possible for you—but only in the abstract, and in a Pickwickian sense—to distinguish between absolute truth and what you do not doubt." ("What Pragmatism Is", 1905, 5.420–421)

This being the case, there seems to be a deep connection between the dialogic structure of reasoning and self-control on the level of semiotics and logic—and the central place enjoyed by shared attention on the level of human psychology according to Tomasello's hypothesis. The parent-child dyad interaction trains the child in the first human level of self-control with the parent as the teacher, of course, but with the continuous exchange of positions making it possible for the child to experience the dialogue structure and internalize it for the benefit of its critical self-control abilities (and for later social interactions as well, of course). Thus, a hypothesis can be stated that there is a connection between the human ability to use signs about signs and thereby exercise semiotic self-control, on the one hand, and the ability of human beings to engage in joint attentions with other subjects shaping a shared world informed by shared thoughts in the shape of shared diagram experiments. The overall argument of this chapter, then, is that the gradual appearance of logic and semiotic capabilities during evolution forms the backbone of the increase of cognitive competencies from simple biology to higher animals and human beings. This appearance takes the shape of the ongoing articulation, subdivision and making explicit of a basic argument structure inherent in perception-action loops. The basic reason is that biological semiosis must be oriented toward adequacy truths for survival reasons, making biological cognition acutely dependent upon the ability to perceive and act in a way which is adequate to the environment, thus expressing the linking of quasi-propositions. This is not to say that issues like the emergence of communication, awareness, consciousness, emotions, episodic memory, human language and much else are not important. Quite on the contrary, in this framework, such capabilities arise during evolution in order to enhance, speed up, widen, and control the basic, biological process of argumentative cognition.

Chapter 7

Dicisigns Beyond Language

A very important implication of the Dicisign doctrine is the extension of propositions to cover not only a wide range of biological signs, but also a vastly expanded field of human signs often not recognized as propositions. Instead of taking propositions to be linguistic only, the decisive criterion, here, is that the sign has truth conditions due to its functional doubleness—a generalized version of Umberto Eco's classic criterion that signs comprise everything which may be used to lie.

This insight opens a vast vista, recategorizing and regrouping many human expressions, sign types and media which appear in a different light—particularly, it provides the foundation for understanding the centrality of diagrammatical reasoning inferring new Dicisigns from others in the medium of diagrammatical predicates. I already covered some of this ground in *Diagrammatology* (2007); in this chapter I shall highlight five crucial implications. One is the decisive role played by pictures and diagrams, both as predicates in truth claims and in reasoning directly manipulating diagrammatical structure. Another is the fact that differences which are usually believed to rely upon dualisms like perception-reason or image-language now rather should be analyzed as differences within the field of propositions, i.e. differences in the types of predicates used—so that a new taxonomy of subtypes of predicates appear as a major task. A third is the variegated range of different combinations of perception modes, sign types and media satisfying the functional definition of Dicisigns which calls out for investigation. A fourth is that the Dicisign doctrine appears as an important first version of Clark's Extended Mind hypothesis—which may, in turn, receive important sophistications from the Dicisign doctrine. Finally, language itself does not remain unchanged in the Dicisign perspective: rather, it emerges as a special diagrammatical tool, combining loosely coupled parts in order to serve as a representing and reasoning organ with potentially universal application.

Let us recapitulate the diagram reasoning doctrine—by quoting Peirce's most concise description of it (from the article "Reasoning" in Baldwin's Dictionary, 1901, 2.278): "We form in the imagination some sort of diagrammatic, that is, iconic, representation of the facts, as skeletonized as possible. The impression of the present writer is that with ordinary persons this is always a visual image, or mixed visual and muscular; but this is an opinion not founded on any systematic examination. If visual, it will either be geometrical, that is, such that familiar spatial relations stand for the relations asserted in the premises, or it will be algebraical, where the relations are expressed by objects which are imagined to be subject to certain rules, whether conventional or experiential. This diagram, which has been constructed to represent intuitively or semi-intuitively the same relations which are abstractly expressed in the premises, is then observed, and a hypothesis suggests itself that there is a certain relation between some of its parts—or perhaps this hypothesis had already been suggested. In order to test this, various experiments are made upon the diagram, which is changed in various ways. This is a proceeding extremely similar to induction, from which, however, it differs widely, in that it does not deal with a course of experience, but with whether or not a certain state of things can be imagined. Now, since it is part of the hypothesis that only a very limited kind of condition can affect the result, the necessary experimentation can be very quickly completed; and it is seen that the conclusion is compelled to be true by the conditions of the construction of the diagram. This is called 'diagrammatic, or schematic, reasoning.'"

Thus, the diagram in itself is a Dicisign involving a predicate presenting the relations involved "intuitively or semi-intuitively".[1]

7.1 Dicisigns with Picture and Diagram Predicates

In a certain sense, the claim that propositions may include non-linguistic elements, even to the extent of not involving language at all, ought not to be very controversial. The decisive criterion being whether the sign has truth conditions, numerous cases can be mentioned where the truth of a claim has been contested exactly because of the controversial status of pictorial evidence, that is, the predicate part of a Dicisign structure.

---

[1]"Diagram" thus may refer both to the full propositional sign (like a map with place names) and to the predicate part of it (like a map with the place names bracketed).

A couple of recent public cases in Denmark show how important controversies may develop around visual predicates of propositional claims. In 2011, the brain researcher Milena Penkowa at the University of Copenhagen was criticized in public, made the subject of critical investigation and subsequently dismissed from academia because of a series of irregularities in her published papers referring to laboratory findings in rat experiments. We should not unravel all of the details of this comprehensive case here, rather focus upon a detail of it concerning the repeated use of the same immunohistochemical image as evidence in several articles on different issues in different journals.

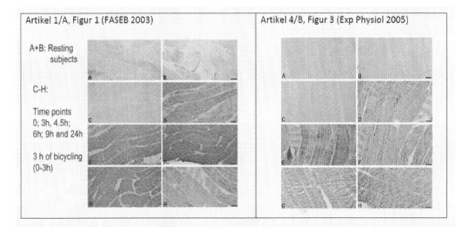

Figure 7.1: Illustrations from two different articles, panel H in a 2003 paper reappearing as panels D and F in a 2005 paper.[1]

---

[1] The illustration is from co-author Bente Klarlund Pedersen's answer against the complaint against her (2013), 3. The two illustrations stem from the two papers:

1) Penkowa M, Keller C, Keller P, Jauffred S, Pedersen BK. "Immunohistochemical detection of interleukin-6 in human skeletal muscle fibers following exercise" *FASEB* J. 2003 Nov;17(14):2166-8. Epub 2003 Sep 4;

2) Penkowa M, Keller P, Keller C, Hidalgo J, Giralt M, Pedersen BK. "Exercise-induced metallothionein expression in human skeletal muscle fibres" *Exp Physiol.* 2005 Jul;90(4):477-86. Epub 2005 Jan 7

Both of the papers have been withdrawn from the journals mentioned.

In the decision proposal of the UVVU against Klarlund, reference is made to the earlier decision against Penkowa pertaining to the same pictures: "UVVU fandt, at dette kan sidestilles med *uoplyst konstruktion af data eller substitution med fiktive data* [...] og derved udgør genbruget af figurer et alvorligt brud på god videnskabelig praksis." (UVVU, 2013, 8)—"The UVVU found that this can be equated with unreported data construction or the replacement by fictive data [...] and thereby the reuse of figures constitutes a serious breach of good scientific practice."

The picture in question was manipulated, turned, differently coloured and slightly differently cut so that it appeared to be different pictures referring to different tests, which prevented even Penkowa's senior collaborator, Professor Bente Klarlund Pedersen from discovering the fraud. Pedersen filed a formal complaint over Penkowa to the Danish Committees for Scientific Dishonesty (UVVU) which led to the Council deciding against Penkowa.[2] The important issue in our context is that this central part in the case aginst Penkowa relies upon a piece of evidence in the shape of a photographic image. As a sign, this image at the same time was claimed to be indexically connected to the experiments and to present graphic content predicatively describing experimental results in rat tissue—cf. the Peircean insistence that photographs may, given collateral knowledge, function independently as Dicisigns. The fact that versions of the very same image occurred in two different papers addressing different issues effectively rules out that it could possess indexical connections to both of the two different experimental setups claimed in the papers, addressing two different compounds, Interleukin 6 and Metallothionein, respectively (a signaling protein in the immune defense and a protein believed to be involved in detoxification against metals). This basic argument—seen from our context—shows that the investigative committee UVVU, making its decision, actually relied upon a conception of the relevant images as Dicisigns, as quasi-propositions.

A case with certain parallels in news journalism concerns the use of news-reel footage in TV news. On July 29 2007, the news journalist Jeppe Nybroe showed, in the state-financed Danish TV-network Danmarks Radio, footage of Danish soldiers on a driving military vehicle. Nybroe's corresponding voiceover text explained this was Danish troop contingents in the process of finally leaving Iraq after years of deployment. In reality, subsequent criticism revealed that the footage did not show this event but rather depicted the soldiers actually *entering* a Danish military camp in Iraq. As Danish troops were actually leaving Iraq at the time the newsreel was broadcast, the accompanying verbal claim was not, in the general picture, untrue. Still, the use of images not actually showing what was claimed in the text gave rise to a minor scandal—critics classed it along with a couple of parallel cases in Danish television with different misfittings between text and picture to form part of a general tendency of fraud in Danish tv news and documentary productions, and Nybroe was sub-

---

[2]Later, other professors filed a complaint against Klarlund Pedersen for her collaboration in the publication of the Penkowa papers involving forged data—the claim against her being that, being the senior researcher she ought to have better controlled the image analyses of her junior partner. This case has not yet been decided; it is not the contention of this author that Klarlund Pedersen, relying upon normal scientific trust between collaborators, is guilty in gross neglect such as claimed by the complaint against her.

sequently dismissed from his position. In our context, this case serves as an example of how images occurring as predicates in a mixed-media Dicisign context acquire their role due to the truth claim emerging from the characteristic, propositional subject-predicate coupling.

The issue of truth in Dicisigns involving non-linguistic material is not, of course, confined to the claim of single, isolated Dicisign complexes such as the cases here discussed might, at a first glance, suggest. Pictures presented may play a pivotal role in inferred claims reached by the practice of diagrammatical reasoning. In the Penkowa papers, thus, the differently colored histochemical picture of tissue played a role in the very argument presented as the core of the scientific results of those papers.

In these cases, text-image conglomerate Dicisigns were prosecuted for fraud. In certain cases, however, the experimental production and manipulation of such diagrams, forming the argumentative core of a truth claim, may even take place without the support of language. A major piece of evidence in the never-ending discussions about the assassination of President Kennedy November 22 1963 has been the so-called Zapruder film, a small piece of amateur footage filmed on location by Abraham Zapruder from among the crowd when the presidential motocade was subjected to shooting. No account of what happened could possibly ignore this piece of iconical evidence. In this context, it goes without saying that the Dicisign character of the film clip derives from the fact that the spatiotemporal origin of the footage stably connects it indexically to the fatal events at the Dealy Plaza. All of the three shots established to have been fired are documented on the Zapruder film, including the much-discussed second and third shots. The second shot, penetrating the neck of the President and prompting him to take his hands to his throat, later gave rise to puzzlements about the "magic bullet", strangely assumed to having hit not only the President but also, after that, the right side chest and left wrist of Governor Connally sitting in front of him in the limousine, finally ending in the Governor's left thigh, causing no less than seven entrance and exit wounds in total.

The third and fatal shot, prompting the President's head to move backwards, gave rise to suspicions about a shot coming from the front of the car rather than from the school depository in Elm Street behind him. Such arguments, in themselves, are immediate examples of diagrammatical reasoning.

An interesting recent development goes to show how such pictorial evidence may give rise to diagrammatical reasoning also in a more technical sense of the word. The computer scientist Dale Myers[3] spent the better part of a decade constructing a computer supported 4-D diagram of the Dealy Plaza area dur-

---

[3] Myers 1995-2008

184

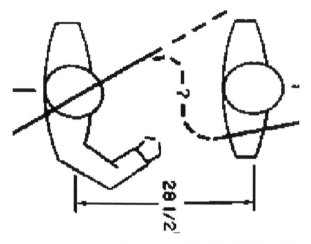

Source: HIGH TREASON

Figure 7.2: A Diagram experiment addressing the so-called magic bullet (from Groden and Livingstone (1990)). The bullet trajectories indicated by four of the entrance/exit wounds of the President and the Governor seem to indicate they could not be caused by the same bullet, as claimed by the Warren Commission investigation, hence the nickname the "magic bullet."

ing the decisive seconds of the assassination, based upon the totality of visual evidence available of the assassination environment: topographical maps of the area, the Zapruder film, other amateur film, newsreel and photographs taken during the incident, forensic reports and autopsy photographs recording the wound locations on the bodies of the President and the Governor, etc. Integrating all this iconical evidence into one 4-D spacetime-framework, triangulation based on the different points of view of the same landmarks recorded in the different documentations, allowed for a high-resolution reconstruction of the whole of the scene, while the precise dating of each single frame of the films allowed for a fine-grained temporal resolution of the events. Collecting all this pictorial evidence into one, schematic computer-based diagram allowed for a striking piece of inference. Taking this comprehensive 4-D diagram as a premise, it was now possible to draw the diagrammatical conclusion of observing the evolving scene from any possible vantage point in the surroundings with a high degree of both spatial and temporal resolution. We cannot here recapitulate all of the detailed argumentation Myers derives from his 4-D diagram. An important inference, however, pertains to the second shot whose trajectory appears much less mysterious given the fact that the President, at the decisive moment, leaned far to his right with his right elbow on the car frame.

Figure 7.3: Relative positions of JFK and Governor Connally, temporally corresponding to Zapruder frame 223 with bullet trajectory added from forensic evidence of wounds. (Dale Myers' reconstruction (Myers (1995–2008)), ©1995–2014 Dale K. Myers. All Rights Reserved).

Indicating the entrance and exit wounds on the President's neck and the entrance wound on the Governor's right back, the diagram makes it possible to project the trajectory cone indicating the probable route of a bullet causing those injuries (highest probability in the cone center, falling towards its periphery). This cone actually hits the famous window in the Elm St. school book depository. This result thus seems to dispel the alleged mystery of the "magic bullet".[4] In terms of diagrammatical reasoning, this result, based on the synthesized premises of all available visual evidence, gives as good an account as possible for the position of every figure in the area at every point during the events, with a margin of centimeters only.[5]

---

[4]If the Governor sat with his legs crossed, left thigh over right thigh and with his right hand leaning upon his left thigh, this might explain the additional three wounds claimed for the second bullet. Being below the car frame, the position of the Governor's legs, however, is not covered by any of the sources for Myers' simulation.

[5]As to the third shot, Myers' 4-D diagram also shows that immediately after the fatal shot, the President's head actually is briefly pushed forward, until it begins its subsequent stronger

186

Figure 7.4: A trajectory cone projected backwards from the relative positions of the wounds of President and Governor hits the open window at the Elm Street school book depository (Dale Myers' reconstruction, Myers (1995–2008), ©1995–2014 Dale K. Myers. All Rights Reserved).

In our context, the important principal observation is that the very core of the diagrammatical experiment—taking the 4-D synthesized representation of the overall layout of the crime scene during the decisive seconds and inferring the trajectory of the second shot to emerge from around the school book depository window—takes place without any intervention of language at all. This is not to say that the collection and synthesis of the visual premise information took place without language, nor is the claim that the conclusion, in order to be communicated, does not need to be reprhrased and expressed linguistically (as it is in the present text). But the *logical* core of Myers' argument is a

backward movement. This first movement, supposedly, was prompted by the impact of the bullet from behind, while the countermovement was due to the amount of powderized brain material leaving the head through the much larger open exit wound in the front, propelling the head backwards in the direction of the supposed shot from the school book depository. Disappointing to conspiracy theorists, thus, this detailed piece of diagrammatical reasoning based upon a meticulous diagrammatical synthesis of all visual evidence available, seems to support the hypothesis that no more than three shots were actually fired during the events. No conclusion, however, is possible on the basis of the diagram as to the precise spatial origin of the third shot—other than that it came from behind. The hypotheses about additional shots being fired by a "badge man" on the "grassy knoll" to the right of the motorcade would imply wounds penetrating to the left side of the President's head and are thus contradicted by these diagrammatical arguments. Myers's argument thus supports that Oswald was the only assassin (even if this does not say anything about whether he was part of a conspiracy).

pure piece of diagram manipulation with computer support.[6] Moreover, it is difficult to see how this inference, based upon the structure of a vast, essentially continuous predicate and granted by its bundle of indexical connections to the real event, could be exhaustively translated into any formal language of modern logic. The diagram here does not serve any merely heuristic purpose (as was the claim of anti-diagram philosophers of mathematics from Moritz Pasch, David Hilbert, Husserl, to the French collective of Bourbaki about the role of diagrams in reasoning) which would be better translated into a proof in a linear language formalism. Such inferences aided by computer technology seem to be better understood by the Peircean doctrine of deduction as being essentially diagrammatical. Just like the case with linguistically represented proofs, the truth of the conclusion of course depends upon that of the premises: if parts of the visual evidence going into Myers' synthesis could be proved to be fallacious, corrupt or lacking in some important sense, the conclusion would no longer have to be held true.

7.2   Types of Predicates

Predicates occurring in Dicisigns, then, admit of a very wide variety of types— and much of the discussion pitching logic and language against icons, pictures and diagrams (e.g. as different "Representational Genera", Haugeland 2000)

---

[6]Such reasoning directly in the visual material can be found in many different media. Brown (2008), against the tradition in philosophy of mathematics, argues that graphical diagrams may serve as proofs on a par with formal proofs (algebraic diagrams); Brown (2010) discusses the power of a series of ground-breaking thought experiments in science. A conspicuous example may be found in cinema. The piecing together and drawing inferences from visually presented information is part and parcel of understanding any feature movie or tv-series. The piecing together of shots to form a scene, of scenes to form a sequence, is an inference process normally not requiring conscious attention to the reasoning undertaken. In scenes involving interacting human beings, reasoning on the basis of perceived gaze directions, objects perceived, persons perceived, eye contacts, accepted eye contacts, avoided eye contacts, perceived eye contacts etc. is crucial for inferring the intersubjective relations of a scene, the changing intentions of each character, etc. These facts are well known under the headline of "eyeline matching" in film studies. Of course, such reasoning also crucially relies upon dialogue, but in most cases both visual and auditory information go together in the reasoning process establishing the understanding of a scene. The seamlessness of such inference facilitated by skilled mainstream visual media products may be interrupted by jump shots, suddenly bringing together seemingly unrelated material in two neighboring shots—revealing that such seamlessness is not a basic given, but rather the product of an ongoing reasoning process which may falter given the appearance of difficult or uninterpretable material (be it in bad productions or in aesthetically advanced art cinema. The seamlessness of ensuing match shots in cinema, however, is shaped so as to facilitate easy reasoning on part of the observer, thereby approaching the seamlessness of (most, not all) average visual reasoning in everyday life.

actually seems to address the issue of different predicate types rather than the supposed deep difference between logic and images.

Linguistic predicates seem to form one end of a range with very detailed, essentially continuous predicates like Myers' 4-D computer model or topographical maps in the other end. The full investigation of subtypes of diagrams is still a desideratum of future research; let us here focus upon the difference between discontinuous and continuous diagrams. A "continuous diagram" we shall define as one of which every connected part of the same dimension is, in itself, a diagram (up to coarse-graining). Thus, any patch of a topographical map is, in itself, a topographical map (of a lesser area). Any 4-D part of Myers's model is, in itself, a diagram of part of the Dealy Plaza area during the relevant seconds (not necessarily a very interesting diagram, of course). Obviously, the same thing does not hold for an algebraical or linguistic diagram (unless we severely restrict what could be counted as parts of such a diagram)—Haugeland notes this by referring the the "relative" and "absolute" characters of the parts of what he calls linguistic vs. iconic signs.

This property, of course, only holds up to granularity—parts of a size chosen below measurement uncertainty (like pixel or voxel size) cease to function as diagrams of anything. An interesting relation holds between Dicisign claims using such predicates and linguistically or algebraically expressed propositions. The whole of Myers's 4-D computer model can be conceived of as one large Dicisign granted by the continuity of its predicate and the unambiguousness of its object reference to the small section of space-time embedding the assassination event. Such a Dicisign directly refers to a whole continuum of objects present in the 4-D space-time slice which is depicted. For the same reason, such a Dicisign allows for the translation into an indefinite amount of linguistically expressible propositions ("The grassy knoll is to the right seen from the motorcade", "A shot from the school book depository would hit the President from behind" etc). In our account of Myers's argument, we have ourselves inferred some such linguistic propositions; many others, relevant or irrelevant, may be inferred, such as detailed claims about the distance between any two chosen points on various objects of the scene covered by the model.[7] The more sketchlike, stylized and simple a diagram predicate, the greater the relevant granularity, and consequently, the less the resolution into potential diagram parts will be. Another dimension which may vary is that of variability itself. Myers's 4-D predicate allows for the experimental Euclidean translation of objects across diagram space (even if only relatively few such translations are interesting such as those of the bullets). Tied to metrical space-time, variation

---

[7]This is essentially the argument made by Kitcher and Varzi (2000) with respect to a map sketch of Manhattan.

of object shapes is an experiment not allowed. In other diagrams, such variation is, quite on the contrary, required for the understanding and use of them. Diagrams depicting types, pure or empirical (e.g. the triangle, the elephant species *Loxodonta africanus*, the structure of the Congress, etc.) come with different, more or less implicit rules for the variation of the diagram so as to cover all possible individual instantiations of them—the identity of the type being determined by which variations will keep constant the type *vs.* which variations will change it (cf. Husserl's notion of eidetic variation). A huge field of investigations addressing different structures, objects, purposes of subtypes of diagram predicates is potentially inaugurated by the Dicisign doctrine.

7.3 Propositions in the Wild—Combining Available Signs into Dicisigns

It is surprising to what degree the widespread co-occurrence of pictures and words in propositions and quasi-propositions is often overlooked. To take some examples: paintings with a title or legend; art exhibitions with catalogues; newspaper photographs with an accompanying caption as well as accompanying article; spoken tv news accompanied by newsreel footage; feature films involving dialogue, narrator's voice-over, title sequence etc.; comics featuring speech balloons and onomatopoetic words indicating noisy events etc.; caricatures involving legends indicating the person or state-of-affairs caricatured; maps with geographical and other names indicated; books with illustrations; scientific papers with graphs, tables, matrices, etc. summing up empirical results or theoretical models; mathematical articles with figures; websites constructed from intricate tissues of images and texts, and much, much more. This omnipresence of word-image conglomerates is so pervasive that we should rather see the occurrence of pure text without any pictures—or the appearance of isolated images unaccompanied by any text—as rare, marginal special cases selected for particular effects.[8]

---

[8]Maybe the idea of text and images as isolated media is an erroneous generalization of recent cultural history. In early art, pictures most often were untitled because the context provided collateral knowledge of what was depicted—cf. most church art where the parish was supposed to know the relevant narratives and characters beforehand. Later, paintings most often were provided with titles; only modernism has, since late 19 C, employed as a specific aesthetic strategy the use of strange, alienating titles or "No title"—with the intention of creating an aesthetic riddle to the observer or prompting him or her to experiment with the isolated image predicate in order to remain in the space of the possible (or to fix reference for themselves). This strategy of isolating images has given great and stunning results in modernist art—but this should not lead us to assume this is the normal condition for the text-image relation. Here, the Dicisign combination of text and image is the rule rather

The reinterpretable subject-predicate divide of Dicisigns, however, does not fit one-to-one with the empirical media facilities of text and picture; rather we can say that the multiplicity of media makes possible many different ways of satisfying the functional doubleness of Dicisigns. Thus we can investigate the different combination possibilities of different expression types within the S-P framework of Dicisigns. Consider a preliminary combination matrix as the following:

Predicate	Subject	Examples
Text	Text	Linguistic propositions
Text	Picture	Newsreel of speaker on location, speaking about local news
Text	Gesture	Pointings acc. by description
Picture	Text	Painting with legend; newsphotos with caption
Picture	Picture	Photos with collateral information
Picture	Gesture	Pointings acc. by showing picture
Gesture	Text	Spoken proper name acc. by gesture predicate
Gesture	Picture	Photo acc. by gesture predicate
Gesture	Gesture	Pointings acc. by gesture predicate

Choosing prototypical means of expression like text, gesture, and picture, we may consider how they combine into Dicisigns. Some combinations seem obvious (like a picture predicate and a text subject); others may seem more rare but by no means impossible—like indicating the object by a picture and predicating something about it by means of a gesture (pointing to a picture of chairman Mao and circling your finger at your temple in order to express something like "Mao was crazy"). My main reason for giving this table is not to present a proposal for a final or exhaustive distinction between Dicisign subtypes—rather to indicate a first charting of the wide field of combination possibilities satisfying the Dicisign S-P structure. Further subtypes may easily be harvested in the wild—e.g. the combination of a subject diagram (showing by an arrow on a map which house you address) and a predicate picture (a photo showing what the house looks like), as in real estate advertisements. Adding further distinctions might yield a more fine-grained taxonomy, e.g. introducing a distinction between diagrams and pictures, the introduction of further sense modalities on top of vision, a distinction between representations depicting time or not (like movies vs. photographs), a distinction between

---

than the exception. A similar case can be made for the isolation of text without picture in modern literature; 19 C novels were often illustrated throughout.

purely mentally represented Dicisigns and Dicisigns dependent upon external support like physical pictures, printed matter, computer interfaces, what could be called Extended Dicisigns.

7.4   Extended Dicisigns

Psychologically, there are certain limits to the processing of complex diagrams in the imagination. Few people, if any, can memorize a topographical map close to perfection for use in their inner contemplation and experimentation, and even if certain autists are reported to be able to observe and infer information from much larger imagined diagrams than ordinary people, even their imagination will have an upper bound. This is of course what makes externally stored representations—in paintings, photos, books, newspapers, maps, DVDs, computers, etc.—so effective for many purposes, artistically, politically, scientifically, personally, etc. Working with such representations supplements the complexity of controllable, imagined imagery in individuals and thus provides important tools for the "extended mind"[9] relying upon externally stored information and external processing of many sorts for economical thinking and acting. Moreover, such externalized signs may be the co-product of several individuals which may collaborate on developing them, simultaneously or not, just as they may, in turn, serve as tools for even further individuals.[10] Thus, diagrammatical reasoning in the public sphere forms a central node for the development of science, politics, the arts—for enlightenment and civilization. Many scientific papers revolve around establishing the synthesis of empirical findings and theoretical assumptions in diagrams which formalize and integrate the central Dicisign chains composing the core of arguments of those papers, thereby communicating them to other scientists, challenging them to repeat and take further the empirical experiments as well as the ideal experiment of the diagram presented.

Andy Clark's recent development (2008) of his Extended Mind hypothesis (originally proposed with David Chalmers in 1998) may favorably cross-fertilize with the Peircean doctrine of Dicisigns and inference as irreducible to the mental support they may recruit. Actually, Peirce may count as an important early proponent of Extended Mind:

---

[9]Cf. Clark (2008).

[10]This excess of information in external pictures and diagrams is probably a basic part of our recurrent tendency to ascribe a certain subjectivity or even a sort of "life" to such representations, cf. Mitchell's (2005) question "what do pictures want?" or Bredekamp's (2010) notion of *Bildakte*, "picture acts" - see Stjernfelt (2012b).

"A psychologist cuts out a lobe of my brain (*nihil animale me alienum puto*) and then, when I find I cannot express myself, he says, "You see your faculty of language was localized in that lobe." No doubt it was; and so, if he had filched my inkstand, I should not have been able to continue my discussion until I had got another. Yea, the very thoughts would not come to me. So my faculty of discussion is equally localized in my inkstand. It is localization in a sense in which a thing may be in two places at once." ("Minute Logic", 1902, 7.366)

Compare Clark's "Parity Principle":

"If, as we confront some task, a part of the world functions as a process which, *were it done in the head*, we would have no hesitation in recognizing as part of the cognitive process, then that part of the world *is* (so we claim) part of the cognitive process. Cognitive processes ain't (all) in the head." (Clark and Chalmers 1998, reprinted in Clark 2008, 220-232; later dubbed "The Parity Principle" when quoted in Clark 2008, 77)

Let us sum up some basic developments in Clark (2008) in order to judge the possible contributions of the Dicisign doctrine: Chalmers' and Clark's initial idea involved examples very close to Peirce's inkstand: "Think of a group of people brainstorming around a table, or a philosopher who thinks best by writing, developing her ideas as she goes" (Clark 2008, 225). Peirce evidently was incapable of doing much thinking without pen in hand. Clark and Chalmers centrally address the manipulation of different types of external diagrams: "... consider the use of pen and paper to perform long multiplication (...), the use of physical rearrangements of letter tiles to prompt word recall in Scrabble (...), the use of instruments such as the nautical slide rule (...), and the general paraphernalia of language, books, diagrams, and culture" (221).

As to the role of perception, Clark generally emphasizes the notion of "Active sensing" (11–12) in contrast to the idea of passive reception. Often, problems involve the manipulation in the imagination of parts of the setup, and there is no sharp difference between such thought experiments and actually turning to physical manpulation of the very model itself—if one is at hand. Perception is also taken to be much more continuous with cognition than often presupposed; perception is importantly performing generalizations—in Clark's cautious wording, perception is "systematically insensitive": that is, sifting away detail—and thus generalizing: "... there is considerable evidence that perceptual experience is linked to specific forms of neural processing that are systematically insensitive to much of the fine detail of the sensorimotor loops themselves" (176). Compare Peirce: "Generality, Thirdness, pours in upon us in our very perceptual judgments, and all reasoning, so far as it depends on necessary reasoning, that is to say, mathematical reasoning, turns upon the perception of generality and continuity at every step" ("Lectures on Pragmatism", 1903, EPII 207, 5.150).

The activity of the Extended Mind is summed up in the Principle of Ecological Assembly, emphasizing a mixed-media approach to reasoning with little regard to the internal-external boundary, akin to the Dicisign doctrine: "... the canny cognizer tends to recruit, on the spot, whatever mix of problem-solving resources will yield an acceptable result with a minimum of effort" (13). Different such sub-tasks may be subserved by internal or external means depending upon the purpose and affordances offered by the situation. The wide fauna of possible Dicisigns combining different media and different internal/external predicates and references perfectly realizes this ecumenical doctrine of cognitive-logical tool use.

But this immediately implies the multiple realizability of the same cognitive task—the task's generality and its relative independence of particular internal-external strategies for its solution. This implies Cognitive Eclecticism: "computational, representational, information-theoretic, and dynamic approaches ... deeply complementary elements in a mature science of the mind." (24)—supporting a Dicisign-doctrine kind of multiple realization of propositions.

The integration of perception with cognition on the one hand and action on the other recalls Peircean pragmatism; in Clark it implies that the "Inner-outer boundary is both analytically unhelpful and computationally far less significant ..." (73). Indeed, this boundary is now so relative that Clark may attack the idea that representations with non-derived contents could only appear in brains as being due to "... anthropocentrism and neurocentrism ..." (92-93). The availability of a wide array of different subtask tools—different Dicisigns, as it were—implies an important criticism of supporters of restrictive notions of the Embodied Mind hypothesis. Clark critically remarks "... a tension at the heart of the program that is sometimes so easily (so unitarily) glossed as the study of "embodied, embedded cognition". It is the tension between seeing body (and world) as expanding the palette of opportunities for the realization of cognitive processes and mental states and something more fundamentally—but I fear mysteriously—fleshy: the idea that embodiment vastly restricts the space of "minds like ours", tying human thought and reason inextricably and nontrivially to the details of human bodily form" (204). Clark here senses a danger parallel to that of psychologism—it could be called embodimentism—taking specific bodily features to form unnegotiable boundaries for thought and thus impinging upon the validity of reason. The free combination of Dicisigns from different systems, using different modalities, different material support, makes evident the multiple realizability of many cognitive problems and processes, thus counter-arguing the threatening relativism stemming from the attempt at binding very tightly cognitive capabilities to particular bodily features of human beings.

Here, Peirce's doctrine of the relation of signs to minds dispenses with the subject-object dichotomy which rarely if ever appears in the received sense in Peirce: "... I do not make any contrast between Subject and Object, far less talk about "subjective and objective" in any of the varieties of the German senses, which I think have led to a lot of bad philosophy, but I use "subject" as the correlative of "predicate," and speak only of the "subjects" of those signs which have a part which separately indicates what the object of the sign is" (Letter to Lady Welby Dec. 14 1908, SS, 69).

Actually, the Peircean approach in this regard seems even more radical. Signs are not only external means scaffolding mental action; they define mental action through and through: "But as there cannot be a General without Instances embodying it, so there cannot be thought without Signs. We must here give "Sign" a very wide sense, no doubt, but not too wide a sense to come within our definition. Admitting that connected Signs must have a Quasi-mind, it may further be declared that there can be no isolated sign." ("Prolegomena to an Apology of Pragmaticism", 1906, 4.450). It is the very existence of Dicisigns connecting via inferences to other Dicisigns which constitutes a mind no matter whether conscious or not—such Dicisigns may be located internally or externally and often it is not easy to determine which is which:

> "Again, the psychologists undertake to locate various mental powers in the brain; and above all consider it as quite certain that the faculty of language resides in a certain lobe; but I believe it comes decidedly nearer the truth (though not really true) that language resides in the tongue. In my opinion it is much more true that the thoughts of a living writer are in any printed copy of his book than that they are in his brain." ("Minute Logic", 1902, 7.364)

In the last chapter we touched upon Peirce's notion of Hypostatic Abstraction and its use in self-control of thoughts as a possible candidate for the specificity of human thought. Hypostatic Abstraction makes second-order objects out of properties, relations, facts, etc—making it possible to address, analyze, control, and criticize them as if they were ordinary first-order objects. Here, Clark takes a similar path. When discussing Second-order Cognitive Dynamics (Metacognition) whereby "... articulating a thought in words or on paper makes it an object for ourselves and others" (58), Clark hypothesizes that

"... we are animals who can think about any aspect of our own thinking", so that he finds "... 'thinking about thinking' a good candidate for a distinctively human capacity" (58). Here, Peirce adds the idea that it is the very capacity of hypostazising an abstract relation, representing it as if it were a thing, which is the key to self-control: "The process consists, psychologically, in catching one of the transient elements of thought upon the wing and converting it into one of the resting places of the mind. The difference between setting down spots in a diagram to represent recognised objects, and making new spots for the creations of logical thought, is huge" ("The Critic of Arguments", 1892, 3.424). It is not far from this idea when Clark speaks about "... the ability to associate concrete tokens with abstract relations" (148)—you need only add the Peircean idea that this association is not an outer, arbitrary one but one which retains the abstract content in a new shape as if it were concrete.

7.5   Diagrams in Linguistics

Diagrams—being responsible for all deductive reasoning—span a wide range of media and instantiation possibilities in the Peircean view. Maps, graphs, algebra, matrices, schemata and much more form examples of diagrams facilitating expression of Dicisigns and inference by diagram manipulation. Importantly, linguistic grammar also counts among those examples. This might not appear strange, as inferences involving linguistically represented propositions form the standard source, in everyday language, of spontaneous logic formalizations, from Aristotle to our days. Still, the claim that language *in itself* possesses diagrammatical aspects is not the least unexpected result of the Peircean reorganization of the cognitive field. Thus, accepting this idea makes received distinctions like that between language and pictures cease to be definitive and become matters of degrees only.

The diagrammatical reinterpretation of language is an especially complicated task. The overall claim, of course, is that the structuralist doctrine of the arbitrariness of language is incorrect—mistaken because it takes as its prototypical example the relationship between the sounds and meanings of single words.[11] Motivation, in the shape of diagrammatically organized signification

---

[11] It should be added, of course, that structualism did not entirely subscribe to the arbitrarity hypothesis. As Cassirer argued (1945), a central aspect of structuralism is the notion of linguistic wholes (connecting it to field theories of physics and gestalt theories of psychology)—and its charting of such structural wholes in grammar, myth, narratology, may easily be reinterpreted diagrammatically.

seems to be present at many different levels in language. [12] The issue, of course, is which kinds of diagrams pertain to which levels of language.

A basic tendency seems to be that the distinction between grammar and morphology on the one hand, and lexical semantics on the other, roughly corresponds to diagrams pertaining to formal and material ontologies, respectively. Which diagrams pertain to the level of grammar? According to Peirce,

> "... if you take at random a half dozen out of the hundred odd logicians who plume themselves upon not belonging to the sect of Formal Logic, and if from this latter sect you take another half dozen at random, you will find that in proportion as the former avoid diagrams, they utilize the syntactical Form of their sentences." ("Prolegomena to an Apology of Pragmaticism", 1906, 4.544)

Peirce's argument here, of course, is that logic is formal *and* diagrammatical, even when it is clothed in the garb of ordinary language. The idea here is thus that grammatical forms make logical reasoning possible—which is why such forms must embody diagrams facilitating such reasoning. The immediate linguistic phenomena referred to are, of course, the conjunctions which are formalized as logical connectors in propositional logic (*and, or, not, therefore, if-then, if and only if* etc.):

> "That icons of the algebraic kind, though usually very simple ones, exist in all ordinary grammatical propositions is one of the philosophical truths Boolean logic brings to light." ("That Categorical and Hypothetical Propositions are one in essence, with some connected matters," c. 1895, 2.280)

Likewise, linguistic quantifiers which may be equally formalized (*all, no, some,* etc.) are the linguistic structures which make it possible for ordinary language to involve in reasoning corresponding to first order predicate logic. Peircean logic, however, does not stop here.

Very basic structures of grammar also pertain to this domain. To Peirce, the basic grammatical distinction on the sentence level is that between icon rhemes and their saturation by means of index rhemes to form Dicisigns—or, translated into linguistics, predicates (verbs, common nouns, and adjectives) and their saturation by means of subjects (represented by nouns, proper names, pronouns etc.) to form sentences. This distinction, in turn, refers to (but is not identical to) the ontological distinction between objects and their relational properties.

---

[12]This general argument is also made by Nöth (2008).

We saw how Peirce took pains to analyze the syntax of Dicisigns as, itself, an iconical structure depicting the fact represented. Thus, basic sentence grammar has a diagrammatical quality:

> "The arrangement of words in sentences, for instance, must serve as *Icons* in order that the sentence may be understood. The chief need for the icon is in order to show the Forms of the synthesis of the elements of thought. For in precision of speech, Icons can represent nothing but Forms and Feelings." ("Prolegomena to an Apology for Pragmaticism", 1906, 4.544)

Related ideas about the iconicity of syntax have gained renewed currency in the Cognitive Linguistics movement, with the outset, e.g., in Haiman (1985). Another main iconic—and hence diagrammatical—part of the sentence is the predicate, in all its linguistic garments, verbs, nouns, adjectives, etc. But this takes us into lexical semantics. Thus we have a basic distinction between the diagrammaticity of the conjunctions and sentence structure as such and the diagrammaticity of the rhemes—predicates—involved in it.

If we remain on the grammatical level, we may make the following observations:

1. Grammatical transformations have logical content—the active-passive transformation allows for the inference that if Peter beats Paul, Paul is beaten by Peter.

2. Grammar and morphology (distinctions between word classes) mostly, but not exclusively, concern formal ontological properties—while lexical structures generally account for regional ontological properties.[13]

Thus, the morphological distinction between *nouns—adjectives* will correspond to the formal ontological distinctions, *objects—properties*; *verbs— nouns* to *processes—objects*; *tempus* to *time categorized from the point of view of the present*; *numerus* to *simple number*; *adverbs* to *process properties*; *aspect* to

---

[13]The distinction between formal ontology and regional (or material) ontologies is due to the early Husserl. Formal ontology deals with general categories pertaining to existing entities across regions; regional ontologies to specified subsets of reality. Husserl himself outlined regional ontologies of physics, biology, and psychology (from above, as it were); some of his disciples like Reinach or Ingarden constructed elaborated regional ontologies rather form below, for social acts, for language and literature. The claim is that domains of reality are characterized by specific types of objects, events and modes of existence given by the ontological commitments of scientific results in those domains; Peirce makes a parallel claim when saying that the special sciences all rest on specific metaphysical assumptions which it is one of the tasks of philosophical and scientific investigation to make explicit.

parts and wholes of processes; *prepositions* to *relations*. Grammar may also concern a few (but still very general) material ontological issues: gender, persons vs other objects (pronouns), force dynamics (modalities, cf. Len Talmy's analysis of modal verbs in terms of force dynamics)[14], etc.

Thus, as maintained by cognitive linguistics, there is no sharp distinction between grammar and semantics. So grammar/semantics may not be mapped directly onto the sharp distinction between formal and regional ontology—but still, the overall tendency seems to remain that grammar provides a formal ontological framework with rather few material ontological additions—while detail of material ontologies is filled in by means of lexical semantics of single word roots of predicates: adjectives, common nouns, and verbs.

These ideas are, of course, related to Husserl's distinction between categorematica and syncategorematica inherited from the scholastics[15] and they have further correlations in Talmy's and others' distinction between open and closed word classes such that syncategorematica form closed classes (pronouns, conjunctions, inflection morphemes, prepositions, modal and auxiliary verbs), establishing in the sentence a general, topological framework presenting a scene—the contents of which is then specified in the single case by the lexical semantics of the single roots of the categorematical open classes (noun roots, adjective roots, most verb roots):

> "The meanings that open-class forms can express are almost unrestricted, whereas those of closed-class forms are highly constrained. This constraint first applies to the conceptual categories they can refer to. For example, many languages around the world have closed-class forms in construction with a noun that indicate the number of the noun's referent, but no language has closed-class forms indicating its color. A positive abstractive universal accordingly is that the grammatical morphemes of a language can represent an approximately closed set of conceptual categories, such as those for number, gender, tense, aspect, causality, and status. Excluded are color, and indefinitely many more such as food and religion—the corresponding negative absolute universal." (Talmy 2010, 755)

The picture is further complicated by the fact that subclasses of formal ontological concepts as well as many high-level material ontological concepts also

---

[14]Cf Talmy 2000, vol.1, 409ff

[15]Husserl (1970; 1984), see also Bundgaard (2004). The distinction has its roots in ancient Greek grammar: "syncategorematica" are words which can not appear in any of Aristotle's 10 categories and hence can not serve as the subjects or predicates of sentences. Categorematica or open classes easily admit for neologisms, syncategorematica or closed classes only rarely.

permit formalization and the construction of logical and diagrammatical calculi to chart them. To the former belong modal logic, temporal logic, higher order logic; to the latter belong epistemic logic, deontic logic, speech act logic, etc.– with linguistic equivalents in modal verbs, in tempus morphemes of verbs, in propositional stance verbs, in speech act verbs, etc. and all their derivatives in other word classes. At the level of lexical semantics, structural linguistics (e.g. Tesnière) and the cognitive semantics tradition (e.g. Fillmore) have investigated in great detail the reliance of nouns and verbs upon schematic— that is, diagrammatical—content, as well as their combination in metaphors, blendings, etc. (Lakoff, Turner, etc.)

The general upshot of these sketchy deliberations, however, is that, conceived from a diagrammatical point of view, language has two levels, one general, formal and vague, formalized in grammar and closed-class syncategorematica—and another in lexical semantics and open-class categorematica. The former level yields a framework of general diagrams on the grammatical and morphological levels; the latter adds material specification by adding more particular diagrams yielding schematic representations of particular kinds of objects, properties and processes in the shape of particular nouns, adjectives and verbs.[16] The former level has a restricted system consisting of few forms which are not amenable to quick linguistic change; the latter is rich and plastic, open to neologisms, on-line metaphors, blending and other linguistic creativity. It is this double character which enables language to be universal in the sense that it—unlike other diagrams—may speak about virtually everything, because widely different material ontological stuff may be inserted in the sparse formal ontological general diagram framework of grammar, and open-ended classes indeed facilitate the ongoing creation of new lexical material to cover emerging content. This doubleness—rather than the Frege-Russell idea of one reference domain which is all of reality—forms the reason why language is universal in the sense of being able to address any possible subject. This is also the reason why ordinary language—despite many claims to the contrary—is not tied to any specific metaphysics or world view. It is true that distinctions at the grammatical level are not without metaphysical implications, and it is true that the carving up of the world in linguistic paradigms at the level of lexical semantics may reflect aspects of particular world views—but the large degree of relative autonomy of the two levels indicated allows for language to reflect upon its own distinctions, modify them, deny them, and thus to house widely different world views. This is also the case because language is *not* universal in another sense of the word: it does not provide the only semiotic access to the

---

[16]See, e.g., the analysis of the adjective "safe" in Bundgaard, Østergaard, and Stjernfelt 2006

world. Different types of diagrams proper—in the shape of diagram tokens of mental imagery, or externally represented on a page or on a screen—constantly interfere with language and may correct language distinctions or claims, just as the opposite may be the case. In actual discourse, language seamlessly interacts with graphical, gestural, and many other diagrams which may easily be substituted for, e.g., linguistic predicates in Dicisigns. This implies that the existence of many competing representations of one and the same fact is the rule rather than the exception.

This follows from a crucial observation by Hintikka tied to his distinction between two strands in 20 C philosophy, that of language as a universal representation, and that of language as a calculus. The former claims language forms one closed representation system—and from this idea follows the idea that the limits of language forms the limit of the world for the users of that language, giving rise to various prisonhouse-of-language hypotheses (Hintikka 1997a.). A further corollary of this claim is the ineffability of semantics—because the only possibility of addressing semantics is using the very same language, leading to circularity. This leads, again, to the impossibility of defining or discussing truth, because any reference to extralinguistic reality is also caught up within the same language. Interestingly, Hintikka finds that this tradition cuts across the analytical-continental divide in philosophy, thus including not only Frege, Russell, Wittgenstein, and Quine, but also Heidegger and Derrida. The alternative tradition, then, involves Boole, Peirce, Schröder, Hilbert, Husserl, the later Carnap—and Hintikka himself. This tradition conceives of logic and language not as one closed system, but as a multiplicity of different representation systems with different degrees of generality, granularity, different aims and techniques. Maybe surprisingly, this representational pluralism, unlike the claims for linguistic universality, is compatible with robust realism: different diagrams, formalizations, and linguistic representations of the same object are possible, thus in a sense semiotically triangulating that object. Furthermore, the semantics and truth claims of one representation system may be critically assessed by another (graphical diagrams may be discussed in language; aspects of linguistics may be investigated in graphical diagrams, etc.). This effectively refutes the ineffability claim about semantics, making semantics the possible object of scientific study, and making truth claims of one representation the possible object of investigation by others.

The diagrammatical point of view would add to this picture that language does not even constitute *one* such system. Ordinary languages may not only embed highly different logics; they basically consist of two different systems, closed class diagrams and open class diagrams, which are only loosely coupled. To this coupling between grammar and lexical semantics on the sentence level must be added their trans-phrastic combination into different genres of speech and text. All this provides languages with an internal representational plurality giving them a plasticity already removing them from the simplistic language-as-universal-representation view. This also explains why non-linguistic representations may easily fit in and play the functional role of one or several of these subsystems.

The loose coupling of the open-closed class systems is evident from the fact that grammatical distinctions may, in many cases, be expressed also by semantic means.[17] What one language expresses by means of grammar, another language may express by means of semantic constructions—and one and the same language often has several, competing ways of expressing the same thing. Thus, the distinction between the two is not sharp and is subjected to a sort of rivalism even within one and the same language. Language, then, in this diagrammatical perspective, is not *one* system; rather, it is the loosely coupled collaboration between several rather different diagrammatical systems, conjunctions, grammar, lexical semantics, genre systems, etc. - therefore easily integrating gestural, pictorial, diagrammatical and other means when the actual online task calls for it. This very loose coupling of linguistic levels, then, also forms a basic reason why the relation between language and icons-pictures-diagrams-gesture is not a secondary, outer one. The same loose coupling as between language levels may be entertained with selected such levels and non-linguistic signs—and always has been. Because language itself is already diagrammatical, it easily mixes with diagrams expressed in non-linguistic media (cf. ch. 8). What keeps these loose couplings together, then, is rather that all of them contribute to the articulation of the ongoing chain of Dicisigns.

The isomorphism between basic structures in formal (and material) ontology, in formal logic, and in grammar/morphology, respectively, is a very important issue: analogous structures seem to appear in ontology (object-relation), logic (subject-predicate), morphology (noun-verb) and grammar (noun phrase-verb phrase). This does not imply, however, that these levels necessarily refer to the same entities. Neither the subjects of logical formulae nor the noun phrases of grammatical expressions necessarily refer to ontological objects (or to each other)—their analogy only grants that they *may* so refer. Because of the hypostatic abstraction device of nominalization, properties, relations and other ontological phenomena may make their appearance as subject nouns ("redness", "distance", etc.) and thus occur as logical subjects and grammatical noun phrases. Similarly, the logical subject of an argument need not

---

[17]French and many other Roman languages have a future tense verb inflection; Germanic languages like English and Danish do not, but represent future by means of a semantic paraphrase using a grammaticalized closed-class version of the verb "will".

appear as the grammatical noun phrase in its corresponding linguistic representation. ("Socrates is mortal"—"Mortality is a property rightly ascribed to Socrates"). Thus, this doubleness of isomorphism and independence between ontology, logic, and language enhances the plasticity of language: it allows for it to investigate higher-order-objects and their behavior, to articulate counterfactual, contradictory, ontologically unsound claims or claims confounding different material ontologies. This implies language is very far from forming a *mathesis universalis*—even in well-formed true claims we should not expect noun phrases to refer directly to first-order ontological objects in the world. Quite on the contrary, this is what facilitates language to effectively function as a trial-and-error *calculus ratiocinator*—language may be used to investigate the diagrammatical implications of very different hypotheses, fine-tuning linguistic representation to express even very complicated, strange and counterintuitive claims.[18]

This allows for language to speak about objects and their properties without 1) logical consistency ("the round square") and 2) without ontological commitment (breaking material laws: "talking stones"—supposing merely physical objects to be alive and capable of intention; mixing different (onto-) logical levels: "green virtue"). This makes language an experimental tool where different such combinations may be investigated in an experimental perspective. This, again, fits the idea of "fallibilistic apriorism"—if it is indeed the case that the *a priori* structures of different material domains are far from known in detail and, in fact, form central parts of the goal of the ongoing scientific investigation rather than its point of departure, we should expect language to be able to express many different, conflicting accounts of those ontologies and furnish the possibility for experimenting diagrammatically with such expressions. By contrast, if Kantian apriorism were correct, language would simply be unable to express propositions breaking apriori laws, because all our intuitions and understandings would necessarily conform to such laws, so that the only open issue remaining would be their composition in schemata. In fallibilistic apriorism, such schemata and their experimental combination in language rather form the royal road to the investigation of such structures.

Thus, a Peircean diagrammatological revolution in semiotics will involve the arduous task of reanalyzing language in terms of diagrams and diagrammatical reasoning. As indicated, the cognitive semantics and cognitive linguistics tra-

---

[18]Diagrammatical reasoning allowing for two participants taking turns in manipulating one and the same diagram also makes such reasoning the object of a pragmatic, intersubjective approach to semiotics. Pietarinen (2006) points to the fact that Peirce's diagram graphs involve such a dialogical structure with two persons playing a game trying to prove, viz. disprove a given claim (cf. ch. 6). With respect to the realization of such games in linguistics, this points to the interconnection of semantics and pragmatics.

dition during the recent 30 years—Fillmore, Lakoff, Johnson, Turner, Talmy, Sweetser, Fauconnier, etc.[19]—already provides many detail analyses of particular linguistic structures in terms of mappings and variations of schemata which may be integrated in such a diagrammatological linguistics.

---

[19]Among diagrammatical issues covered by this tradition, the following is but a brief overview: Kinaesthetic image schemata, idealized cognitive models, metaphor as structure preserving mappings between semantic domains (Lakoff/Johnson); blending and conceptual integration based on structures in "generic space" (Fauconnier/Turner); scripts as diagrams of semantic scenes (Shank/Abelson); landmark/trajectory diagrams in cognitive grammar (Langacker); force dynamics in modal expressions, linguistic attention distributions (Talmy).

Chapter 8

Operational and Optimal Iconicity in Peirce's Diagrammatology

In this book, we have unproblematically assumed Peirce's concept of iconicity as referring to the semiotic function of similarity between sign and object. For a closer look, however, two different conceptions of iconicity compete in Peirce's diagrammatical logic. One is articulated in his general reflections on the role of diagrams in thought, in his diagrammatology—the other is articulated in his specific construction of Existential Graphs as an iconic system for representing logic. One is operational and defines iconicity in terms of which information may be derived from a given diagram or diagram system—the other has stronger demands on iconicity, adding to the operational criterion a demand for as high a degree of similarity as possible and may be termed optimal iconicity. Peirce himself does not clearly distinguish these two iconicity notions, a fact that has caused some confusion. By isolating them, we get a clearer and more refined conceptual apparatus for analyzing iconic signs. This chapter investigates the two iconicity notions and addresses some of the problems they involve.

8.1   The Basic Iconicity Definition

The basic concept of iconicity in Peirce's semiotics and logic is presented in his second trichotomy of sign types, the well-known distinction between icons, indices, and symbols, respectively.[1] This trichotomy deals with the relation between the sign and its dynamic object, and the idea is that this relation may take three different forms. Icons function by means of a similarity between the sign and the object, or, as Peirce may also say, by shared characteristics between the sign and its object. Indices function by means of an actual connection between the sign and its object, either of a causal character (the footprint on the beach) or of a purposive character (pointing gestures, deictics, pronomina or proper names in language). Symbols, finally, function by means of a habit, in mind or in nature, of connecting two otherwise unconnected entities to a sign. It should be clear by now that the sign types of this trichotomy, just as is the case in the later Peirce's other ten tricotomies, do not correspond directly to distinct, independent classes of signs. They rather pertain to *aspects* of signs, so that pure icons, indices, and symbols, respectively, may be conceived of as borderline cases only, while most typical (and indeed most interesting) signs involve all three aspects to different degrees.[2] It is possible, though, in many cases, to point out which of the three aspects is *basic* in a given sign or a given sign type—so, for instance, diagrams being basically icons, and only secondarily (but still necessarily) having also indexical and symbolical aspects.

These basic definitions do not, however, state any clear criterion for the "similarity" between sign and object. This has caused some confusion. Is similarity detected by the immediate psychological experience of resemblance such as is often assumed? Or is it a relational property that may, in some cases, be difficult to establish? And which signs are subsumed by the definition of iconicity? Most semioticians will agree that pictures, paintings, photographs, movies, etc., have iconical qualities. In Peirce, as we have seen, iconicity also pertains to diagrams, algebra, grammar, etc. This issue, of course, requires a criterion for iconicity. This is what Peirce gives in what I call *operational* iconicity.

8.2   Operational Iconicity

In the basic iconicity definition by similarity or shared characteristics, as outlined above, neither of the two iconicity concepts to be discussed here become

---

[1]The trichotomy is the second out of Peirce's three major trichotomies, referring to the sign's relation to itself, to its object, and to its interpretant, respectively. In Peirce's more developed series of ten trichotomies from his later years, it is the fourth.

[2]Thus, Peirce sees such signs as appearing as aspects of propositions only: "... no sign of a thing or kind of thing—the ideas of signs to which concepts belong—can arise except in a proposition; and no logical operation upon a proposition can result in anything but a proposition; so that non-propositional signs can only exist as constituents of propositions" ("An Improvement on the Gamma graphs," 1906, 4.583).

obvious. They only appear when a further determination of similarity is attempted. The first, operational, definition appears in the discussion of the semiotics of diagrams, and it is developed by Peirce already in the 1880s, even if the full articulation of it awaits Peirce's mature philosophy of the years around the turn of the century.

Diagrams can be initially defined by reference to Peirce's detailed taxonomy of signs from his late period. Here, icons come in three subtypes: images, diagrams, and metaphors, respectively. Images are to be taken in a special, technical sense not corresponding to our everyday image notion: they are icons whose similarity functions by means of simple qualities only; color, sound, pitch, shape, form, etc. Thus, images are very simple icons, functioning by one or few such qualities only. The crescent shape as a sign for the moon may serve as an example. The simplicity of images is made clear by their contrast to diagrams. Diagrams are skeletal icons, representing their object as analyzed into parts among which "rational relations" hold, be they explicit or implicit. Such relations may be spatial, temporal, logical, mathematical, or any other type that may make clear the specific type of connection holding between parts. So, as soon as the icon consists of parts whose relations mirror the relations between the corresponding parts of the object, and the sign is used to gain information about those parts and their interrelations, a diagram is at stake.[3] In contrast to this technical notion of image, being much more narrow than the everyday use of the word, Peirce's technical notion of diagram is much wider than the everyday diagram notion: it will include any use of, e.g., a painting, in which the relation between its parts plays a role in the interpretation—and it will include also algebraic notations that may not, at a first glance, seem diagrammatical. Metaphors, to finish this trichotomy, are icons functioning through the mediation of a third object, for instance, an ancestral tree, charting family relationships in a branching diagram structure through the intermediate icon of a tree. The important notion here is the very wide sense of the notion of diagram that stems, in fact, from the operational criterion for iconicity. An icon is a sign "...from which information may be derived," Peirce simply says (*Syllabus* 1903, 2.309), and this is the basic idea in the operational criterion: icons as the only sign type

---

[3]It is important to note that Peirce's distinctions pertain to sign use rather than to the specific sign vehicles, based on his dictum "A sign is only a sign in actu ..." ("Truth and Falsity and Error," 1901, 3.569). Thus, the very same sign token may be used in some contexts as an image—paying no attention to what can be learned from the relation between its parts—and in other contexts as a diagram, focusing upon those relations. If, for instance, we took the simple crescent shape image of the moon, and performed observations on it pertaining to the relation between its parts—if we, say, measured the angle sizes at its two singularities—we would treat exactly the same sign token as a diagram.

able to provide information. This is why all more complex sign types must involve or lead to icons in order to convey information. Later in the same paper, Peirce adds that "An Icon, however, is strictly a possibility involving a possibility..." (ibid., 2.311), and in this enigmatic formula, the first "possibility" should be read as referring to an icon being a possible sign of everything that resembles it in the respect so highlighted (only an index may make explicit which object or class of objects the sign more precisely refers to—in the shape of a proposition). The second "possibility," however, refers to the fact that the similarity characteristics defined by the first possibility in themselves involve possibilities that are not explicit and that may be further developed:

> "For a great distinguishing property of the icon is that by the direct observation of it other truths concerning its object can be discovered than those which suffice to determine its construction." ("That Categorical and Hypothetical Propositions are one in essence, with some connected matters" c. 1895, 2.279)

I have earlier argued (Stjernfelt 2000a, 2007) that this idea constitutes an epistemologically crucial property of the icon: it is an operational specification of the concept of similarity. The icon is not only the only kind of sign directly presenting some of the qualities of its object; it is also the only sign by the contemplation of which more can be learned than lies in the directions for the construction of the sign. This definition immediately separates the icon from any psychologism: it does not matter whether sign and object for a first (or second) glance seem or are experienced as similar; the decisive test for iconicity lies in whether it is possible to manipulate or develop the sign so that new information as to its object appears. Icons are thus signs with implicit information that may be made explicit. This definition is non-trivial because it avoids the circularity threat in most definitions of similarity which has so often been noted.[4] At the same time, it is what connects the concept of icon intimately to that of deduction. This is because, in order to discover these initially unknown pieces of information about the object involved in the icon, some deductive experiment on the icon must be performed. The prototypical icon deduction in Peirce's account is the rule-governed manipulation of a geometrical figure in order to prove a theorem—but the idea is quite general: an icon is characterized by containing implicit information about its object that, in order to appear, must be made explicit by some more or less complicated deductive manipulation or experiment procedure accompanied by observation.

---

[4]It is an interesting fact in the history of science that such attacks on the notion of similarity have come from otherwise completely opposed camps, namely, the analytical tradition (e.g., Nelson Goodman) on the one hand, and the (post-) structuralists in the continental tradition on the other (e.g., Umberto Eco). See Stjernfelt (2000b) and Stjernfelt (2007).

Thus, Peirce's diagrammatical logic rests on the basic idea that all knowledge, including logical knowledge, indispensably involves a moment of observation. Peirce thus writes, as early as 1885, in the context of presenting his first, algebraic notation for first order predicate logic:

> "The truth, however, appears to be that all deductive reasoning, even simple syllogism, involves an element of observation; namely, deduction consists in constructing an icon or diagram the relations of whose parts shall present a complete analogy with those of the parts of the object of reasoning, of experimenting upon this image in the imagination, and of observing the result so as to discover unnoticed and hidden relations among the parts." ("On the Algebra of Logic: A Contribution to the Philosophy of Notation," 1885, 3.363)

This operational criterion makes the breadth of the diagram category within icons obvious. As soon as rationally related parts of an icon are distinguished, and the manipulation of such parts is undertaken, we perform a diagram manipulation, developing some of the implicit possibilities involved in the icon. A very important effect of this operational criterion of similarity is now the appreciation of iconicity where at first glance it may not be obvious. Peirce himself makes use of this operational criterion when arguing that syllogistic logic or algebra are, in fact, instances of diagrammatical iconicity. In what I believe is Peirce's most detailed account for the diagrammatical reasoning process in general, abstracted from particular diagram systems, he thus argues this point:

> "Now necessary reasoning makes its conclusion *evident*. What is this "Evidence"? It consists in the fact that the truth of the conclusion is *perceived*, in all its generality, and in the generality of the how and the why of the truth is perceived. What sort of a Sign can communicate this Evidence? No index, surely, can it be; since it is by brute force that the Index thrusts its Object into the Field of Interpretation, the consciousness, as if disdaining gentle "evidence." No Symbol can do more than apply a "rule of thumb" resting as it does entirely on Habit (including under this term natural disposition); and a Habit is no evidence. I suppose it would be the general opinion of logicians, as it certainly was long mine, that the Syllogism is a Symbol, because of its Generality. But there is an inaccurate analysis and confusion of thought at the bottom of that view; for so understood it would fail to furnish Evidence. It is true that ordinary Icons—the only class of Signs that remains for

necessary inference—merely suggest the possibility of that which they represent, being percepts *minus* the insistency and percussivity of percepts. In themselves, they are mere Semes, predicating of nothing, not even so much as interrogatively. It is, therefore, a very extraordinary feature of Diagrams that they *show*—as literally *show* as a Percept shows the Perceptual Judgment to be true—that a consequence does follow, and more marvellous yet, that it *would* follow under all varieties of circumstances accompanying the premisses." ("PAP", 1906, a parallel version to "Prologomena to an Apology for Pragmaticism" from the same year, NEM IV 317–318)

Here, the operational criterion is used in order to include traditional syllogistic reasoning within the field of diagrams: the structure of syllogism simply *is* a diagram, even when presented in the clothing of ordinary language. The same criterion was early used by Peirce in order to include algebra as icons, even involving icons "par excellence", in the manipulation rules of the algebra:

"As for algebra, the very idea of the art is that it presents formulae which can be manipulated, and that by observing the effects of such manipulation we find properties not to be otherwise discerned. In such manipulation, we are guided by previous discoveries which are embodied in general formulae. These are patterns which we have the right to imitate in our procedure, and are the icons par excellence of algebra." ("On the Algebra of Logic: A Contribution to the Philosophy of Notation," 1885, EP I, 228; 3.363)

In this very paper, Peirce develops his linear notation of logic that, unlike his later graphs, sticks to traditional algebraic representations—the notation that, via Schröder and Peano, became the standard representation of first-order predicate logic and thus forms the backbone of modern formal logic notation. But already here, he acknowledges at the same time that such formal representations must necessarily be diagrammatic, as measured on the operational criterion of iconicity. Elsewhere, cf. ch. 7, he extends that criterion to include aspects of linguistic grammar in the diagram category. This operational criterion of iconicity thus becomes a very strong tool for a Peircean in trying to chart the limits of iconicity. Unfortunately, Peirce never went into a further taxonomical exercise in order to chart the possible subtypes of diagrams—the only reference in this direction is a brief comment upon the diagram types of maps, algebra, and graphs, respectively ("On Quantity," ca. 1895, NEM IV, 275). In any case, the operational criterion forms a very strong argument in a Peircean diagrammatology—yielding the means of a logical similarity test that is immune against psychologism and any subjective similarity impressions or confusions. This broad iconicity and diagram criterion is not, however, without problems. One terminological issue is that the technical, Peircean notion of diagram is now extended to such a degree that the common-sense notion of diagrams vanishes in the haze and seems to constitute only a small subset of the new, enlarged category. Another more serious problem is that Peirce still tends to take such diagrams as *prototypical* diagrams in many discussions, generalizing diagram notions taken from them to the whole category of diagrams. This goes, e.g., for his distinction between corollarial and theorematic reasoning, distinguishing conclusions that may be directly read off the diagram, on the one hand, and more difficult inferences requiring the introduction of manipulation or new entities in the diagram (cf. ch. 10). This distinction is taken from the prototypical diagram case of Euclidean geometrical diagrams where the new entities introduced are auxiliary lines, etc. As Hintikka says it was Peirce's "brilliant insight (...) that this geometrical distinction can be generalized to all deductive reasoning" (1983, 109). The most serious problem, however, in the generalization of the diagram concept, is connected to the lack of a rational subtaxonomy of diagrams; namely, by which semiotic means should we now distinguish between, e.g., algebraical representations and topological-geometrical representations of the same content as, for instance, the graphical and algebraical-arithmetical representations of the same mathematical functions? If the same amount of information may be derived from such representations, they are, to the exact same degree, diagrammatical representations, and Peirce's diagram category offers no means for us to distinguish the particular properties of these different representations.

8.3 Optimal Iconicity

This problem seems, indeed, to lie behind Peirce's introduction of a second, stricter notion of iconicity. It is well known that Peirce, in the latter half of the 1890s, left behind his early algebras of logic, now preferring the development of graphical systems known as Entitative and Existential graphs. Especially the development of the latter was seen by Peirce himself as one of his major achievements, and they have been an inspiration for diagrammatical or multimodal logics of our day, because they involve "iconical" representations in two or more dimensions that differ highly from algebraical or "symbolical" representation systems of linear formal logic, e.g., in the Peano-Russell tradition. I place "iconical" and "symbolical" in scare quotes here to emphasize that the use of such words in this context runs directly counter to Peirce's operational iconicity criterion. For, according to this criterion, such representation systems are indeed diagrammatical and iconical *to the exact same degree*, provided they yield similar possibilities for extracting new information about their object. If the same theorems may be inferred from two such systems they are, on the operational criterion, to the same degree operationally iconical. And if we take Peirce's two finished systems of "iconical" logic graphs, the Alpha and Beta systems of existential graphs, they have indeed been proved complete and consistent representations of propositional logic and first-order predicate logic, respectively. So, in terms of which theorems may be derived from them, the Alpha and Beta graphs are just as iconical as propositional logic and first-order predicate logic, as developed within mainstream formal logic.

Peirce's operational iconicity criterion does, it is true, provide the strong insight that these results of mainstream formal logic are *not,* contrary to widespread belief, "symbolical" in the sense that they do not involve iconical representations. They may, of course, be termed "symbolical," understood in the sense that they employ symbols to a larger degree than Peirce's graphs (which, it should be noted, also employ symbols), but this term may no longer be taken, implicitly, also to mean that they do not contain iconical representations of their object. This is, indeed, a very strong and maybe to some extent counter-intuitive result of Peirce's operational iconicity criterion. But it immediately raises a further question: *What is then the difference between "symbolical" and "iconical" logic representations (examples: Peirce's algebra of logic vs. Peirce's graphs) when it may no longer be expressed in terms of iconicity?*

Even if Peirce does not explicitly pose the question in these terms, this issue is involved in his introduction of a second, stronger iconicity criterion. He does not introduce technical terms to distinguish the two kinds of iconicity. It takes place, however, particularly in his discussion of the adoption of different conventions used in his Beta system, which is equivalent to first-order predicate logic, so it goes without saying that it transgresses operational iconicity. While the Alpha system requires only a sheet of assertion, letters representing propositions, same location of graphs indicating conjunctions, and cuts representing negations, the Beta system adds to these entities further conventions representing quantifications, variables, and predicates. The whole machinery of these issues is introduced by means of a very simple convention. Predicates with up to three variables (equivalent to functions with arguments in the Fregean tradition) are introduced by means of the verbal/predicative kernel of the predicate written directly on the graph with the corresponding subject slots indicated by hooks ending in blanks to be filled in or connected to symbols for the subjects involved (nouns, pronouns, or proper names). In ordinary text, such blanks are indicated by blanks delineated by underscores, as in "_gives_to_" involving three blanks. In the Existential Graphs, similar lines are interpreted as "lines of identity" so that any further determination of the identity of the subjects of these blanks are to be added to the ends of the lines. The single piece of line of identity thus refers to a variable, and the line may branch in order to tie to different slots in different predicates, indicating that the individual(s) referred to by that line takes those predicates. The spots at the end of such lines are subject, consequently, to the second convention added. They refer, as indices, to the binding of the variables bearing the predicates in issue. Thus, the whole logical machinery of quantification, variables, and predicates is represented by these very simple means. If a line of identity abuts on the sheet of assertion (or on any evenly enclosed part of it, that is, by 2, 4, 6,... cuts), then this immediately indicates the existential quantifier of "Something exists that ..." and the three dots are then filled in by the predicates to which the line of identity connects this implicit quantification. Similarly, any such line of identity having its outermost end in an unevenly enclosed cut immediately indicates a negative universal quantifier.[5] Peirce is proud of this very simple sign of *Line of Identity* being able to perform so many logical tasks at the same time (thus preempting the Frege-Russell claim about the ambiguity of the copula): the representation of variables, their quantification and their predication at one and the same time. This is why he subjects it to an analysis making clear the indexical, symbolical, and especially the iconical aspects of the Line of Identity:

"Remark how peculiar a sign the line of identity is. A sign, or, to use a more general and more definite term, a *representamen*, is of one or other of three kinds: it is either an *icon*, an *index*, or a *symbol* (...) The value of an icon consists in its exhibiting the features of a state of things regarded as if it were purely imaginary. The value of an index is that it assures us of positive fact. The value of a symbol is that it serves to make thought and conduct rational and enables us to predict the future. It is frequently desirable that a representamen should exercise one of those three functions to the exclusion of the other two, or two of them to the exclusion of the third; but the most perfect of signs are those in which the iconic, indicative, and symbolic characters are blended as equally as possible. Of this sort of signs the line of identity is an interesting example. As a conventional sign, it is a symbol; and the symbolic character, when present in a sign, is of its nature predominant over the others. The line of identity is not, however, arbitrarily conventional nor

---

[5]In his algebras of logic and independently of Frege, Peirce had already invented the "symbolic" quantifier notion. Peirce's version later became, through Schröder and Peano, the standard notation of $\forall$ and $\exists$ (in Peirce's version Π and Σ, respectively).

purely conventional. Consider any portion of it taken arbitrarily (with certain possible exceptions shortly to be considered) and it is an ordinary graph for which [Figure 8.1] might perfectly well be substituted.

—is identical with—

Figure 8.1: Peirce's alternative graph for identity

But when we consider the connection of this portion with a next adjacent portion, although the two together make up the same graph, yet the identification of the something, to which the hook of the one refers, with the something, to which the hook of the other refers, is beyond the power of any graph to effect, since a graph, as a symbol, is of the nature of a *law*, and is therefore general, while here there must be an identification of individuals. This identification is effected not by the pure symbol, but by its *replica* which is a thing. The termination of one portion and the beginning of the next portion denote the same individual by virtue of a factual connection, and that the closest possible; for both are points, and they are one and the same point. In this respect, therefore, the line of identity is of the nature of an index. To be sure, this does not affect the ordinary parts of a line of identity, but so soon as it is even *conceived*, [it is conceived] as composed of two portions, and it is only the factual junction of the replicas of these portions that makes them refer to the same individual. The line of identity is, moreover, in the highest degree iconic. For it appears as nothing but a continuum of dots, and the fact of the identity of a thing, seen under two aspects, consists merely in the continuity of being in passing from one apparition to another. Thus uniting, as the line of identity does, the natures of symbol, index, and icon, it is fitted for playing an extraordinary part in this system of representation." ("Logical Tracts, No. 2" 1903, 4.447–448)

The Line of Identity in the Beta and Gamma graphs is thus praised for two outstanding qualities. One is that it unites symbolic, indexical, and iconic qualities. It is a symbolic convention that receives its general meanings within the system of conventions defining those graphs. It is indexical because it points out individuals. And it is iconical because of its continuity being an iconic sign of the existence/identity/predication/subsumtion relations between its indexical end points. This last aspect constitutes its second outstanding quality: it is "in the highest degree iconic." Here is introduced the idea of iconicity coming in degrees. This is why I name it *optimal* iconicity. In his development of the Beta system, Peirce places a large emphasis on the fact that the representation of quantification, bound variables, and identity by the means of lines of identity is *more iconical* than the logically equivalent representation of the same issues by means of the repeated identification of the same bound variables represented by symbols,[6] for instance, when he writes that "A diagram

---

[6]The issue of the iconicity of aspects and conventions of Existential Graphs is far wider than the alternative between Lines of Identity and Selectives that is chosen as the main case in our context because Peirce himself highlights it so thoroughly. The overall iconical motivation in the construction of the graphs is well indicated by Peirce when introducing the details of the graphs: "I dwell on these details which from our ordinary point of view appear unspeakably trifling—not to say idiotic—because they go to show that this syntax is truly *diagrammatic*, that is to say that its parts are really related to one another in forms of relation analogous to those of the assertions they represent, and that consequently in studying this syntax we may be assured that we are studying the real relations of the parts of the assertions and reasonings; which is by no means the case with the syntax of speech" ("Fragments on Existential Graphs", 1909 Ms. 514, 15). Shin (2002, 53–58) lists three basic iconical features of Beta graphs: lines of identity, quantifiers and scope. Quantifiers do seem to come naturally because the end of an identity line in an unenclosed graph is simply taken to mean "something is...," but it deserves mention that in his earlier formalization attempt from the 1890s known as Entitative Graphs, in many respects dual to Existential Graphs, the very same sign is taken to stand for the universal quantifier. Maybe it could be argued that a point in a plane does indeed more naturally mean "something" than "all." Scope seems to come naturally in the endoporeutic, outside-in, reading of the graphs (which Shin is otherwise out to dismantle), because the outermost occurrence of part of an identity line defines the scope of the corresponding quantifier, and more inner quantifiers are taken to lie inside the scope of the more outer ones. In addition to these iconicities, a basic iconicity in Existential Graphs is one of its very motivating ideas in Peirce, namely, the representation of material implication by means of a "scroll"; that is, two nested cuts where the premise is placed within the outer cut but outside the inner cut, while the conclusion is placed in the inner cut. The geometrical inclusion of the conclusion within the premise furnishes a simple iconic representation of the idea that the conclusion lies in, is inherent in, or is implicated by the premiss. Peirce proudly refers to this ("The Bedrock beneath Pragmaticism," 1906, 4.553, note 1) while at the same time complaining about the lack of iconic representation of modality in the Graphs, a lack he attempts to remedy not much later, cf. below. Another issue discussed by Shin—but not in relation to iconicity—is Peirce's distinction between logic systems as result-oriented calculi and logic systems as representations of logical thought process (a distinction she strangely thinks loses its relevance in graphical systems). Here, the former aims at quick and easy results, and a plurality of logical connectors and rules may be used to further that aim as expediently as possible. In the dissection of logical inference steps, on the other hand, as few connectors and rules as possible should be chosen, in order to be able to compare the single steps—a guideline explicitly followed in Peirce's graphs. In this connection, Peirce remarks that it is "...a defect of a system intended for logical study that it has two ways of expressing the same fact, or any superfluity of symbols, although it would not be a serious defect for a calculus to have two ways of expressing a fact" ("Symbolic Logic," 1901/1911, 4.373). This requirement—which Existential Graphs do not perfectly satisfy—is obviously iconical, demanding the extinction of arbitrary, that is,

ought to be as iconic as possible, that is, it should represent relations by visible relations analogous to them." ("Logical Tracts, vol. 2," 1903, 4.432) In quotes such as this, it may remain ambiguous which iconicity concept is exactly at stake, but the fact that Peirce considers alternative, more or less iconic, representations of the very same propositions and arguments represented in the Graphs, shows an alternative iconicity conception being considered. Consider the Beta Graph in Figure 8.2.

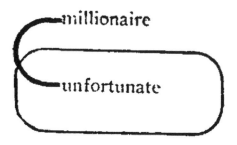

Figure 8.2: Beta Graph (4.569)

The graph reads "There is a millionaire who is not unfortunate"; this graph now will be more iconic than the corresponding first-order predicate logic notation of it:

$$\exists(x) : M(x) \& \neg U(x)$$

—already for the simple reason that the Line of Identity of the former uses one sign to refer to one variable—while the variable notation of FOPL represents the same object by no less than three consecutive x's. This is explicitly addressed when Peirce considers an alternative representation as substitutes for Identity Lines in Beta and Gamma Graphs (here "Ligatures" refer to systems

non-iconical, choices between parallel representations. Finally, Pietarinen's (2006 128–131) argument against Shin runs along these lines: her rewriting of the inference rules of Peirce's graphs gives us many more rules and connectors than does Peirce's own version, and so is less analytical and iconical than his (even if maybe facilitating easier readability on some points). In his defence of the endoporeutic, outside-in, interpretation of the graphs against Shin's attacks, Pietarinen highlights a further and very basic iconical feature in them: the dialogic structure, rhythmically changing between a Graphist and a Grapheus, responsible for existentially and universally quantified propositions, respectively, and thus responsible for taking turns in a dialogue where each of them manipulates the graph according to Peirce's rules. Pietarinen, of course, makes this point in order to facilitate his interesting, Hintikkan interpretation of the graphs in terms of game-theoretical semantics. Here, we may emphasize the basic iconicity inherent in this conversational structure of the graphs, motivated in the supposedly dialogical structure of thought, be it between persons or between positions in one person's thought and mind.

of Identity Lines meeting across negation cuts) under the headline of *Selectives*: "A Ligature crossing a Cut is to be interpreted as unchanged in meaning by erasing the part that crosses to the Cut and attaching to the two Loose Ends so produced two Instances of a Proper Name nowhere else used; such a Proper name (for which a capital letter will serve) being termed a *Selective*" ("Prolegomena to an Apology for Pragmaticism," 1906, 4.561).

Using this convention on the graph discussed, it would now appear as in Figure 8.3.

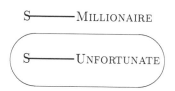

Figure 8.3: The proposition "There is a Millionaire who is not Unfortunate" expressed in Beta Graphs with Selectives (S)

Now, the S's in figure 8.3 only serve to identify the two pieces of Identity Line as referring to one and the same object—just as the x's in ordinary First Order Logic. In cases where many different variables are involved and the web of Lines of Identity in a Beta or Gamma graph becomes so entangled that may be difficult to survey, some of these lines may be cut, and the identity of the now severed and scattered bits of Identity Line may be secured by the addition of identical symbolical letters to the outermost end of the remaining identity line bits. When reading the graph outside-in, the reader must now take note of the quantification indicated by the location of that outermost identity line end, remember the letter representing the selective, and identify the more inner appearances of the same letter with the first quantified variable. Peirce explicitly and strongly regrets the introduction of these Selectives exactly because they lack the iconicity of identity granted by the continuous line connecting the different predicates that this Identity Line takes:[7]

"[The] purpose of the System of Existential Graphs, as it is stated in the Prolegomena [4.533], [is] to afford a method (1) as *simple* as possible (that is to say, with as small a number of arbitrary conventions as possible), for representing propositions (2) as *iconically* or

---

[7]Given the equivalence between Line of Identity and Selective representations, we might use this idea in reconsidering ordinary Peano-Russell-style formal logic—here, we might see the different instances of the same bound variable in a symbolic expression as connected by an erased identity line running in an additional line parallel to the line of the normal expression.

diagrammatically and (3) as *analytically* as possible... These three essential aims of the system are, every one of them, missed by Selectives." ("The Bedrock beneath Pragmaticism" [2], 1906, 4.561, note 1)

The substitution of selectives for the line of identity is less iconic because it requires the symbolic convention of identifying different line segments by means of attached identical symbols. The line of identity, on the other hand, is immediately an icon of identity because it makes use of the continuity of the line that, so to speak, just stretches the identity represented by the spot—and that is, at the same time, a natural iconical representation of a general concept: "The second aim, to make the representations as iconical as possible, is likewise missed; since Ligatures are far more iconic than Selectives. For the comparison of the above figures shows that a Selective can only serve its purpose through a special habit of interpretation that is otherwise needless in the system, and that makes the Selective a Symbol and not an Icon; while a Ligature expresses the same thing as a necessary consequence regarding each sizeable dot as an Icon of what we call an "individual object"; and it must be such an Icon if we are to regard an invisible mathematical point as an Icon of the strict individual, absolutely determinate in all respects, which imagination cannot realize" ("The Bedrock beneath Pragmaticism" [2], 1906, 4.561 note 1). The Peircean Selective, of course, does exactly the same as quantification with bound variables undertakes in the traditional system: the first presentation of the variable determines the quantification of it, and later occurrences of that variable in the logical expression remains under the scope of that quantifier. But it remains an offensive, anti-iconic representation when one and the same bound variable is no longer represented by one entity only (the line of identity) but is, instead, represented by a series of different lines of identity segments identified only by the addition of symbolical indices, or, as in ordinary formal logic, by the series of xs or ys, identified only by their merely symbolical identity. The reason why Peirce considers the introduction of Selectives at all is, of course, that in sufficiently complicated Beta graphs involving many variables taking many predicates, the network of identity lines may form a thicket hard to get a simple visual grasp of. The reason for introducing Selectives is thus heuristic and psychological, pointing to the specific visual faculties of a human observer; we might imagine a mind better equipped than ours that would be able to survey in one iconic glance any complicated web of identity lines without having to resort to Selectives. But the important issue here is Peirce's very motivation for preferring identity lines to Selectives in the first place: they are *more iconical*, because they represent in one icon entity what is also, in the object, one entity. This thus forms an additional, stronger iconicity criterion in addition to the operational iconicity criterion. One could object that Peirce was in no position to know the informational equivalence between his Beta system and what was only later named first-order predicate logic—but, still, his argument was implicitly aimed against his own earlier algebraical logic formalization (the first version of modern mainstream "symbolic" formal logic). In any case, Peirce realized that the two versions of Beta graphs, with identity lines and with Selectives, respectively, were logically equivalent, and the latter even in some cases heuristically superior. And still he preferred the former version in as many cases as possible, thereby indicating a criterion for distinguishing more and less iconical (2) representations among iconical (1) representations being equivalent under the operational criterion. We may indicate these two different concepts of iconicity by iconicity (1), referring to the operational criterion, and iconicity (2), referring to the "more iconical," optimal type of iconicity. Peirce's arguments for and against identity lines and Selectives display two different sets of constraints on logic representations. What counts for the Selectives were heuristic, practical issues tied to the psychology and aims of the reasoner—obviously a constraint deemed less noble by an avowed anti-psychologist like Peirce. What counts for the identity lines is rather an *ontological* argument: the idea that using them, Beta graphs more appropriately depict logical relations *like they really are*, thus adding to the pragmatist operational criterion of iconicity an ontologically motivated extra criterion. According to this criterion, if two icons are equivalent according to iconicity (1), the representation that is most iconical according to iconicity (2) must still be preferred—if heuristic arguments do not count against it, that is.

This implies that the addition of iconicity (2) to Peirce's iconicity doctrine is connected to his *realism*. It is well known that Peirce's realism developed over the years, such as is documented most famously by his own diamond example from the very birthplace of pragmatism, *How To Make Our Ideas Clear* (1878), to which he returns in *Issues of Pragmatism* (1905) in order to correct what he now sees as a youthful error. In his early doctrine, he claimed that if a diamond was formed within a bed of cotton and remained there until it was consumed by fire, it would be a mere convention to call that diamond hard, because it was never put to any test. In his mature correction, Peirce says that his earlier idea was nominalist and tied to a conception of being that was actualist only and thus focused upon the present moment. Now, he refers to the "real possibilities" inherent in the very concept of diamond, which implies that it is hard because it *would be* tested hard if subjected to the adequate testing—the hardness of the diamond is not only subject to testing but connected to other pieces of knowledge of diamonds' molecular structure, reflection abilities, heat development during burning, etc. While earlier only admitting subjective possibilities—possibilities due to the fact that we possess incomplete knowledge about the fact in issue (thus, it is possible that there are living beings on other planets, because we do not know it is not the case)—Peirce now admits that certain possibilities such as this also have a *real* character, laws of nature being the most clear expressions of such real possibilities (if I held a stone and let go, the stone would fall to the ground). Peirce's admission of such real possibilities from the latter half of the 1890s considerably changes and enriches his concept of Thirdness as well as his conception of the pragmatic maxim in terms of *would-bes*. Still, this realism was never really incorporated into his logic graphs. In Max Fisch's (1986) famous charting of Peirce's almost life-long development into a still more extreme—or consequent, if you like—realism, the last step, only hinted at in some of Peirce's late writings, was a tendency to see material implication in logic as insufficient. The normal logical interpretation of the implication $p \Rightarrow q$ states its equivalence to "either non-p or q." Of course, the traditional uneasiness with this interpretation is that, according to this interpretation, all cases of p being false automatically render $p \Rightarrow q$ true, in contrast to different versions of strong implication, among those implication in everyday language where p being false rather makes the implication irrelevant than true. For most of his lifetime, Peirce was a strong defender of material implication (under the title of "Philonian," as opposed to "Diodoran" implication, the names stemming from Cicero's reference to two competing Roman logicians), but Fisch is right in indicating that the mature Peirce expressed increasing doubts as to the possible nominalism inherent in material implication, admitting as early as 1898 that it does indeed seem strange that an occurrence of non-lightning should in any way support the implication that "If it is lightening, it will thunder":[8] "For my part, I am a Philonian; but I do not think that justice has ever been done to the Diodoran side of the question. The Diodoran vaguely feels that there is something wrong about the statement that the proposition "If it is lightening, it will thunder," can be made true merely by its not lightening" ("Types of Reasoning," 1898, NEM IV 169). One even stronger locus of such doubt appears eight years later, and interestingly it addresses the interpretation of

---

[8]Two years earlier, not long before the introduction of Real Possibilities in January 1897, doubt is awakening: "It may, however, be suspected that the Diodoran view has suffered from incompetent advocacy, and that if it were modified somewhat, it might prove the preferable one" ("The Regenerated Logic," 1896 3.442–3.443). But as early as the second "On the Algebra of Logic," Peirce states that "If, on the other hand, A [the premise] is in no case true, throughout the range of possibility, it is a matter of indifference whether the hypothetical be understood to be true or not, since it is useless. But it will be more simple to class it among true propositions, because the cases in which the antecedent is false do not, in any other case, falsify a hypothetical." (1885, 3.374,) Here, Peirce observes the problem, but accepts material implication out of simplicity (and not iconicity) reasons.

exactly the issue of Identity Lines in Beta and Gamma graphs. In order to follow the argument, we have to reproduce a fairly long quote:

"Second, In a certain partly printed but unpublished "Syllabus of Logic," which contains the only formal or full description of Existential Graphs that I have ever undertaken to give, I laid it down, as a rule, that no graph could be partly in one area and partly in another; and this I said simply because I could attach no interpretation to a graph which should cross a cut. As soon, however, as I discovered that the verso of the sheet represents a universe of possibility, I saw clearly that such a graph was not only interpretable, but that it fills the great lacuna in all my previous developments of the logic of relatives. For although I have always recognized that a possibility may be real, that it is sheer insanity to deny the reality of the possibility of my raising my arm, even if, when the time comes, I do not raise it; and although, in all my attempts to classify relations, I have invariably recognized, as one great class of relations, the class of references, as I have called them, where one correlate is an existent, and another is a mere possibility; yet whenever I have undertaken to develop the logic of relations, I have always left these references out of account, notwithstanding their manifest importance, simply because the algebras or other forms of diagrammatization which I employed did not seem to afford me any means of representing them. I need hardly say that the moment I discovered in the verso of the sheet of Existential Graphs a representation of a universe of possibility, I perceived that a reference would be represented by a graph which should cross a cut, thus subduing a vast field of thought to the governance and control of exact logic.

Third, My previous account of Existential Graphs was marred by a certain rule which, from the point of view from which I thought the system ought to be regarded, seemed quite out of place and inacceptable, and yet which I found myself unable to dispute. I will just illustrate this matter by an example. Suppose we wish to assert that there is a man every dollar of whose indebtedness will be paid by some man or other, perhaps one dollar being paid by one man and another by another man, or perhaps all paid by the same man. We do not wish to say how that will be. Here will be our graph, [Figure 8.4]. But if we wish to assert that one man will pay the whole, without saying in what relation the payer stands to the debtor, here will be our graph, [Figure 8.5a].

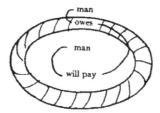

Figure 8.4: Peirce's Beta Graph for "There is a man every dollar of whose indebtedness will be paid by some man or other, perhaps one dollar being paid by one man and another by another man, or perhaps all paid by the same man. We do not wish to say how that will be." (4.580)

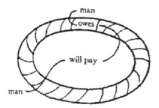

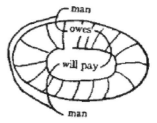

(a) Peirce's graph for "There is a man every dollar of whose indebtedness will be paid by one man who will pay the whole, without saying in what relation the payer stands to the debtor."

(b) Peirce's graph for "There is a man every dollar of whose indebtedness will be paid by a man who is the very same man who owes them."

Figure 8.5: Beta Graphs (4.580)

Now suppose we wish to add that this man who will pay all those debts is the very same man who owes them. Then we insert two graphs of teridentity and a line of identity as in [Figure 8.5b]. The difference between the graph with and without this added line is obvious, and is perfectly represented in all my systems. But here it will be observed that the graph *"owes"* and the graph *"pays"* are not only united on the left by a line *outside* the smallest area that contains them both, but likewise on the right, by a line *inside* that smallest common area. Now let us consider a case in which this inner connection is lacking. Let us assert that there is a man A and a man B, who may or may not be the same man, and if A becomes bankrupt then B will suicide. [Figure 8.6a] Then, if we add that A and B *are* the same man, by drawing a line outside the smallest common area of the graphs joined, which are here bankrupt and suicide [Figure 8.6b], the strange rule to which I refer is that such outer line, because there is no connecting line within the smallest common area, is null and void, that is, it does not affect the interpretation in the least ... The proposition that there is a man who if he goes bankrupt will commit suicide is false only in case, taking any man you please, he will go bankrupt, and will not commit suicide. That is, it is falsified only if every man goes bankrupt without committing suicide. But this is the same as the state of things under which the other proposition is false; namely, that every man goes broke while no man suicides. This reasoning is irrefragable as long as a mere possibility is treated as an absolute nullity. Some years ago, however, when in consequence of an invitation to deliver a course of lectures in Harvard University upon Pragmatism, I was led to revise that doctrine, in which I had already found difficulties, I soon discovered, upon a critical analysis, that it was absolutely necessary to insist upon and bring to the front, the truth that a mere possibility may be quite real. That admitted, it can no longer be granted that every conditional proposition whose antecedent does not happen to be realized is true, and the whole reasoning just given breaks down. I often think that we logicians are the most obtuse of men, and the most devoid of common sense. As soon as I saw that this strange rule, so foreign to the general idea of the System of Existential Graphs, could by no means be deduced from the other rules nor from the general idea of the system, but has to be accepted, if at all, as an arbitrary first principle—I ought to have asked myself, and should have asked myself if I had not been afflicted with the logician's bêtise, What compels the adoption of this rule? The answer to that must have been that the interpretation requires it; and the inference of common sense from that answer would have been that the interpretation was too narrow. Yet I did not think of that until my operose method like that of a hydrographic surveyor sounding out a harbour, suddenly brought me up to the important truth that the verso of the sheet of Existential Graphs represents a universe of possibilities.

This, taken in connection with other premisses, led me back to the same conclusion to which my studies of Pragmatism had already brought me, the reality of some possibilities. This is a striking

224

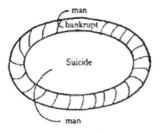

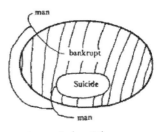

(b) Peirce's graph for "There is a man A and a man B, who may or may not be the same man, and if A becomes bankrupt then B will suicide."

(a) Peirce's graph for "There is a man A and a man B, who are the same man, and if A becomes bankrupt then B will suicide."

Figure 8.6: Beta Graphs (4.580)

proof of the superiority of the System of Existential Graphs to either of my algebras of logic. For in both of them the incongruity of this strange rule is completely hidden behind the superfluous machinery which is introduced in order to give an appearance of symmetry to logical law, and in order to facilitate the working of these algebras considered as reasoning machines. I cannot let this remark pass without protesting, however, that in the construction of no algebra was the idea of making a calculus which would turn out conclusions by a regular routine other than a very secondary purpose ..." ("For the National Academy of Sciences, 1906 April Meeting in Washington", 4.579-581)

In this long quotation, Peirce considerably revises parts of the foundation of Beta and Gamma graphs. Cuts no longer represent negation, but merely possibility—they only represent negation if they enclose a further blank cut (meaning everything can be derived from the contents of the first cut, evidently making those contents false). Furthermore, material implication is relativized: not all conditional propositions with false antecedents are true. References as relations are included as represented by graphs connecting actuality and possibility, evenly and unevenly enclosed cuts, making modal logic expressions possible referring to possibilities of actual existing things. Finally, there is the relation of identity line conventions and real possibilities that Peirce admitted in his metaphysics from the later 1890s onwards (cf. the diamond discussion). The "strange rule" that Peirce refers to is presented earlier that very same year and says in its brief form that "...there is some one individual of which one or other of two predicates is true is no more than to say that there either is some individual of which one is true or else there is some individual of which the other is true" ("Prolegomena to an Apology for Pragmatism," 1906, 4.569). Now, this rule will imply that the two graphs saying "if A becomes bankrupt, B will suicide," and "if A becomes bankrupt, A will suicide," are identical. Both are falsified if every man goes bankrupt without committing suicide. However, the two propositions are, evidently, not identical, A and B being potentially different persons in the former proposition, not so in the latter. Peirce's hasty and difficult reasoning at this point must refer to the fact that the possibility of A and B being identical is not a mere subjective possibility but a real possibility, given by the possible causal link between bankruptcy and suicidal tendencies, forming a real tendency in social life. But the "strange rule" exactly makes of such possibilities mere "nullities." The "strange rule" allows us to identify and disidentify A and B at will by the introduction or removal of Identity Line between them. The ontological correlate to this rule is that properties are taken to be independent: it does not have any significance whether two properties occur in the same object or whether they occur in different objects (cf. ch. 9). In both cases, it is true that there is an x having property 1 and property 2. But the ontological assumption of Real Possibilities is that properties come in clusters: some of them imply others in different ways, and the property of bankruptcy is objectively related, with some weight, to the occurrence of suicidal tendencies. What Peirce is looking for, hence, is a way of logically expressing a stronger implication than material implication, an implication expressing the dependency of properties, a sort of "ontological implication." This points to some important ontological issues. The British philosopher Barry Smith has pointed to the fact that superficial features of first order logic have led many analytical philosophers to assume simplistic ontological doctrines (Smith 2005). First order logic places all that is general in logic in the predicates—thereby giving rise to important misunderstandings. One is that property universals ("red") is given priority at the expense of kind universals ("electrons"). Another is that these property universals are conceived of as atomistic—they may be combined at random, leading to nominalism. It is this random combination of properties that Peirce indirectly addresses in his withdrawal of the "strange rule." There is a link, a "real possibility" connecting bankruptcy and suicide that is not addressed if you adopt the "strange rule." But is that link made evident by the mere giving up of the "strange rule"? Real possibilities, after all, is a matter of ontology, not of logic, just like Smith points to the need of keeping logic and ontological languages separate. The investigation of which universals and particulars exist and how they combine is an ontological task, not a logical task. What would be Peirce's response to this? The abolishment of the "strange rule" leads to the distinction between the cases of

$$\exists(x) : A(x) \ \& \ B(x) \tag{8.1}$$

and

$$\exists(x) : A(x) \ \& \ \exists(y) : B(y)) \tag{8.2}$$

—but it does not in any way give an analysis of the relation between the predicates A and B making (8.1) true. It merely removes a hindrance in the use of Lines of Identity from considering predicates occurring in the same variable and thus for considering the virtual Real Possibility holding between them. Thus, the removal of the "strange rule" could be said to motivated in general, formal ontology—but not in the material ontology which determines the relation between single predicates.[9]

This change in the conventions for the Line of Identity has further iconicity implications. The fact that it is the very system of Existential Graphs that leads Peirce to these conclusions is taken to count among the chief virtues of that system. While his own earlier algebras hid such facts as the problems with the "strange rule" behind "superfluous machinery" constructed with their (secondary) aim as reasoning machines, the Existential Graphs are not so constructed, but with the aim of displaying to the highest degree of detail and clarity every single logical step taken in reasoning. The heuristic efficiency of the algebras is thus contrasted to the higher iconicity, logical detail and simplicity of the graphs—this is an argument referring to the larger degree of iconicity (2) of the graphs, even if they may be equivalent as reasoning machines; that is, with respect to iconicity (1). This leads to a further reinterpretation of the iconicity inherent in Identity Lines:

> "The System of Existential Graphs recognizes but one mode of combination of ideas, that by which two indefinite propositions define, or rather partially define, each other on the recto and by which two general propositions mutually limit each other upon the verso; or, in a unitary formula, by which two indeterminate propositions mutually determine each other in a measure. I say in a measure, for it is impossible that any sign whether mental or external should be perfectly determinate. If it were possible such sign must remain

---

[9]The distinction between formal or general ontology, pertaining to all existing objects, on the one hand, and material or regional ontology, pertaining to objects of a specific field (physics, biology, psychology, ... etc.) stems from Husserl (the 3rd Logical Investigation). Both ontologies, in turn, are distinct from formal logic. When removing the "strange rule," I think it is in order not to prevent the expressivity of logic to represent connectedness between predicates in general—a formal ontological requirement. Any particular such connectedness—as that between bankruptcy and suicide—of course pertains to a material ontology, in this case that of human psychology, and falls outside of logic.

absolutely unconnected with any other. It would quite obviously be such a sign of its entire universe, as Leibniz and others have described the omniscience of God to be, an intuitive representation amounting to an indecomposable feeling of the whole in all its details, from which those details would not be separable. For no reasoning, and consequently no abstraction, could connect itself with such a sign. This consideration, which is obviously correct, is a strong argument to show that what the system of existential graphs represents to be true of propositions and which must be true of them, since every proposition can be analytically expressed in existential graphs, equally holds good of concepts that are not propositional; and this argument is supported by the evident truth that no sign of a thing or kind of thing—the ideas of signs to which concepts belong—can arise except in a proposition; and no logical operation upon a proposition can result in anything but a proposition; so that non-propositional signs can only exist as constituents of propositions. But it is not true, as ordinarily represented, that a proposition can be built up of non-propositional signs. The truth is that concepts are nothing but indefinite problematic judgments. The concept of man necessarily involves the thought of the possible being of a man; and thus it is precisely the judgment, "There may be a man." Since no perfectly determinate proposition is possible, there is one more reform that needs to be made in the system of existential graphs. Namely, the line of identity must be totally abolished, or rather must be understood quite differently. We must hereafter understand it to be potentially the graph of teridentity by which means there always will virtually be at least one loose end in every graph. In fact, it will not be truly a graph of teridentity but a graph of indefinitely multiple identity. We here reach a point at which novel considerations about the constitution of knowledge and therefore of the constitution of nature burst in upon the mind with cataclysmal multitude and resistlessness." ("For the National Academy of Sciences, 1906 April Meeting in Washington", 4.583-584)

All identity lines are now to be considered implicitly polyadic. The basic argument is that objects represented in the graph are necessarily not completely determined, which is why an open end of the Line of Identity should always be left (if only implicitly) in each Identity Line variable in order to indicate further, yet undetermined properties of that variable. An open end of the continuum of the Line of Identity would thus serve as an iconic (2) sign of the openness of the object represented. Variables thus being under-determined, their polyadicity implies that the entities referred to may have other predicates in common than the ones explicitly mentioned in the graph, thus potentially sharing real possibilities which are not referred to in the explicit graph. These musings on the status of Identity Lines are connected to Peirce's conception of the blank Sheet of Assertion on which the graphs are scribed: its continuity depicts the continuity of implicit truths that the users of the graphs agree to hold within the Universe of Discourse they consider. The polyadicity of the single Identity Lines thus refers to their forming part of that real continuum. Peirce never consistently revised the Graphs after the "cataclysms" of ideas proposed here, but it is obvious that the proposals discussed pertain to the overall idea of iconicity (2)—the attempt at making the graphs match general ontological structure to as large a degree as possible and to leave the system open for material ontological determinations.

8.4 The Two Iconicity Notions in Pictures

The distinction between two iconicity notions becomes obvious in Peirce's logic diagrammatizations because of the explicit difference between the proof power of a logical representation (operational), on the one hand, and the ontological depiction aspect of the representation on the other (optimal). Can this difference be generalized to iconicity in the broader sense? Consider the well-known fact that any pixelated picture may be represented as a picture, in print or on a screen, on the one hand, and as a linear sequence of digital information on the other. Like the case with linear logic representations and existential graphs, these two representations are informationally equivalent; the same amount of information can be derived from each, and it is possible to transform one into the other. It is a psychological fact pertaining to human perception that the image representation is far easier for a human being to decode. But this is due not only to the specific architecture and the special abilities of the human visual system (surface smoothing, contour sharpening in the retina, object detection, etc.). It is also due to the fact that, in the pictorial representation, object contours are represented in the shape of continuous line structures, object surfaces are represented in the shape of continuous plane segments—which is, of course, not the case in the linearized digital representation, where those informations are disseminated over large parts of the code. Here we thus find an analogous relation: the two representations are equivalent as measured on iconicity (1), but the image is superior as measured on iconicity (2). More fluid distinctions appear, of course, if we vary the granulation of the pixels; with pixel growth, we will find an inverse proportional change of both iconicities,

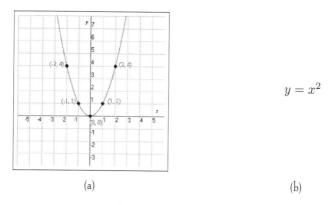

$$y = x^2$$

(a)   (b)

Figure 8.7: A geometric diagram and an algebraic diagram partially depicting the same mathematical state-of-affairs

and the difference between them harder to distinguish. Consider the simple mathematical example in Figure 8.7.

The graphical representation in Figure 8.7 and the arithmetic equation (**??**) partially refer to the same mathematical function. Still, they differ in many ways. The algebraic representation is universal and has unlimited precision. For any x, the corresponding y value may be computed, given the algebraic rules of transformation constituting the iconicity of algebra. And the computation is as precise as the input x value given. The parabola graph has none of these qualities. It only represents the values of the function for $-3 < x < 3$, and correspondingly $0 < y < 8$. And computation may be made with approximately one decimal only using the naked eye; maybe up to $\frac{1}{20}$ using a ruler or other measurement instruments. The graph, however, has other facilities. It permits to grasp the overall structure of the function in one glance, it permits to see the solution to the equation immediately; namely, where the graph touches the x-axis ($x = 0$), it permits one to see the differential properties of the equation (maxima, minima, saddles, etc.), in this case the function minimum in $(0, 0)$, it permits to judge the function goes to ∞ for x going to plus or minus ∞.[10] This information may also be derived, it is true, from the algebraic representation, this requiring the use of a bit of calculus. Here, the algebraic representation evidently is the stronger as measured on iconicity (1). But as to the selected segment indicated around the origin, the graphical representation could be argued to be stronger as to iconicity (2): the continuity of the func-

---

[10] This result depends, of course, upon the assumption that all of the differentially important parts of function structure are present in the interval chosen.

tion, its overall shape and its differential properties are directly represented. Thus, Peirce's unspoken distinction between operational iconicity and optimal or ontological iconicity may be extrapolated from logic representations also to the iconicity of diagrams and pictures in the broader sense of the word.

8.5 The Pragmatic Maxim and the Two Iconicity Notions

The coexistence of two competing iconicity criteria in the mature semiotics of Peirce raises further questions. What about the pragmatic maxim, Peirce's basic idea that the content of all conceptions may be exhausted by considering which practical effects those conceptions would be conceived to have under imagined circumstances? The operational iconicity criterion seems molded after the pragmatic maxim due to the reductivist action foundation of both: any aspect of an idea that does not have conceivable consequences, practically or theoretically, may be discarded. The investigation of possible practical consequences in the former case mirrors the investigation of possible theorems to be inferred in the latter. But this interpretation seems to leave iconicity (2) in a strange vacuum. If optimal iconicity remains without any practically conceivable consequences, it may be thought to belong to what may be discarded by the maxim as superfluous, empty verbiage. For is there any conceivable practical difference between Lines of Identity and Selectives in Existential Graphs, if the difference in formalism does not give any difference in terms of provable theorems? Of course there is the realist conviction that Lines of Identity may refer to real generals that may be easier grasped (in some cases, at least) by identity lines than by Selectives. And, of course, there is the practical issue that, in complicated cases, Selectives may facilitate an easier use of the graphs than Lines of Identity. But, at the same time, the amount of theorems, of new information, accessible by the two means are supposed to be exactly the same. Maybe this difference corresponds to two different readings of the pragmatic maxim, cf. Peirce's own two readings without and with the hardness of the untested diamond, respectively. The untested diamond hardness and the realist interpretation of the pragmatic maxim seem to correspond to the addition of iconicity (2) as a criterion with its possibilities for distinguishing between more and less iconical representations in addition to the provision of new information, while the earlier, nominalist version of the maxim where it charts testable regularities and nothing more corresponds to purely operational iconicity (1). Just like existence is no predicate, it seems like Peircean reality is no predicate neither (but rather the relation between several predicates), and the addition of reality does not add to the amount of information that may be taken out of any given predicate. But Iconicity (2) may add, in some cases, to the heuristics of working with representation systems, just as it presents the same information in an ontologically more valid form, so to speak. If that interpretation is correct, then the introduction of iconicity (2) as a criterion constitutes yet another step in Peirce's lifelong movement towards realism, as charted by Max Fisch (1986). In that case, Iconicity (2) is tightly interwoven with the step leading from the Real Possibilities introduced in the latter half of the 1890s as the central mode of Thirdness, on the one hand, and, on the other hand, to Peirce's last and most realist position in search for stronger, ontological implication constraints than material implication in the years after 1900. Doing so, it constitutes a realist step in the solution of an ontological problem of natural classes which preoccupied the young Peirce already 35 years earlier.

Chapter 9

Cows, Red Cows, and Red Herrings

9.1 A Graphical Experiment Addressing Natural Classes in the Young Peirce

Peirce's unpublished manuscript pages contain numerous drawings, drafts and illustrations—ranging from margin doodles to technical diagrams integrated into the argument structure of the papers. In the difficult task of cataloguing and indexing this large inventory of drawings, the basic methodological rule that must be followed (if possible) is to interpret the single drawing in the context of the paper with which it occurs (if it does so at all). This is not to presume that all drawings serve illustration purposes for the accompanying text—many drawings obviously do not—but the method may safeguard us against erroneously overlooking such a connection where one does exist. In this paper, I shall attempt to interpret the puzzling sheets containing 99 small drawings (in fact 98, plus one deletion) which accompany Ms. 725. The manuscript does not explicitly refer to these drawings at all (unlike some preceding illustrations also found at the end of the manuscript), and their presence at the end of the manuscript might, at first glance, be taken as a coincidence.[1]

---

[1] Benjamin Meyer-Krahmer has gone so far as to propose that these drawings are not by Peirce but have been added by another hand (personal communication). As becomes evident, my interpretation argues against this idea by taking them to be a graphical experiment prompted by the claims of the preceding paper. The argument that they were added by another hand seems to draw on the fact that similar drawings do not appear elsewhere in Peirce's unpublished papers. These papers, however, clearly establish Peirce as a skilled

Ms. 725 is undated in the Robin catalogue of Peirce's manuscripts—it is handwritten and accompanied by the cutout pages of the printed journal version of his early text "On Logical Extension and Comprehension" from the *Proceedings of the American Academy of Arts and Sciences* (here referred to as OLEC).[2] Apparently, the handwritten parts of Ms. 725 were not composed much later,[3] containing comments and additions to the published paper, but they address issues which continued to occupy Peirce up to the end of his career.[4]

Both texts—the printed pages and the additional handwritten margin comments and text—address the classical logical issues of extension versus comprehension, reference and meaning.[5] In the OLEC Peirce lists the traditional renderings of this opposition:

Extension	Intension	
Extension	Comprehension	(the Port-Royal Logic)
Umfang	Inhalt	("the Germans")
Scope	Force	(Augustus de Morgan)
Denotation	Connotation	(John Stuart Mill)
Breadth	Depth	(William Hamilton)

draughtsman, which is why there seems to be no reason he could not have made them. As there is no known evidence in favor of a different author, this conclusion seems less likely than the simpler assumption that he drew them himself.

[2]The text was presented as a paper on Nov. 13th 1867 and was subsequently published in *The Proceedings of the American Academy of Arts and Sciences* 7, 416–32 (2.391–426). In the version contained in the *Writings* (W 2, 70–86) the title of the paper title is given as "Upon Logical Comprehension and Extension".

[3]The *Writings* vol. 2 dates Ms. 725 to the spring of 1870, and according to André de Tienne of the Peirce Edition Project, the handwriting of the Ms. "leaves no doubt" that its dating must be ca. 1870 (personal communication). The version of Ms. 725 published in the notes of *Writings* vol. 2 omits the drawings after the text; the three groups of circles are mentioned, and the drawings discussed in this chapter are described as follows: "The remaining four pages of the notebook are covered with what appear to be neatly drawn doodles." (W 2, 512)

[4]For instance, the *Grand Logic* of 1893 (MS 421), Peirce's contributions to *Baldwin's Dictionary* (1901), such as the entry on "Kind" (6.384) and the unpublished entry on "Information" (Ms. 1147), the discussions of science and natural classes in the *Minute Logic* of 1902 (CP 1.203ff; EP II 115ff), the Lowell Lectures of 1903 (Ms. 469), or the unfinished "Rationale of Reasoning" of 1910 (Ms. 664).

[5]Not much has been written about these early theories of Peirce's; they are not dealt with in the large Nathan Houser/Don D. Roberts/James van Evra (eds.): *Studies in the Logic of Charles Sanders Peirce*, Bloomington 1997. Pietarinen (2006), 345–369 treats them as forerunners of Peirce's diagrammatical logic; de Tienne (n.d.) provides an introduction and discussion.

Peirce adopts Hamilton's terminology (which he intermittently uses until late in his career). He immediately argues against the widespread conviction that there is, in general, an inverse proportionality between the two such that

$$\text{Breadth} \times \text{Depth} = k$$

where k is a constant—implying that the larger the extension is, the smaller the intension will be, and vice versa. This idea, of course, is easy to obtain if one restricts one's focus to the Breadth and Depth of single terms only, where, e. g., a term like "lion" has smaller extension and larger intension than the term "animal". "Lion" adds further semantic content as compared to "animal" and consequently refers to a smaller group of individuals. Peirce, however, does not consider the logic of terms to be basic, but rather the Dicisign level of propositional and predicate logic. The issue of breadth and depth thus points to the double structure of what he later called the Dicisign: the indexical sign which points out the extension, and the iconical sign which provides the intension. Subject and predicate, index and icon, breadth and depth thus characterize the two aspects of the proposition, and each of the two may, to some extent, vary independently of the other within the Dicisign. This obviously precludes the idea of inverse proportionality between the two within the framework of the proposition. An isolated term, in this perspective, is merely the predicate part of a proposition left unsaturated by indices, which is why its extension may not vary independently. The different roles of the two aspects are indicated by the claim that "Nominantur singularia, sed universalia significantur", as Peirce liked to say, quoting John of Salisbury (e.g., in "Signification", 1901, 2.434): The extension aspect refers to singular objects, while the intension aspect signifies universal aspects of those objects. The proposition, therefore, is only informative in case it possesses both extension and intension.[6] If no object or set of objects is referred to, or if no description is put forward about an object indicated, the proposition remains empty as to information. A proposition only informs us about an object if neither B nor D is empty. If there is no reference, the proposition shrinks to a mere unsaturated predicate; if there is no signification, it shrinks to a mere indexical pointing out of an object. In the OLEC, this gives Peirce the idea that, far from being a constant, Breadth $\times$ Depth gives

---

[6] Peirce later, in 1893, adds the following generalization: "I restricted myself to *terms,* because at the time this chapter was first written (1867), I had not remarked that the whole doctrine of breadth and depth was equally applicable to *propositions* and to *arguments*. The breadth of a proposition is the aggregate of possible states of things in which it is true; the breadth of an argument is the aggregate of possible cases to which it applies. The depth of a proposition is the total of fact which it asserts of the state of things to which it is applied; the depth of an argument is the importance of the conclusions which it draws. In fact, every proposition and every argument can be regarded as a term" (2.407n).

a measure of the amount of information inherent in a proposition—the result
of a multiplication being zero if any one of the multiplicands is zero. In the
geometrical metaphor adopted from Hamilton, Peirce consequently names this
information concept "Area":

$$\text{Breadth} \times \text{Depth} = \text{Area} = \text{Information}$$

This formula is a formalization of the common sense intuition that if a sign says
a lot of things about a lot of objects, it contains much information, but it does
not yield to explicit quantification because of the issue of quantifying intensions
(depths). A quarter of a century later, in the "Kaina Stoicheia" (1904), Peirce
retains this theory: "Besides the logical depth and breadth, I have proposed (in
1867) the terms *information* and *area* to denote the total fact (true or false)
that in a given state of knowledge a sign embodies" (EP II, 305). This notion
of the information presented by a proposition is thus related to the fact which
determines the truth of that proposition. In chapter 3, we discussed Peirce's
theory of *facts* which belongs to the same tradition as the Austrian notion of
Sachverhalt developed by Stumpf and made famous by Wittgenstein: "What
we call a 'fact' is something having the structure of a proposition but supposed
to be an element of the very universe itself" (EP II, 304). According to this,
facts are the truth-makers of propositions, and the information contained by
a proposition is information about that fact. We remarked that Peirce thus
distinguishes the fact—or "state-of-things", as he sometimes calls it—from the
reference of the proposition. The latter pertains to the object which is pointed
out by the reference part of the proposition—but that object is not the truth-
maker. A false proposition may succeed in pointing out an extension, but fail
to connect it with a correct intensional description. The truth-maker, then, is
the fact comprising both the object and the property described in the intension
part of the proposition. Certain facts, now, pertain to the existence of natural
classes—cf. Peirce's "scholastic realism" which claims the reality of (some) universals. This "extreme realism", however, does not imply that these universals
are necessarily exhaustively defined.[7] Quite to the contrary, a natural class
has "other properties than those which are implied in its definition" (W 1418,
1866).[8] This distinction between explicit and implicit information was going

---

[7]Already in 1866, Peirce writes that "...it must be admitted that there are exceptions to
almost every rule. Thus many of the characters which seem to belong to a class universally
only belong to a part of it" (W 1:419).

[8]This claim may sound as if any concept had one exclusive definition. Peirce's idea is
rather that a concept may be defined in any number of ways, providing the definition satisfies
the aim of picking out the right extension. Definitions are thus taken to be reference tools,
while the closer investigation of the properties characterizing a class is left for a higher grade
of clearness (*How to Make our Ideas Clear*, 1878). "Nonfeathered biped" may thus be a

to grow over the years to occupy a central place in Peirce's philosophy, the mature Peirce seeing icons as signs that allow the discovery of information about the sign's object (cf. previous ch.), although this information is not explicitly stated in the sign. This is why diagrammatic icons become the designated tool for discovering such properties that are not implied by the definition itself (cf. Peirce's concept of "theorematic reasoning with diagrams"[9]).

The investigation of the OLEC into extension, intension, information, facts, and natural classes now constitutes the starting point of Ms. 725—the handwritten addenda to the OLEC continue this discussion. The first, handwritten parts of Ms. 725 are marginal notes to the OLEC copy and begin with a reference to Aristotle: "Aristotle remarks in several places that genera (and differences) may be regarded as parts of species and species as parts of genera," followed by the relevant quote from the *Metaphysics*. This creates the frame for his comments—how is it possible, intensionally, for genera to be subgroups of species, while, conversely, species extensionally form a subgroup of genera? The first half of the handwritten text mostly consists of scattered, commented quotes from the classics, the Schoolmen, Descartes, Leibniz, etc., which address the extension-intension issue, along with comments on his own text, placed directly on the margins of the cutout pages from the OLEC. This continues until the last half of Ms. 725, which directly precedes the drawings and explicitly presents a draft for a new, additional sixth paragraph of the 1867 paper.[10] Here Peirce enters into a discussion of Mill's conception of natural kinds. What follows is the entirety of the short text from Ms. 725 that is intended as an additional paragraph, and which is succeeded by drawings of the three circle diagrams referred to in the text.

9.2   The New Paragraph "On Natural Classification"

"Classes are divided into natural and artificial. This doctrine which is the essence of the doctrine of the Predicables and which was implied in the system of scholastic realism, which indeed it may be said to constitute, was thought of little moment by the nominalists and finally slipped out of the logical treatises. But the students of Botany and Zoölogy revived the conception, and have

---

successful definition of human beings in a certain Universe of Discourse without for that reason saying much of the essential differences between humans and other higher animals.

[9]See next chapter and Stjernfelt: *Diagrammatology* (2007), ch. 4.

[10]Actually, the paragraph number ought to have been 7 rather than 6, because the printed version of the OLEC erroneously has two §5s, the latter of which properly should have been §6, so the hand-written addendum, in turn, should have been §7.

reëstablished a doctrine of natural classes very similar to that of Aristotle, especially in the feature of ranging classes in a sort of hierarchy. The doctrine of a hierarchy of classes is contained in the second antepredicamental rule: τῶν ἑτέρων γενῶν καὶ μὴὑπ᾽ ἀλλήλα τετανμένων ετεραι τῶειδει καὶ αἱ διαφοαί, οἱον ζώον καί ἐπιστήμζ [11] "The differences of different & not subordinated genera are different."

This plainly forbids cross-classification and hence ranges classes in hierarchy.

I do not know that any successful attempt has hitherto been made to say in what a *natural class* consists. In order to investigate the matter we may take the two classes

Cows
& Red Cows

The former is a natural class, the latter is not. Now one predicate more may be attached to Red Cows than to Cows; hence Mr. Mill's attempts to analyze the difference between natural and artificial classes is seen to be a failure. For, according to him, the difference is that a real kind is distinguished by unknown multitudes of properties while an artificial class has only a few determinate ones. Again there is an unusual degree of accordance among naturalists in making Vertebrates a natural class. Yet the number of predicates proper to it is comparatively small.

As Mr. Mill is an extremely popular writer and therefore numbers among his followers many men who have read but little else in logic & philosophy and who have therefore not acquired the calmness and impartiality of mind which comes from longer reading, it is not to be expected that this objection to Mr. Mill's position will satisfy the smaller men among his followers. They will argue as though he were *creating* a distinction and not endeavoring to *analyze* one. We may have erected two classes of classes, but are they *real kinds* among classes, either according to an estimate formed after the manner of the naturalists, of *even according to his own definition*?

What are the innumerable properties or some of them, which belong to that class of classes which is defined as consisting of

---

[11] Aristotle:*Categories*, 3, 1b16–18: "The differentiae of genera which are different and not subordinate one to the other are themselves different in kind. For example, animal and knowledge." (transl. J. L. Ackrill).

classes of which innumerable properties may be truly asserted?— to that class which includes trout, bees, cows whose tails are two feet 3 inches long, men with their hands behind their backs &c and excludes vertebrates, radiates, mollusks, articulates, monocotyledonous plants, &c.

Why is *red cows* not a natural class, while *cows* is one? Because the former can be defined as the common extent of the classes *red* and *cows* and nothing can be universally predicated of *red cows* which is not predicable either of *red* or *cows*; whereas *cows* cannot be defined as the common extent of two or more classes such that nothing can be universally predicated of the former which is not predicable of one or other of the latter. In other words *cow* is a term which has an area; *red cow* has no area, except that area which every term has, namely that it excites a particular emotion in the mind.

I now propose to show by ocular demonstration that a class which has an area is one which is marked in nature, and that the more area it has, the more it is marked in nature.

Let the classes be defined thus

1. Circles not shaded
2. Circles shaded
3. — with a horizontal line across
4. — without —
5. — with a vertical line across
6. — without — " (Ms. 725)

Then follow three circle diagrams on two pages, Figures 9.1 and 9.2.

240

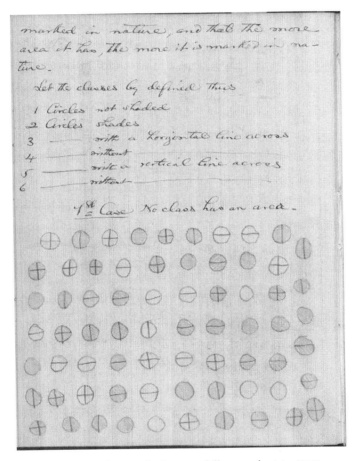

marked in nature, and that the more
area it has, the more it is marked in nature.

Let the classes by defined Thus

1 Circles not shaded
2 Circles shaded
3 ——— with a horizontal line across
4 ——— without
5 ——— with a vertical line across
6 ——— without ———

1ˢᵗ Case No class has an area.

Figure 9.1: The first circle diagram following the Ms. 725 text.

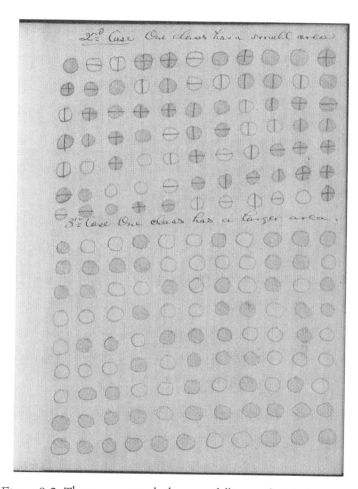

Figure 9.2: The two next circle diagrams following the Ms. 725 text.

9.3   Three Circle Diagrams

The first diagram is presented with the headline "*1st Case* No class has an area." This diagram contains 69 circles, in 7 × 9 rows and columns, plus an additional column with 6 circles only. The second is titled "*2nd Case* One class has a small area."; this diagram contains 77 circles in 7 × 11 rows and columns. The third diagram is titled "*3rd Case* One class has a larger area." and it contains 99 circles in 9 x 11 rows and columns. The diagrams are not further commented on and are immediately followed by the 4-page 98-object diagram which is the focus of this chapter

Let us first attempt to understand the three circle diagrams. The first diagram contains all the eight possible combinations of the three properties (and their negatives) listed in the text. The line properties comprise 33 verticals (36 non-verticals) and 41 horizontals (28 non-horizontals); combined they amount to 19 crosses, 14 sole verticals, 22 sole horizontals, 14 bare circles (as opposed to the expected 17,25 average of each subset). The shadings are a bit more difficult to make out exactly, but there seem to be some 45 shaded and 24 unshaded circles[12], resulting in the following eight subsets for the combination of all three classes:

Shaded crosses	11
Unshaded crosses	8
Shaded verticals	13
Unshaded verticals	1
Shaded horizontals	11
Unshaded horizontals	11
Shaded bare circles	10
Unshaded bare circles	4

All eight classes, of course, are mere intersections of simpler property classes (compare the Red Cow example). The distribution of properties is not even, but except for the subset of unshaded verticals not far from average (1/8 of 69 = 8,625). No property seems significantly connected to another except for one regularity: that a sole vertical is almost always shaded. Unshaded isolated verticals tend not to exist (only one specimen found) so that verticality minus horizontality tends to imply shading. One of the 8 classes thus hardly exists

---

[12]In an earlier published version of this chapter, I relied upon the Microfilm version of the Ms.; shadings were somewhat difficult to judge in that reproduction which lead to the erroneous numbers of 43 shaded and 26 non-shaded. This and other errors have been corrected also in the tables given.

(if at all; Peirce would later dismiss such outliers in samples from infinite sets from a continuity argument[13]) but none of the other seven count, for that reason, as a natural class. This must be what the headline "No class has an area" is intended to refer to.[14]

In the second case, the category numbers are as follows:

Shaded crosses	18
Unshaded crosses	0
Shaded verticals	12
Unshaded verticals	13
Shaded horizontals	10
Unshaded horizontals	9
Shaded bare circles	10
Unshaded bare circles	5

Remarkably, here all crossed circles are shaded and number 18 exemplars. Thus, crossed circles are a) a category numbering almost the double of 1/8 of 77 (9.625), as one would statistically expect; and b) a category that excludes the category of non-shaded crossed circles. Consequently, in this universe, crossed circles constitute a (weak) natural class in which the additional property of being shaded depends upon the presence of the two other properties making up the cross, sufficient to define the category. So the definition of "crossed" refers to a class that is connected by a dependence relation to the property of "shaded"—to phrase it using Peirce's idea of natural classes as having further properties than merely those given by their definition. The fact that certain intersection classes are ruled out is equivalent to the existence of dependence relations between some of the properties. Therefore the category of crossed

---

[13]"We may find that such and such a proportion of calves have five legs. But we never can conclude with any probability that the ratio is strictly zero; and even if we knew that the proportion of men with golden thighs is exactly zero, that would be no argument at all against Pythagoras having had a golden thigh. For something might be true of one man, or any number of men, and yet might occur in the long run in a finite number of cases out of an infinite series. Now a finite number divided by infinity is exactly zero." (*Principal Lessons of History of Science*, 1896; 1.88)

[14]Some problems remain here. The class "isolated verticals" permits with some certainty to predict the additional property "shadedness" (with the one outlier mentioned). Peirce clearly did not take natural classes to be mutually exclusive and defined by necessary and sufficient conditions but envisioned, more flexibly, the possibility of continuity and overlap between them. But given this idea, it seems as if vague natural classes begin to appear as soon as you depart from a completely free and equal combination of properties.

circles must be taken to correspond to that one class "with a small area" to which Peirce refers in the headline of the second diagram.[15]

The third diagram is claimed to involve one class with "a larger area" and is completely devoid of the vertical/horizontal lines, that is, it pertains only to the first of the three dichotomies shaded/unshaded. Of the 99 circles, 57 are shaded. It presents just two of the eight combinatorial classes, the other six remaining unrepresented. This is obviously intended to correspond to the "cow" case with the large area, but how?

Here we face two possibilities:

a) In this universe of discourse, shaded, non-crossed circles constitute a natural class with a large area, because the property of shading excludes the other two properties (and hence the three other possible property combinations of shaded circles with crossing lines) which might have appeared. The same thing, however, could be said about the unshaded circles, which also preclude crossings of all types. Both shading-options exclude the occurrence of vertical as well as of horizontal lines. The definitions both of "shaded" and "unshaded" thus pick out the relevant classes with the additional properties of non-vertical-lines and non-horizontal-lines. Therefore, they could be said to form two natural classes in this universe of discourse.

b) The third and last diagram remains unfinished. Peirce gave up the addition of lines indicating the two other property-types which should have resulted in an even stronger natural class than the second diagram.

Red Cows are not a natural class because they do not share a property aside from being red and being cows, such was Peirce's idea.[16] Mere intersections

---

[15]Peirce here makes the crossed circles category conspicuous by two means: by exterminating non-shaded crosses, but also by giving it a high number of members. But these two must be independent. If, among the 77 individuals, there was only one shaded cross and no unshaded crosses—would crossed circles not still be a natural class in Peirce's definition (it would still have the extra-property of non-shadedness)? In that case, it would be a natural class, even if rare in the Universe of Discourse.

[16]But does this really imply that the term "red cows" has no area at all? It has breadth (the non-empty intersection set of existing red cows) and it has depth (the added depths of "red" and "cows"). So the information of "red cows" seems to be equal to that of "cows" by the inverse proportion rule holding for terms (but not for propositions), and the passage from "cows" to "red cows" to be one of decreasing breadth by increasing depth—such as Peirce referred to as "specification" and "determination by restriction" in 1893: "In order to express an extension by depletion, and a determination by restriction, without change of information, we obviously stand in need of the words *generalization* and *specification*" (*Syllabus*, 1903, 2.249). We shall return to this.

between property classes do not yield natural classes. Natural classes should stably possess at least one universal property in addition to a set of shared properties sufficient for defining them. Of course, different definitions may select the same natural class—but in all cases, definitions must exist which do not include certain shared properties

If we take the third diagram as finished and propose a definition for the natural class "unshaded bare circles" comprising the whole Universe of Discourse, it could be defined as "unshaded circles without horizontal crossings". These would then possess the necessary additional quality on top of this definition, namely that of being without vertical crossings. The problem, of course, is that the definition of the same set of individuals as "unshaded circles without any crossings at all" is exhaustive and therefore does *not* possess any further qualities that are not mentioned in the definition. So, on one definition, all individuals of case 3 form a natural class, in another, they do not. Could this be mended by narrowing the demand from any definition to the existence of at least one definition which leaves further properties?

These problems might be the reason why Peirce dismissed these diagrams and instead turned his attention to the construction of the diagrams occupying the following sheets (see below).

9.4 The "Kandinskys"

After the three circle diagrams just discussed, announced in the text and presented as diagrams of classes with no, small, and a larger area, respectively, four rather different diagram pages follow that do not show any corresponding captions (see illustrations at the end of the chapter). They also consist of rows and columns of smaller figures, the single pages containing 32 (including one crossed over and marked "delete this"[17]), 28, 32, and 7 smaller figures, respectively—all in all numbering 99, just like the third circle diagram. Stylistically, these are much more elaborated figures, more meticulously executed, resembling small constructivist, pre-Kandinsky sketches. Given that they share the overall column-and-row format of the three circle diagrams at the end of

[17]Figure no. 28 on the first page has been crossed over with many pencil strokes making it difficult to reconstruct what it may have looked like; and is accompanied by the handwritten note: "dele[te] this". It appears to have been one of the "soft triangles" with a curved base line and a bold lower right hand corner. To the left, it seems to have had a couple of curved "antennae", each terminating in a dot, and the lower antenna spiraling one and a half rounds. As this spiraling of the lower antenna does not occur in any other K, this feature may have prompted the deletion of this K. As it, moreover, is explicitly deleted, we do not include it in the following observations and arguments.

the text part of the manuscript, it seems obvious to hypothesize that they continue the preceding diagram experiment pertaining to natural classes. Indeed, these drawings also relate to types:

a) Several of them are repeated—as if forming tokens of one and the same type (as is the case in the simpler circle diagrams)

b) Several single-feature graphic properties are repeated across types (also like in the circle diagrams)

Let us call the 98 small complex drawings Ks (for "Kandinskys") to distinguish them from the property parts of which each of them consists, here referred to as Ps. Let us begin by outlining an inventory of these Ps along with the number of Ks in which each of them appears:

List of Ps[18]

1. Central bold circle (14, including one lacking a segment on the right)
2. Horizontal wavy bottom line (41)
3. Vertical oval at the top (18)
4. Central S (20)
5. SW-NE zigzag line (18)
6. Central square with open right side (35)
7. Central black ball (14)
8. Top white circle segment (22; difficult to ascertain)
9. NW-pointing arrow in SE corner (17)
10. Hairy rim (41)
11. Central "soft" triangle with curved left side (6)
12. Three descending parallel lines at the NW corner (31)
13. Central white ball (4)
14. Long spiral-segment curve going right and back left (4)

---

[18]The amount of Ps recorded here may be less than exact, for several reasons: 1) Despite their beauty, the drawings are executed with different degrees of precision, 2) The Ps vary continuously in size and shape from one K to the next, and in some cases it may be difficult to determine whether two P tokens are of the same type or whether they constitute different types, 3) in some cases, the Ps may combine in ways that make it difficult to distinguish the individual features. Another issue is that the parsing of the Ks into Ps may, in certain cases, have proceeded differently. The central bold circle and the central triangle in some cases open up to the right (in 1 and 3 cases, respectively). As one of the main Ps represents an "E", a square with part of the right side missing, all of these figures might have been intended as a simple circle, a triangle, and a square, respectively, meaning that the removal of the right side was counted as an additional P, always occuring with the square; rarely or almost never with the triangle and circle.

15. Central triangle, pointing upward (20)
16. Central, cloudy ball (11)
17. Shaded SW half (24)
18. Curve descending NW–SE (13)
19. Large black SW blot with a NE-facing right angle (11)
20. Three parallel lines at the right side (14)
21. S-shape with blots on the SW end, in the SW corner (23)
22. Small central vertical line at the bottom, with blot at the S end (often combines with 20 to an inverted U-shape with blots at each end) (15)
23. Double black blot or oblong blot in the SE corner (23)
24. A pair of "antennae" with blots on each end pointing NW; the lower antenna forming the base of a cut-off triangle (6)
25. Large dotted V-shape with same symmetry axis as the whole K (10)
26. Large circle segment on the right (17)
27. Central horizontal line (17)
28. Central vertical line (6)
29. Small vertical line at the top with a N dot (1)
30. Three small dots in the NE corner (11)
31. Shading of the central figure (9)
32. Feather-like figure in the NE corner (9)
33. Small triangle pointing down at the top (1)
34. The rim of the central figure supplied with an inner row of dots (9)

All of these 34 properties P are introduced in the course of 30-odd figures of the first page and the top of the second page (except for $P29$ occurring on the last page only). The remaining two pages merely recombine these properties or repeat previous combinations. Two of the Ps ($P29$ and $P33$) have one appearance only and thus might not be counted as stable, typical properties of the universe of Ks, which leaves 32 basic properties. The appearance of the individual Ps may vary continuously from one K to the next to a considerable extent, changing their size and (to some degree) their shape. This might be ascribed to the lack of precision inherent in hand drawing; some of the variations, however, appear too pronounced to pass off as spontaneous hand-drawing variations given the meticulous execution. This variation, then, rather points to the deliberate insistence that the identity of the Ps is that of tokens belonging to the same type, not that of complete qualitative indiscernibility.[19]

---

[19] Take as an example P4—the central S-shape—which comes in very open, oblong versions where the upward end of the S ends before turning around to point downwards (and vice versa for the downward end), such as in the very first K on the first page, or, even more

All of these 32 Ps may be present or absent, as was the case with the three property possibilities of the circle diagrams. But as opposed to the circles, there is a restriction to the combination of Ps, because only some 5 out of the 32 properties appear in each K, so their number is not the total sum of free combinations that would equal 2^{32}. As each K realizes 5 (sometimes 4, sometimes 6 or 7) of these Ps, and none of them appear more than once in a single K, the free combination of five Ps in each K would result in a large amount of possible Ks, exceeding

$$\frac{32!}{27! \times 5!} = \frac{32 \times 31 \times 30 \times 29 \times 28}{120},$$

amounting to some 200,000 Ks. These are, needless to say, not exhaustively realized. This is not, however, only because the sample of Ks given here merely numbers 98—but also because of the fact that the Ps do not combine freely. Unfortunately, there is no text accompanying the four K pages and thus no explicit indication of any syntax of combination, and there is probably no complete rule system to be induced from the small sample. But the very issue of restrictions of P combinations, as we saw in the previous chapter, is the key to the Peircean approach to natural classes—later under headlines such as Would-Bes or Thirdness. The whole natural class issue Peirce has set out to investigate assumes that some properties tend to come in bundles, so to speak, while other properties mutually exclude each other. It is striking, for one thing, that the large, central (maybe "defining") Ps of each complex figure K—the bold circle, the square open to the right, the soft triangle, the hard triangle, the cloudy circle—do not seem to combine at all. You easily get the idea they correspond to genera involving the possibility of further specifications by the addition of more peripherally attached Ps. Each of the Ks realize one and only one of each of these Ps—seemingly because of their geometrically central position in the K.[20] Most other Ps are found towards the periphery of the Ks or cutting through their centres, and hence may be more easily dispensed with. Unlike the case with the circle diagrams, there's no explicit sign here for the *object* bearing the properties (like the circles with 8 possible property combinations added)—here, the object is only indicated by the 2-D region of space occupied by a physically connected selection of Ps.

If—as my hypothesis presumes—these diagrams were actually intended to continue the investigation commenced by the circle diagrams, the central ques-

---

articulated, in the seventh K from the bottom on the third page. It also comes in much more compressed versions, with each of the two halves of the S representing a full half circle, such as in the ninth K on the third page.

[20]The only possible exception to this rule is K 2.28 (number three from the bottom of page 2) which may be interpreted as a combination of the bold circle and the large "E".

tion would be: Which of these Ks form natural classes in Peirce's sense in this K-universe of discourse? As we may recall, Peirce's idea was that signs referring to natural classes had a large "area"—meaning high information.[21]

Let us focus upon what immediately appears to be one of the most "typical" and stable of these Ks (9.1). Let us call it the Ball and Balloon (B&B). No less than 14 Ks are tokens of this type, displaying all of the following five, stably connected P properties:

1. a bold circle ($P1$) on a

2. wavy ground line ($P2$),

3. topped by a vertical oval ($P3$),

4. equipped with a central S ($P4$) and

5. a zigzag line through it ($P5$)—(Figures 9.3 and 9.4a–9.4e).

These Ks are numbers 1.1, 1.18, 2.3, 2.4, 2.10, 2.17, 2.18, 2.28, 3.7, 3.19, 3.24, 3.26, 4.5, 4.6. They may vary in three respects: 1) They may be continuously deformed as to the size and relative locations of the Ps; 2) they may vary by having one or two further Ps added—Ps they share, of course, with other figures: a shady lower left ($P14$), a hairy contour to the circle ($P10$), a thin line half circle, spiral section or sinus section ($P17$), a small arrow ($P9$), a dot ($P23$), etc.; 3) they may lack parts, e.g. a section to the right of the bold circle (like fig. 8, number three from the bottom of page 2, approaching it to the "hairy E" square which opens in the same direction, see note on central Gestalts). Despite this, they are immediately recognizable as tokens of a type because of the stable co-occurrence of all the five Ps mentioned—the most immediately striking natural class in this universe of discourse (the very first figure on the first page is a B&B, and one of only four of the 98 Ks to be depicted in double size is the almost pure B&B specimen 3.7).

---

[21] In the passing, we recall Lévi-Strauss' (1966) observation about animal species being so useful for categorizing other structures (family structure, social structure, geographical, cosmological, mythical, theological structure). Many animal species are, at the same time, easily identifiable natural kinds (easy to "define" in terms of appearance and behavior features)— and, at the same time, they come with lots of "additional" properties offering an abundance of material for thought.

250

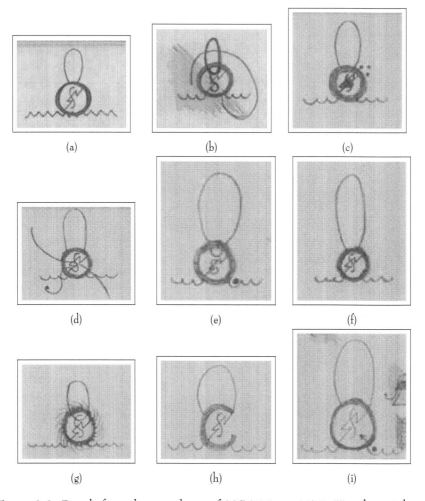

Figure 9.3: Details from drawing sheets of MS 725 ca. 1870, Houghton Library, Harvard University

There is only one other example in which five properties from among the 32 Ps occur together in 14 cases (see below). This does not imply, of course, that the occurrence of each of the five Ps involved in the B&Bs is restricted to these 14 Ks. There are numerous other cases in which some of them appear in other Ks (numbers refer to Ks by page and location on the page, read textwise from upper left):

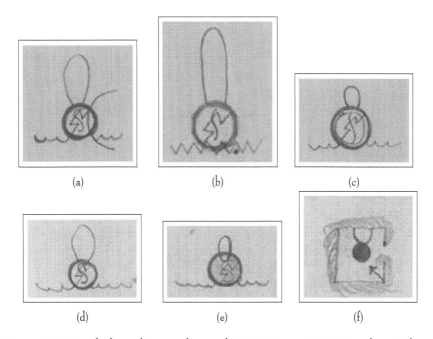

Figure 9.4: Details from drawing sheets of MS 725 ca. 1870, Houghton Library, Harvard University

a) the wavy ground, $P2$ (1.4, 1.5, 1.7, 1.17, 1.19, 1.24, 1.25, 1.26, 1.28, 1.29, 1.30, 2.6, 2.11, 2.12, 2.15, 2.20, 2.28, 2.29, 2.30, 3.6, 3.14, 3.15, 3.16, 3.21, 3.28, 3.32, 4.1, 4.2, 4.7) = 29, all in all, in 43 Ks;

b) a bold circle, $P1$ (in 1.8, the straight triangle appears with a bold contour) = 1, all in all, in 15 Ks:

c) with an S, $P4$ (1.10, 2.29, 3.9, 3.17, 3.23) = 5, all in all, in 19 Ks;

d) and a zigzag line through it, $P5$ (1.22, 2.11, 2.26, 3.12) = 4, all in all, in 18 Ks;

e) topped by a vertical oval, $P3$ (1.31, 2.1, 3.20, 4.3) = 4, all in all, in 18 Ks.

The five Ps of this K occur stably together, but compared to their other occurrences, they fall into three classes:

a) $P1$ only occurs if all of the other four also occur (with one, albeit doubtful, exception);

b) $P2$ occurs in further 29 Ks, which implies that it is present in some 44 % of all Ks;

c) $P3$ occurs an additional 4–5 times besides its occurrence in B&Bs.

d) $P4$ occurs an additional 4–5 times besides its occurrence in B&Bs.

e) $P5$ occurs an additional 4–5 times besides its occurrence in B&Bs.

In a sample of 100 Ks, with roughly 5 different Ps for each K, the probability that one of the 32 possibilities will occur presuming an arbitrary distribution is 0.156, meaning it will be present in approximately 15–16 Ks. In the rest population of 86, omitting the B&Bs, this probability becomes 0.134, which is still significantly more than is found in c)–e). Thus the B&B, as a natural kind, may be defined by b)—the bold circle, with c)–e) forming 3 additional properties that characterise B&Bs, because all B&Bs display them, while they only occur in around half of the average of the rest of the population. Case a) is, of course, different—it is almost evenly distributed among the whole population, so that even if it occurs in all B&Bs, it cannot serve to characterize this group specifically. (So B&Bs should properly be renamed Bold Circles with Balloons, S's, Zigzags and Waves).

Another natural class candidate is the second figure on the first page, the "Hairy E": a broken square with a hairy rim, a black circle in the middle with a white circle segment on top of it and an arrow pointing to NW in the SE corner—thus also combining 5 stable properties, in this case $P6$–$P10$ (Figure 9.4f). The question is how to determine the defining centre of the category.[22] Like the B&B with its 14 cases in which five Ps stably connect, the Hairy E also appears in 14 stable cases. If we tentatively take the conspicuous Hairy E as being central, some 35 Ks display the combination of these two Ps. Of these 35 Es none lack hairiness (even if it varies considerably in length), some 18 lack the white circle, some 21 the black circle, and some 20 the small

---

[22]For Gestalt reasons, P6 and P1 may seem to mutually exclude each other—they both occupy and delineate the center space of the Ks they appear in and there is no K in which both appear (even if $K3$ from the bottom of page 2 may be seen as a compromise between the two). We have not, however, assumed that there are purely graphical dependencies among the Ps excluding certain combinations from the outset. While P1 turns out to be defining for the B&Bs, P6 turns out *not* to be defining for the Hairy Es. Therefore, we should probably not be misled by Gestalt perception into presuming that large central Ps play different roles than smaller or more peripheral Ps. So the argumentation here presupposes that all Ps are, in principle, graphically compatible and might be combined—in result, all lack of combination is taken to be ontologically, rather than graphically, relevant.

arrow. The two circles and the arrow co-occur stably, meaning that in all cases in which the black circle appears, the white circle and the arrow also appear. Thus, the co-occurrence of these three Ps—in 14 cases—might be interpreted as the defining centre of this category. If we trace the overall occurrence of the 5 Ps aside from their 14 cases of co-occurrence, which we focused on above, we get the following:

a) Square with open right side, $P6$: 21—all in all 35 Ks;

b) central black ball, $P7$: 0—all in all 14 Ks;

c) top white ball, $P8$: 4—all in all 18 Ks;

d) NW-pointing arrow in SE corner, P9: 3—all in all 17 Ks;

e) hairy rim, $P10$: 24—all in all 38 Ks

Hence, the central black ball seems to be the defining feature of this category, narrowly taken, while the top white ball and arrow only rarely occurs outside of the category. The E and the hairy rim often appear outside the category, but almost always together (only three hairy rims are not on Es), which is why they seem to form a larger, more vague category with $P7$–$P9$ as its centre. Just like the existence of a black ball allows us to infer the presence of a white ball and an arrow, the existence of an E allows us to infer the presence of hair. They thus seem to form two natural classes, one nested within the other. I would guess that Peirce here attempts to present a less stable candidate for a natural class than the B&B— in agreement with the idea that natural classes may have more or less area and thus may come in a continuous gradient of stabilities, just as they may overlap without thereby becoming any less natural.[23]

9.5 Defining Natural Classes

As mentioned, there is no written comment at all to the 98 small Kandinskys. Yet just like the circle diagrams preceding them, they experiment by constructing small graphical universes inhabited by individuals forming natural classes

---

[23]In Ms. 725, Peirce explicitly addresses the idea that natural classes may come in a continuum of different degrees of well-definedness ("area"), but he only later (e.g. in the part of the 1902 "Minute Logic" on classification, EP II, 115ff; 1.203 ff) made explicit the idea inherent in the "Kandinsky"-experiment that natural classes may unproblematically overlap, so that the lack of a definite borderline between them should neither count as proof of their nonexistence nor of their not being natural.

that are defined by stable property clusters and exclude certain other such clusters. In this account, Peirce seems to articulate a notion of natural class which is continuous in the sense that such classes may be of different clarity and delimitation, i.e. of different "area".

They also seem to overlap, to allow exceptions and to shade into each other—which may seem to contradict or at least relativize Peirce's strong support of an Aristotelian genus-species hierarchy in the text. Being a fallibilist, Peirce probably treated the Aristotelian hierarchy as a general rule—a rule of thumb—permitting exceptions that do not lead to the total nominalist arbitrariness that would stem from adopting a completely free combination of single properties. Thus, this account of natural classes contrasts with a "spreadsheet ontology" (David Armstrong's free combination of simple ontological properties, critically characterized by Barry Smith[24]) where simple properties form the only universals and natural kinds may, in turn, be selected from the free combination of properties in various empirical objects. Such an ontology is, of course, untenable: If only simple property universals exist, kind universals (widespread in science from physics to the humanities) cease to have any explicable stability. Peirce's quest for natural kinds, by contrast, pertains to classes of objects—or events—characterized by the binding of single properties into distinctive clusters that exclude free combination.

In the fictitious universe of discourse populated by the 98 Ks, co-occurrence, however, is the only access to dependency relations between properties—thus this experiment, just like Armstrong's spread-sheets, completely brackets any possible explanations, empirical or a priori (by statistical, causal and ontological necessities, respectively), for the reason behind the co-occurrence of certain Ps and not of others. In the real world, such co-occurrences will of course have explanations both in form of empirical laws (stably charting the dependence of gravitation forces upon masses, or the dependence of political power upon access to violence in the last resort, for instance) and a priori regularities (determining the dependence of colour on space, or of obligations on promises, for instance). By bracketing the access to any such reasons behind dependencies in these diagram experiments, it was Peirce's aim to define natural kinds as more or less stable clusters of interdependent properties—so that some dependent properties become unnecessary for a definition and thus might constitute the "surplus" of properties required in Peirce's natural kind definition. Peirce was always a realist of sorts, but maybe it was this bracketing that led him, in the 1870s, from his early version of realism towards a more empiricist skepticism against the presence of any property which is not directly evident or measurable in each single case (as indeed holds true for the

---

[24] Smith (2005)

small world of Ks)—compare his famous diamond example from "How to Make our Ideas Clear" (1878) which was later revised from a more realist point of view.[25] Here, he claimed that a diamond whose hardness was never measured could not reasonably be described as hard. In his "Lectures on Pragmatism" of 1903, some 25 years later, he revised this idea: the knowledge of diamonds pertains to a cluster of properties, and if some of these properties are present to convince us of its being a diamond, the dependency between properties allows us to infer its hardness without measuring it. Later in his career, Peirce would describe such stable combinations of properties as "would-bes", connecting the properties in groups of "general principles" or tendencies—what are nowadays often called dispositions. This generalization, of course, pertains to the real universe, which—unlike the artificial experiment-world of Ks—never allows us to ascertain all properties of any single object, but which—also in contrast to the K-universe—enables research into the reasons, empirical and a priori, why certain properties form dependency clusters and certain others never co-occur. This would also indicate that Peirce was wrong in assuming that classes which are mere intersections of natural classes— e.g Red Cows—have no area in his own definition of this term. In the brief paragraph preceding the graphical experiments of Ms. 725, Peirce proposes no less than three different definitions of natural classes, two of them negative: they are 1) classes which are not mere intersections of simpler natural classes,[26] 2) classes which have more properties than their definition, 3) classes without an Area. Peirce assumes, without any further explication, that these definitions are co-extensive. Maybe this is not the case, however, with the third definition: It is hard to see why Red Cows should not have an Area in the simple $b \times d$ sense defined in the OLEC. So the possession of Area could not simply be a measure of the naturalness of a class, such as the circle experiment—and probably also the "Kandinsky" experiment—explicitly aimed to prove. The definition of natural classes by their having properties in addition to any definition is equivalent to defining them by the characteristic of not being mere intersections of simpler classes— but it seems to be independent of the attempted Area definition. Even if the "Kandinsky" experiment did allow giving (artificial) examples of natural classes

---

[25] See the discussion in Stjernfelt: *Diagrammatology* (as fn. 9), ch. 2.

[26] Peirce here articulates a parsimony principle for the acceptance of natural classes: conjunction of such classes does not produce further classes of the kind—see Barry Smith/Werner Ceusters: "Ontological Realism: A Methodology for Coordinated Evolution of Scientific Ontologies", in: *Applied Ontology*, 5 (2010), 139–188, and their rejection of universals brought about by the conjunction, disjunction, and negation of other universals. As to negation, Peirce's circle experiments in Ms. 725 gave the same prominence to properties (shaded) as to their negations (non-shaded), while the subsequent diagram experiment with the Ks implicitly rejects negative properties in composing the Ks out of positive Ps only. So here, Peirce seems to agree with the rejection of negatively defined universals as well.

using the former definition, it did not fit with this definition's Area definition, because even Ks which were only defined as intersections of property classes still would have both breadth and depth, and hence an area. Maybe these were the reasons why Peirce never got around to writing a text to accompany the K diagrams—he realized that the mere extensions of properties and their combinations could never determine the intensions pertaining to the kinds of connections which make them appear in clusters, thus sharpening his realism? Maybe he noticed that the Area definition did not select natural classes?

Later on (in The "Minute Logic" 1902), he emphasized that exactly this kind of observation of connections represented a major road to finding natural classes: "There are cases where we are quite in the dark, alike concerning the creating purpose and concerning the genesis of things; but [there are cases] where we find a system of classes connected with a system of abstract ideas— most frequently numbers—and that in such a manner as to give us reason to guess that those ideas in some way, usually obscure, determine the possibilities of the things. For example, chemical compounds, generally—or at least the more decidedly characterized of them, including, it would seem, the so-called elements—seem to belong to types, so that, to take a single example, chlorates $KClO_3$, manganates $KMnO_3$, bromates $KBrO$, rutheniates $KRuO_3$, iodates KIO_3, behave chemically in strikingly analogous ways. That this sort of argument for the existence of natural classes—I mean the argument drawn from types, that is, from a connection between the things and a system of formal ideas—may be much stronger and more direct than one might expect to find it, is shown by the circumstance that ideas themselves—and are they not the easiest of all thin gs to classify naturally, with assured truth?—can be classified on no other grounds than this, except in a few exceptional cases" (1902, EP II 125; 1.223).[27]

Such a connection between "the things and a system of formal ideas" is completely lacking in the K sheets, where there is no systematic indication in the graphical formalism of which Ps are compatible with which other Ps and why.[28] This seemingly iconic experiment is, in this respect, completely lacking in iconic qualities that would explicate the combination possibilities of the Ps.

---

[27]Editors' notes in the CP correct two of these chemical formulae - K_2MnO_4 and K_2RuO_4, respectively.

[28]We can add that the issue raised by Ms. 725 and Peirce's ensuing graphical experiment is far from settled to this day; there seems to be a wide agreement on the existence of (some) natural kinds, but only little agreement on how to define or describe the category in general. To take an actual example: within the practical framework of articulating ontologies for biomedical data engineering, nominalists (like Gary Merrill) and realists (like Smith and Ceusters) are taking further the strife over universals, where we find the latter articulating a distinction between natural and artificial classes along lines not far from Peirce's ideas in Ms. 725 and later.

The syntax of P combinations is not *itself* iconically represented apart from co-localization (Peirce might, e.g., have formed them as jigsaw puzzle pieces showing which Ps combine and which do not).

In the most developed reflection upon natural classes in the mature Peirce, occurring in the context of the classification of the sciences, exactly in the "Minute Logic" of 1902, Peirce took the surprising step of defining natural classes from their *purpose*, taking human artifacts like lamps as the prototype of such classes, cf. Hulswit (1997). All lamps belong to the same class for the basic reason that they have been constructed for related aims. Here, Peirce boldly generalizes this idea to all natural classes claiming that, in non-human cases, we just do not know the teleological definition of them. This indeed sounds scary, and in connection to the more speculative parts of Peirce's cosmology, this might give rise to almost providential interpretations. There is, however, a more modest interpretation. Peirce did not take teleology in nature to take the same shape as human purposes which he considered a special case. Rather, his strong Darwinism made him think natural selection was the basic natural mechanism for the working out of what appears as teleologies in nature, that is, dependent upon local interactions rather than any pre-given goal or vitalist force. In that sense, the "teleology" of the "Minute Logic" should rather be seen as *forms*—the "systems of formal ideas" referred to in the quote above, forms subjected to Darwinian conditions of selection for their realization in the world.

But in the realm of such forms, we are back to diagrams and diagrammatical reasoning. And here, again, it remains central to Peirce that such diagrams may give occasion of "theorematic reasoning" whose aim it is exactly to discover properties of their objects which were not mentioned in the explicit construction of the diagram—corresponding to the definition of the class.

So the idea of the additional, hidden properties to be deduced kept their place in Peirce's doctrine, so that the "system of forms" of the "Minute Logic" may give rise to natural classes for the same reasons sketchily outlined in Ms. 725. So, the strange drawings at the end of that Ms. may have put him on an important track, realizing that the fascinating diagrammatic experiments with Cows and Red Cows were originally motivated by a red herring.

258

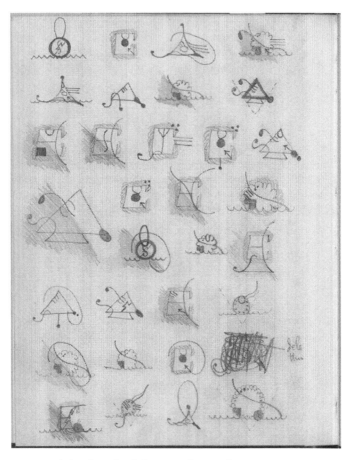

Figure 9.5: First of the four final drawing sheets of MS 725 ca. 1870, Houghton Library, Harvard University

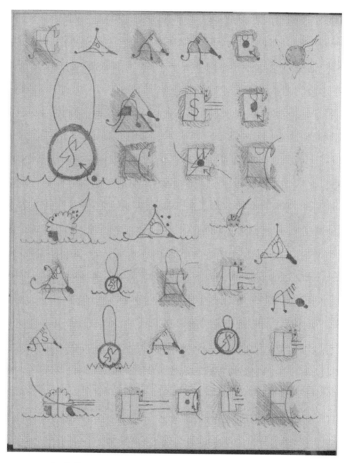

Figure 9.6: Second of the four final drawing sheets of MS 725 ca. 1870, Houghton Library, Harvard University

260

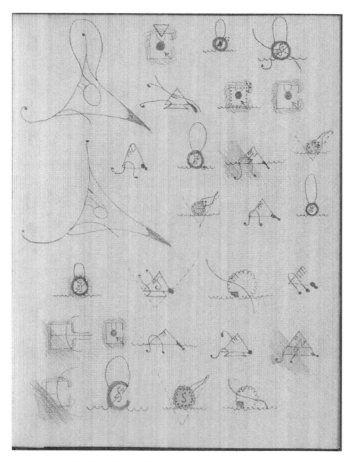

Figure 9.7: Third of the four final drawing sheets of MS 725 ca. 1870, Houghton Library, Harvard University

Figure 9.8: Fourth of the four final drawing sheets of MS 725 ca. 1870, Houghton Library, Harvard University

Chapter 10

Corollarial and Theorematic Experiments With Diagrams

> I hope that, before I cease to be useful in this world, I may be able to define better than I now can what the distinctive essence of theoric thought is. I can at present say this much with some confidence. It is the directing of the attention to a sort of object not explicitly referred to in the enunciation of the problem at hand ...

("Specimens of Mathematical Amazes", 1908, NEM III, 622)

The central aspect of Peirce's doctrine of diagrammatical reasoning is the idea of using diagrams as tools for making deductions by performing rule-bound experiments on the diagram. Famously, Peirce distinguished between two classes of diagram proofs, "corollarial" and "theorematic", respectively—a distinction he himself saw as his first major discovery. As opposed to the simpler corollarial reasoning with diagrams, theorematic reasoning concerns diagram experimentation involving the introduction of new material—this chapter investigates the issue of the structure of theorematic diagram experiments and proposes three types of such experiments

The increasing interest in Peirce's philosophy of logic as well as his philosophy of science highlights the importance of his notion of deductive reasoning as based on diagrams. As argued by several authors in Moore (2010)—Tiercelin and Cooke—this can be taken as providing an original solution of the so-called Benacerraf's Dilemma which has haunted much philosophy of mathematics since Benacerraf's famous 1973 "Mathematical Truth" article against Platonism (in Benacerraf and Putnam 1983). Benacerraf's paper argued against Platonism and the existence of abstract objects in mathematics by setting up the following dilemma: 1) Mathematics claims the existence of abstract objects outside of time and space; 2) Acquisition of knowledge takes place by means of a causal process connecting an object with a knowing subject. But as abstract objects are causally inert, we must either accept Platonism and reject causal epistemology—or we must embrace causal epistemology and refuse Platonism. Due to the prominence of causal reference theories at the time, Benacerraf's choice seemed obvious: abstract objects and Platonism must be discarded in the face of the seeming evidence of causal epistemology. Literally taken, Benacerraf's argument would, in fact, eliminate not only abstract objects but a series of other aspects of the world, such as many properties (color, pitch, shape . . .) which may also be suspected of being causally inert in the billard-ball causation theory of the second horn of the dilemma.

Causal reference theories hardly hold the attraction which they did in the 1970s, and the role of diagram experiments in an alternative, Peircean way of cutting the cake is the following. To Peirce, deduction and mathematical reasoning are one and the same. Mathematics is defined by two things, methodologically and substantially, respectively. The former comes from the definition of mathematics that Peirce inherited from his father, the mathematician Benjamin Peirce: mathematics is the science that draws necessary conclusions. Peirce's own addition to this doctrine pertains to the status of the subject matter of those necessities: the object of mathematics is hypotheses concerning the forms of relations. All mathematical knowledge thus has a hypothetical structure: if such and such entities and structures are supposed to exist, then this and that follows. We might call this weaker variant of commitment to abstract objects "hypothetical Platonism". This admission liberates you, of course, from the presupposistion of a strange, space-timeless realm of real existence—but it commits you, on the other hand, to further modes of being in addition to that of particular individuals, which is why diehard nominalists will hardly feel attracted by Peirce's alternative. As mentioned in chapter 4, Peirce's doctrine operates with no less than two further modes of being than that of individuals, namely that of possibility—"May-Bes"—and that of real possibility—"Would-Bes". Mathematics being hypothetical through-and through then forms a fundamental subset of the latter. The crucial roles of diagrams, now, is that the notion of reasoning by diagram experiments furnishes an epistemological alternative to Benaceraffian causal reference. The idea is that diagrams form the epistemological means of accessing hypothetical abstract objects. They do that in two steps, as it were. One step is taking a diagram token, a drawing on paper, blackboard, computer screen, or in the imagination, and subjecting it to "prescission", the imaginary stripping it of accidental qualities so that only few relevant, controllable, general, schematic relations are left—permitting the observer to grasp, through the token, its type. This process of prescission, of course, is neither arbitrary nor subjective and is governed by symbols and rules, explicitly or implicitly. Once the type is grasped, it may, by the intermediary of its physical token, be subjected to experimental manipulation, in the imagination or using a physical diagram replica, or both. Certain types of transformation are allowed, others not so, corresponding to truth-preserving logical reasoning steps. So diagram experimentation incarnates the if-then hypothetical structure of mathematics and thus gives mathematical knowledge its conditional, modal character. The observation of diagram tokens/types, of course, is prefigured in the perception of ordinary objects as tokens of types—just like the prescission process stripping the token of its accidental qualities in order to access its type is a more formalized version of similar processes when we address natural kinds by stripping away accidental properties in order to constitute categories like red, chairs, running—or even the category of an individual persisting in time despite its changing appearances. General structures and shapes of reality are present already in the perceptual stream, and it is no wonder that we, as biological beings, have become adapted to focus upon such features in perceptual structures. This very ability, however, may now be recycled apart from its basis in real objects to be put to use vis-a-vis purified imaginary objects like those of mathematics.

This argument pertains to pure, mathematical diagram reasoning; now what about the vast amount of applied diagrams representing empirical states-of-affairs? Peirce's system of the sciences offers an explanation of the efficacy of such diagrams—namely that they inherit, explicitly or implicitly, some mathematical structure of pure diagrams and add further constraints to those diagrams, constraints stemming from the special science or practical conditions of the domain to which they pertain.[1] Thus, all deductive reasoning, everyday or scientific, is taken to involve a mathematical-diagrammatical scaffolding, and necessary inferences in all sciences as well as in everyday reasoning employ mathematics, implicitly or explicitly. In Stjernfelt (2007) I attempted a reconstruction of Peirce's overall doctrine of diagrams and diagrammatical reasoning, arguing that this cluster of ideas forms the center of a Peircean epis-

---

[1] Taking Comte's principle (a science is below another science from which it takes its principles, and above another science whose principles borrows from it) as basis for his classifications of the sciences, Peirce places mathematics on top as the science from which all other sciences borrow principles.

Figure 10.1: The perimeter of a square with the side s

temology as well as it constitutes an important contribution to contemporary realist semiotics in general.

In this chapter, I shall take a closer look at the notion of diagram experiment based on Peirce's famous distinction between two such classes of experiments, giving rise to Corollarial and Theorematic reasoning, respectively. On the base of the introduction of this distinction, a series of issues are addressed. To what degree does this distinction capture different formal classes of problem difficulty? How may we distinguish between different types of Theorematic reasoning? And what is the relation between diagram experiments and hypostatic abstraction?

In the years after 1900, Peirce returns over and over again to the Corollarial/Theorematic-distinction, famously celebrating it as his own first "real discovery" (in his Carnegie application 1902). The overall idea is that corollarial deduction gives a conclusion which may be read off the diagram, once it succeeds in fashioning a synthesis of the premises—thus conforming to the Kantian idea of logical conclusions offering nothing which was not already there in the premises. By contrast, theorematic (or theorematogenic, or theoretic, or theoric, or theôric) reasoning forms a more demanding and creative type of reasoning where some new activity or elements must be experimentally added to the premises in order to reach the conclusion.

Take a simple example: asking the question of the size of the perimeter of a square with the side s, the conclusion may be reached based on the very definition of a square as a quadrangle with four equal sides—or by a very simple diagram experiment of counting sides, using the following diagram:

The result of $4s$ is easily reached by both of these means. By comparison, the famous Euclidean proof of the angle sum of the triangle being equal to two right angles may serve as a simple example of theorematic reasoning:

This proof requires the addition of auxiliary lines to the triangle—here CE and CD, parallel to AB and prolonging BC, respectively—to establish the proof based on the fact that the three angles now meeting at C have the same sizes as those of the triangle. $\angle BCA$ participates in both of the two sums,

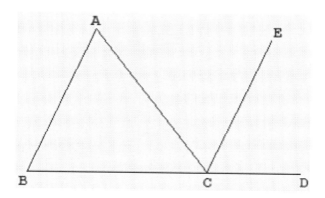

Figure 10.2: The angle sum of a triangle

$\angle ACE$ is equivalent to $\angle BAC$, while $\angle ECD$ is equivalent to $\angle ABC$.[2] The sum of the three angles meeting at C—$\angle BCA$, $\angle ACE$, and $\angle ECD$—is obviously two right angles. But this is impossible to derive from mere definitions of "angle" and "triangle" just as it is impossible to prove from the triangle diagram without any additions.

The terminology of corollarial/theorematic comes from Euclid whose later editors named simple inferences *corollaries* (from the margin indication of them by means of a wreath—Greek "corolla")—while propositions to be proved were theorems. Peirce judges that some of Euclid's theorems are, in fact, mere corollaries—the overall distinction is taken to rely upon the necessity of experimenting by adding new elements to the diagram, elements which disappear again in the final, general statement of the proof. The theorem that the angle sum of a triangle equals two right angles does not, for example, in any way refer to the subsidiary lines necessary to reach the proof. The basic issue behind this distinction is, of course, the doublesidedness of mathematics, being apodictic and inexhaustible at one and the same time. How is it possible that mathematicians find results by necessity while at the same time new, unexpected discoveries abound among these results, just like in the empirical sciences? This issue troubled Peirce for a long time. Already when constructing his first formal language for logic, in his 1885 masterpiece "On the Algebra of Logic", he reasoned: "It has long been a puzzle how it could be that, on the one hand, mathematics is purely deductive in its nature, and draws its conclusions apodictically, while on the other hand, it presents as rich and apparently

---

[2]These equivalences between alternate angles, of course, are granted by Euclid's Proposition 29 : *If two straight lines are parallel, then a straight line that meets them makes the alternate angles equal.*

unending a series of surprising discoveries as any observational science. Various have been the attempts to solve the paradox by breaking down one or other of these assertions, but without success. The truth, however, appears to be that all deductive reasoning, even simple syllogism, involves an element of observation; namely, deduction consists in constructing an icon or diagram the relations of whose parts shall present a complete analogy with those of the parts of the object of reasoning, of experimenting upon this image in the imagination, and of observing the result so as to discover unnoticed and hidden relations among the parts" ("On the Algebra of Logic", 1885, 3.363). Here, the inexhaustibility of mathematics is explained by means of Peirce's first, germ-like diagram reasoning doctrine—as a generalization, interestingly, of his linear algebra of logic, far from the ordinary conception of diagrams. The "unnoticed and hidden" relations obtainable by diagram observation, of course, are what are later taken to require theorematic deduction, in addition to mere inference from definitions.

Even if the problem addressed by the distinction is thus an early concern in Peirce, it seems to be only in the years after 1900 that he makes the corollarial/theorematic distinction explicit and sets out to elaborate it. Only in 1901 do we seem to witness the nascent terminology of the distinction appearing: "1901 Oct 12 If my present view, held for four or five years, is right that Abduction Deduction Induction are Premarian, Secundarian, and Tertian, then there ought to be two types of Deduction & three of Induction (...) Now I don't recognize any such two types of Deduction. (...) We can distinguish Deductions into those which are corollarific and those which are theorematogeneous. The former merely require the careful consideration of the conclusion, the latter involve outside considerations,—subsidiary lines, etc. But this seems a methodeutic not a critical distinction" (Logic Notebook Ms. 339, 362; earlier on the page, Peirce attempts to distinguish proposition deductions and term deductions). Later, Peirce will include the corollarial/theorematic distinction in his critical table of inference types—but this early quote points to the fact that the latter part of the distinction sits uneasily on the critical/methodeutic divide (today, we would rather speak of logic versus heuristics or theory of science). Theorematic reasoning requires an inventiveness or even ingenuity which makes it alien to a narrow concept of logic—even if its results, on the other hand, remain purely deductive. This apparently simple distinction covers a whole bunch of interesting issues: that of the much more outspoken experimental character of theorematic reasoning as compared to corollarial reasoning, that of the strategy of finding suitable new elements to add, that of instantiating those elements in particulars (only particular sets of lines in the angle sum example will lead to the proof), that of the character of those elements, that of the relation of the diagram experiment to verbal instructions and definitions. Probably for this reason, Peirce's description of theorematic reasoning differs to some extent from time to time and is in need of a synthetic reconstruction.

10.1   Theorematic Diagram Experiments in Peirce

Let us run through Peirce's different definitions.

1) The basic idea is the indirect conception that theorematic reasoning, unlike corollarial reasoning, is not reducible to inferences from concept definitions, that is, conceptual analysis: "An accurate definition of Corollarial Demonstration would require a long explanation; but it will suffice to say that it limits itself to considerations already introduced or else involved in the Explication of its conclusion; while *Theorematic* Demonstration resorts to a more complicated process of thought" ("A Neglected Argument for the Reality of God" 1908, EP II 442, 6.471). This brief definition of theorematic reasoning, of course, is merely negative and contrastive vis-à-vis Kant's description of logic as tautological, and most of Peirce's descriptions of the pair of concepts take their point of departure in the inability of certain theorems to be proved by corollarial reasoning: "Deductions are of two kinds, which I call *corollarial* and *theorematic*. The corollarial are those reasonings by which all corollaries and the majority of what is called theorems are deduced; the theorematic are those by which the major theorems are deduced. If you take the thesis of a corollary, i.e., the proposition to be proved, and carefully analyze its meaning, by substituting for each term its definition, you will find that its truth follows" ("On the Logic of Drawing History ...", 1901, EPII, 96, 7.204—after which the quote continues with a more positive definition of theorematic reasoning—cf. below). Even if corollarial reasoning counts as the ideal and should be preferred whenever possible because of its simplicity, a certain class of "major theorems" require more than careful description in terms of conceptual analysis. This necessity stems from the general impossibility of defining things, in all cases, so that all their properties will be corollaries from their definition. This impossibility, of course, is connected to the conception of natural classes as possessing properties transgressing definitions. Peirce addresses this when claiming that the best translation of Greek "episteme" is "comprehension"—which is "...the ability to define a thing in such a manner that all its properties shall be corollaries from its definition. Now it may be that we shall ultimately be able to do that, say for light or electricity. On the other hand, it may equally turn out that it forever remains as impossible as it certainly is to define number in such a way that Fermat's or Wilson's theorems should be simple corollaries from the definition" ("On Science and Natural Classes", 1902, EPII 129, 1.232). Even if

much in arithmetics is corollarial (such as Kant's famous 7+5=12 which Peirce refuses to grant the status of synthetic a priori for the same reason), complicated theorems of arithmetics are not. So the impossibility of defining things, in all cases, so that all their essential properties easily flow from the definition, obviously forms the first argument for the necessity of theorematic reasoning.

2) A basic way of describing theorematic reasoning more positively, now, is as involving the addition of new elements to the premises (abstractions or not, foreign ideas or existential instantiations of general objects the existence possibility of which is granted by the universe of discourse). Peirce seems to have received this idea about the introduction of a new element from no less than George Boole's widow in 1898: "The widow of the great Boole has lately written a little book in which she points out that, in solving a mathematical problem, we usually introduce some part or element into the construction which, when it has served our purpose, is removed. Of that nature is a scale of quantity, together with the apparatus by which it is transported unchanged from one part of the diagram to another, for the purpose of comparing those two parts. Something of this general description seems to be indispensable in mathematics" ("The Logic of Mathematics in Relation to Education", 1898, 3.561)—and Peirce's overall development of the corollarial/theorematic distinction now covers the following decade. Here, as simple an addition as that of a ruler counts as theorematic. The addition of such objects is taken to be the subject of an additional lemma to the premises, supported by a postulate. Continuing the above quote from "On the Logic" (1901), Peirce writes: "But when it comes to proving a major theorem, you will very often find you have need of a *lemma,* which is a demonstrable proposition about something outside the subject of inquiry; and even if a lemma does not have to be demonstrated, it is necessary to introduce the definition of something which the *thesis* of the theorem does not contemplate. In the most remarkable cases, this is some abstraction; that is to say, a subject whose existence *consists* in some fact about other things. Such, for example, are operations considered as in themselves subject to operation; *lines,* which are nothing but descriptions of the motion of a particle, considered as being themselves movable; collections; numbers; and the like" ("On the Logic", 1901, EP II 96, 7.204). In Peirce's debatable analysis, lines are abstractions from the trajectories of particles (why not from contours of objects or the intersections of planes, etc.?)—so the auxiliary lines in the angle sum proof are taken to be examples of the introduction of abstractions. Be that as it may,[3] the quote given here overlooks the important

---

[3] As abstractions come in many levels, and abstract/concrete is not coextensive with general/particular, the issue whether the subsidiary lines should be taken as abstractions or particulars or both needs not bother us deeply.

issue of the *selection* of those lines. The postulate in Euclid that given a line and a point, a line through the point may be drawn which is parallel to the line given, obviously lies behind the lemma of introducing the two particular auxiliary lines in the proof. But not any old lines added to the original triangle would lead us to the proof. So the selection of which particular objects to add becomes an important issue. Hintikka, in his development of Peirce's notion of theorematic reasoning, takes this "existential instantiation" in the shape of "witness individuals" to constitute the core of theorematic reasoning, adding further quantified variables to those referred to in the premises. Sun-Joo Shin (2010) emphasizes the importance of this individualizing step in reasoning: much has been spoken, since the British empiricists, of the access to the triangle in general, but the inverse movement, that of selecting the right individuals to add in a proof, has received much less attention. But the right selection of individuals is seminal for conducting the proof. Hintikka insists that the addition of individuals to the premises constitutes the very core of Peirce's idea: "What makes deduction theorematic according to Peirce is that in it we must envisage other individuals than those needed to instantiate the premise of an argument" (1980, 110)—also other than needed to express its conclusion, we may add. This is what constitutes the basis of Peirce's "brilliant insight (...) that this geometrical distinction can be generalized to *all deductive reasoning*" (109). Thus, in Hintikka's reconstruction, "...a valid deductive step is theorematic, if it increases the number of layers of quantifiers in the proposition in question" (110). To Hintikka, this solves the ancient Aristotelian riddle of logical incontinence—how can it be that one may fail to grasp the sum total of logical consequences of the amount of knowledge in one's possession? This is because many of those consequences require the theorematic addition of further individuals for their proof, and Hintikka surmises that the difficulty of a problem is roughly proportional to the number of new individuals needed for its solution (113; Stjernfelt 2007 107-8). This particularity of auxiliary individuals, much discussed after Hintikka's reinterpretation of theorematic reasoning, is surprisingly rarely addressed in Peirce; however, this late quote connects the basis of the additional elements in a general postulate with the particularity of those elements: "Of my two divisions of Deductions, one is into *Corollarial* and *Theorematic Deduction*. The former requires nothing more than a logical analysis of the premises to furnish the conclusion. The latter involves as one of its premises a *postulate*, or proposition asserting the possibility of any object which lies in certain definite general relation to any existing objects of a certain kind. E.g. Between any two points on a line it is possible to place a third. Now to derive from this postulate the particular consequence that will lead to the conclusion required, [one needs] not merely *sagacity* or Aristotle's *eustokha* (...) but also imaginative genius in all its complexity of resources" (Ms. 764, unpaginated, the 29th page in the Ms, late, seemingly 1910-11). Here, the requirement of imaginative genius—implicitly compared to the laborious teasing out of corollarial definition consequences—is highlighted as required for finding the appropriate particular elements to add. Shin (2010) more precisely insists upon the importance of selecting the *right* individuals, among many possible, to conduct the proof.[4]

Other times, it is rather the *general* or *abstract* (which is not the same) character of the added elements which is emphasized: "To the Diagram of the truth of the Premises something else has to be added, which is usually a mere May-be, and then the conclusion appears" (letter to James 25. dec 1909, EPII, 502). A May-be, in Peirce's late metaphysics, is a possibility which is, of course, vague. Again, selecting the right one among possibilities is crucial. Especially when talking about the added elements in this general way, Peirce insists they are *foreign* to the theorem which the proof intends to establish: "What I call the *theorematic* reasoning in mathematics consists in so introducing a foreign idea, using it, and finally deducing a conclusion from which it is eliminated. Every such proof rests, however, upon judgments in which the foreign idea is first introduced, and which are simply self-evident" (Carnegie Application 1902, Ms. L75, NEM IV 42).[5]

So are the additional elements particular instantiations selected on the basis of general possibilities granted in the relevant universe of discourse (like the subsidiary lines of the angle sum proof granted by Euclid's postulates), or do they consist in the addition of a new general principle or idea? Judson Webb, in an important paper on Hintikka's philosophy of logic, also points to the fact that, in discussing different proofs of Desargues' theorem, Peirce mentions different types of theorematic reasoning: "There are just two distinct kinds of things we can introduce into a proof that do not appear in such a theorem: auxiliary *lines* and the idea of *length*. The former are only new *objects* of the same kind occurring in the theorem, while the latter is a new *concept* that is 'foreign' to it" (Webb 2006, 249). Peirce, however, did not seem to pay explicit

---

[4]The selection of the right elements to add is abductive. In the angle sum case, the addition of parallel lines is probably prompted by the previous knowledge of Proposition 29 dealing with the relation between parallel lines and the size of alternate angles—because the theorem to be proved is about angle sizes. So even if the selection itself is not deductive but merely abductive, the abduction is motivated by a certain likeness between the theorem and possibilities offered by previous theorems proved.

[5]A parallel quote, emphasizing the theorematic step as the addition of a new idea, is the following: "I shall term the step of so introducing into a demonstration a new idea not explicitly or directly contained in the premises of the reasoning or in the condition of the proposition which gets proved by the aid of this introduction, a theoric step" ("Amazing Mazes", 1908, 4.613).

attention to this important distinction to which we shall return later. He did, however, introduce another distinction between subtypes of theorematic reasoning. In the famous description of the two kinds of deduction in the Carnegie application, the description in terms of new elements gives rise to a subdivision of theorematic reasoning based on the abstract or non-abstract character of that reasoning: "My first real discovery about mathematical procedure was that there are two kinds of necessary reasoning, which I call the corollarial and the theorematic, because the corollaries affixed to the propositions of Euclid are usually arguments of one kind, while the more important theorems are of the other. The peculiarity of theorematic reasoning is that it considers something not implied at all in the conceptions so far gained, which neither the definition of the object of research nor anything yet known about could of themselves suggest, although they give room for it. Euclid, for example, will add lines to his diagram which are not at all required or suggested by any previous proposition, and which the conclusion that he reaches by this means says nothing about. I show that no considerable advance can be made in thought of any kind without theorematic reasoning. When we come to consider the heuretic part of mathematical procedure, the question how such suggestions are obtained will be the central point of the discussion. Passing over smaller discoveries, the principal result of my closer studies of it has been the very great part which an operation plays in it which throughout modern times has been taken for nothing better than a proper butt of ridicule. It is the operation of *abstraction*, in the proper sense of the term, which, for example, converts the proposition 'Opium puts people to sleep' into 'Opium has a dormitive virtue'. This turns out to be so essential to the greater strides of mathematical demonstration that it is proper to divide all theorematic reasoning into the non-abstractional and the abstractional. I am able to prove that the most practically important results of mathematics could not in any way be attained without this operation of abstraction. It is therefore necessary for logic to distinguish sharply between good abstraction and bad abstraction" (Carnegie Application 1902, Ms. L75, Draft C, 90-102, NEM IV 49). This distinction between abstractional and non-abstractional theorematic reasoning has been taken up by Stephen Levy and Michael Hoffmann (1997; forthcoming) in their efforts to outline taxonomies of theorematic reasoning—is it so that this idea might, simultaneously, constitute a basis for the distinction between theorematic reasoning by means of existential instantiation on the one hand and the introduction of new, foreign ideas on the other? Peirce does not further develop his distinction between abstractional and non-abstractional theorematic reasoning, so it is difficult to decide. Suffice it to say that it is not evident that these two distinctions are identical or even co-extensive; the introduction of certain abstract objects may be permitted in the formalism used and in that sense not being new or foreign (just like the introduction of lines in a geometry proof or a variable in an equation)—the foreign idea seems to comprise a special class of abstractions only.

3) An interesting feature of the descriptions in terms of added elements quoted here is that they do *not* refer to deductions in terms of diagram experiments. Diagram experiment, however, is taken to constitute the center of deduction in general, and of theorematic deduction in particular. In a parallel draft of the Carnegie application, Peirce thus characterizes theorematic reasoning as follows: *"Theorematic deduction* is deduction in which it is necessary to experiment in the imagination upon the image of the premiss in order from the result of such experiment to make corollarial deductions to the truth of the conclusion. The subdivisions of theorematic deduction are of very high theoretical importance" (Carnegie Application 1902, Ms. L75, NEM 4:38, 1902). The year after, in the *Syllabus* accompanying his Lowell lectures, Peirce connects the experimental character of theorematic reasoning to the ingenuity required as well as to observation; it "...is one which, having represented the conditions of the conclusion in a diagram, performs an ingenious experiment upon the diagram, and by the observation of the diagram so modified, ascertains the truth of the conclusion" (*Syllabus*, 1903, EP II 298, 2.267). In one of the drafts of the Lowell lectures, Peirce connects these two descriptions, now taking the addition of new material to be a subtype of experiment: "I draw a distinction between Corollarial consequences and Theorematic consequences. A corollarial consequence is one the truth of which will become evident simply upon attentive observation of a diagram constructed so as to represent the conditions stated in the conclusion. A theorematic consequence is one which only becomes evident after some experiment has been performed upon the diagram, such as the addition to it of parts not necessarily referred to in the statement of the conclusion" (Lowell Lectures, Ms. 456, 49; transcription by Helmut Pape). Here, it is not made explicit which other types of experiment there might be besides the addition of new elements—but such addition is in itself experimental for the reason that it may be an issue of trial-and-error to find the right instantiations. In an early account for diagram experimentation, however, Peirce provides such an example: "Deduction is that mode of reasoning which examines the state of things asserted in the premises, forms a diagram of that state of things, perceives in the parts of that diagram relations not explicitly mentioned in the premises, satisfies itself by mental experiments upon the diagram that these relations would always subsist, or at least would do so in a certain proportion of cases, and concludes their necessary, or probable, truth. For example, let the premise be that there are four marked points

upon a line which has neither extremity nor furcation. Then, by means of a diagram, we may conclude that there are two pairs of points such that in passing along the line in any way from one to the other point of either pair, one point of the second pair will be passed an odd number of times and the other point an even (or zero) number of times. This is deduction" (Untitled manuscript, c. 1896, 1.66).[6]

Figure 10.3: Peirce's figure illustrating diagrammatic deduction (1.66)

In this example, the diagram experiment is undertaken by following a trajectory along the closed curve, until realizing that each full turn will add 2 to the number of passages of each point pair—so with respect to odd/even, the result will stay the same as the very first half trajectory, passing one point 1 time, the other point 0 times. This experiment hardly introduces any new ideas at all, but it does involve instantiation, this time of following a trajectory moving in the diagram. So the new elements added may also be actions performed on the diagram. In the "Minute Logic" of 1902, Peirce hints at those other experiment possibilities: "Just now, I wish to point out that after the schema has been constructed according to the precept virtually contained in the thesis, the assertion of the theorem is not evidently true, even for the individual schema; nor will any amount of hard thinking of the philosophers' corollarial kind ever render it evident. Thinking in general terms is not enough. It is necessary that something should be DONE. In geometry, subsidiary lines are drawn. In algebra permissible transformations are made. Thereupon, the faculty of observation is called into play. Some relation between the parts of the schema is remarked. But would this relation subsist in every possible case? Mere corollarial reasoning will sometimes assure us of this. But, generally speaking, it

---

[6]The shortest presentation is probably: "For mathematical reasoning consists in constructing a diagram according to a general precept, in observing certain relations between parts of that diagram not explicitly required by the precept, showing that these relations will hold for all such diagrams, and in formulating this conclusion in general terms. All valid necessary reasoning is in fact thus diagrammatic" ("Lessons from the History of Science", 1896, 1.54). The object of mathematics will be pure diagrams of any kind, while ordinary reasoning as well as the empirical sciences will use diagrams applied in being constrained by existing relations—empirical data and regional ontology—as well.

may be necessary to draw distinct schemata to represent alternative possibilities. Theorematic reasoning invariably depends upon experimentation with individual schemata" ("Minute Logic", 1902, 4.233).

Here, the mere introduction of new elements or ideas as additional general terms is not deemed sufficient—the experiment is supposed to perform an action manipulating the diagram—drawing the auxiliary lines—or, in the algebraic example undertaking transformation granted by the relevant symbol manipulation rules. In the Euclidean example, transformations including the movements of geometrical objects in the plane permitted (rotations, mirrorings, translations, etc.) obviously form a class of experiments different from those of introducing new elements, just like, in arithmetics, the transformation possibilities given by calculation rules (and more generally, in algebra, symbol manipulation rules), provide such experiment possibilities.

An important issue here—both related to the "addition of new elements or foreign ideas" and to the "experiment" aspects—is the relation between theorematic reasoning and abduction. A finished piece of theorematic reasoning, of course, is deductive—the conclusion follows with necessity from the premises. But in the course of conducting the experiment, an abductive phase appears when investigating which experimental procedure, among many, to follow; *which* new elements or foreign ideas to introduce. This may require repeated, trial-and-error abductive guessing, until the final structure of the proof is found—maybe after years or centuries. Exactly the fact that neither premises nor theorems need to contain any mentioning of the experiment or the introduction of new elements makes the abductive character of experimentation clear. Of course, once the right step has been found, abductive searching may cease and the deductive character of the final proof stands out.

4) A further description of the corollarial/theorematic distinction makes it correspond to reasoning with words or schemata, respectively. The quote just given from the "Minute Logic" continues with the conclusion that "We shall find that, in the last analysis, the same thing is true of the corollarial reasoning, too; even the Aristotelian 'demonstration why.' Only in this case, the very words serve as schemata. Accordingly, we may say that corollarial, or 'philosophical' reasoning is reasoning with words; while theorematic, or mathematical reasoning proper, is reasoning with specially constructed schemata" ("Minute Logic", 1902, 4.233). This complicated claim identifies corollarial reasoning with philosophical reasoning in words (implicitly placing a severe limitation on the powers of such reasoning), as compared to the constructive power of theorematic reasoning using specially constructed schemata and be-

ing able to make "demonstration that".[7] Immediately, however, words are *also* taken to constitute such schemata, even if simpler and less directly accessible than "specially constructed" schemata. The ubiquity of schemata also outside of science (maps, graphs and tables in newspapers, media, commodities, etc.) points to the fact that the distinction between words and constructed schemata does not, as it might be immediately assumed, coincide with that of everyday reasoning and science. The issue becomes even more complex when we consider that also corollarial reasoning is often able to use diagrams. So words/simple schemata/simple use of schemata are all opposed to theorematic reasoning. Rather, the idea that conceptual reasoning forms a simple version of schematic reasoning points to the idea of the distinction between corollarial and theorematic as being a gradient continuum rather than two mutually exclusive classes—also supported by the fact that theorematic reasoning examples differ enormously in complexity and the amount of new elements required. We shall return to this below.

5) A final characterization of theorematic reasoning is that of requiring a new point of view of the problem, as e.g. a Gestalt shift. We find a simple version of this in Ms. 773 ("Third Lecture on Methodeutic Induction", undated (but late), one unpaginated sheet, page 2-3 of the microfilm): "I spoke of Deduction as the compulsive kind of reasonings. Almost all the theoric inferences are positively *creative*. That is, they create, not existing things, but *entia rationis* which are quite as real. This blackboard is black. Theoric deduction concludes that the board possesses the quality of blackness and that *blackness* is a simple object, called an *ens rationis* because that theoric thought created it." Here, the hypostatic abstraction from "black" to "blackness" is taken as an example of theoric deduction.

Here is a terminological problem. In many cases, "theoric" is used interchangeably with "theorematic"; in other contexts, Peirce seems to intend a slightly different meaning by the concept "theoric" (or "theôric"). One of his paradigm examples is that of Desargues' theorem (two triangles which are centrally in perspective are also axially in perspective, usually referred to by Peirce as "the ten point theorem")[8]—a 17th C geometry proof recently rediscovered

---

[7] In scholastic proof theory "demonstration that" differs from "demonstration why" which is able to go all the way from definitions. "Demonstration that" is taken to fall short of this ideal; Peirce obviously takes explanations not reducible to definitions to require more complicated machinery.

[8] A detailed attempt at developing the distinction between corollarial and theorematic reasoning in "The Logic of History" (1901, NEM IV) takes the proof of $(x+y)+x = x+(y+z)$ as example of the former and the proof that "every multitude is less than a multitude" (there is no largest set) as example of the latter. The overall argument, however, is not very clear. Especially the latter proof which seems to be a sort of diagonal argument implying a power set construction is not very clearly presented, and even if Peirce concludes it "requires the

in Peirce's time by von Staudt in the context of projective geometry. Here, Peirce uses the notion of "theoric" to refer to the "new point of view" which may introduce a third dimension to the diagrammatical representation of the 2-d theorem, thereby making it much more immediately graspable than much more cumbersome proofs using lengths of lines:

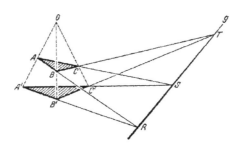

Figure 10.4: The Ten-Point Problem in 3-D after Hilbert and Cohn-Vossen

The two triangles lying in a central perspective as seen from the point 0 have the intersections of their sides coinciding on the same line (axial perspective). This figure (Hilbert and Cohn-Vossen, quoted from Hoffmann, forthcoming, 18) shows how a three-dimensional interpretation of the originally 2-D planar diagram makes it easy to grasp that the two planes of the triangles meet at the line g, because the 2-D case now appears as a special case of the more general 3-D problem. Peirce returns over and over again to this proof, taking it as a central example of "theoric" or "theorematic" reasoning. An alternative proof restricted to two dimensions is possible but rests upon another theorematic addition, namely that of the length of lines which is also not mentioned in the original theorem.

---

invention of an idea not at all forced upon us by the terms of the thesis", he does not make explicit what that new idea should be, apart from not being derivable from the definition of the concept "fewer" (a clearer example of Peirce's version of Cantor's power set theorem can be found a few years earlier in "The Logic of Relatives", 1897, 3.548). Similarly, at the end of "Logic of History", Peirce has a brief and clear summary of the Power Set Theorem: "I proved that there is no maximum multitude by considering the collection of all possible collections of the numbers of a collection. Now a *collection* is an abstraction ..." (1901, NEM IV, 11), but still there is no indication of what the "new idea" introduced should be. Certainly not the abstraction of "collection" which is presupposed by the multitudes of the premises—rather the power set notion of the set of all possible subsets of a given set. Peirce seems to have realized the early discussion of corollarial/theorematic in "The Logic of History" was less than satisfying; according to the Robin catalogue on the Ms. (691), Peirce added the following note to the Ms.: "These pages are to be used in the chapter of the Logic treating Deductive Reasoning. But the theory needs completion."

Michael Hoffmann has made a strong case that this adoption of a new point of view should be called "theoric", differing from theorematic reasoning because simply constituting a gestalt shift in the conception of the problem rather than the necessary experimental introduction of new elements in the deduction process (Hoffmann, forthcoming). Hoffmann's interpretation is based on the use of the term "theoric" in Ms. 318 and Ms. 754, both of them from 1907. From the large Ms. 318 on pragmatism, Hoffmann quotes the following description of "theoric" reasoning which consists ". . . in the transformation of the problem,—or its statement,—due to viewing it from another point of view" (ibid., 68). In the brief Ms. 754 (notes for a "talk to the Phil. club" April 12 1907), Peirce writes: "I formerly, quite dubiously, divided Deductions into the Corollarial & the Theorematic. Explain these. Deduction will better be called Demonstration. But further study leads me to lop off a corollarial part from the Theorematic Deductions, which follows that part that originates a new point of view. This part of the theorematic procedure, I will call theôric reasoning. It is very plainly allied to retroduction, from which it only differs as far as I now see in being indisputable" (Hoffmann, forthcoming, p. 27, n13).[9] The core of theorematic reasoning, following this quote, is taken to be the theoric introduction of a new viewpoint—the rest seems to be mere corollarial reasoning. I am not convinced, though, that Peirce, by the introduction of the term "theoric" in 1907 intends a wholly new concept, completely different from that of "theorematic". In the Ms. 754 quote just given—which forms a *hapax,* the only place, to my knowledge, where Peirce uses both of the notions "theoric" and "theorematic" simultaneously—the former is introduced as the central part of the latter. Shortly afterwards, in the April 1908 issue of *The Monist,* Peirce publishes the "Amazing Mazes" in whose "First curiosity" he defines "theoric" in complete parallel to the usual definitions of "theorematic" contrasting "corollarial": "I shall term the step of so introducing into a demonstration a new idea not explicitly or directly contained in the premises of the reasoning or in the condition of the proposition which gets proved by the aid of this introduction, a theoric step" (4.613). So, I just take "theoric" to be another example of Peirce's proliferating neologisms where the same concept gives rise to the coining of many different terminological expressions for that concept. Hoffmann, on the other hand, remains right in pointing to the fact that Peirce's analysis of the recurrent example of Desargues' theorem does not coincide with his other examples and descriptions of theorematic reasoning—I would say it adds a further aspect to the description of varieties of theorematic reasoning. Adding a third dimension to the diagram of Desargues' theorem is adding a

---

[9]Here, I quote Ms. 754 from Hoffmann (forthcoming) as the relevant page is missing from the Microfilm edition where it seems to belong between pages 5 and 6.

new element in an importantly different way than adding a particular line to an Euclidean diagram, because it induces a "transformation" in the whole way of viewing the problem. When returning to Desargues' theorem the next year, in a letter to William James in 1909 (Ms. L224, NEM III, 471), Peirce now characterizes the Desargues proof as "theorematic" and the introduction of a third dimension as yet another example of "additions to the diagram." The "theoric" examples thus rather point to the fact that the range of possible additions and experiments in theorematic reasoning is fairly large, involving elements of highly different dimensionality, generality, and abstractness.

To sum up Peirce's different descriptions of theorematic reasoning, we can say they exceed the mere explication from the combination of definitions by introducing something further, be it new elements (particular or general), be it experiments by diagram manipulation, be it the substitution of schemata for words, or be it the gestalt shift of seeing the whole problem from another point of view.[10]

10.2 Theorematic Reasoning, Relative to Intelligence?— Or to Logic Systems Chosen?

But why could we not conceive of the differences between corollarial reasoning and the different types of theorematic reasoning as a difference in reasoning capacity only? The former reasonings are generally taken to be easy while the latter require ingenuity—could we not reduce the difference between them to a difference between psychological resources needed to solve the problems? When we are taught which lines to select in the angle sum proof or how to introduce the third dimension in Desargues' proof, these proofs become just as easy to conduct as corollarial proofs. Would the corollarial/theorematic distinction then be reducible to one of psychology of learning, of the peculiarity of human reasoning capabilities to which some problems may appear easy and others may appear more difficult? Peirce, always hostile to psychologism in logic, does not consider this possibility and maintains the idea that it is the very structure of the problem and the formal resources for its proof itself which

---

[10]Maybe the very concept of theorematic reasoning is necessarily open—given the inexhaustibility of mathematics, it may not be granted we should be able to chart all possible subtypes of such reasoning beforehand?

gives rise to the distinction.[11] Here, we take Peirce's stance in assuming that the difference in problem complexity is no purely psychological phenomenon.

A related idea rests on the fact that proofs of the same theorem may take many different forms—cf. the Desargues example—and so a logical parallel to such psychological proposals will be the following question: After a successful theorematic proof, could we not simply add the theorematic ideas to the original set of premises, the original statement of the problem—then the ensuing proof would become corollarial only and easy to perform? From time to time, Peirce toyed with the idea that proofs once having been theorematic might be transformed into the simpler form of corollarial reasoning by the change of logical system: "Perhaps when any branch of mathematics is worked up into its most perfect form all its theorems will be converted into corollaries" ("Sketch of Dichotomic Mathematics", c. 1903?, NEM III 289). That corollarial proofs must be preferred to theorematic proofs for the same theorems, if available, follows from the obvious ideal that simpler proofs must be preferred to more complicated proofs of the same theorem—but this ideal does not grant that all of the latter may, in fact, be translated into the former. And even if some theorematic proofs may be translated into corollarial proofs, Peirce generally finds such an idea— comparable to a positive solution to Hilbert's *Entscheidungsproblem* – impossible, as we already saw in the 1902 quote where he deemed it impossible "... to define number in such a way that Fermat's or Wilson's theorems should be simple corollaries from the definition" ("On Science and Natural Classes", 1902, EPII 129).

On one occasion, in the "Amazing Mazes", Peirce clearly distinguished between theorematic reasoning as such and the repetition of an already established theorematic proof, as well as between proofs necessarily requiring theore-

---

[11] A related issue is the degree of conscious access to reasoning processes: "If, however, as the English suppose, the feeling of rationality is the product of a sort of subconscious reasoning–by which I mean an operation which would be a reasoning if it were fully conscious and deliberate–the accompanying feeling of evidence may well be due to a dim recollection of the experimentation with diagrams" ("Minute Logic", 1902, 2.172). The experience of evidence resulting from rational reasoning may, in some cases, depend upon subconscious reasoning. A recurring argument in Peirce, however, points to the fact that such reasoning (cf. ch. 6)—and, even more, that of computers—lacks self-control as the hallmark of real reasoning. As to mechanization of reasoning, Peirce often discusses the corollarial/theorematic distinction with reference to computers ("logic machines"). His overall idea is that the former will generally be mechanizable, while the latter lie beyond mechanization because their introduction of new elements by experiment requires creativity and ingenuity. These ideas might be seen as a vague anticipation of later discoveries of decision limitations in the philosophy of mathematics and computation (Gödel's incompleteness theorem, or Turing's related halting problem), but they are not simply equivalent. These limitations has another character than Peirce's distinction, because they limit the range even of purely mechanical decision procedures which Peirce would, in all probability, categorize as corollarial.

matic tools and theorematic proofs reducible to corollaries (as in the "Amazing Mazes" in general, Peirce here uses "theoric" for "theorematic"). A theorematic proof which may—if possible—be transformed into a simpler corollarial proof caused by the introduction of a better formal representation system, is called a "theorem-corollary"—somewhat a misnomer. The repetition of a theorematic proof, once it has become familiar, "a matter of course", and thus as easy as corollarial reasoning, he terms "theoremation"—this must, of course, be distinguished from the former by still possessing the theorematic structure. Finally, the theorematic introduction of the new element in order to establish the proof is, by contrast, named a "major theorem": "Now to propositions which can only be proved by the aid of theoric steps (or which, at any rate, could *hardly* otherwise be proved), I propose to restrict the application of the hitherto vague word '*theorem*,' calling all others, which are deducible from their premises by the general principles of logic, by the name of *corollaries*. A theorem, in this sense, once it is proved, almost invariably clears the way to the corollarial or easy theorematic proof of other propositions whose demonstrations had before been beyond the powers of the mathematicians. That is the first secondary advantage of a theoric step. The other such advantage is that when a theoric step has once been invented, it may be imitated, and its analogues applied in proving other propositions. This consideration suggests the propriety of distinguishing between varieties of theorems, although the distinctions cannot be sharply drawn. Moreover, a theorem may pass over into the class of corollaries, in consequence of an improvement in the system of logic. In that case, its new title may be appended to its old one, and it may be called a *theorem-corollary*. There are several such, pointed out by De Morgan, among the theorems of Euclid, to whom they were theorems and are reckoned as such, though to a modern exact logician they are only corollaries. If a proposition requires, indeed, for its demonstration, a theoric step, but only one of a familiar kind, that has become quite a matter of course, it may be called a *theoremation*. If the needed theoric step is a novel one, the proposition which employs it most fully may be termed a *major theorem*; for even if it does not, as yet, appear particularly important, it is likely eventually to prove so. If the theoric invention is susceptible of wide application, it will be the basis of a mathematical method" ("Amazing Mazes", 1908, 4.613).

The terminology of these distinctions seems not particular well-chosen, one referring to the process ("theoremation") two to the result ("theorem-corollary", "major theorem"), and the syncretistic notion "theorem-corollary" ill-chosen to indicate that the proposition in question is a corollary of one set of axioms, but not of another. The overall conceptual argument, however, clearly establishes the distinction between theorematic reasoning as such on the one hand, the issue of its dependency upon axiom and rule systems on other hand—and, finally, the psychological issue of its becoming familiar with repetition. As Hintikka (1983, 112) argues, the fact that some theorematic proofs become corollarial under other rule systems does not at all obliterate the corollarial-theorematic distinction, rather it makes clear that the distinction is relative to the logic system used and will remain, albeit differently, in any such system.

10.3   Types of Theorematic Diagram Experiments

As we have seen, Peirce developed the distinction of corollarial and theorematic diagram deductions during the last 15 years of his life, and both explicitly and implicitly, he proposed different subtypes of theorematic deductions. He explicitly proposed a distinction between theorematic reasoning with or without abstractions, and more implicitly, distinctions may be inferred from his examples: manipulating with the diagram versus adding new material; the new elements added being objects, foreign ideas or new points of view. Apparently, he realized that all this laid out a whole field for further investigation: "I wish a historical study were made of all the remarkable theoric steps and noticeable classes of theoric steps. I do not mean a mere narrative, but a critical examination of just what and of what mode the logical efficacy of the different steps has been. Then, upon this work as a foundation, should be erected a logical classification of theoric steps; and this should be crowned with a new methodeutic of necessary reasoning" ("Amazing Mazes", 1908, 4.615).

The ultimate goal for such a research, as so much in Peirce, is heuristic ("methodeutic"): it should be undertaken in order to find better methods for deduction within the confines of the research process as such. The plurality of theorematic subtypes involved, already more or less vaguely glimpsed, may be no wonder, given the basic negative definition of somehow transgressing the merely definition-based corollarial reasoning. In how many ways is it possible to transcend corollarial reasoning? Given Peirce's overall continuism, we might surmise that these different subtypes of theorematic reasoning rather form a continuum from the simplest corollarial examples in the one end to the most complicated theorematic specimens in the other end. Hintikka proposed one arithmetic measuring stick for such a gradual scale—the number of additional individuals needed in the proof. But this only goes for one subtype of theorematic reasoning, that of the introduction of further quantified particulars.

Among the many species of theorematic reasoning to investigate, we shall propose three logical levels of theorematic diagram experiment. Let us go back to the simple Euclidean example with the angle sum proof. Here, the introduction of auxiliary lines gives a basic example of the introduction of new particular objects. They are not in any way extraordinary—their very possibility is granted by basic Euclidean axioms and postulates. The only extraordinary thing about them is, as Shin argues, the selection of the right lines among the infinity of those possible.

A higher level of diagram experiment addresses the change of selected details of the very formalism making the former experiment possible. The famous geometrical example, of course, is the change of the parallel axiom[12] which made possible the angle sum proof in the first place. As is well known, this axiom was originally changed in order to try to find an ad absurdum proof: if a negated parallel axiom lead to inconsistencies in geometry, this would prove the parallel axiom was a theorem of the theory, and the rather cumbersome postulate could change status and become a theorem of geometry rather than part of the premises. Famously, these attempts failed and led, instead, to new, consistent systems of non-Euclidean geometries by Bolyai, Lobachevsky, Riemann, etc. in the mid-19th century. The parallel axiom could be changed, now, in two basic directions: instead of one possible parallel, given a line and a point, no parallel lines could be drawn through the point, or an infinity of parallel lines could be drawn—resulting in elliptic and hyperbolic geometries, respectively. But the change of the parallel axiom is obviously an experiment of a wholly different status than the addition of auxiliary lines in the angle sum proof. Here, the very definition of which objects are taken to be possible in the formalism is changed—and a theorem such as the angle sum theorem will consequently be revised—in the former case, the angle sum will be more than 180 degrees, in the latter, less. Generally, experiments varying axioms, postulates, object definitions, transformation rules etc. of a theory must be ascribed a different status than the mere introduction of an object allowed by the existing system.

A still higher level, now, may be grasped from the same example. After the realization that three different types of geometries may result from the change of the parallel axiom, an experiment on an even higher level was possible: to vary and synthesize all such geometries and organize them on one continuum so that Euclidean geometry now forms a point with zero curvature of space on a line with a continuum of different elliptic geometries having different positive curvatures, hyperbolic geometries having different negative curvatures (Bolyai, Riemann). By doing so, those pioneers undertook a step characterized by Peirce before he discovered the corollarial-theorematic distinction: "Mathematical reasoning consists in thinking how things already remarked may be conceived as making a part of a hitherto unremarked system, especially by means of the introduction of the hypothesis of continuity where no continuity

---

[12]Strictly speaking, the parallel postulate; it has become common usage to call it an axiom.

had hitherto been thought of" ("Review of Spinoza's *Ethic*" (1894), in Peirce, 1975-1987 II, 84-85). This third step realizes how Euclidean geometry and the infinite number of elliptic and hyperbolic geometries form part of "a hitherto unremarked system" given by variation of curvature—exactly by taking them to be connected by the continuous variation of curvature. Of course, still higher syntheses are possible—in geometry, the generalizations of the Erlangen program, defining different geometries by which invariances their transformation procedures allow for (thus finding a higher-order unremarked system of which both (non-)Euclidean geometries, projective geometry, and topology form a part)—or the generalization by Hilbert, taking the axiomatic structure of geometries as fixed while the interpretation of which model of objects they refer to could be subject to variation—or, again, the generalization of category theory allowing for the coarticulation of geometry with different branches of mathematics, etc. Such syntheses, however, seem to repeat the two latter types of theorematic experiments on higher levels. Thus, the three theorematic levels distinguished here - the introduction of a new object, and the two types of introducing a foreign idea, the experiment with one or more of the basic object or rule definitions, and the establishment of a system of different versions of those definitions, seem to to give us a hypothesis of three different levels of theorematic diagram experiment.

10.4 The Three Levels in Applied Diagrams

Let us argue by example in discussing diagram experiments of these three kinds in applied diagrams, taking the geographical example of topographical maps. Here, the tracing of a route on the map from one location to another must constitute an example of corollarial reasoning. It does introduce new elements—the real or imaginary drawing of a line on the map, respecting, in addition to the mathematical aspects of the diagram, additional features of physico-geographical ontology: the trajectory should follow roads, not cross lakes, swamps, buildings, mountains etc. Geography, of course, is no fully axiomatized science, and the regional ontology of geography makes the additional geographical diagram constraints considerably more vague than the exact mathematical aspects of the same diagram.

A practical example of corollarial map reasoning may be the Danish police detective Jørn "Old Man" Holm's computer program, immediately plotting on a topographical map huge amounts of cell phone information related to suspects:

The map shows locations of calls made in a selected, typically shorter, period; calls from the same cell phone are marked by the same colour. This diagram representation does not add anything new to previously existing

Figure 10.5: Jørn "Gamle" Holm's computer map showing the geographical movements of cell phones

information—except for the synthesizing a lot of isolated informations on one map, information which would otherwise have to be gathered from long lists of single pieces of longitude-latitude information of cell phone masts, cell phone numbers and call-up times. The synthesis of such information on one and the same diagram makes it possible to grasp in one glance gestalt information about cell phone trajectories on the map which would otherwise require complicated, time-demanding and not immediately convincing argumentation in court. Diagrammatic argumentation, by contrast, proves highly efficient in court where Holm has been called as an expert witness in many severe cases about drug smuggling, trafficking etc. Obviously, it becomes harder for a defendant to stay with his explanation that he spent the whole day in front of his tv set when a diagram proves that his cell-phone travelled from one end of the country to the other and back again the same day. Such information synthesis on a diagram constitutes an example of corollarial reasoning—unproblematically adding to the geometrical diagram aspects of points and lines those of the regional ontologies of geography and human communication.

Now, we may argue, like Peirce above, that the introduction of a new object in the diagram, e.g. in the shape of a ruler, marks a first small step in theorematic reasoning. It permits us to compare distances across the map—and even if having become an everyday utensil in our time and automatized in GPS and elsewhere, the ruler must have been a major breakthrough when the first distance calculation on a map was actually performed.

Still higher species of diagram experiment with maps may be gathered from science. A recent such example stems from Jared Diamond's celebrated volume *Guns, Germs, and Steel*, tracing the roots of domesticated agriculture on Earth since the beginning of the neolithic era. A basic argument in the book comes from Diamond's diagram experiment with a world map (Diamond 2005, 177):

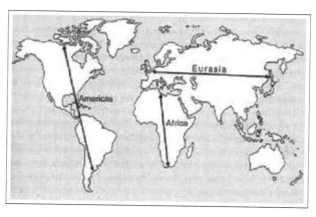

Figure 10.6: Jared Diamond's world map showing overall directions of continents

Diamond's basic observation is that among the three major continental complexes, Eurasia, Africa, and the Americas, there is a seminal difference—the former is grossly oriented East-West, while the latter two are both oriented North-South. This almost trivial diagram experiment receives its nontriviality (which qualifies it as a piece of theorematic reasoning) from the underlying combination of biogeography with human culture in the regional ontology of the diagram. The domestication of plants and animals is a watershed event in human culture giving rise to the agricultural revolution and the development of large-scale, layered societies. Domestication presupposes the presence of easily domesticated species and the stable human settlement over many generations in the environment favoring the survival of these species. But local domestications only get the ability to deeply influence the development of human civilization if they are able to spread from there to other areas and cultures. Biogeographically, species are tied to local climate,—and local climate roughly depends on the latitude, forming isotherms across a temperature gradient falling from Equator towards the Poles. So the piecing together of these pieces of geographical ontology into a system depends upon a diagram experiment: once you have domesticated a species, where may it spread? Most favourably it spreads in the overall East-West direction, along isotherms, keeping climate conditions approximately constant—as opposed to traveling in the North-South direction where climate changes drastically with latitude. By this piece of a priori diagram reasoning—based on the combination of biogeographical ontology and the ontology of human culture development—Eurasia stands out as a privileged site for the original domestication of agricultural species (as opposed to Africa which might immediately be taken as a better candiate, original cradle of the human species as it is). Empirical findings subsequently corroborate this piece of theorematic reasoning: the fertile crescent of present-day Israel, Palestine, Syria, Turkey, and Iraq seems to form the origin of many of the most important domestic species of the whole world, while the Far East comes in second. These areas were able to communicate domestications along the East-West axis and thus export them to Europe and the Far East. Of course, theorematicity must be a less precise concept in empirical examples like this, where the ontologies of biogeography and of culture are not exhaustively described, but still an argument may be made which runs as follows. The complex of three basic propositions 1) domestication of a species is a local event, 2) requiring stable human settlement in the natural niche of the species, 3) and the spread of such species must favor isotherms, combined with the diagram experiment of searching the world map where the most favorable isotherms occur, constitutes a piece of theorematic reasoning. It introduces a new object on the map—the possible spreading trajectories of domesticated animal and plant species— and thus hypothesizes a general regularity on the globe. This experiment on the map involves the combination of concepts from different regional ontologies, of geography, biogeography, meteorology, cultural history—in some sense, it synthesizes different world maps charting findings in these different disciplines as a prerequisite of the experiment. Thus, it provides a new argument for which cultures were able to survive. But it does not introduce a foreign idea.

A further geographical example may be the more famous diagram experiment by the German geographer and explorer Alfred Wegener, ultimately leading to the plate-tectonics of current geology. Famously, Wegener was observing a map and noticing that the West coast of Africa strangely fit like a puzzle piece into the East coast of South America;[13]

This lead to Wegener's groundbreaking 1912 idea ("Die Entstehung der Kontinente") that these continents had once been one—a controversial argument initially ridiculed, but later corroborated by the findings of geological

---

[13] Wegener was not the first to observe the similarity between the coastlines which seems to have been a theme already in the 17. Century. He seems to have been the first, however, to actually take the similarity as an argument, investing geological ontology in his diagram experiment.

Figure 10.7: Ill. The coastline fit of South America and Africa, supplemented with geological similarities, from Wegener 1929, 73. (The illustration adapted by Wegener from Alexander du Toit.)

and biological similarities along the two coasts and finally accepted after the discovery of the mid-Atlantic mountain range as the decisive indication that the ocean does in fact "grow" in the middle. This diagram experiment would then belong to a second level as compared to the Jared Diamond example. Here, not only new objects or connections are introduced—here a completely novel idea is introduced, namely that of continents moving over time. Taken on the level of pure diagrams, of course, nothing is strange—all Wegener did was to take a geometrical object and make a classical rigid Euclidean movement in order to let it face another object. This is permitted by geometry, of course, but not by the regional ontology of pre-Wegener geography. So Wegener's diagram experiment changed an axiom of geography, as it were—the assumption of long-term stability of large-scale features of the Earth surface—and so introduced not only a new object, but a foreign idea, that of continents moving on a geological timescale.

An example of a third level diagram experiment in geography might be taken from the same piece of history of science: the reinterpretation of the whole of the surface of the Earth in terms of moving continental plates, inverting their present movements and extrapolating them into the past in order to trace the origins of the continents. Mountain ranges now became seen as the results of continent collisions and volcanic areas as the result of chasms between plates going in different directions. This permitted the systematic, coordinated diagram experiment on a global scale reconstructing the original ur-continent of Pangaea. Wegener had already presented the idea of the ur-continent in his 1915 book; it was baptized Pangaea at a 1928 conference, and was presented like this in the 1929 version of his book *Die Entstehung der Kontinente und Ozeane* (19) shortly before his death in 1930:

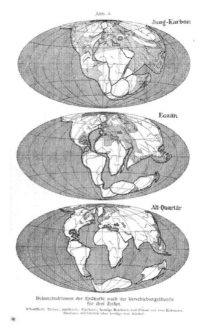

Figure 10.8: Rekonstruktionen det Erdkarte nach der Versciebungstheorie für drei Zeiten. (Reconstruction of the world map according to the displacement theory for three ages.)

Here, the particular change of an axiom leads to the systematic reinterpretation of the whole conceptual structure of geographical and geological ontology, effectively integrating the two into one discipline by seeing the same forces at work all over the surface of the Earth—in some ways comparable to the systematization of geometries after degrees of curvature.

10.5 Conclusion

Based on the hypothesis of these three levels of Theorematic reasoning:

1) Addition of new individuals to the premises, already allowed for in the ontology of the Universe of Discourse

2) Higher-level experiment with variation of axiom, transformation rule, or ontological assumption

3) Establishment of system of different axioms or rules

– how do they now relate to Hypostatic Abstraction—the procedure Peirce described as making a second-level substantive out of a first-level predicate, thereby creating a new object of thought? As we have seen in this paper, Peirce sometimes distinguishes non-abstract from abstract theorematic reasonings; but in an early quote he almost identifies abstraction with theorematic reasoning. Immediately, the talk about individual instantiation in the first theorematic reasoning type seems to preclude that abstraction should play any role here. Peirce's debatable analysis of lines as abstractions from the trajectories of moving particles would make the subsidiary lines in the angle sum proof abstract objects added in the proof. In any case, the importance of this step lies in the selection of the particular individual lines needed for the proof which is not a matter of abstraction. Likewise, such lines do not add an idea which could be said to be foreign to the theorem to be proved. Maybe the first-level addition of new individuals could comprise both abstract and non-abstract cases

Different, however, seems the case of the second level of theorematic reasoning, implying that some basic feature in the rule system is taken as the object of an experiment, leading to the introduction of a "foreign idea". If the parallel axiom is what defines the hypostatic abstraction of "parallelness" or "being parallel", then the variation of that axiom introduces competing definitions of that abstraction—the "foreign ideas" of that example; the abstraction of "continental drift" in the map example.

The third level, then, would be that of making a whole system out of hypostatic abstractions—this system constituting in itself, then, a complex hypostatic abstraction on a higher level, involving such new hypostatic terms as "curvature of space", or in geology, the whole doctrine of "plate tectonics".

This level seems characterized by a generalized version of Poncelet's continuity principle, "the introduction of the hypothesis of continuity where no continuity had hitherto been thought of", as Peirce had it—establishing continua of hypostatic abstractions from the second level.

No doubt, the relation between theorematic reasoning and abstraction allows for further sophistications which it lies beyond our scope to investigate here. This must be left for future investigations.

Chapter 11

Strategies of Research: Peirce's Enlightenment Maxims

This last chapter reviews what could be called Peirce's three Enlightenment maxims: the Pragmatic Maxim, 'Symbols Grow', and 'Do not block the way of inquiry.' The three of them constrain the growth of knowledge, of true Dicisigns, in Peirce's cognitive semiotics conception of the progress of science converging in the limit. Thus, they characterize Peirce's semiotics as an Enlightenment doctrine.

The fact that Charles Peirce's theory of science implies a scientific optimism is well known. From early on, Peirce held the idea that progress not only of science but of truth in general depends upon the collective effort of scholars—leading to his well-known definition of truth as convergence of human knowledge in the limit (in, for instance, *How to Make Our Ideas Clear*, 1878, EPI), and, correlatively, reality as the sum of states-of affairs which are referred to by true sentences of scientific knowledge in the limit. This doctrine of reality and truth with its emphasis on the cognitive effort of mankind Peirce aptly calls 'cognitionism'.[1] This correlation between truth, reality and the community of researchers in a broad sense has been taken as inspiration by later philosophers of democracy—in Germany, Karl-Otto Apel (e.g., 1974) and Jürgen Habermas (e.g., 1968)[2] have taken these Peircean ideas as central

---

[1] In "Quest of Quest", 1910 (Ms. 655), Peirce uses 'cognitionism' to describe the convergence stance that reality is what reasoning would finally result in, a stance inherited from Chauncey Wright and shared with James.

[2] Habermas, it is true, finds a tension between Peirce's convergence definition of reality and truth, on the one hand, and his scholastic realism on the other, claiming the former

293

to their political philosophies making public deliberation crucial to democracy; recently Peircean themes have been discussed in American political philosophy by Robert Talisse (2007) and Rosa Maria Mayorga (2009).

More rarely, however, have these basic Peircean ideas been brought into connection with what could be called his Enlightenment maxims regarding the semiotics of the research process. The whole of Peirce's semiotics and logic is developed in order to serve the overall aim of the development of the sciences and epistemology. Convergence to truth in the limit is subject to a complicated set of constraints in Peirce—hedged by the maxims of his 'methodeutic', the doctrine of the heuristics of the research process. The fact that these maxims are indeed developed from Enlightenment standards may be seen from the often-overlooked fact that basic tenets of Peirce's pragmatism come directly out of central Enlightenment figures such as Spinoza, Locke, Berkeley, and Kant. In Peirce's renewed focus upon pragmatism in the years after the turn of the century, this appears again and again, as when he characterizes his own position in the third person:

> "... yet in the writings of some philosophers, especially Kant, Berkeley, and Spinoza, he sometimes came upon strains of thought that recalled the ways of thinking of the laboratory, so that he felt he might trust to them; all of which has been true of other laboratorymen." (*What Pragmatism Is*, 1905, EPII, 332; 5.412)[3]

This inheritance is crystallized in Peirce's brief Enlightenment maxims of which at least three may be counted—one stated conditionally, one in the indicative, and one in the imperative.

11.1 The Pragmatic Maxim

In the public emergence of philosophical pragmatism around 1900 after the publication of William James's *The Will to Believe* (1896), James pointed back to Peirce's 1878 papers and their discussions in the Metaphysical Club

---

implies a 'linguistic-logic' foundation, ultimately basing science in structures of intersubjectivity. Habermas, however, commits the mistake of taking Peirce's semiotics to be a theory of communicative language only, thereby failing to realize its general cognitive and logical status, transcending human language in order to cover processes of cognition in general. This paves the way for Habermas' erroneous identification of specific human interests with certain scientific objects in *Knowledge and Human Interest*.

[3] Another example: "Of those who have used this way of thinking [pragmaticism, FS] Berkeley is the clearest example, though Locke (especially in the fourth book of his Essay), Spinoza, and Kant may be claimed as adherents of it" (Letter to Signor Calderoni 1905, 8.206).

in the early 1870s as the origin of the doctrine (even if the term 'pragmatism' was used by neither of them in print at that time), and Peirce vigorously entered the discussion of the basics of pragmatism (or 'pragmaticism' as he would rename it in 1905 in order to distinguish his own version from that of James). The famous first articulation of the maxim goes as follows: "Consider what effects, which might conceivably have practical bearings, we consider the object of our conception to have. Then, our conception of these effects is the whole of our conception of the object" (*How to Make our Ideas Clear*, 1878, EPI, 132; 5.402). In the years after 1900, Peirce reformulated the maxim numerous times, for instance as follows:

> "Pragmatism is the principle that every theoretical judgment ex-
> pressible in a sentence in the indicative mood is a confused form of
> thought whose only meaning, if it has any, lies in its tendency to en-
> force a corresponding practical maxim expressible as a conditional
> sentence having its apodosis in the imperative mood." (*Lectures on
> Pragmatism*, 1903, 5.18)

The basic intention of the maxim is that of clarifying the meaning of proposi-
tions. The idea is that all sorts of metaphysical ideas which do not have any 'practical bearings' or 'effects' (1878), any ensuing 'imperative practical max-
ims' (1903), are null and void. It goes without saying that Peirce did not host any positivist ideas that this would do away with metaphysics as such—rather it would cleanse science, including metaphysics, of empty and superfluous assumptions of all kinds. As a meaning theory, it may be compared to the mature Peirce's idea that the immediate meaning of a sign is the sum of all the ob-
vious logical implications of that sign (to be distinguished from the dynamic meaning of the sign, inferable from the context of utterance, on the one hand, and the final meaning of the sign, on the other, comprising all implications of it in the state of knowledge in the limit). At the same time, the pragmatic maxim is a generalization of the lab experience of the empirical scientist to sci-
ence and meaning in general, cf. the reference to 'thinking of the laboratory' in the Enlightenment philosophers. The practical effects which are found to follow, in the laboratory experiment, from a specific setup, constitute a special case of meaning more generally, where the sum of conceivable implications of any belief forms the exhaustive definition of its meaning. The relation of that meaning to practical issues comes from Alexander Bain's definition of belief, often quoted by Peirce, as "that upon which a man is prepared to act" (e.g. 5.12), ruling out lip-service paid to all sorts of ideas which are not, in reality, connected to possible action. A basic Enlightenment urge thus characterizes the maxim: that of getting rid of superfluous metaphysical assumptions. An

important tension, of course, remains between the conceived effects of a conception at any given time, on the one hand, and the conceivable effects of that conception in the limit; the research process having the aim of approaching from the former to the latter.

11.2 Symbols Grow

With this motto, the process of convergence to the limit is taken to be part and parcel of the historical development of man's symbol use—and, by extrapolation, of the growth of symbols already in pre-human nature. This forms an often misunderstood aspect of Peirce's doctrine (such as when Habermas takes symbols to refer to human linguistic usage only and thus reduces Peircean semiotics to a sort of human transcendental pragmatics): the biosemiotic claim that the growth of semiotics is a process inherent in nature, predating the origin of man. This idea gives rise to an indicative maxim (but, as the pragmatic maxim above made clear, indicatives are concealed conditional imperatives), the brief Enlightenment proverb that 'Symbols Grow'—competing in brevity with Horace's and Kant's more well-known imperative 'Sapere aude.' In his *Grand Logic* of 1894 (2.301-02), Peirce explains this idea:[4]

> "A symbol, as we have seen, cannot indicate any particular thing; it denotes a kind of thing. Not only that, but it is itself a kind and not a single thing. You can write down the word 'star,' but that does not make you the creator of the word, nor if you erase it have you destroyed the word. The word lives in the minds of those who use it. Even if they are all asleep, it exists in their memory. So we may admit, if there be reason to do so, that generals are mere words without at all saying, as Ockham supposed, that they are really individuals. Symbols grow. They come into being by development out of other signs, particularly from icons, or from mixed signs partaking of the nature of icons and symbols. We think only in signs. These mental signs are of mixed nature; the symbol-parts of them are called concepts. If a man makes a new symbol, it is by thoughts involving concepts. So it is only out of symbols that a new symbol can grow. *Omne symbolum de symbolo.* A symbol, once in

---

[4]This quote contains a seeming contradiction: first we learn that symbols may come into being out of other signs such as icons, a bit later we are taught that all symbols come from symbols. I think this tension may be solved by assuming that all signs, also from the earliest biological beginning, have a symbolic aspect. These symbols may, as is most often the case, contain icons which may evolve into separate symbols themselves. See the discussion in ch. 3.

being, spreads among the peoples. In use and in experience, its meaning grows. Such words as *force, law, wealth, marriage,* bear for us very different meanings from those they bore to our barbarous ancestors. The symbol may, with Emerson's sphynx, say to man,

Of thine eye I am eyebeam."

The basic idea of Peirce's cognitive semiotics that all thought takes place in signs,[5] has the converse corollary that as soon as you have signs giving rise to other signs, however simple, you have thought—and the process of the development of signs and thoughts can be studied not only apart from the individual mind, but apart from any special symbolisms put to use by man. Thus Peirce holds a special version of objective idealism: thought and ideas have intrinsic structures which are not invented by man (or by any other thinking being); rather the signs and minds of man, animals and other possible thinking beings must evolve in order to conform to the structure of thoughts. Such intrinsic structures of thoughts, however, are not conceived of in isolation from the world—general structures of the world (in a broad sense) are the same as those of thought, cf. the identification of reality with knowledge in the limit. The growth of symbols, then, is the Enlightenment process of self-evolving semiotic systems approaching reality in the limit. In an important quote from the "Minute Logic" in 1902, this process is directly linked to the concept of Enlightenment:

"...there is no more striking characteristic of dark ages, when thought was little developed, than the prevalence of a sentiment that an opinion was a thing to be chosen because one liked it, and which, having once been adopted, was to be fought for by fire and sword, and made to prevail. Take any general doctrine you please, and it makes no difference what facts may turn up: an ingenious logician will find means to fit them into the doctrine. Ask the theologians if this is not true. As civilization and enlightenment advance, however, this style of thought tends to weaken. Natural selection is against it; and it breaks down. Whatever one's theory may be as to the invalidity of human reason, there are certain cases where the force of conviction practically cannot be resisted; and one of these is the experience that one opinion is so far from being as strong as another in the long run, though it receives equally warm support, that on the contrary, ideas utterly despised and frowned

---

[5]"...all thought is in signs." ("Questions Concerning Certain Faculties Claimed For Man", 1868, 5.253).

upon have an inherent power of working their way to the governance of the world, at last. True, they cannot do this without machinery, without supporters, without facts; but the ideas somehow manage to grow their machinery, and their supporters, and their facts, and to render the machinery, the supporters, and the facts strong. As intellectual development proceeds, we all come to believe in this more or less. Most of us, such is the depravity of the human heart, look askance at the notion that ideas have any power; although that some power they have we cannot but admit. The present work, on the other hand, will maintain the extreme position that every general idea has more or less power of working itself out into fact; some more so, some less so. Some ideas, the harder and more mechanical ones, actualize themselves first in the macrocosm; and the mind of man receives them by submitting to the teachings of nature. Other ideas, the more spiritual and moral ones, actualize themselves first in the human heart, and pass to the material world through the agency of man. Whether all this be true or not, it must at any rate be admitted by every candid man that he does believe firmly and without doubt that to some extent phenomena are regular, that is, are governed by general ideas; and so far as they are so, they are capable of prediction by reasoning." ("Minute Logic", 1902, 2.149; see also 2.24)

The commonplace Enlightenment idea of Dark Ages gradually yielding to the spread of reason is interpreted in two surprising ways: it takes the shape of a process of natural selection, gradually letting better ideas survive at the expense of lesser ideas; and it is a process in which ideas themselves are agents attracting instantiations in signs and sign-users rather than being passive memes as in our days' parallel proposals regarding the selection and survival of ideas. The laws of physics are taken to be the most obvious example of general ideas having effect in the behavior of particulars. At the same time, ideas do not form an isolated realm apart from their instantiation in signs: it is only this incarnation that makes possible their expression and mutual fight for survival: "A pure idea without metaphor or other significant clothing is an onion without a peel" ("The Basis of Pragmaticism in the Normative Sciences", 1906, EPII, 392).[6] It is the growth of symbols which allows for ideas to become explicit and thus influence the course of evolution of the world. This is why diagrams and diagrammatical reasoning form the royal road to the development of ideas: they facilitate the direct observation of as well as the manipulation

---

[6]On Peirce's recurrent use of the onion metaphor to underline the necessary support of ideas by signs see de Tienne 2003 and Redondo 2008.

and experimentation with ideal entities, quite in parallel to the observation and experiment with empirical objects (cf. ch. 10; see also Stjernfelt 2007). In this doctrine of evolutionary convergence towards knowledge in the limit lies an important insensitivity to specific points of departure. Even if the present position is highly path-dependent, the attractor in the limit remains identical. No matter where one begins reasoning, knowledge in the limit forms an attractor making thought gravitate towards it. Thus, reasoning may reach the same results by very different trajectories from very different points of departure. Cultural, psychological, and historical particularities may slow down or force the process into long detours, but in the long run, the process is insensible to such particularities of individuals or particular groups of arguers. This does not imply, on the other hand, that all cultural or other differences will necessarily vanish in the limit: all signs necessarily retain some degree of 'material' aspects of their expression which are bound to their particular users—as long as they do not bar their trajectory towards the limit.

Given the Pragmatic Maxim and the naturalist doctrine of Symbols Grows, it might seem that the Enlightenment process towards the limit is an automatic, natural process of organic growth. In some sense it indeed is, but among the many different trajectories towards the limit, some are more direct than others which are delayed or even forever blocked by sticking to false conceptions. The better trajectories, however, may be found by adhering to Peirce's third Enlightenment maxim, smoothing the process of inquiry.

11.3 Do Not Block the Way of Inquiry

The development of reason as an objective process in the universe does not preclude us from influencing it. Quite on the contrary, as we are ourselves co-constituents of the universe, our actions may have effects on the process. This is why the indicative ascertainment of the existence of the growth of symbols is compatible with normative claims about how to further it most efficiently:

> "...the development of Reason requires as a part of it the occurrence of more individual events than ever can occur. It requires, too, all the coloring of all qualities of feeling, including pleasure in its proper place among the rest. This development of Reason consists, you will observe, in embodiment, that is, in manifestation. The creation of the universe, which did not take place during a certain busy week, in the year 4004 B.C., but is going on today and never will be done, is this very developement of Reason. I do not see how one can have a more satisfying ideal of the admirable than

the development of Reason so understood. The one thing whose admirableness is not due to an ulterior reason is Reason itself comprehended in all its fullness, so far as we can comprehend it. Under this conception, the ideal of conduct will be to execute our little function in the operation of the creation by giving a hand toward rendering the world more reasonable whenever, as the slang is, it is 'up to us' to do so. In logic, it will be observed that knowledge is reasonableness; and the ideal of reasoning will be to follow such methods as must develop knowledge the most speedily ..." ("Ideals of Conduct—Lowell Lectures," 1903, 1.615)

That it is 'up to us' to further the ongoing process of making the world more reasonable entails we should do some things rather than others in order to promote the process. This imperative governing what we should do is articulated in 1898 under the headline of *The First Rule of Logic*—taken in the broad, heuristic sense of the logic of inquiry. This rule is taken to be that in order to learn, you must desire to learn—in short: you must wonder. But wondering implies you are not satisfied with the present state of knowledge and so refuse at least some part of tradition and aim to correct and further the process of inquiry:

> "Upon this first, and in one sense this sole, rule of reason, that in order to learn you must desire to learn, and in so desiring not be satisfied with what you already incline to think, there follows one corollary which itself deserves to be inscribed upon every wall of the city of philosophy: Do not block the way of inquiry." (EPII, 48; 1.135)

In some sense, this imperative may seem so self-evident as to be easily overlooked. Why should any researcher wish to block the way of inquiry? Peirce's elaboration of this corollary, however, takes important implications from it. Most importantly, he claims that the central sin of metaphysicians of all times is exactly that of blocking the way of inquiry. In that sense, this maxim is a further detailing of the impetus against established metaphysics (and ideologies, religions, etc.) contained in the pragmatic maxim already from 1878.[7] Such blocking may take, Peirce claims, four basic shapes.

---

[7]Religiously, Peirce's background was Unitarian though he converted to Evangelicalism when marrying Melusina Fay; he seemed to be a sort of Christian with Buddhist leanings, approaching a version of deism—while at the same time being deeply sceptical against established churches as instruments of power (cf. "...can anybody who understands the procedure of science [...] assent for a moment to the idea that any science, be it theology or any other, can be rightly developed under the impulses of ecclesiastical ambition and the **odium** of priests?", "Politics and Religion" c. 1895, 6.450). We shall not go deeply into

1) One is "absolute assertion" or "over-confident assertion" (EPII, 49; 1.137) —Peirce here takes the Euclidean parallel axiom as his example, being careful to note that Euclid himself did not make of it more than a postulate. Later geometers, however, skipped this hypothetical aspect of the parallel postulate to make it into an absolute assertion (thereby halting the development of geometry for two thousand years until the emergence of non-Euclidean geometries in the 19th C). Peirce's hypothesis is that such over-confident assertion is a fault for third- or fourth-rate men interested more in teaching than in learning, that is, more oriented towards appearing as sources of truth to an audience than in actually searching for truth.

2) The second road block is the converse of the first: the claim "...maintaining that this, that, and the other never can be known" (EPII, 49, 1.138), thereby effectively attempting to halt further research in that direction. Peirce takes as his example Comte's famous claim that the chemical composition of stars will forever be beyond the reach of science—which was refuted not long after by the discovery of spectral line radiation patterns, specifically characterizing each element. Had Comte's contention been generally accepted by bodies governing the funding of research, we may imagine an alternative timeline in which spectral analysis had never been discovered.

3) The third and fourth blocking strategies temporalize, in effect, the two first ones: the third consists in "...maintaining that this, that, or the other element of science is basic, ultimate, independent of aught else, and utterly inexplicable—not so much from any defect in our knowing as because there is nothing beneath it to know" (EP II, 49, 1.139). It is the claim that some ultimate point has been reached beyond which further research can never penetrate. To some extent, this characterizes the role which the Big Bang has held for decades in cosmology—or, more generally physicalism, psychologism, historicism or any other sweeping reduction claim in the sciences. Peirce does not offer an example but rather an a priori refutation: such a claim of unattainability can be reached by abduction only, but abduction provides a possible explanation, and thus cannot possibly declare anything inexplicable.

Peirce's writings pertaining to religion here, suffice it to say that his anti-institutional type of faith has similarities to Enlightenment stances such as that of Voltaire, or even that of Spinoza:"The **raison d'être** of a church is to confer upon men a life broader than their narrow personalities, a life rooted in the very truth of being. To do that it must be based upon and refer to a definite and public experience. Fears of hell and hopes of paradise have no such reference; they are matters all sane men confess they know nothing about. Even for the greatest saints, the active motives were not such hopes and fears, but the prospect of leaving behind them fertile seeds of desirable fruits here on earth" (ibid. 6.451). The idea that the true purpose of religion is social cohesion and earthly influence on people's behaviour is close to the Spinozist stance of the *Tractatus*.

4) The fourth strategy is "... holding that this or that law or truth has found its last and perfect formulation—and especially that the ordinary and usual course of nature never can be broken through" (EP II, 49–50, 1.140). The claim of perfection regarding a certain piece of knowledge immunizes it from further scrutiny. The special example Peirce adds pertains to his 'tychism'—the Maxwellian idea that real chance exists and makes larger or lesser deviations possible in any empirical law. Peirce himself makes use of the anti-roadblock maxim over and over, mostly implicitly, as when refusing rationalist dogmatism as well as empiricist beliefs in beginning with absolute, simple facts, or when introducing fallibilism requiring us to admit that every single piece of our current knowledge at any time could in principle be doubted, at the same time as claiming that the overall sum of that knowledge is probably sound and parts of it should only actually be doubted when some particular reason calls for it.

That the refutation of such roadblock stratagems is closely connected to Peirce's own pragmatist methodology and fallibilism comes as little surprise; its connection to his own metaphysics may be less evident. Peirce, of course, was a monist; the refutation of all sorts of dualisms comes directly from the refusal to block the way of inquiry: claiming the world consists of two (or more) irreconcilable realms is the same as claiming that the road to finding laws of regularities for the interaction between those realms is forever blocked—for if not they would, effectively, merge into one. Similarly, the refusal of roadblocks is what makes Peirce's metaphysics inclusive, going against excessive ontological reduction. Most significantly, of course, in his refusal of nominalism claiming the nonexistence of any universals of thirdness as the result of excessive use of Ockam's razor—but also more generally in his refusal of all of the 6 types of metaphysical systems which do not allow the full triad of Peircean categories to co-exist (*The Seven Systems of Metaphysics*, EP II, 179ff; 5.93ff.). Finally, Peirce's adherence to the Principle of Continuity is connected to this maxim: science proceeds by constructing continuous connections between realms earlier believed to be unconnected. This is why the scientist must assume—until proven wrong—continuity to reign rather than discontinuity which might lead to blocking the way of inquiry. An explicit example of Peirce's use can be seen when we find him writing to Dewey in order to refute his claim that all scientific explanations be genetic: "Never permanently bar the road of any true inquiry ..." (1905, 8.243). Effectively, it is the fourth roadblock stratagem he finds put to use in Dewey when he claims that all scientific explanations should be genetic; Peirce of course realizing that such an idea will inevitably entail relativism.[8] Hintikka once claimed that the only thing preventing Peirce's dialogical conception of logic from being fully fledged game-theoretical semantics was his lack of a notion of *strategy*. Hintikka claims the closest Peircean equivalent to such a notion is his concept of *habit*.[9] To Hintikka, an important distinction in epistemology is that between constitutive rules and strategic rules (cf. Hintikka 2009)—with the basic illustration of the simplicity of chess rules vs. the vast complexities of chess strategies. The implication, of course, is logic needing the addition of strategic rules of investigation in order to bridge the way to the understanding of scientific investigations. Here, however, Peirce's Enlightenment maxims form, as part of his heuristic theory of science, his "methodeutics", an elementary set of such strategic rules with huge consequences. They may not translate directly into individual competitive stratagems of Hintikkan proof games, but they do provide important rules of scientific strategy: do not assume absolute starting points, do not accept separated ontological realms, do not accept fields definitely closed to any investigation, do never take questions to be completely settled, do not believe in absolute doubt, do not refuse the existence of universals, do not believe in the wholesale reduction of one field to another, do not accept the erroneous hypostatization of limit cases into independent objects, prefer bundles of inferences over single counterexamples ... such roadblock assumptions may bar the player from moves which may, unexpectedly, prove fruitful ...

11.4 Peirce's Enlightenment

The three maxims discussed briefly here frame, taken together, a Peircean conception of Enlightenment as the ongoing reasoning process carried on in-

---

[8]In an earlier letter from the same year, Peirce warns Dewey against letting logic depend genetically upon sciences which, themselves, depend upon logic: "There are three sciences according to me to which Logic ought to appeal for principles, because they do not depend upon Logic. They are Mathematics, Phenomenology, and Ethics. There are several sciences to which logicians often make appeal by arguments which would be circular if they rose to the degree of correctness necessary to that kind of fallacy. They are Metaphysical Philosophy, Psychology, Linguistics [...], History, etc." (1905, 8.242). Evidently, this argument is a generalization of Peirce's thoroughgoing anti-psychologism of logic (see ch. 2); at the same time, the argument is that such genetic explanation blocks the way of inquiry.

[9]As Hintikka says, often quoted by Pietarinen: "I suspect, in other words, that inside each Peircean habit there lurks (at least in the area of epistemology) a strategic rule trying to get out" ("What is abduction? The fundamental problem of contemporary epistemology", in Hintikka (1999) 100). Pietarinen (2011a) provides a strong argument for the fact that Peirce's notion of habit, in his attempts at articulating a proof of pragmaticism after 1900, actually came very close to a concept of strategy.

tersubjectively by humanity. The beginning as well as the end of that process are not absolute and may never be made explicit—both of them are subject to Peirce's continuism and may be grasped as limits only. Before man, this implies that the process of Enlightenment was already brewing in organic nature. In the opposite end, Enlightenment continues indefinitely, its end point only existing at the limit. Peirce's main emphasis, as a scientist and philosopher of science, obviously lies on the cognitive content of the process. But he is not blind to ethical or even political aspects of the process. Peirce generally saw established morality as conservative, conformist and traditionalist and thus blocking the way of the reasoning process[10]—but at the same time he envisioned a future development of ethics intertwined with scientific progress on

---

[10]As to seminal political questions of the period, Peirce's father Benjamin was an anti-abolitionist; Peirce's stance on that issue is harder to determine. Peirce sometimes proposed a distinction between the role of reason in science and in "human affairs" which may have taken observers to portray him as a conservative (e.g. Louis Menand in his 2001 book): "Men many times fancy that they act from reason when, in point of fact, the reasons they attribute to themselves are nothing but excuses which unconscious instinct invents to satisfy the teasing 'whys' of the *ego*. The extent of this self-delusion is such as to render philosophical rationalism a farce. Reason, then, appeals to sentiment in the last resort. Sentiment on its side feels itself to be the man. That is my simple apology for philosophical sentimentalism. Sentimentalism implies conservatism; and it is of the essence of conservatism to refuse to push any practical principle to its extreme limits—including the principle of conservatism itself" ("Detached Ideas", 1898, 1.631-1.633). In the very same paper, however, he continues: "I would not allow to sentiment or instinct any weight whatsoever in theoretical matters, not the slightest. Right sentiment does not demand any such weight; and right reason would emphatically repudiate the claim if it were made. True, we are driven oftentimes in science to try the suggestions of instinct; but we only *try* them, we compare them with experience, we hold ourselves ready to throw them overboard at a moment's notice from experience. If I allow the supremacy of sentiment in human affairs, I do so at the dictation of reason itself; and equally at the dictation of sentiment, in theoretical matters I refuse to allow sentiment any weight whatever" (ibid. 1.634). Sentiment seems to play the role of guiding reason on selecting the most fertile abductions for further testing, rather than forming a conservative ground immune to reason. You can add that with all we know about Peirce's tumultuous personal life it is difficult to believe much in any portrayal of him as a conservative. Rather, science and reason act as radical dissolvents with respect to conservative morals: "Hence, morality is essentially conservative. Good morals and good manners are identical, except that tradition attaches less importance to the latter. The gentleman is imbued with conservatism. This conservatism is a habit, and it is the law of habit that it tends to spread and extend itself over more and more of the life. In this way, conservatism about morals leads to conservatism about manners and finally conservatism about opinions of a speculative kind. Besides, to distinguish between speculative and practical opinions is the mark of the most cultivated intellects.

Go down below this level and you come across reformers and rationalists at every turn—people who propose to remodel the ten commandments on modern science. Hence it is that morality leads to a conservatism which any new view, or even any free inquiry, no matter how purely speculative, shocks. The whole moral weight of such a community will be cast against science. To inquire into nature is for a Turk very unbecoming to a good Moslem;

the basis that both of them prosper from the increasing self-control of reason-ers. Thus the collaboration of scientists prefigures the ethical collaboration of human beings more broadly, supported by the dialogic structure of logi-cal argumentation (cf. ch. 6). Peirce did not develop these ideas anywhere nearly as deeply as his theory of science, and we cannot go further into them here; suffice to say that the standard of self-control, common to science and ethics, individually and intersubjectively, also in this respect places Peirce in the Enlightenment tradition emphasizing human autonomy and liberty.

Given the ongoing discussion of 'moderate' versus 'radical' Enlightenments after Jonathan Israel's important 2001 book, you might ask, a bit anachro-nistically, to which camp Peirce might be counted. Israel's distinction mainly turns upon whether to politically compromise with princely or clerical author-ities (moderates) or not (radicals), and Peirce only marginally treats political issues explicitly. His ontological monism, of course, pulls him towards the radical side, while his religious sentiments rather draw him towards moderate Enlightenment. His staunch refusal of religious institutions as power appara-tuses,[11] however, along with his equally strong refusal of authority arguments in the reasoning process and his emphasis on intersubjective deliberation in science, rather tend to place him in the radical camp.

---

just as the family of Tycho Brahe regarded his pursuit of astronomy as unbecoming to a nobleman" (*Lessons from the History of Science*, c. 1896, 1.50).

In general, the Peircean stance plays an important role for free speech. Justice Oliver Wendell Holmes who famously instituted the modern interpretation of the First Amendment in the US Superior Court in 1919 was an original member of the Metaphysical Club in the early 1870s. In our time, one of the most important voices in the discussions of free speech and "political correctness", Jonathan Rauch, explicitly takes Peirce and the motto "Do Not Block the Way of Inquiry" as his foundation (Rauch 2013, 170ff).

[11] As when he comments upon the method of tenacity (authority) in religions by the following classical Enlightenment quip: "Every distinctive creed was as a historical fact invented to harm somebody" (Note added to "The Fixation of Belief" 1893, 5.380n).

Chapter 12

Perspective

It is my hope this book will contribute to the development of a cognitive semiotics which is no longer blocked by the persistent dualisms so widespread in cognitive science and philosophy of mind. As soon as you take the starting point as being hard divisions like those between inner and outer, body and soul, mind and matter, perception and cognition, images and logic, you will be sure to spend the rest of your conceptual life by trying, in vain, to bridge those dualisms. Your very point of departure will serve as a trap from which you will never escape, with ever so many conceptual sophistications and experimental investigations.

The modern version of that quagmire is often dated to the Cartesian *res extensa/res cogitans* distinction, but you might just as well pass the trophy to the competitors of the rationalists—the empiricists with their conception of ideas in the head, ever struggling to reunite those ideas with a supposed or hypothetical world out there. The concept of sign, from the outset, involves meanings as well as objects, not falling apart in any of the versions of the subject-object dichotomy mentioned. The crooked and not very succesful history of modern semiotics, however, is no testimony to the idea that it should be easy to steer such a conception of signs away from the dangers of received subject-object dichotomies.

I hope this book makes a case for Peircean semiotics being able to follow that course, with a conception of signs in which biological intentionality must, from the very beginning, be taken to instantiate simple inferences. Such a view, a semiotics in a certain sense naturalized, where a cognitive appreciation of logic becomes a central axis, will allow us to integrate biosemiotics and human semiotics in a broader picture, just like man's plural set of different, externalized semiotic systems with all their varied action purposes will be seen to share, in different ways, the fundamental reliance upon truth claimed by Dicisigns and their ongoing development in reasoning. This does not wed us to any overarching teleology in the cosmos, nor to mysterious dreams of prebiological pan-semiotism, but it gives us a hint of why it is that the—in a certain sense very narrow—continuous windows of proposition and argument structure allow us to attain idealized and general objectives, in myth, arts, science, politics, technology, and other large human endeavours.

References

Adler, J., Hazelbauer, G. L. & Dahl, M. M. (1973) "Chemotaxis Toward Sugars in Escherichia Coli", *Journal of Bacteriology*, 115 (3), 824-847

Almeder, Robert F (1970) "Peirce's Theory of Perception", *Transactions of the Charles S. Peirce Society,* vol 6, no. 2, 99-110

Amini, Majid (2008) "Logical Machines: Peirce on Psychologism", *Disputatio*, vol. II, no. 24, 336-348

Anellis, Irving H. (1995) "Peirce Rustled, Russell Pierced: How Charles Peirce and Betrand Russell Viewed each Other's Work in Logic, and an Assessment of Russell's Accuracy and Role in the Historiography of Logic", *Modern Logic* 5 (1995), 270-328

– (2012) "How Peircean was the 'Fregean' Revolution in Logic?", working paper, http://arxiv.org/pdf/1201.0353.pdf (accessed July 10, 2013)

Apel, K.O. (1974) "From Kant to Peirce. The Semiotical Transformation of Transcendental Logic", in: L.W. Beck (ed.) *Kant's Theory of Knowledge*, Dordrecht: Reidel 1974: 23–37

Aristotle (1975) *Categories and De Interpretatione*, Oxford: Oxford UP

Austin, J.L. (1961) *Philosophical Papers*, Oxford: Oxford UP

Baggersgaard, Carsten (2013) "Klarlund: Sandheden er taberen", in *Uniavisen* Sept. 5 2013, http://universitetsavisen.dk/videnskab/klarlund-sandheden-er-taberen, accessed Nov. 27 2013

Baldwin, James Mark (1902) *Dictionary of Philosophy of Psychology,* N.Y.: Macmillan Co.

Barsalou, Lawrence (1999) "Perceptual Symbol Systems", in *Behavioral and Brain Sciences* 22, 577-660

– (2003) "Abstraction in Perceptual Symbol Systems", in *Phil. Trans. R. Soc. Lond.*, vol. 358, 1177–1187

Bellucci, Francesco (2013) "Diagrammatic Reasoning: Some Notes on Charles S. Peirce and Friedrich A. Lange", *History and Philosophy of Logic*, DOI:10.1080/01445340.2013.777991

– (2013a) "Peirce's Continuous Predicates", *Transactions of the Charles S. Peirce Society*, vol. 49, no. 2, 178-202

– (in preparation) "The Deduction of the Dicisign. Peirce on Propositions and Other Signs"

Benacerraf, Paul with H. Putnam (1989), (eds.) *Philosophy of Mathematics*, Camb.Mass.: Cambridge University Press

Berg, H.C. (1988) "A Physicist Looks at Bacterial Chemotaxis", *Cold Spring Harbor Symposia on Quantitative Biology*, 53, 1-9

Bermúdez, José and Cahen, Arnon (2012) "Nonconceptual Mental Content", *The Stanford Encyclopedia of Philosophy* (Spring 2012 Edition), Edward N. Zalta (ed.), plato.stanford.edu/archives/spr2012/entries/content-nonconceptual/

Bird, C. D. and Emery, N. J. (2009) "Insightful Problem Solving and Creative Tool Modification by Captive Nontool-using Rooks", *Proc Nat Acad Sci* 106, 10370-10375

Boole, George (1854) *The Laws of Thought* www.gutenberg.org/files/15114/15114-pdf.pdf

Bredekamp, Horst (2010) *Theorie des Bildakts*, Berlin: Suhrkamp

Brock, Jarrett (1981) "An Introduction to Peirce's Theory of Speech Acts" in *Transactions of the Charles S. Peirce Society*, XVII, 319-326

Brown, James Robert (2008) *Philosophy of Mathematics: A Contemporary Introduction to the World of Proofs and Pictures* (2.ed.), N.Y. and London: Routledge

– (2010) *The Laboratory of the Mind: Thought Experiments in the Natural Sciences* (2.ed.), N.Y: and London: Routledge

Brøndal, Viggo (1948) *Les parties du discours: partes orationis. Études sur les catégories linguistiques*, Copenhagen: Munksgaard (Danish version 1928)

Bruck, Jason N. (2013) "Decades-long social memory in bottlenose dolphins", *Proc. R. Soc. B* vol. 280 no. 1768, 20131726, http://rspb.royalsocietypublishing.org.ez.statsbiblioteket.dk:2048/content/280/1768/20131726.full.pdf

Bruner, Jerome (1977) "Early social interaction and language acquisition", H.R. Schaffer (ed.): *Studies in Mother-Infant interaction*, New York: Academic Press

Brunning, Jacqueline and Forster, Paul (1997) (eds.) *The Rule of Reason. The Philosophy of Charles Sanders Peirce* Toronto: University of Toronto Press

Buchsbaum, Bradley R., Rosanna K. Olsen, Paul Koch, and Karen Faith Berman (2005) "Human Dorsal and Ventral Auditory Streams Subserve Rehearsal-Based and Echoic Processes during Verbal Working Memory", *Neuron*, Volume 48, Issue 4, 687-697

Bundgaard, Peer (2004) "The Ideal Scaffolding of Language: Husserl's fourth *Logical Investigation* in the light of cognitive linguistics", *Phenomenology and the Cognitive Sciences* 3: 49-80

Bundgaard, Peer, S. Østergaard, and F. Stjernfelt (2006) "Waterproof Fire Stations. Conceptual schemata and cognitive operations involved in compound constructions", in *Semiotica*, vol. 161 – 1/4, 362-393

Burch, R.W. (1997) "Peirce's Reduction Thesis", Houser et al. (eds.) 234-251

Byrne, Alex (2004) "Perception and Conceptual Content", *Contemporary Debates in Epistemology*, (eds. E. Sosa and M. Steup) Oxford: Blackwell, 231-250

Caro, T.M. and M. D. Hauser "Is There Teaching in Nonhuman Animals?" *The Quarterly Review of Biology*, Vol. 67, No. 2 (Jun., 1992), 151-17

Cassirer, Ernst (1944) "The Concept of Group and the Theory of Perception", in *Philosophy and Phenomenological Research* 5: 1-35 (original French version 1938)

– (1945) "Structuralism in Modern Linguistics" in *Word*, vol. I, nr. II, 99-120

– (1954) *Philosophie der symbolischen Formen* I-III, Darmstadt 1954 (1923-29)

– (1956) "Zur Logik der Symbolbegriffs", in *Wesen und Wirkung des Symbolbegriffs*, Darmstadt (1938)

– (1985) "Die Sprache und die Aufbau des Gegenstandswelts", in *Symbol, Technik, Sprache*, Hamburg: Felix Meiner (1927)

Cheney, Dorothy L. and Robert M. Seyfarth (1980) "Vocal Reccognition in Free-Ranging Vervet Monkeys", *Anim. Behav.*, 28, 362-367

– (1988) "Assessment of meaning and the detection of unreliable signalsby vervet monkeys", *Anim. Behav.*, 36, 477-486

– (1990) *How Monkeys See the World: Inside the Mind of Another Species* Chicago: University of Chicago Press

Clark, A. (2008) *Supersizing the Mind: Embodiment, Action, and Cognitive Extension.* Oxford: Oxford University Press.

Coffa, J. Alberto (1991) *The Semantic Tradition from Kant to Carnap*, Cambridge: Cambridge University Press

Colapietro, Vincent (2003) "The Space of Signs: C.S.Peirce's Critique of Psychologism", in Jacquette 2003, 157-80

Collier, John (submitted) "Signs Without Minds", http://web.ncf.ca/collier/papers/Signs%20without%20minds.pdf

Cooke, E. (2010) "Peirce's General Theory of Inquiry and the Problem of Mathematics", in Moore (2010), 169-292

Copeland, Jonathan and James E. Lloyd (1983) "Male Firefly Mimicry", *Science*, New Series, Vol. 221, No. 460, 484-485

Crane, Tim "Is Perception a Propositional Attitude?", *The Philosophical Quarterly*, vol. 59, no. 236, 452-469

Cussins, Adrian (1990) "The Connectionist Construction of Concepts", *The Philosophy of Artificial Intelligence* (ed. Margaret Boden), Oxford:Oxford University Press, 368-440

Deacon, T. (1997) *The Symbolic Species*, N.Y.: W.W.Norton

– (2012) "Beyond the Symbolic Species", in Schilhab, Deacon, and Stjernfelt (eds., 2012) 9–38

– (2012b) *Incomplete Nature*, N.Y.: W.W.Norton

Deely, John (2001) *Four Ages of Understanding*, Toronto: University of Toronto Press

Diamond, Jared (2005) *Guns, Germs and Steel* London: Vintage, 2005 [1997]

Dipert, Randall (1995) "Peirce's Underestimated Place in the History of Logic: A Response to Quine", in Ketner 1995, 32-58

– (1997) "Peirce's Philosophical Conception of Sets", in Houser et al. (eds.) 1997, 53–76

– (2004) "Peirce's Deductive Logic: Its Development, Influence, and Philosophical Significance", in Misak 2004, 287-324

Dougherty, Charles J. (1983) "Peirce's Phenomenological Defense of Deduction", in Freeman 1983, 167-177

Eco, Umberto (1976) *A Theory of Semiotics,* Bloomington: Indiana U.P.

– (1999) *Kant and the Platypus*, London: Secker

El-Hani, C., Queiroz, J., and Stjernfelt, F. (2010) "Firefly femmes fatales: A Case Study in the Semiotics of Deception. *Journal of Biosemiotics*, vol. 3.1, April 2010, 33-55

Elqayam, Shira & Evans, Jonathan (2011) "Subtracting "ought" from "is": Descriptivism versus normativism in the study of human thinking", *Behavioral and Brain Sciences* (2011) 34, 233–290 doi:10.1017/S0140525X1100001X

Emery, Nathan & Nicola Clayton (2004) "The Mentality of Crows: Convergent Evolution of Intelligence in Corvids and Apes", *Science* 306 (5703): 1903–7

Engel, Pascal (1998) "The Psychologist's Return", *Synthese* 115, 1998, 375-393

Evans, Gareth (1982) *The Varieties of Reference*, Oxford: Oxford University Press

Fauconnier, G. & Turner, M. (2002) *The Way We Think. Conceptual Blending and the Mind's Hidden Complexities* N.Y.: Basic Books

Fisch, Max (1986) "Peirce's Progress from Nominalism Towards Realism", in Fisch (eds. K.L.Ketner and C.J.W.Kloesel) *Peirce, Semeiotic, and Pragmatism*, Bloomington: Indiana University Press, 184-200

Forster, Paul (2011) *Peirce and the Threat of Nominalism*, Cambridge: Cambridge University Press

Frasnelli, Johannes, Johan N. Lundström, Veronika Schöpf, Simona Negoias, Thomas Hummel, and Franco Lepore (2012) "Dual processing streams in chemosensory perception", *Front Hum Neurosci*; 6: 288 doi:10.3389/fnhum.2012.00288

Frisch, Karl von (1965) *Tanzsprache und Orientierung der Bienen*, Berlin-Heidelberg-New York: Springer Verlag

– (1967) *The Dance Language and Orientation of Bees*, Cambridge Mass.: Harvard University Press

Freeman, Eugene (ed.) (1983) *The Relevance of Charles Peirce*, La Salle, Illinois: The Hegeler Institute

Frege, Gottlob (1995) *Begriffsschrift und andere Aufsätze* (ed. Ignacio Angelelli), Hildesheim: Georg Olms (*Begriffsschrift* org. 1879)

– (1986) *Grundlagen der Arithmetik*, Ditzingen: Reclam (1884)

Gardner, Esther P. (2008) "Dorsal and Ventral Streams in the Sense of Touch", in Jon H. Kaas and Esther Gardner (eds.) *The Senses: A Comprehensive Reference* vol. 6 *Somatosensation* Amsterdam etc.: Elsevier, 233-258

Goldfarb, Warren B. (1979) "Logic in the Twenties: The Nature of the Quantifier", *The Journal of Symbolic Logic*, Vol. 44, No. 3 (Sep., 1979), 351-368

Goodale, Melvyn A. and A. David Milner "Separate visual pathways for perception and action", *Trends in Neurosciences*, Vol. 15, No. I, 1992, 20-25

Goodman, Nelson (1976) *Languages of Art*, Indianapolis: Hackett Publishing Company

Gould, James L. (2002) "Can Honey Bees Create Cognitive Maps?", in Mark Beckoff, Colin Allen, and Gordon M. Burghardt (eds.) *The Cognitive Animal. Empirical and Theoretical Perspectives on Animal Cognition*, Cambridge Mass.: MIT Press, 41-45

Groden, Robert J. and Livingstone, Harrison Edward (1990) *High Treason*, N.Y.: Berkley Books

Haack, S. (1992) "Extreme Scholastic Realism: Its Relevance to Philosophy of Science Today", *Transactions of the Charles S. Peirce Society*, XXVIII (1), 19-50

Habermas, Jürgen (1968) *Erkenntnis und Interesse* [*Knowledge and Human Interest*], Frankfurt: Suhrkamp

Haiman, John (1985) *Natural Syntax: Iconicity and Erosion*, Cambridge: Cambridge University Press

Hanks, Peter (2009) "Recent Work on Propositions", *Philosophy Compass* 4/3, 469–486

Haugeland, John (2000) *Having Thought*, Camb. Mass.: Harvard University Press

Hilpinen, Risto (1992) "On Peirce's Philosophical Logic: Propositions and Their Objects", *Transactions* XXVIII, no. 3,, 467-488

– (2007) "On the Objects and Interpretants of Signs: Comments on T. L. Short's Peirce's Theory of Signs", *Transactions of the Charles S. Peirce Society*: Volume 43, Number 4, pp. 610-618

– (in press) "Conception, Sense, and Reference in Peircean Semiotics", in *Synthese, special issue on "Peirce's Logic"*

Hintikka, J. (1983) "C.S. Peirce's "First Real Discovery" and Its Contemporary Relevance", In E. Freeman (Ed.), *The Relevance of Charles Peirce*, La Salle, Ill.: The Hegeler Institute, 107-118.

– (1997) "The Place of C.S. Peirce in the History of Logical Theory", J. Brunning and P. Forster (eds.), *The Rule of Reason*, Toronto: University of Toronto Press, 13-33 (also in Hintikka 1997, 140-61)

– (1997a) *Lingua Universalis vs. Calculus Ratiocinator. An Ultimate Presupposition of Twentieth-Century Philosophy*, Dordrecht etc.: Kluwer

– (1999) *Inquiry as Inquiry*, Dordrecht: Kluwer

– (2007) *Socratic Epistemology. Exploration of Knowledge-Seeking by Questioning*, Cambridge: Cambridge University Press

Hintikka, J. and J. Symons (2007) "Systems of Visual Identification in Neuroscience: Lessons from Epistemic Logic", in Hintikka (2007), 145-160

Hoffmann, Michael (2006) "Seeing Problems, Seeing Solutions. Abduction and Diagrammatic Reasoning in a theory of Scientific Discovery", Working Paper #2006.15, Georgia Institute of Technology

– (2010) "'Theoric Transformations' and a New Classification of Abductive Inferences", *Transactions of the Charles S. Peirce Society* vol. 46, no. 4, 570-590

Hoffmeyer, J. (1996) "Evolutionary Intentionality", E. Pessa, A. Montesanto, and M.P.Penna (eds.), *Proceedings from The Third European Conference on Systems Science*, Rome: Edzioni Kappa, 699-703

– (2008) *Biosemiotics. An Examination into the Signs of Life and the Life of Signs* Scranton: University of Scranton Press

– (2010) "Semiotic freedom: an emerging force", P. Davies and N. H. Gregersen (eds.), *Information and the Nature of Reality From Physics to Metaphysics* Cambridge: Cambridge University Press, 185-204

Hoffmeyer, J. and Stjernfelt, F. (in press) "The Great Chain of Semiosis: Investigating the Steps in the Evolution of Biosemiotic Competence", in Kull, Kalevi (ed.) *Semiotic Approaches to Evolution*, Dordrecht: Springer

Hookway, Chr. (2002) "'...a sort of composite photograph'. Pragmatism and Schematism", in? *Transactions of the Charles S Peirce Society* XXXVIII, 29-45

Houser, N. (1992) "On Peirce's Theory of Propositions: A Response to Hilpinen", *Transactions* XXVIII, no. 3, 489-504

Houser, Nathan, Don D. Roberts and James van Evra (eds.) 1997 *Studies in the Logic of Charles Sanders Peirce*, Bloomington: Indiana University Press

Hulswit, Menno (1997) "Peirce's teleological approach to natural classes", *Transactions of the Charles S. Peirce Society* 33 (3), 722-772

Hurford, James (2003) "The neural basis of predicate-argument structure", *Behavioral and Brain Sciences* 26, 261–316 (Target article with comments and rejoinder, all of which are referred, in the text, to Hurford (2003) and page numbers.)

– (2007) *The Origin of Meaning*, Oxford: Oxford University Press

– (2011) *The Origin of Grammar*, Oxford: Oxford University Press

Husserl, Edmund (1970) *Logical Investigations* (transl. J.N.Findlay), London and Henley: Routledge and Kegan Paul

– (1970a) *Philosophie der Aritmetik, Hua* XII, Den Haag: Martinus Nijhoff

– (1971) *Ideen zu einer reinen Phänomenologie und Phänomenologischen Philosophie*, drittes Buch *Husserliana* vol. V Tübingen: Max Niemeyer

– (1975) *Logische Untersuchungen, Hua* XVIII, Den Haag: Martinus Nijhoff, (1900)

– (1979) *Aufsätze und Rezensionen (1890-1910), Hua* XXII, Dordrecht etc.: Martinus Nijhoff

– (1980) *Phantasie, Bildbewusstsein, Erinnerung, Hua* XXIII, Dordrecht etc.: Martinus Nijhoff

– (1980a) *Ideen zu einer reinen Phänomenologie und Phänomenologischen Philosophie*, Tübingen: Max Niemeyer (1913)

– (1984) *Logische Untersuchungen* II, I.-II. Teil (Text nach *Hua* XIX/1-2), Hamburg: Felix Meiner (1901)

– (1985) *Erfahrung und Urteil* [EU], Hamburg: Felix Meiner (1939)

– (1991) *Ideen zu einer reinen Phänomenologie und Phänomenologischen Philosophie*, zweites Buch *Husserliana* vol. IV Tübingen: Max Niemeyer

Israel, Jonathan (2001) *Radical Enlightenment* Chicago: Chicago University Press

Jacquette, Dale, ed. (2003) *Philosophy, Psychology, and Psychologism*, New York: Kluwer

316

Jappy, Tony (2013) *Introduction to Peircean Visual Semiotics*, London: Bloomsbury

Kaplan, F. and V.V. Hafner (2004) "The Challenges of Joint Attention", in Berthouze, L., Kozima, H., Prince, C. G., Sandini, G., Stojanov, G., Metta, G., and Balkenius, C. (Eds.) *Proceedings of the Fourth International Workshop on Epigenetic Robotics, Lund University Cognitive Studies 117*, ISBN 91-974741-3-4, 67-74 (also in *Interaction Studies*, 7(2), 35–69)

Kasser, J. (1999) "Peirce's Supposed Psychologism", www.cspeirce. com/menu/library/aboutcsp/kasser/psychol.htm#docinfo, accessed Oct. 2010f

King, Jeffrey (2007) *The Nature and Structure of Content* Oxford: Oxford UP

– (2012) "Structured Propositions", *The Stanford Encyclopedia of Philosophy* (Winter 2012 Edition), Edward N. Zalta (ed.), plato.stanford.edu/ archives/win2012/entries/propositions-structured/

King, Stephanie L. and Vincent M. Janik (2013) "Bottlenose dolphins can use learned vocal labels to address each other", *Proceedings of the National Academy of Sciences* vol. 110 no. 32 13216-13221

Kitcher, Philip and Achille Varzi (2000) "Some Pictures are Worth $2^{\text{Aleph}-0}$ Sentences", in *Philosophy*, 75-3 (2000), 377-381

Kusch, Martin (1995) *Psychologism: A Case Study in the Sociology of Philosophical Knowledge*, London: Routledge

– (2007) "Psychologism", *Stanford Encyclopedia of Philosophy* (accessed Oct. 2010)

Lakoff, George (1987) *Women, Fire, and Dangerous Things*, Chicago: Chicago U.P.

Lakoff, George and Mark Turner (1989) *More Than Cool Reason. A Field Guide to Poetic Metaphor*, Chicago: University of Chicago Press

Lakoff, George and Johnson, Mark (1999) *Philosophy in the Flesh*, Chicago: University of Chicago Press

Lakoff, George and Rafael Nuñez (2001) *Where Mathematics Comes From. How the Embodied Mind Brings Mathematics into Being* New York: Basic Books

Lange, Friedrich Albert (1877) *Logische Studien. Ein Beitrag zur Neubegrundung der formalen Logik und der Erkenntnistheorie*, Iserlohn: Verlag von J. Baedeker

Lévi-Strauss, C. (1966) *The Savage Mind*, Chicago: University of Chicago Press (1962)

Levy, S. H. (1997) "Peirce's Theoremic/Corollarial Distinction and the Interconnections between Mathematics and Logic", Houser et al. (eds.), 85-110

Livingstone, M. and Hubel, D. (1987) "Psychophysiological evidence for separate channels for the perception of form, colour, movement and depth", *Journal of Neuroscience*, 7, 3416-3468

Lloyd, James E. (1980) "Male Photuris Fireflies Mimic Sexual Signals of their Females' Prey", *Science*, New Series, Vol. 210, No. 4470, 669-671

Mayorga, Rose Maria (2009) "Rethinking Democratic Ideals in Light of Charles Peirce", *Contemporary Pragmatism* vol. 6 no. 1, June 2009, 1–10

McDowell, John (1994) "The Content of Perceptual Experience", *Philosophical Quarterly* XLIV, 190-205

McGrath, Matthew 2012 "Propositions", *The Stanford Encyclopedia of Philosophy* (Summer 2012 Edition), Edward N. Zalta(ed.), plato.stanford.edu/archives/sum2012/entries/propositions

Menand, Louis (2001) *The Metaphysical Club: A Story of Ideas in America*, New York: Farrar, Straus, and Giroux

Millikan, Ruth (2000) "Naturalizing Intentionality", in *The Proceedings of the Twentieth World Congress of Philosophy* (eds. *Jaakko Hintikka, Robert Neville, Ernest Sosa, and Alan Olson)*, vol. 9, "Philosophy of Mind", Philosophy Documentation Center, 83-90, DOI: 10.5840/wcp202000997

Milner A. David and Goodale Melwyn A. (1995) *The visual brain in action* (Oxford UP, Oxford)

Mitchell, W.J.T. (1994) *Picture Theory*, Chicago: University of Chicago Press

– (2005) *What do Pictures Want? The Lives and Loves of Images*, Chicago: University of Chicago Press

Moore, Matthew E. (2010) (ed.) *New Essays on Peirce's Mathematical Philosophy*, Chicago and La Salle: Open Court

Mulligan, Kevin, Peter Simons and Barry Smith (1984) "Truth-Makers", *Philosophy and Phenomenological Research*, 44, 287-321

Mulligan, Kevin (1995) "Psychologism and its History Revalued" (Review of Martin Kusch, *Psychologism*), *Metascience* vol. 8, 17-26

Mullin, A.A. (1966) "C.S.S.Peirce and E.G.A.Husserl on the Nature of Logic", *Notre Dame Journal of Formal Logic*, vol. VII, no. 4

Murphey, Murray (1961) *The Development of Peirce's Philosophy*, Camb. Mass.: Harvard University Press

Myers, Dale K (1995-2008) *Secrets of a Homicide: JFK Assassination* http://www.jfkfiles.com/

Nguyen, Angela P., Marcia L. Spetch, Nathan A. Crowder, Ian R. Winship, Peter L. Hurd, and Douglas R. W. Wylie (2004) "A Dissociation of Motion and Spatial-Pattern Vision in the Avian Telencephalon: Implications for the

318

Evolution of "Visual Streams"", *The Journal of Neuroscience*, 24(21), 4962-4970

Noë, Alva (2004) *Action in Perception*, Camb.Mass.: MIT Press

Norman, J. (2002) "Two visual systems and two theories of perception: An attempt to reconcile the constructivist and ecological approaches", *Behavioral and Brain Sciences* 25, 73–144

Nöth, Winfried (2008) "Semiotic foundations of natural linguistics and dia-grammatic iconicity", in Willems, Klaas and Ludovic De Cuypere (eds.), *Naturalness and Iconicity in Language*, 73–100

Pattee, H.H. (2007) "The Necessity of Biosemiotics: Matter-Symbol Complementarity", in Marcello Barbieri (ed.), *Introduction to Biosemiotics* Dordrecht: Springer, 115-132

Pedersen, Bente Klarlund (2013), "Redegørelse til UVVU. Afsluttende Bemærkninger vedrørende den faglige del", attached to Baggersgaard 2013

Peirce, Charles Sanders (1909) Manuscript 514 (Michel Balat & J. F. Sowa eds.), http://www.jfsowa.com/peirce/ms514.htm (accessed 12 April 2011)

– (1966) *Selected Writings*, (ed. Ph. Wiener), N.Y.: Dover Publications

– (1975-87) *Contributions to the Nation,* I-IV (ed. K. Ketner & J.E. Cook), Lubbock TX: Texas Technological University Press

– (1976) *New Elements of Mathematics*, [referred to as NEM] (ed. C. Eisele) I-IV, The Hague: Mouton

– (1977) *Semiotics and Significs. The Correspondence Between Charles S. Peirce and Victoria Lady Welby*, [referred to as SS] (ed. Ch.S. Hardwick, with the assistance of J. Cook), Bloomington and London: Indiana University Press

– (1982ff) *Writings* vols. I-IV; VIII, [referred to as W] Bloomington: Indiana University Press

– (1992) *Reasoning and the Logic of Things*, (eds. K. Ketner and H. Putnam), Camb.Mass.: Cambridge University Press

– (1992) *The Essential Peirce*, vol. I. (1867-1893) [referred to as EP I] (eds. N. Houser and C. Kloesel), Bloomington: Indiana University Press

– (1997) *Pragmatism as a Principle*, (ed. A. Turrisi), Albany: SUNY Press

– (1998) *Collected Papers* [CP, references given by volume and paragraph numbers], I-VIII, (ed. Hartshorne and Weiss; Burks) London: Thoemmes Press 1998 (1931-58)

– (1998a) *The Essential Peirce*, vol. II (1893-1913) [referred to as EP II] (eds. N. Houser and C. Kloesel), Bloomington: Indiana University Press

– (2010) *Philosophy of Mathematics. Selected Writings*, ed. M. Moore, Bloomington and Indianapolis: Indiana University Press

– (n.d.) "Logic, Considered as Semeiotic", constructed from manuscript L 75 by Joseph Ransdell members.door.net/arisbe/menu/library/bycsp/l75/ver1/l75v1-01.htm

– (n.d.) Manuscripts at the Houghton Library referred to by Ms. numbers in the Microfilm edition 1966 *The Charles S. Peirce Papers, Microfilm Edition, Thirty Reels with Two Supplementary Reels Later Added* Cambridge: Harvard University Library Photographic Service, numbers simultaneously referring to the Robin catalogue of the Mss. (Robin 1967). As to manuscript page numbers, reference is to Peirce's pagination (which is not unanimous since several parallel drafts may belong to the same Ms.)

Pepperberg, Irene (1999) *The Alex Studies: Cognitive and Communicative Abilities of Grey Parrots*, Camb.Mass.: Harvard University Press

Petitot, Jean (1985) *Morphogenèse du sens*, Paris: PUF

– (1992) *Physique du sens*, Paris: Éditions du CNRS

Pietarinen, Ahti-Veikko (2006) *Signs of Logic: Peircean Themes on the Philosophy of Language, Games, and Communication*, Dordrecht: Springer

– (2006a) "Early cognitive science – a challenge to analytic philosophy?", H.J. Koskinen, S. Pihlström and R. Vilkko (eds), *Science - A Challenge to Philosophy?* (Scandinavian University Studies in the Humanities and Social Sciences), Frankfurt am Main: Peter Lang, 327-346

– (2006b) "Peirce's Contribution to Possible-World Semantics," in: *Studia Logica*, 82, 345-369

– (2011) "Existential Graphs: What a Diagrammatic Logic of Cognition Might Look Like", in *History and Philosophy of Logic*, 32 (August 2011), 265–281

– (2011a) "Moving Pictures of Thought II: Graphs, Games, and Pragmatism's Proof", in *Semiotica*, 186 1/4, 315-331

– (2012) "Some Myths about EGs", www.helsinki.fi/~pietarin/brpage/Ten%20Myths%20about%20EGs.pdf

– (in prep) "The Genesis of Peirce's Beta Part of Existential Graphs", www.helsinki.fi/~pietarin/brpage/The%20Genesis%20of%20Peirce's%20Beta%20Part%20of%20Existential%20Graphs-Pietarinen.pdf

Poli, Roberto (2003) "Descriptive, Formal, and Formalized Ontologies", in D. Fisette (ed.) *Husserl's Logical Investigations Reconsidered* Dordrecht: Springer, 183-210, www.formalontology.it/essays/descriptive-ontologies.pdf

Putnam, Hilary (1982) *Realism with a Human Face*, Camb.Mass.: Harvard University Press

Pylyshyn, Zenon W. (1989) "The role of location indexes in spatial perception: A sketch of the FINST spatial-index model", *Cognition* 32, 65–97

– (2000) "Situating vision in the world", *Trends in Cognitive Sciences* 4(5), 197–207

Queiroz, Joao (2012) "Dicent Symbols in Non-Human Semiotic Processes", *Biosemiotics* vol. 5 no.3, 319-329

Raftopoulos, A. and Müller, V. C., (2006) "The phenomenal content of experience", *Mind and Language*, 21(2), 187âĂŞ219

Rauch, Jonathan (2013) *Kindly Inquisitors. The New Attacks of Free Thought*, Chicago and London: Chicago University Press

Redondo, I. (2008) "Embodiment and Mediation: Towards a More Robust Philosophy of Communication", *COGNITIO-ESTUDOS: Révista Electronica de Filosofia*, Vol. 5. No. 1, Sao Paolo 2008: 93–103

Robin, Richard (1967) *Annotated catalogue of the Papers of Charles S. Peirce*, Amherst: University of Massachusetts Press

– (1971), "The Peirce Papers: A Supplementary Catalogue." *Transactions of the Charles S. Peirce Society* 7.1 (Winter 1971): 37-57

Roepstorff, Andreas "Navigating the brainscape: When knowing becomes seeing" in Grasseni, C. (ed) *Skilled Vision*, Oxford 2007: Berghahn, 191-206

Russell, B. (1903) *Principles of Mathematics*, New York: W.W.Norton & Co.

– (1905) "On Denoting", *Mind* 14, 479–493

– (1994) "On the Nature of Truth and Falsehood", in *Philosophical Essays*, London: Routledge (1910)

Santaella, Lucia (1995) "Peirce's Broad Concept of Mind", in *S European Journal of Semiotic Studies*, vol. 6 (3,4), 399-412

Savage-Rumbaugh, E.S., Stuart G. Shanker, and Talbot J. Taylor (2001) *Apes, Language, and the Human Mind*, Oxford: Oxford U.P.

Schneider, Gerald E. (1969). "Two visual systems", *Science* 163 (3870), 895–902

Scott-Philips, T.C. (2008) "Defining biological communication", *J. Evol. Biol.* 21, 387–395

Seyfarth, Robert M., Dorothy L. Cheney (1986) "Vocal development in vervet monkeys", *Anim. Behav.*, 34, 1640-1658

Seyfarth, Robert M., Dorothy L. Cheney and Peter Marler (1980) "Vervet Monkey Alarm Calls: Semantic Communication in a Free Ranging Primate", *Anim. Behav.*, 28, 1070-1094

Shin, Sun-Joo (1994) *The Logical Status of Diagrams*, Cambridge: Cambridge University Press

– (1997) "Kant's Syntheticity Revisited By Peirce", *Synthese* 113, 1–41

– (2000) *The Iconic Logic of Peirce's Graphs*, Camb. MA: MIT Press

– (2010) "Peirce's Two Ways of Abstraction", in Moore 2010, 41-58

– (2013) "Visualization of Quantificational Logic", paper presented at the Extended Problem Solving conference, Aarhus University, January 2013

Short, T.L. (1984) "Some Problems Concerning Peirce's Conceptions of Concepts and Propositions", *Transactions* XX, No. 1, 20–37

– (2007) *Peirce's Theory of Signs* Cambridge: Cambridge University Press

Smith, Barry (1978) "Frege and Husserl: The Ontology of Reference", *Journal of the British Society for Phenomenology*, 9, 111–25

– (1989) "Logic and Formal Ontology", J. N. Mohanty and W. McKenna (eds.) *Husserl's Phenomenology: A Textbook*, Lanham: University Press of America, 29-67

– (1992) "An Essay on Material Necessity", in P.Hanson and B. Hunter (eds.) *Return of the A Priori (Canadian Journal of Philosophy*, Supplementary Vol. 18), 301–322

– (1994) *Austrian Philosophy*, Chicago: Open Court 1994

– (1996) "In Defense of Extreme (Fallibilistic) Apriorism", in *Journal of Libertarian Studies*, 12, 179-192

– (2005) "Against Fantology", M. Reicher & J. Marek (eds.), *Experience and analysis* Vienna: ÖBV & HPT, 153-170

Smith, Barry, and Werner Ceusters (2010): "Ontological Realism: A Methodology for Coordinated Evolution of Scientific Ontologies", *Applied Ontology*, vol. 5 no. 3-4, 139-88

Spiegelberg, Herbert (1956) "Husserl's and Peirce's Phenomenologies: Coincidence or Interaction", *Philosophy and Phenomenological Research*, vol. 17, no. 2, 164-185

Spinoza, B. (1998) *Theological-Political Treatise*, Indianapolis: Hackett (1670)

Stevens, Martin and Graeme D. Ruxton (2012) "Linking the evolution and form of warning coloration in nature", *Proc. R. Soc. B* 2012 279, 417-426, doi: 10.1098/rspb.2011.1932

Stjernfelt, F. (2000) "Diagrams as centerpiece in a Peircean epistemology", *Transactions of the Charles S. Peirce Society* 36(3), 357–392

– (2007) *Diagrammatology. An Investigation on the Borderlines of Phenomenology, Ontology, and Semiotics*, Dordrecht: Springer Verlag

– (2008) "Spatial Cognition Strategies in Map and Diagram Reasoning", P.A.Brandt og C. Carstensen (eds.) *The Map is not the Territory*, Esbjerg: Esbjerg Kunstmuseum, 167-73

– (2009) "Simple Animals and Complex Biology. The double von Uexküll inspiration in Cassirer's philosophy," in *Synthese*, Volume 179, Number 1, 169-186

– (2011) "Signs Conveying Information. On the range of Peirce's notion of propositions: Dicisigns", *International Journal of Signs and Semiotic Systems*, 1(2), July-December 2011, 40–52

– (2012a) "Peirce and Cassirer – The Kroisian Connection: Vistas and Open Issues in John Krois' Philosophical Semiotics.", in *Bodies in Action and Symbolic forms: Zwei Seiten der Verkörperungstheorie*, eds. Horst Bredekamp; Marion Lauschke; Alex Arteaga; Berlin: Akademie Verlag, 37-46

– (2012b) "How Do Pictures Act? Two Aspects of Picture Activity", in U. Feist & M. Rath (eds.) *Et in imagine ego*, Berlin: Akademie Verlag, 16-29

– (2013) "Forgotten Twins. Reason and Visuality", in Kristensen, Tore, Michelsen, Anders, Wiegand, Frauke (eds.), *Transvisuality*, Liverpool University Press, Liverpool, 75-86

Stjernfelt, F. and S. Østergaard (in press) " FONK! HONK! WHAM! OOF! Representation of events in Carl Barks - and in the aesthetics of comics in general", in *Picturing the Language of Images*, eds. Nancy Pedri and Laurence Petit, Cambridge: Cambridge Scholars Press

Talisse, Robert (2007) *A Pragmatist Philosophy of Democracy*, N.Y.: Routledge

Talmy, Leonard (2000) *Toward a Cognitive Semantics*, I-II, Camb. Mass: MIT Press

– (2010) "Universals of Semantics", in P. Hogan (ed.) *Cambridge Encyclopedia of the Language Sciences*, Camb.Mass: Cambridge University Press, 754-757

Thom, René (1972) *Stabilité Structurale et Morphogénèse*, Paris: Ediscience

– (1975) *Structural Stability and Morphogenesis*, Reading MA: Benjamin (English version of Thom 1972)

– (1988) *Ésquisse d'une sémiophysique. Physique aristotélicienne et théorie des catastrophes*, Paris: Dunod

de Tienne, André (2003) "Learning Qua Semiosis", *S.E.E.D. Journal*, 2003 (3), 37–53

– (n.d.) "Peirce's Logic of Information," Working paper, at www.unav.es/gep/SeminariodeTienne.html(07.10.2011)

Tiercelin, C. (2010) "Peirce on Mathematical Objects and Mathematical Objectivity", in Moore (ed.) (2010), 81-122

Tomasello, M. (1999) *The Cultural Origins of Human Cognition*, Cambridge MA: Harvard University Press

- (2008) *Origins of Human Communication*, Camb. Mass: MIT Press

Turner, Mark (1996) *The Literary Mind*, N.Y.: Oxford U.P.

Tye, Michael (2006) "Nonconceptual content, richness, and fineness of grain", in Tamar S. Gendler & John Hawthorne (eds.) *Perceptual Experience*, Oxford: Oxford University Press

Ungerleider, Leslie G. and Mortimer Mishkin (1982) "Two Cortical Visual Systems", in David J. Ingle, Melvyn A. Goodale, and Richard J. W. Mansfield (eds.) *Analysis of Visual Behavior*, Camb. Mass: MIT, 549-586

UVVU [The Danish Committees on Scientific Dishonesty] (2013) "Udkast til afgørelse i høring", file attached with Baggersgaard (2013)

Wang, Ian J. and H. Bradley Shaffer (2008) "Rapid Color Evolution in an Aposematic Species: A Phylogenetic Analysis of Color Variation in the Strikingly Polymorphic Strawberry Poison-Dart Frog", *Evolution*, Vol. 62, No. 11 (Nov., 2008), 2742-2759

Wang, Quanxin, Olaf Sporns, and Andreas Burkhalter (2012) "Network Analysis of Corticocortical Connections Reveals Ventral and Dorsal Processing Streams in Mouse Visual Cortex ", *The Journal of Neuroscience* 32(13), 4386-4399

Webb, Judson (2006) "Constructions, Intuitions, and Theorems", in Randlall E. Auxier and Lewis Edwin Hahn (eds.) *The Philosophy of Jaakko Hintikka* Chicago etc.: Open Court, 196-301

Wegener, Alfred (1912) "Die Entstehung der Kontinente", *Geologische Rundschau* 3(4), 276–292

– (1929) *Die Entstehung der Kontinente und Ozeane [The Origin of Continents and Oceans]* (4 ed.). Braunschweig: Friedrich Vieweg & Sohn

Whiten, A. (2011) "The Scope of Culture in Chimpanzees, Humans and Ancestral Apes", *Philos Trans R Soc Lond B Biol Sci.*, 366(1567): 997âĂŞ1007

Wittgenstein, Ludwig (1922) *Tractatus Logico-Philosophicus*, German orig. 1921, http://www.gutenberg.org/ebooks/5740

Index

328

Made in the USA
Lexington, KY
15 June 2014